Lecture Notes in Computer Science 11186

Commenced Publication in 1973
Founding and Former Series Editors:
Gerhard Goos, Juris Hartmanis, and Jan van Leeuwen

Editorial Board

More information about this series at http://www.springer.com/series/7409

Steffen Staab · Olessia Koltsova
Dmitry I. Ignatov (Eds.)

Social Informatics

10th International Conference, SocInfo 2018
St. Petersburg, Russia, September 25–28, 2018
Proceedings, Part II

 Springer

Editors
Steffen Staab ⓘ
University of Koblenz
Koblenz
Germany

Olessia Koltsova ⓘ
National Research University Higher School
of Economics
St. Petersburg
Russia

Dmitry I. Ignatov ⓘ
National Research University Higher School
of Economics
Moscow
Russia

ISSN 0302-9743 ISSN 1611-3349 (electronic)
Lecture Notes in Computer Science
ISBN 978-3-030-01158-1 ISBN 978-3-030-01159-8 (eBook)
https://doi.org/10.1007/978-3-030-01159-8

Library of Congress Control Number: 2018955276

LNCS Sublibrary: SL3 – Information Systems and Applications, incl. Internet/Web, and HCI

This Springer imprint is published by the registered company Springer Nature Switzerland AG
The registered company address is: Gewerbestrasse 11, 6330 Cham, Switzerland

Preface

This volume contains the proceedings of the 10th Conference on Social Informatics (SocInfo 2018), held in Saint Petersburg, Russia during September 25–28, 2018. Continuing the tradition of this conference series, SocInfo 2018 brought together researchers from the computational and the social sciences with the intent of closing the gap that has traditionally separated the two communities. The goal of the conference was in fact to provide a forum for academics from many disciplines across social and computational sciences to define common research objectives and explore new methodological advances in their fields. The organizers welcomed a broad range of contributions, ranging from those that apply the methods of the social sciences in the study of socio-technical systems, to those that employ computer science methods to analyze complex social processes, as well as those that make use of social concepts in the design of information systems. The most welcomed were the papers that belonged to more than one discipline.

This year SocInfo received 110 submitted papers from a total of 306 distinct authors, located in 38 different countries. We were glad to have a broad and diverse Program Committee of 138 experts with a strong interdisciplinary background from all over the world. The Program Committee reviewed all submissions and provided the authors with in-depth feedback on how to improve their work. As a novelty, this year SocInfo employed a double-blind peer review process. Papers received at least three reviews by the Program Committee.

The Program Committee selected 34 submissions for oral presentation (30.9% acceptance rate) and 36 submissions to be presented as posters (32.7% acceptance rate). In line with the goal of fostering participation from fields with different publication practices than those of computer science, authors were given the chance to present their work without having it included in the proceedings. Eight submissions opted out from the proceedings, taking the total number of contributions included in these volumes to 62.

In addition to posters and paper presentations, SocInfo 2018 hosted six great keynotes delivered by Ingmar Weber (Qatar Computing Research Institute), Jonathan J. H. Zhu (City University of Hong Kong), Harith Alani (The Open University), Bettina Berendt (KU Leuven), Alexander Boukhanovsky (ITMO University), and Olga Megorskaya (Yandex).

We would like to congratulate and thank all the authors and attendees for selecting this venue to present and discuss their research. We would like to thank everybody involved in the conference organization that helped us in making this event successful.

We owe special thanks to the Steering Committee of this conference for their input and support, particularly the chair of the Steering Committee, Adam Wierzbicki, and Luca Maria Aiello, who is another active member of the committee.

The organizers are extremely grateful to all the reviewers and the members of the Program Committee for their tireless efforts in making sure that the contributions adhered to the highest standards of scientific rigor and originality. We thank our two hardworking program co-chairs, Steffen Staab and Olessia Koltsova, who oversaw the process and put together a great program for this event. We are also grateful to our Organizing Committee chair, Sergei Koltcov and our proceedings chair, Dmitry Ignatov. This event would not have been possible without the generous support of the staff and the faculty of the Laboratory for Internet Studies at Higher School of Economics: Yadviga Sinyavskaya, Oleg Nagorny, Vera Ignatenko, and Daria Yudenkova.

We are extremely grateful to the National Research University Higher School of Economics that kindly provided us with the venue and amazing logistic support.

We are very thankful to our sponsors, particularly the Association for Computing Machinery, Springer, National Research University Higher School of Economics, The Centre for German and European Studies (St. Petersburg State University, Bielefeld University, and German Academic Exchange Service (DAAD) with funds from the German Foreign Office), and the Russian Foundation for Basic Research.

September 2018   Olessia Koltsova
Steffen Staab

Organization

Program Committee Chairs

Olessia Koltsova (Co-chair)	National Research University Higher School of Economics, Russia
Steffen Staab	University of Koblenz-Landau, Germany

Proceedings Chair

Dmitry I. Ignatov	National Research University Higher School of Economics, Russia

Workshop Chairs

Luca Maria Aiello	Bell Labs, UK
Sergei Koltsov	National Research University Higher School of Economics, Russia

Steering Committee

Chairs

Adam Wierzbicki	Polish-Japanese Academy of Information Technology, Poland
Karl Aberer	École polytechnique fédérale de Lausanne, Switzerland
Katsumi Tanaka	Kyoto University, Japan
Anwitaman Datta	Nanyang Technological University, Singapore
Ee-Peng Lim	Singapore Management University, Singapore
Noshir Contractor	Northwestern University, USA
Michael Macy	Cornell University, USA
Hsinchun Chen	University of Arizona, USA
Sue B. Moon	Korea Advanced Institute of Science and Technology, South Korea
Andreas Ernst	University of Kassel, Germany
Andreas Flach	University of Groningen, The Netherlands
Dirk Helbing	ETH Zurich, Switzerland

Program Committee

Palakorn Achananuparp	Singapore Management University, Singapore
Robert Ackland	Australian National University, Australia
Luca Maria Aiello	Nokia Bell Labs, UK

Daniel Alexandrov	National Research University Higher School of Economics, Russia
Mikhail Alexandrov	Autonomous University of Barcelona, Catalonia, Spain
Stuart Anderson	The University of Edinburgh, UK
Pablo Aragón	Universitat Pompeu Fabra, Catalonia, Spain
Yasuhito Asano	Kyoto University, Japan
Vladimir Barash	Cornell University, USA
Marco Bastos	University of London, UK
Dominik Batorski	University of Warsaw, Poland
Ginestra Bianconi	Queen Mary University of London, UK
Livio Bioglio	University of Turin, Italy
Svetlana Bodrunova	St. Petersburg State University, Russia
Alexander Boukhanovsky	ITMO University, Russia
Ulrik Brandes	ETH Zurich, Switzerland
Pavel Braslavski	Ural Federal University, Russia
Colin Campbell	Washington College, USA
Claudio Castellano	Institute of Complex Systems, Italy
Michael Castelle	University of Chicago, USA
Fabio Celli	University of Trento, Italy
Nina Cesare	University of Washington, USA
David Corney	Dunnhumby, UK
Michele Coscia	Harvard University, USA
Andrew Crooks	George Mason University, USA
Manlio De Domenico	Fondazione Bruno Kessler, Italy
Gianluca Demartini	The University of Queensland, Australia
Bruce Desmarais	The Pennsylvania State University, USA
Jana Diesner	University of Illinois at Urbana-Champaign, USA
Sofia Dokuka	National Research University Higher School of Economics, Russia
Victor M. Eguiluz	Universitat de les Illes Balears, Spain
Tim Evans	Imperial College London, UK
Katayoun Farrahi	University of Southampton, UK
Rosta Farzan	University of Pittsburgh, USA
Andrey Filchenkov	ITMO University, Russia
Vanessa Frias-Martinez	University of Maryland, USA
Gerhard Fuchs	University of Stuttgart, Germany
Chris Fullwood	University of Wolverhampton, UK
Floriana Gargiulo	GEMASS - CNRS and University of Paris Sorbonne, France
Kwang-Il Goh	Korea University, South Korea
Jennifer Golbeck	University of Maryland, USA
André Grow	Katholieke Universiteit Leuven, Belgium
Christophe Guéret	Accenture, Ireland
Alex Hanna	University of Toronto, Canada
Mohammed Hasanuzzaman	ADAPT Centre, Ireland
Kim Holmberg	University of Turku, Finland

Vera Ignatenko	National Research University Higher School of Economics, Russia
Dmitry Ignatov	National Research University Higher School of Economics, Russia
Adam Jatowt	Kyoto University, Japan
Marco Alberto Javarone	University of Kent, UK
Mark Jelasity	University of Szeged, Hungary
Pablo Jensen	ENS de Lyon and CNRS, France
Hang-Hyun Jo	Asia Pacific Center for Theoretical Physics, South Korea
Andreas Kaltenbrunner	NTENT, Spain
Kazuhiro Kazama	Wakayama University, Japan
Andreas Koch	University of Salzburg, Austria
Sergei Koltsov	National Research University Higher School of Economics, Russia
Olessia Koltsova (Co-chair)	National Research University Higher School of Economics, Russia
Salla-Maaria Laaksonen	University of Helsinki, Finland
Renaud Lambiotte	University of Oxford, UK
Walter Lamendola	University of Denver, USA
David Laniado	Eurecat – Technology Centre of Catalonia, Spain
Georgios Lappas	Technological Educational Institute of Western Macedonia, Greece
Yanina Ledovaya	St. Petersburg State University, Russia
Deok-Sun Lee	Inha University, South Korea
Juyong Lee	National Heart, Lung, and Blood Institute/National Institutes of Health, USA
Sang Hoon Lee	Korea Institute for Advanced Study, South Korea
Sune Lehmann	Technical University of Denmark, Denmark
Zoran Levnajic	Faculty of Information Studies in Novo Mesto, Slovenia
Elisabeth Lex	Graz University of Technology, Austria
Yu-Ru Lin	University of Pittsburgh, USA
Matteo Magnani	Uppsala University, Sweden
Rosario Mantegna	Università di Palermo, Italy
Gianluca Manzo	CNRS (GEMASS), France
Afra Mashhadi	University of Washington, USA
Emanuele Massaro	Ecole Polytechnique Fédérale de Lausanne, Switzerland
Naoki Masuda	University of Bristol, UK
Peter McMahan	McGill University, Canada
Yelena Mejova	Qatar Computing Research Institute, Qatar
Hisashi Miyamori	Kyoto Sangyo University, Japan
Jose Moreno	Institut de Recherche en Informatique de Toulouse, France
Tsuyoshi Murata	Tokyo Institute of Technology, Japan

Oleg Nagornyy

National Research University Higher School
of Economics, Russia

Shinsuke Nakajima
Kyoto Sangyo University, Japan

Keiichi Nakata
University of Reading, UK

Mirco Nanni
Institute of Information Science and Technology/Italian
National Research Council, Italy

Alexandra Nenko
National Research University Higher School
of Economics, Russia

Finn Årup Nielsen
Technical University of Denmark, Denmark

Carlos Nunes Silva
Universidade de Lisboa, Portugal

Jason Nurse
University of Kent, UK

Alexander Panchenko
University of Hamburg, Germany

Daniela Paolotti
Institute for Scientific Interchange Foundation, Italy

Mario Paolucci
Institute of Cognitive Sciences and
Technologies/National Research Council Italy

Symeon Papadopoulos
Centre for Research and Technology Hellas, Greece

Luca Pappalardo
Institute of Information Science and Technology/Italian
National Research Council, Italy

Jaimie Park
Korea Advanced Institute of Science and Technology,
South Korea

Sergei Pashakhin
National Research University Higher School
of Economics, Russia

Leto Peel
Universite catholique de Louvain, Belgium

Orion Penner
École polytechnique fédérale de Lausanne, Switzerland

María Pereda
Universidad Carlos III de Madrid, Spain

Nicola Perra
University of Greenwich, UK

Gregor Petrič
University of Ljubljana, Slovenia

Alexander Porshnev
National Research University Higher School
of Economics, Russia

Hemant Purohit
George Mason University, USA

Giovanni Quattrone
University College London, UK

Matthias R. Brust
University of Luxembourg, Luxembourg

Jose J. Ramasco
Universitat de les Illes Balears, Spain

Giancarlo Ruffo
University of Turin, Italy

Mostafa Salehi
University of Tehran, Iran

Kazutoshi Sasahara
Nagoya University, Japan

Michael Schaub
Massachusetts Institute of Technology, USA

Rossano Schifanella
University of Turin, Italy

Frank Schweitzer
ETH Zurich, Switzerland

Pål Sundsøy
Norges Bank Investment Management, Norway

Xian Teng
University of Pittsburgh, USA

John Ternovski
Yale University, USA

Thanassis Tiropanis
University of Southampton, UK

Michele Tizzoni
Institute for Scientific Interchange Foundation, Italy

Klaus G. Troitzsch
University of Koblenz-Landau, Germany

Milena Tsvetkova
University of Oxford, UK

Lyle Ungar   University of Pennsylvania, USA
Onur Varol   Northeastern University, USA
Dani Villatoro   Openbank (Grupo Santander), Spain
Wenbo Wang   Wright State University, USA
Ingmar Weber   Qatar Computing Research Institute, Qatar
Joss Wright   University of Oxford, UK
Kevin S. Xu   University of Toledo, USA
Elena Yagunova   St. Petersburg State University, Russia
Taha Yasseri   University of Oxford, UK
Dasha Yudenkova   National Research University Higher School
                            of Economics, Russia
Igor Zakhlebin   Northwestern University, USA
Arkaitz Zubiaga   University of Warwick, UK
Thomas Ågotnes   University of Bergen, Norway

Organizing Committee

Sergei Koltosov (Chair)   National Research University Higher School
                              of Economics, Russia
Vera Ignatenko   National Research University Higher School
  (Proceedings   of Economics, Russia
  Management)
Oleg Nagornyy (Website)   National Research University Higher School
                              of Economics, Russia
Yadviga Sinyavskaya   National Research University Higher School
  (EasyChair,   of Economics, Russia
  Correspondence, and
  News)
Daria Yudenkova (Finance   National Research University Higher School
  and Documentation)   of Economics, Russia

Additional Reviewers

Alexander Beloborodov   Yuri Rykov
Timofey Bryksin   Simon Schweighofer
Arthur Thomas Edward Capozzi   Alfonso Semeraro
Jessie Chin   Panote Siriaraya
Ly Dinh   Salvatore Vilella
Sofia Dokuka   Xiaoyu Wang
Yury Kabanov   Nurudín Álvarez

Sponsors

Association for Computing Machinery
Centre for German and European Studies
National Research University Higher School of Economics
Russian Foundation for Basic Research
Springer

Contents – Part II

Short Papers

City of the People, for the People: Sensing Urban Dynamics via Social
Media Interactions.. 3
   Sofiane Abbar, Tahar Zanouda, Noora Al-Emadi, and Rachida Zegour

Partial and Overlapping Community Detection in Multiplex
Social Networks.. 15
   Nazanin Afsarmanesh Tehrani and Matteo Magnani

Digitalized News on Non-communicable Diseases Coverage - What
Are the Unhealthy Features of Media Content Induced for Chinese?........ 29
   Angela Chang

Network Structure of e-Shops Profile as Factor of Its Success:
Case of VK.com.. 40
   Olga Dornostup and Alena Suvorova

Studying Migrant Assimilation Through Facebook Interests 51
   Antoine Dubois, Emilio Zagheni, Kiran Garimella, and Ingmar Weber

Access-Control Prediction in Social Network Sites: Examining
the Role of Homophily 61
   *Nicolás E. Díaz Ferreyra, Tobias Hecking, H. Ulrich Hoppe,
and Maritta Heisel*

Mobile Applications as Tools of Alternative Communication, Diagnostics
and Language Development for Children with Language Disorders........ 75
   Liudmila Mozheikina and Pavel Emelyanov

Studying the Impact of Trained Staff on Evacuation Scenarios
by Agent-Based Simulation 85
   Daniel Formolo, Tibor Bosse, and Natalie van der Wal

Towards Understanding Communication Behavior Changes During Floods
Using Cell Phone Data 97
   Lingzi Hong, Myeong Lee, Afra Mashhadi, and Vanessa Frias-Martinez

How Happy You Are: A Computational Study of Social Impact
on Self-esteem 108
   Fakhra Jabeen

Influence of Temporal Aspects and Age-Correlations on the Process
of Opinion Formation Based on Polish Contact Survey   118
    Andrzej Jarynowski and Andrzej Grabowski

Using Computer Vision to Study the Effects of BMI on Online Popularity
and Weight-Based Homophily   129
    *Enes Kocabey, Ferda Ofli, Javier Marin, Antonio Torralba,
    and Ingmar Weber*

News Headline as a Form of News Text Compression.   139
    Nataliya Kochetkova, Ekaterina Pronoza, and Elena Yagunova

Designing a Smart Tourism Mobile Application: User Modelling Through
Social Networks' User Implicit Data   148
    Aristea Kontogianni, Katerina Kabassi, and Efthimios Alepis

Monitoring and Counteraction to Malicious Influences in the Information
Space of Social Networks   159
    *Igor Kotenko, Igor Saenko, Andrey Chechulin, Vasily Desnitsky,
    Lidia Vitkova, and Anton Pronoza*

Using Twitter Hashtags to Gauge Real-Time Changes in Public Opinion:
An Examination of the 2016 US Presidential Election   168
    Hannah W. Lee

Text-Based Detection and Understanding of Changes in Mental Health   176
    Yaoyiran Li, Rada Mihalcea, and Steven R. Wilson

Evaluating the Search and Rescue Strategies of Post Disaster   189
    Qianqian Liu, Jianqiu Chen, Guoqing Peng, Qian Wan, and Qiyu Liang

Simulating Mutual Support Networks of Human and Artificial Agents.   202
    Lenin Medeiros, Tibor Bosse, and Jan Treur

Automatic Credibility Assessment of Popular Medical Articles
Available Online.   215
    Aleksandra Nabożny, Bartłomiej Balcerzak, and Adam Wierzbicki

Urban Dynamics Simulation Considering Street Activeness
and Transport Policies.   224
    Hideyuki Nagai and Setsuya Kurahashi

Designing Healthcare Systems with an Emphasis on Relational Quality
and Peace of Mind   234
    *Leysan Nurgalieva, Marcos Baez, Francesca Fiore, Fabio Casati,
    and Maurizio Marchese*

Success Factors of Electronic Petitions at Russian Public Initiative Project:
The Role of Informativeness, Topic and Lexical Information   243
  Alexander Porshnev

With or Without Super Platforms? Analyzing Online Publishers' Strategies
in the Game of Traffic.   251
  Joni Salminen, Dmitry Maslennikov, Bernard J. Jansen,
  and Rami Olkkonen

Location2Vec: Generating Distributed Representation of Location
by Using Geo-tagged Microblog Posts.   261
  Yoshiyuki Shoji, Katsurou Takahashi, Martin J. Dürst,
  Yusuke Yamamoto, and Hiroaki Ohshima

Graph-Based Clustering Approach for Economic and Financial Event
Detection Using News Analytics Data   271
  Sergei P. Sidorov, Alexey R. Faizliev, Michael Levshunov,
  Alfia Chekmareva, Alexander Gudkov, and Eugene Korobov

The Effect of Service Cost, Quality, and Location on the Length
of Online Reviews   281
  Antonio D. Sirianni

Where Is the Memorable Travel Destinations?   291
  Miho Toyoshima, Masaharu Hirota, Daiju Kato, Tetsuya Araki,
  and Hiroshi Ishikawa

How Can We Utilize Self-service Technology Better?   299
  Keiichi Ueda and Setsuya Kurahashi

New/s/leak 2.0 – Multilingual Information Extraction and Visualization
for Investigative Journalism   313
  Gregor Wiedemann, Seid Muhie Yimam, and Chris Biemann

False Information Detection on Social Media via a Hybrid Deep Model.   323
  Lianwei Wu, Yuan Rao, Hualei Yu, Yiming Wang, and Ambreen Nazir

Information Diffusion Power of Political Party Twitter Accounts During
Japan's 2017 Election   334
  Mitsuo Yoshida and Fujio Toriumi

Author Index   343

Contents – Part I

Full Papers

Process Workflow in Crowdsourced Digital Disaster Responses   3
    Najeeb G. Abdulhamid, Mark Perry, and Armin Kashefi

Transitory and Resilient Salient Issues in Party Manifestos, Finland, 1880s
to 2010s: Content Analysis by Means of Topic Modeling   23
    Pertti Ahonen and Juha Koljonen

Diversity in Online Advertising: A Case Study of 69 Brands
on Social Media   38
    Jisun An and Ingmar Weber

Communication Based on Unilateral Preference on Twitter:
Internet Luring in Japan.   54
    Kimitaka Asatani, Yasuko Kawahata, Fujio Toriumi, and Ichiro Sakata

Estimating Group Properties in Online Social Networks with a Classifier. . . .   67
    *George Berry, Antonio Sirianni, Nathan High, Agrippa Kellum,
    Ingmar Weber, and Michael Macy*

Computational Analysis of Social Contagion and Homophily
Based on an Adaptive Social Network Model.   86
    Guusje Boomgaard, Falko Lavitt, and Jan Treur

An Agent-Based Modelling Approach to Analyse the Public
Opinion on Politicians.   102
    Thijs M. A. Brouwers, John P. T. Onneweer, and Jan Treur

A Comparison of Classical Versus Deep Learning Techniques
for Abusive Content Detection on Social Media Sites   117
    Hao Chen, Susan McKeever, and Sarah Jane Delany

March with and Without Feet: The Talking About Protests and Beyond.   134
    *Wen-Ting Chung, Yu-Ru Lin, Ang Li, Ali Mert Ertugrul,
    and Muheng Yan*

Fake News as We Feel It: Perception and Conceptualization of the Term
"Fake News" in the Media.   151
    *Evandro Cunha, Gabriel Magno, Josemar Caetano, Douglas Teixeira,
    and Virgilio Almeida*

Inferring Human Traits from Facebook Statuses 167
   Andrew Cutler and Brian Kulis

Assessing Competition for Social Media Attention Among Non-profits 196
   Rosta Farzan and Claudia López

A Generalized Force-Directed Layout for Multiplex Sociograms 212
   Zahra Fatemi, Mostafa Salehi, and Matteo Magnani

The Anatomy of a Web of Trust: The Bitcoin-OTC Market 228
   Bertazzi Ilaria, Huet Sylvie, Deffuant Guillaume, and Gargiulo Floriana

Gender Wage Gap in the University Sector: A Case Study of All
Universities in Ontario, Canada. 242
   Laura Gatto, Dar'ya Heyko, Miana Plesca, and Luiza Antonie

Analyzing Dynamic Ideological Communities in Congressional
Voting Networks. 257
   Carlos Henrique Gomes Ferreira, Breno de Sousa Matos,
   and Jussara M. Almeira

Quantifying Media Influence and Partisan Attention on Twitter During
the UK EU Referendum. 274
   Genevieve Gorrell, Ian Roberts, Mark A. Greenwood, Mehmet E. Bakir,
   Benedetta Iavarone, and Kalina Bontcheva

Ballparking the Urban Placeness: A Case Study of Analyzing Starbucks
Posts on Instagram 291
   Gaurav Kalra, Minsang Yu, Dongman Lee, Meeyoung Cha,
   and Daeyoung Kim

A Full-Cycle Methodology for News Topic Modeling and User
Feedback Research 308
   Sergei Koltsov, Sergei Pashakhin, and Sofia Dokuka

Network-Oriented Modeling of Multi-criteria Homophily and Opinion
Dynamics in Social Media 322
   Olga Kozyreva, Anna Pechina, and Jan Treur

Restoring the Succession of Magistrates in Ancient Greek Poleis: How to
Reduce It to Travelling Salesman Problem Using Heuristic Approach 336
   Michael Levshunov, Sergei V. Mironov, Alexey R. Faizliev,
   and Sergei P. Sidorov

Keeping up on Current Events! A Case Study of Newcomers
to Wikipedia. 348
   Ang Li and Rosta Farzan

Who Gets the Lion's Share in the Sharing Economy: A Case Study
of Social Inequality in AirBnB   370
  Afra Mashhadi and Clovis Chapman

Offline Versus Online: A Meaningful Categorization of Ties for Retweets . . .   386
  Felicia Natali and Feida Zhu

Network Analysis of Anti-Muslim Groups on Facebook.   403
  Megan Squire

The Evolution of Developer Work Rhythms: An Analysis Using Signal
Processing Techniques.   420
  Benjamin Traullé and Jean-Michel Dalle

Forecasting Purchase Categories with Transition Graphs Using Financial
and Social Data   439
  Danila Vaganov, Anastasia Funkner, Sergey Kovalchuk,
  Valentina Guleva, and Klavdiya Bochenina

Building and Validating Hierarchical Lexicons with a Case Study
on Personal Values   455
  Steven R. Wilson, Yiting Shen, and Rada Mihalcea

Diversity of a User's Friend Circle in OSNs and Its Use for Profiling   471
  Qiu Fang Ying, Dah Ming Chiu, and Xiaopeng Zhang

Vitriol on Social Media: Curation and Investigation.   487
  Xing Zhao and James Caverlee

Author Index   505

Short Papers

City of the People, for the People: Sensing Urban Dynamics via Social Media Interactions

Sofiane Abbar[1(✉)], Tahar Zanouda[1], Noora Al-Emadi[1], and Rachida Zegour[2]

[1] Qatar Computing Research Institute, HBKU, Doha, Qatar
{sabbar,tzanouda,nalemadi}@qf.org.qa
[2] Abderrahmane Mira - Béjaïa University, Béjaïa, Algeria
zegourr@gmail.com

Abstract. Understanding the spatio-temporal dynamics of cities is important for many applications including urban planning, zoning, and real-estate construction. So far, much of this understanding came from traditional surveys conducted by persons or by leveraging mobile data in the form of Call Detailed Records. However, the high financial and human cost associated with these methods make the data availability very limited. In this paper, we investigate the use of large scale and publicly available user contributed content, in the form of social media posts to understand the urban dynamics of cities. We build activity time series for different cities, and different neighborhoods within the same city to identify the different dynamic patterns taking place. Next, we conduct a cluster analysis on the time series to understand the spatial distribution of patterns in the city.

1 Introduction

After the revolutionary growth of the modern industry in the late 18th century, cities have become a niche for new opportunities that attracted huge numbers of local and international migrants. In 2015, we were 53.89% to live in urban areas and this number is projected to reach 70% by the end of 2050 [23]. Until now, much of our understanding about urban dynamics came from traditional surveys conducted by human agents either physically or by phones [12,20]. While this way of collecting data provides detailed information about urban behaviors, it remains hard to update and present many weaknesses regarding generalization and scalability. More recently, researchers have looked into the use of mobile data such as Call Detailed Records (CDRs) to model urban dynamics [6,7,17]. These attempts have been quite successful in building accurate models for different dynamics such as mobility, traffic congestion, and land use at city-wide scales. However, these two methods suffer major drawbacks related to the high financial (CDRs) and labor (human operated surveys) costs required to acquire the data

---

R. Zegour was intern at QCRI during this work.

S. Staab et al. (Eds.): SocInfo 2018, LNCS 11186, pp. 3–14, 2018.
https://doi.org/10.1007/978-3-030-01159-8_1

needed, which makes its availability very limited. For instance, CDRs are not only expensive, but are also highly proprietary posing serious data sharing challenges.

Alternatively, social media is notorious for providing its users with a means of documenting the minutiae of their daily lives, including places they go and activities they engage with [5,19]. In this paper, we investigate the use of large scale and widely available public user generated data, in the form of social media posts, to understand urban dynamics taking place in cities and neighborhoods. We are particularly interested in data that is geo-located, i.e. associated with an accurate pair of latitude and longitude coordinates, that is generated by users on different social media platforms such as Twitter, Foursquare, and Instagram. We argue that analyzing geo-located posts can provide an interesting angle to look at the city as a holistic dynamic system. Our analysis is driven by the following two research questions.

RQ 1. Can we use social media – and Twitter in particular – to get insights into urban dynamics in different cities? Inspired by the work of Reades et al. [17] on exploring the use of mobile data, we hypothesize that spaces can be characterized by the volume of social media use over time. By analyzing the use of social signatures, we can show how social media interactions are related to urban activities.

RQ 2. Is social media data sensitive enough to pick out more fine grained variations at the level of city neighborhoods? To answer this question, we perform a cluster analysis on typical weekly signatures in the format of time-series created for different neighborhoods. To this end, a city is partitioned into different zones corresponding to a particular administrative division such counties (in the US), boroughs (in UK), and districts (in Doha). The objective is to discover the different patterns and urban rhythms that characterize different areas of the city presenting different cultural, social and economic properties.

In order to demonstrate the effectiveness of using social media based time-series to capture the different urban rhythms within cities, we built and released a tool that we call CityPulse[1]. The main objective of CityPulse is to allow a visual inspection of the different spatio-temporal patterns captured in different cities.

2   Data Gathering and Processing

We discuss in this section the geographical context of the study as well as the data gathering processes we used to collect and clean geo-tagged data from Twitter.

Geographical Context. We focus on the two cities of Doha and London spotted in Fig. 1. Doha is a fast growing city located in the middle east. Doha is also home to a rich international mix of people where locals only represent about 10% of the total population estimated to 2.2M in the last 2015 census[2]. The city of Doha is divided into 61 different administrative zones. London on the other

---

[1] Link anonymized for the submission.

[2] https://data.worldbank.org/country/qatar.

hand is an example of a mature and developed city, home to more than 8.2M people. Extended Great London area encompasses 61 district community boroughs[3]. Population composition of the two cities and the different life styles observed in European cold London and middle-eastern hot Doha are good motivations to study their different underlying urban dynamics.

Twitter Data. For this study, we use the *location* filter Twitter Streaming API[4] to retrieve geo-located tweets matching a specified input region. The data used in this study spans three months June–August 2017, and consists of 60,197 tweets posted from Doha and 152,007 tweets from London. Figure 1 gives a glimpse into the spatial distribution of geo-located data in the two cities. We clearly see that activity in London is concentrated around its central business district (CBD), whereas in Doha the activity is spread across the cost-line, with noticeable clusters at the airport (south east), the Souq area (center), and West-Bay (north east).

Population Data. For population data shown in Fig. 1(a) and (b), we use Gridded Population of the World (GPWv4) by NASA [3].

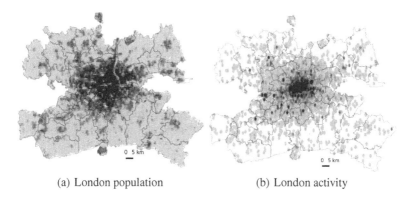

(a) London population   (b) London activity

Fig. 1. Administrative heat maps of population (a) and social activity (b) in London

3   Preliminary Insights

In order to better capture the vibe of cities, we use the methodology presented in [17] to build their average or what can be coined as representative *"typical week signatures"* (TWS). *TWS* of a region is a 168 (24 h × 7 days) long time-series reporting the hourly observed Twitter activity in the whole region. Each value in *TWS* represents the average (typical) count (level) of activity observed in the region in similar hours of the same day on the week throughout the three month period of data.

---

[3] https://data.worldbank.org/country/united-kingdom.
[4] https://dev.twitter.com/streaming/overview.

Insights at the Macro Level of Cities. We focus in this section on comparing the typical weekly signatures of the two cities of Doha and London. We plot in Fig. 2 the two typical weekly signatures of Doha and London. As all timestamps in the data come in GMT timezone, Doha time series has been shifted by three hours to reflect its actual GMT+3 timezone. Examining absolute counts (top panel) for the two cities of Doha and London, reveals big discrepancies as the average activity level in the two cities differs significantly. One could easily spot that London presents a surge in activity on Fridays night and a significant drop in activity on Saturdays (first day of the weekend.) Doha on the contrary, shows a relatively steady levels throughout the week, with a slight increasing tendency towards Saturdays (second day of the weekend in Doha.) In order to correctly compare for the population differences in the two cities, we normalize their TWS time-series using z-score. Normalized time-series have usually a zero mean and a unit standard deviation. Thus, the z-normalized time-series of a given time-series TWS_{city}^{act} is calculated as follows: $TWS_{city}^{norm}(t) = \frac{TWS_{city}^{act}(t) - \mu_{TWS_{city}^{act}}}{\sigma_{TWS_{city}^{act}}}$ Normalized time-series of Doha and London are plotted in the second panel of Fig. 2(a). These time-series show now somewhat similar patterns reflecting the typical circadian rhyme of a city in which people wake up in the morning, go to work, have dinner, and come back home. The max activity happens in both cities toward the end of the day. Interestingly enough, we see that activity in Doha is slightly shifted compared to that in London, in that the morning activity starts later and the last later at night. The residual activity plots shown in the bottom panel of Fig. 2(a) reveal an increasing tendency of activity in the city of Doha on Fridays and Saturdays which form the weekend in Qatar. On the contrary, the activity tends to decrease on the same days in the city of London, before it picks up again on Sunday.

Insights at the Micro Level of Cities. Now, we compare the typical signature of different neighborhoods within the same city to see to which extend social media can unveil differences in local dynamics. We selected four areas in Doha that are dominated by different types of activities: **Souq Wakif**, which is the most visited site in Doha that gathers restaurants, coffee shops, and gift shops. **West Bay**, which is the most westernized neighborhood. **Industrial Area**, and **Hamad International Airport (HIA)**. Figure 2(b) plots the TWS time-series for these four areas. We see some differences in terms of absolute activity (top panel). As expected, Souq Wakif, which is the most visited and most vibrant site in Doha acquires the highest activity, followed by West-Bay, and the airport. The Industrial Area, which is mainly populated by workers, shows lower levels of activity. In order to allow better analysis, we computed again the residual time-series for the four areas. The resulting time-series are plotted in bottom panel in Fig. 2(b). We can see that activity in industrial area always drops around 4pm, which corresponds to the time most workshops close. The airport shows an interesting pattern in which activity mainly happens early in the morning (the growth starts around mid-night) and spikes around 10:00 in the morning, before it starts fading out throughout the day.

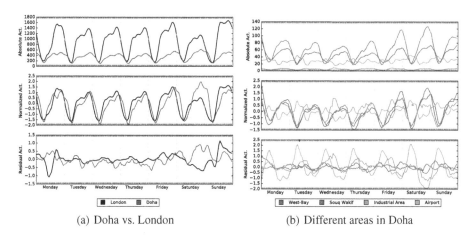

(a) Doha vs. London   (b) Different areas in Doha

Fig. 2. (a) WTS for Doha and London. The top panel plots the average number of tweets. The middle panel plots the $z-score$ normalized time-series. The bottom panel shows residual activity. (b) TWS of four selected landmark areas in Doha.

4   Cluster Analysis

In the previous section, we have demonstrated that using relatively easy and straightforward time-series analysis techniques allows to identify and visualize different urban rhythms happening in different cities or in different areas within the same city. In many cases, the identified patterns matched our a-priori knowledge about the spatio-temporal dynamics of cities such as their overall circadian rhythms, i.e., morning rise of activity, late morning peak, evening drop, etc. In the following, we propose to validate our hypothesis with a more principled methodology. The idea here is to group the typical weekly signatures (TWS) of different areas based on their similarity and then map them back into the urban space.

Time-Series Representation of Urban Activity. To represent geographic partitions with time-series reflecting their urban rhythm, we borrow the technique first introduced in [17] and used later in [7,22] to infer the typical weekly signature of different administrative divisions. The difference is that our time-series are built upon social media activity whereas all previous work have used proprietary mobile phone data activity such as calls and sms. We first map each social media post into its corresponding area (polygon). Next, we build 168 long typical weekly signatures (TWS) for each area.

K-Means. The general scheme of $k-means$ is described as follows [11]: First, randomly select k items and consider them as cluster seeds. Second, use an iterative procedure that performs two steps in every iteration: (i) assignment step in which each item is assigned to the cluster of its nearest centroid, which is determined with the use of a distance function; (ii) reevaluation of cluster centroids to reflect the changes in cluster memberships. Finally, the algorithm

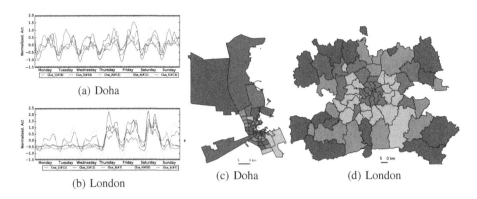

(a) Doha

(b) London

(c) Doha

(d) London

Fig. 3. Results of the independent cluster analysis. Panels (a) and (b) plot the representative (average) TWS time-series for the different clusters found in Doha and London respectively. Panels (c) and (d) project the clusters into the map of the two cities. (Color figure online)

converges either when there is no change in cluster memberships or when the maximum number of iterations is reached. Given that items in our case are TWS time-series, it is important to use an adequate distance function.

Time-Series Distance Function. For any clustering algorithm, we need to define the distance function to use in order to assess how similar are two items (time series in our case.) The two state-of-the-art steps for time-series comparison are to first z-normalize the sequences and then use a distance measure to determine their similarity. The most widely used distance metric is Euclidean distance that compares time-series of the same length by computing the root square of the sum of squared element-wise subtractions. However, despite of its simplicity, Euclidean distance shows several shortcomings related to time-series invariances such as scaling, translation, and shifting [8,18,24]. In this paper, we use an optimized version of Dynamic Time Warping (DTW) [24] known as Keogh Lower-Bound (LB-Keogh) approximation [8] to efficiently and effectively evaluate the similarity of time-series.

Find the Optimum Number of Clusters K. Finding the optimal number of clusters is a fundamental problem in $k - means$ clustering and alike partitioning methods which requires the number of clusters to be provided as an input [9,15, 21]. In our case, we used the optimized version of gap static method proposed in [15] to guide our choice of K. For both cities, we found $K = 2$ to be a good choice as suggested in Fig. 4. However, other possible good values of K are 5 and 8. Obviously, a small value of K favors the creation of large and broadly similar clusters whereas a high value of K favors the creation of smaller yet specific clusters. Thus, we set K to be 5 as a good compromise between specificity and generality. Figure 4 shows the optimal number of clusters for both Doha and London.

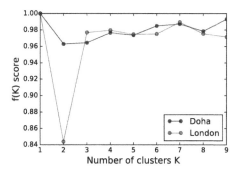

Fig. 4. Using $f - scores$ to find best value(s) of K. Best values coincide with local minima of $f(K)$

4.1 Discussion

We first requested clustering the administrative divisions of each city into five partitions. This is done via independent k-means clustering analysis for each city. In panels (a) and (b) of Fig. 3, we plot the normalized TWS time-series of each cluster centroid found in Doha and London respectively. A close inspection of the Doha's TWS reveals the presence different dynamic patterns taking place in different areas of the city. For instance, zones belonging to cluster #5 (purple) are characterized by an activity pattern that builds up in the early morning, maximizes around noon, and dies around midnight. This pattern is typical of areas dominated by day activity facilities such as schools. Zones belonging to cluster #1 (blue) on the contrary are characterized by a later spike happening around 08:00pm. In fact, the corresponding TWS time-series of this cluster shows a slow yet important rise of activity that starts around 06:00am and keeps building up until it spikes around 08:00pm, then fades out. The important level of late activity is a good indicator of the presence of night life spots (e.g., restaurants, bars, etc.) in the corresponding zones. Zones in cluster #3 show a distinguishable daily bimodal distribution of activity. The first small peak usually occurs before noon whereas the second major peak occurs around midnight.

London's TWS time-series on the other hand also show some interesting insights about the different urban rhythms that characterize different boroughs. The most striking one is related to clusters #1 (blue) and #4 (azure) which have two activity phases: A steady phase recorded on Sunday, Monday, Tuesday, and Wednesday, and a more vibrating phase recorded on Thursday, Friday and Saturday. While the remaining clusters show relatively similar patterns, they greatly differ from each other when we looked into their absolute volume of weekly activity.

Projecting TWS time-series of clusters into the map reveals some geographical grouping of zones belonging to similar clusters. Panels (c) and (d) in Fig. 3 show the result of this projection. The obtained clusters for London demonstrate an interesting geographical structure. That is, boroughs on cluster #5 (purple) are concentrated toward the center of the city. These boroughs are surrounded by another circle of boroughs belonging to cluster #4 (azure). Then come clusters #1 (blue) and #2 (green) in the outer circle of the city. Doha's clusters are organized into a less obvious spatial configuration that makes it difficult to interpret via simple visual inspection.

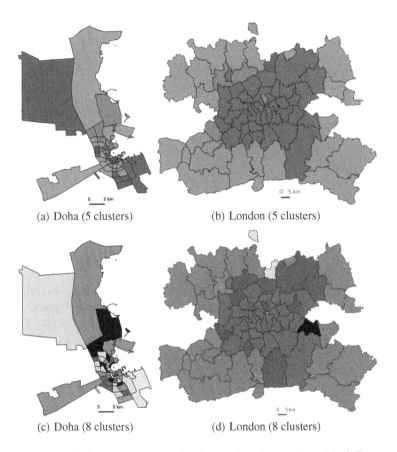

(a) Doha (5 clusters)   (b) London (5 clusters)

(c) Doha (8 clusters)   (d) London (8 clusters)

Fig. 5. Clustering Doha zones and London boroughs all together with different values of K (number of clusters.) For each K, divisions from the two cities sharing the same color have similar TWS. (Color figure online)

So far, we saw that social media data, and Twitter in particular, can be used to reveal different dynamics and patterns grouped into clusters that share similar typical signatures. In order to see the extent to which the two cities are similar, we run a transversal k-means clustering algorithm on both cities of Doha and London at once. To do so, we put all administrative divisions (71 Doha zones and 69 London boroughs) into one bag in which each division is characterized with its normalized typical weekly signature (TWS). Next, we request k-means to digests all divisions together and partition them into clusters of divisions with similar signatures. Figure 5 plots the projection of the clusters into the maps of the two cities, for different values of $K \in \{2, 5, 8\}$. Divisions with the same color in the two cities belong to the same cluster, and thus share similar typical signatures.

There are few interesting observations that we can make here. First, in the case of $K = 2$, we clearly see that central boroughs of London and central zones of Doha are grouped into the same cluster (blue), whereas peripheral boroughs and zones are grouped into another cluster (green). What is happening here is that k-means is mainly partitioning divisions based on level of activities. For the case of $K = 5$, the two cities have shown different distributions of clusters (see Fig. 5(c) and (d)). Now, the mainly common pattern of the two cities in the one concerning boroughs at the periphery of London and zones with low activity in Doha (represented with azure color.) The red cluster seems to be specific to center London, with only one zone in Doha belonging to the same cluster. Note that this zone is close the the central business district of Doha. In contrast, green and blue clusters seem to be specific to Doha. Finally, in the case of $K = 8$ (see Fig. 5(c) and (d)), we see that k-means picked on more specificities for the two cities, with very little transversal clusters.

5   Conclusion

In this paper, we investigated the use of user generated social media posts for modeling urban dynamics in Doha and London. Following previous models that used mobile phone data, we characterized different cities and neighborhoods using typical weekly signatures (TWS) reflecting time-dependent volumes of social-media activity. Initial data analysis enabled the comparison between the circadian rhythms of the two cities. We could also spot change in dynamics taking place during weekends. In order to closely inspect the commonalities and differences of fine-grained neighborhoods, we conducted a cluster analysis in which similar areas are bundled together. The cluster analysis revealed that geographically close neighborhoods tend to share similar rhythms. In the future, we want to exploit the content of social media posts, such as text and images to create more comprehensive profiles for neighborhoods.

Appendix A Related Work

Social Media and Urban Studies. Using social media data to characterize urban dynamics in neighborhoods is not new [1,5,10,13,19]. Therefore, we analyze in the following major works and try to contrast them to our own. In a study by [13], authors looked at modeling human activity and geographical areas via spectral clustering of Foursquare data. The main idea is to split a region into equally sized rectangles, and then characterize each rectangle with a vector containing the total number Foursquare places belonging to different categories. While this approach is interesting, it completely dismisses the temporal aspect of human activity and focuses solely on the geographical distribution and popularity of places (e.g. shops, restaurants, schools, etc.) Our framework's main contribution is to allow a spatio-temporal analysis of human dynamics in cities. The *Livehoods Project* is another influential work in this area [5]. It aims at using Foursquare data for explaining dynamics in cities, and use for that spectral clustering on types of Foursquare venues present in different areas of a city. However, similar the work by [13], this project ignores the temporal aspect in the data, which we believe is very important in modeling human dynamics. Indeed, two areas with similar facilities may show different temporal behaviors (e.g. people may stay late at night in one, but not in another.) More recently, [10] demonstrated that using tweet counts could help identifying the land use profile of a neighborhood in a city. Authors used temporal features such as average number of tweets observed within different hours of the day to train a classifiers to label neighborhoods. The main weakness of this approach resides in the many heuristics introduced in defining land use profiles and selecting the ones to test against. Indeed, while land use has already a well-known classification into commercial, business, residential, industrial, etc. Authors provide their own definition of land use profiles on the only basis of resident and business count. A typical profile in their case would be a one that represents a neighborhood (a square cell) with low number of residents and high number of businesses. Our work is different from this one in two aspects. First we introduce a clustering approach using dynamic time warping on weekly time-series. Second, we study well-defined neighborhoods (represented as polygons) that correspond to actual administrative zones.

Using Mobile Data for Urban Analytics. The wide-spread and adoption of mobile phone technologies have allowed telecommunication companies to gather massive data sets about the spatio-temporal daily activities of people that yield better understanding of how our cities function [2]. These rich mobile phone datasets have unlocked the potential for several urban related applications such as traffic congestion [4], human mobility patterns [6], exposure to air pollution [14], and sensing urban dynamics [16] to name but a few. One of the closest work to ours is the one done by MIT's Senseable City Lab[5] in which they partnered with different telecommunication companies based in Europe and used the call data records (CDRs) to profile cities and neighborhoods using typical weekly signatures (TWS) in the format of time-series. Reades et al. [17] present a nice overview of their related urban computing projects in. Following the same line of research, Grauwin et al. [7] proposed a framework for comparative science of cities by comparing the spatio-temporal dynamics of neighborhoods, represented as time-series featuring different mobile phone activities such as: calls, messages, and data usage. Toole et al. [22] propose also to characterize neighborhoods using mobile data based time-series that are used to classify land use of different neighborhoods in Boston. The main finding is that time-series of mobile activity can be used to figure out what type of urban activities are taking place in different areas by inferring the land use of those areas. Examples of land use classes considered in the study are: residential, commercial and industrial.

---

[5] http://senseable.mit.edu/.

References

1. Arribas-Bel, D., Kourtit, K., Nijkamp, P., Steenbruggen, J.: Cyber cities: social media as a tool for understanding cities. Appl. Spat. Anal. Policy **8**(3), 231–247 (2015). https://doi.org/10.1007/s12061-015-9154-2
2. Batty, M.: Cities and Complexity: Understanding Cities with Cellular Automata, Agent-Based Models, and Fractals. The MIT Press, Cambridge (2007)
3. CIESIN, SEDAC: Gridded population of the world, version 4 (GPWV4): population density. Technical report, Center for International Earth Science Information Network - CIESIN - Columbia University. NASA Socioeconomic Data and Applications Center (SEDAC)
4. Çolak, S., Lima, A., González, M.C.: Understanding congested travel in urban areas. Nature Commun. **7** (2016)
5. Cranshaw, J., Schwartz, R., Hong, J.I., Sadeh, N.: The livehoods project: utilizing social media to understand the dynamics of a city (2012)
6. González, M.C., Hidalgo, C.A., Barabási, A.L.: Understanding individual human mobility patterns. Nature **453**(7196), 779–782 (2008)
7. Grauwin, S., Sobolevsky, S., Moritz, S., Gódor, I., Ratti, C.: Towards a comparative science of cities: using mobile traffic records in New York, London, and Hong Kong. In: Helbich, M., Jokar Arsanjani, J., Leitner, M. (eds.) Computational Approaches for Urban Environments. GE, vol. 13, pp. 363–387. Springer, Cham (2015). https://doi.org/10.1007/978-3-319-11469-9_15
8. Keogh, E., Ratanamahatana, C.A.: Exact indexing of dynamic time warping. Knowl. Inf. Syst. **7**(3), 358–386 (2005)
9. Ketchen Jr., D.J., Shook, C.L.: The application of cluster analysis in strategic management research: an analysis and critique. Strat. Manag. J. **17**, 441–458 (1996)
10. Krumm, J., Kun, A.L., Varsanyi, P.: TweetCount: urban insights by counting tweets. In: Proceedings of the 2017 ACM International Joint Conference on Pervasive and Ubiquitous Computing and Proceedings of the 2017 ACM International Symposium on Wearable Computers, pp. 403–411. ACM (2017)
11. MacQueen, J., et al.: Some methods for classification and analysis of multivariate observations. In: Proceedings of the Fifth Berkeley Symposium on Mathematical Statistics and Probability, Oakland, CA, USA, vol. 1, pp. 281–297 (1967)
12. Morenoff, J.D., Sampson, R.J., Raudenbush, S.W.: Neighborhood inequality, collective efficacy, and the spatial dynamics of urban violence. Criminology **39**(3), 517–558 (2001)
13. Noulas, A., Scellato, S., Mascolo, C., Pontil, M.: Exploiting semantic annotations for clustering geographic areas and users in location-based social networks. Soc. Mob. Web **11**(2) (2011)
14. Nyhan, M., et al.: Exposure track: The impact of mobile-device-based mobility patterns on quantifying population exposure to air pollution. Environ. Sci. Technol. **50**(17), 9671–9681 (2016)
15. Pham, D.T., Dimov, S.S., Nguyen, C.D.: Selection of k in k-means clustering. Proc. Inst. Mech. Eng. Part C J. Mech. Eng. Sci. **219**(1), 103–119 (2005)
16. Ratti, C., Frenchman, D., Pulselli, R.M., Williams, S.: Mobile landscapes: using location data from cell phones for urban analysis. Environ. Plan. B Plan. Des. **33**(5), 727–748 (2006)
17. Reades, J., Calabrese, F., Sevtsuk, A., Ratti, C.: Cellular census: explorations in urban data collection. IEEE Pervasive Comput. **6**(3), 30–38 (2007). https://doi.org/10.1109/MPRV.2007.53

18. Sakoe, H., Chiba, S.: Dynamic programming algorithm optimization for spoken word recognition. IEEE Trans. Acoust. Speech Signal Process. **26**(1), 43–49 (1978)
19. Steiger, E., Westerholt, R., Resch, B., Zipf, A.: Twitter as an indicator for whereabouts of people? Correlating twitter with UK census data. Comput. Environ. Urban Syst. **54**, 255–265 (2015)
20. Theobald, D.M.: Land-use dynamics beyond the american urban fringe. Geogr. Rev. **91**(3), 544–564 (2001)
21. Tibshirani, R., Walther, G., Hastie, T.: Estimating the number of clusters in a data set via the gap statistic. J. R. Stat. Soc. Ser. B (Stat. Methodol.) **63**(2), 411–423 (2001)
22. Toole, J.L., Ulm, M., González, M.C., Bauer, D.: Inferring land use from mobile phone activity. In: Proceedings of the ACM SIGKDD International Workshop on Urban Computing, pp. 1–8. ACM (2012)
23. UNHABITAT: World cities report 2016: urbanization and development. Technical report, UN HABITAT (2016)
24. Wang, X., Mueen, A., Ding, H., Trajcevski, G., Scheuermann, P., Keogh, E.: Experimental comparison of representation methods and distance measures for time series data. Data Min. Knowl. Discov. **26**, 275–309 (2013)

Partial and Overlapping Community Detection in Multiplex Social Networks

Nazanin Afsarmanesh Tehrani[1,2] and Matteo Magnani[1,2(✉)]

[1] Gavagai, Stockholm, Sweden
nazanin.afsarmanesh@gavagai.se
[2] InfoLab, Department of Information Technology,
Uppsala University, Uppsala, Sweden
matteo.magnani@it.uu.se

Abstract. We extend the popular clique percolation method to multiplex networks. Our extension requires to rethink the basic concepts on which the original clique percolation algorithm is based, including cliques and clique adjacency, to handle the presence of multiple types of ties. We also provide an experimental characterization of the communities that our method can identify.

Keywords: Multiplex network · Community detection · Overlapping
Partial · Clique · Clique percolation

1 Introduction

Community detection is one of the most popular social network analysis tasks, for which a large number of algorithms have been developed [1,2]. The number of existing methods is not only justified by the importance of this task, but also by the absence of a unique definition of what a community is: different algorithms are often designed to identify different types of communities, and it is thus practically important for a social network analyst to have a toolbox with alternative algorithms.

The clique percolation method [3] is based on the intuition that the presence of a community can be observed in a social network through the presence of cliques, that is, sets of actors who are all adjacent to each other. This method has a set of features that make it well-suited to the discovery of communities in social networks: (1) it allows to specify how much connectivity is necessary to recognize the presence of a community (minimum clique size k), (2) it allows the same actor to be present in multiple communities (overlapping), and (3) it does not force all actors to be part of a community (partial).

However, this approach is currently only defined for networks with one single type of tie, while in social networks individuals often interact with different groups of people, such as friends, colleagues, and family, and this determines multiple types of relationships, including multiple types of ties between the same

© Springer Nature Switzerland AG 2018
S. Staab et al. (Eds.): SocInfo 2018, LNCS 11186, pp. 15–28, 2018.
https://doi.org/10.1007/978-3-030-01159-8_2

pairs of actors. Therefore, in this paper we extend this approach to deal with multiplex networks, to add clique percolation and the special features of its communities to the multiplex network analysis toolbox.

To increase the expressiveness of models based on simple graphs, multiplex networks [4,5] and heterogeneous information networks [6] have been introduced, among other models, allowing vertices and edges to have different types and to be described by multiple attributes. A specific type of multiplex system, called *multiplex network*, is characterized by vertices that can be connected through multiple types of edges and has been used for almost one century in the field of social network analysis [7,8]. For what concerns community detection, people have developed several methods to find overlapping communities in simple graphs [9]. Clique based methods [3,10,11], fuzzy community detection algorithms [12,13] and link partitioning methods [14,15] are examples of overlapping clustering algorithms.

To the best of our knowledge, these two lines of research have been almost completely distinct so far: while we have methods for overlapping community detection on simple graphs [9], and we have partitioning community detection methods for multiplex networks [16], the problem of detecting overlapping communities in multiplex networks has only been addressed by three methods based on different definitions of community, including the one presented in this paper.

Some approaches convert the multiplex network to a simple graph [17–20], and then employ existing methods. However, this may result in information loss, because the clustering algorithm would not know whether a set of edges belongs to the same or to different edge types, potentially leading to the discovery of communities scattered across a large number of edge types and weak ties.

2   Preliminaries

Multiplex networks are graph-based data structures where the same pair of vertices can be connected by different types of edges.

Definition 1 (Multiplex network). *Given a set of vertices V and a set of edge types $\mathcal{L}$, a multiplex network is defined as a triple $M = (V, E, \mathcal{L})$ where $E \subseteq V \times V \times \mathcal{L}$.*

The objective of the method introduced in this paper is to identify a set of communities, also known as community structure. Here we define a community as a set of vertices combined with a set of edge types, to indicate that for example a group of actors can be part of a *friend and family* community without being part of a *work* or *sport* community.

Definition 2 (Community). *Given a multiplex network $M = (V, E, \mathcal{L})$, a community is defined as a set $C \subseteq 2^V \times 2^{\mathcal{L}}$.*

This definition of community allows both vertices and edge types to overlap across communities, and does not force all vertices and edge types to be included in any community. This is a special case of the type of community that is used for example by the generalized Louvain [21] method, which is defined as a set of pairs $(v, l) \in V \times \mathcal{L}$. However, differently from the generalized Louvain method and in line with the multiplex community detection methods Abacus [22] and Infomap [23], our multiplex clique percolation approach may find communities that are overlapping on the same edge type[1] and also partial.

The clique percolation method was introduced by Palla et al. in 2005 [3]. For a given k, CPM builds up communities from k-cliques, that is, complete subgraphs in the network with k vertices. Two k-cliques are said to be adjacent if they share $k - 1$ vertices. A k-clique community is defined as a maximal union of k-cliques that can be reached from each other through a series of adjacent k-cliques. In general, if the number of links is increased above some critical point, a giant community would appear that covers a vast part of the system. Therefore, k is chosen as the smallest value where no giant community appears. CPM allows overlapping communities in a natural way as a vertex can belong to multiple cliques. Figure 1 shows an example of how CPM works. Given an input graph, first maximal cliques are identified, then adjacent cliques are grouped together to form communities.

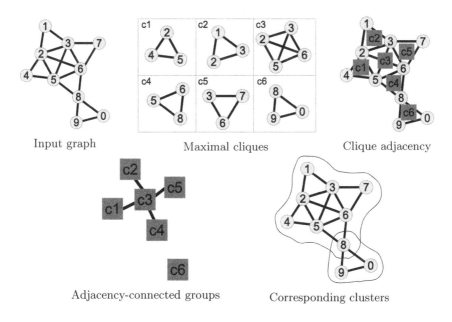

Input graph   Maximal cliques   Clique adjacency

Adjacency-connected groups   Corresponding clusters

Fig. 1. A step-by-step view of the original clique percolation method

---

[1] Using the generalized Louvain method, every pair (v, l) is included in exactly one community.

3   Multiplex Clique Percolation

Our extended CPM algorithm for multiplex networks (CPM^M), of which we describe an implementation in the next section, follows the same main general steps of CPM. However, the concepts on which it is based must be extended to multiplex networks. In particular, we need to define what a clique on multiple edge types is, when two multiplex cliques can be considered adjacent, and how adjacent cliques should be grouped to build communities.

3.1   Cliques on Multiple Edge Types

While a clique on a simple graph is a well understood structure, defined as a set of vertices that are all adjacent to each other, the same concept can be extended in different ways for multiplex networks depending on how multiple edge types are allowed to contribute to the clique connectivity. Considering a specific set of edge types, we might require that a clique contains all the possible edges on all these edge types. In other words, a clique is formed by a combination of cliques on individual edge types. We refer to this type of cliques as AND-cliques.

Definition 3 (k-m-AND-clique). *Let L_{ij} be the set of edge types between vertices i and j. We define a k-m-AND-clique as a subgraph in the multiplex network with k vertices that includes a combination of at least m different k-cliques from m different edge types. In other words, a k-m-AND-clique is a subgraph with k vertices C where*

$$| \bigcap_{i,j \in C} L_{ij} | \geq m \tag{1}$$

Similar to the case of cliques on simple graphs, we can define a concept of maximality for cliques in multiplex networks, where neither k nor m can be increased.

3.2   Adjacency and Communities

When cliques may exist on different edge types, the concept of adjacency should also consider this aspect.

To illustrate why, consider a definition of adjacency where k-m-AND-cliques only need to share $k - 1$ vertices to be considered adjacent. As shown in Fig. 2 (lhs) adjacent cliques do not necessarily share any edge types on all pairs and

Fig. 2. Adjacent cliques

they might share edge types only on their common pairs of vertices. It is worth noting that more diversity among the edge types in external connections of adjacent cliques results in denser internal connectivity. In addition, cliques at distance one still have to share some edge types on some of their pairs of vertices, as in the figure, but when the distance between cliques becomes greater than one, as in Fig. 2 (rhs), they may end up having completely different edge labels. To enforce uniformity among edge types throughout the whole community, we thus need more constraints than what we can define at the level of clique adjacency.

Definition 4 (Multiplex clique-based community). *A multiplex clique-based $[(k - m)\text{-}AND\text{-}clique]_{(m',m'')}$ community is the maximal union of m'-adjacent $k\text{-}m\text{-}AND$-cliques where all cliques share at least m'' edge types on all of their pairs of vertices.*

Please notice that this is a very general definition, and in practice we can just use two parameters: k and $m(=m, m', m'')$.

3.3   Algorithm

In Fig. 3 we have sketched an algorithm to detect communities according to our definitions, where without loss of generality we will assume that $m = m' = m''$. The details of the algorithm, including pseudo-code, are given in the appendix [24], and the algorithm is available in the *multinet* library[2].

The algorithm is divided into three parts, as in the original method: finding cliques, which can be done using an extension of Bron–Kerbosch's algorithm, building the adjacency graph, and extracting communities.

In a simple graph, each clique is included in exactly one community, therefore, communities can be identified from a clique-clique overlap matrix (see [3] for the details). However, this statement is not necessarily true for $k\text{-}m\text{-}AND$-cliques and the corresponding communities. Because of the more complicated relations between cliques, instead of the overlap matrix used in the original method we generate an adjacency graph as in Fig. 3. In the graph we have indicated for each vertex the edge types where the corresponding clique is defined.

Two cliques can be included in at least one community if: (1) there exists a path between the corresponding vertices in the clique-adjacency graph, and (2) for all vertices in the path the corresponding cliques share at least m edge types on all of their pairs. Therefore, each community corresponds to a maximal tree in the clique-adjacency graph where condition (2) holds.

Figure 3 shows all the maximal trees from our clique-adjacency graph for $m \geq 1$. As we see, clique $c4$ can be included in three communities: C1, C2 and C3. No new clique can be added to these sets without reducing the value of m for which the cliques' constraint holds. As an example, community C4 satisfies the cliques' constraint for $m = 2$. Adding any adjacent clique to it, like c3, c5 and c6, the constraint would no longer hold for $m = 2$ because only one edge type would be common for both cliques. In Fig. 3 for each maximal tree we have

---

[2] https://CRAN.R-project.org/package=multinet.

indicated the edge types where the constraint is satisfied, and we also show all communities in this example for $m \geq 1$.

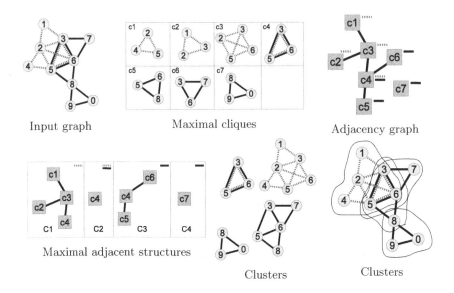

Fig. 3. A step-by-step view of our method

4   Experiments

4.1   Qualitative Analysis

Table 1 shows the result of our experiments on a real multiplex network of five edge types [27] coding five types of relationships inside a university department (Facebook, Work, Lunch, Co-authorship, Leisure) on 61 employees, with $k = 3$ and $m = 2$; we only report communities that share at least two edge types, not those that can be found on single edge types one by one. Our algorithm finds 26 communities where the size of communities vary from 3 to 12 vertices. The edge types Facebook, Work and Lunch which are denser than Leisure and Coauthor appear more frequently among the communities. As expected, some of the 61 vertices in the network are not included in any community.

It can be realized from this table that we can identify different types of overlapping vertices among communities in multiplex networks. If we consider the communities on the two edge types Lunch and Work, e.g. C3 and C5, the structure of communities are more or less similar to the case of single networks as the communities are well-separated with a limited number of overlapping vertices. This can be considered as a general rule for the case where the sets of contributing edge types are the same. On the other hand, we have two communities C21 and C22 where the sets of contributing edge types are not exactly the same. These two communities have 5 overlapping vertices while C21 has only 6 vertices. This is in fact a consequence of what we experienced earlier, that is, cliques can be included in different communities on different combinations of edge types. In addition, we can also have hierarchical community structures: small communities with a larger number of contributing edge types inside larger communities with a smaller number of edge types, such as C16 and C17.

These overlapping structures identified by our method, with core communities built on many edge types and larger communities including more peripheral vertices on less edge types, are compatible with the type of communities often observed in online social networks, as studied by [28].

Table 1. Communities identified in a real data set for k = 3 and m = 2

#	Vertices	Edge types
C01	U107 U1 U29 U32	Facebook lunch
C02	U124 U109 U47	Facebook lunch
C03	U130 U134 U4	Lunch work
C04	U91 U65 U72	Lunch work leisure
C05	U4 U112 U68 U141	Lunch work
. . .		
C16	U59 U91 U110	Facebook lunch work leisure
C17	U59 U91 U110 U113 U138	Work leisure
. . .		
C21	U109 U18 U3 U54 U76 U79	Facebook lunch
C22	U109 U126 U3 U54 U76 U79 U90	Lunch leisure
C23	U106 U118 U41	Lunch work leisure
C24	U123 U59 U71 U91 U130 U47 + 6	Facebook work
. . .		

4.2   A Quantitative Characterization of the Obtained Communities

Table 2 shows various statistics describing the communities found in a multiplex network about co-authorship in the arxiv repository on 13 research fields, corresponding to 13 edge types, using different parameters.

From the statistics we can see that the algorithm actually finds overlapping and partial communities. Notice that this is expected, but not necessary, as depending on the data and parameters not all the types of communities expected in theory necessarily exist or are found, a typical example being the generalized Louvain algorithm where for many values of the interlayer coupling parameter vertices are forced into the same community for all edge types.

We can also see a significant overlapping inside edge types (%over_et), indicating for example that the same individual can part of multiple communities inside the same research field.

Table 2. Quantitative characterization of the community structures identified by the algorithm. #c: number of communities. sc1: size of largest community. sc2/1: relative size of second largest community wrt largest community. %in_com: portion of vertices included in at least one community. %all_et portion of vertices included in the same community for all edge types. %over_v: portion of vertices included in more than one community on different edge types. %over_et: portion of vertices included in more than one community on the same edge type

k	m	#c	sc1	sc2/1	%in_com	%all_et	%over_v	%over_et
3	1	4278	1562	0.96	0.84	0.28	0.35	0.36
3	3	773	144	0.96	0.26	0.31	0.31	0.32
3	5	82	42	0.95	0.04	0.28	0.25	0.25
5	1	1320	70	0.86	0.36	0.47	0.22	0.20
5	3	180	56	0.80	0.10	0.39	0.17	0.17
5	5	9	42	0.95	0.01	0.24	0.20	0.13
7	1	248	60	0.93	0.11	0.60	0.10	0.09
7	3	33	56	0.80	0.03	0.44	0.11	0.08
7	5	1	40	0.00	0.00	0.12	0.00	0.00

The ratio sc2/1 shows that no single giant community is identified with the tested settings. In addition, the number of communities decreases when k increases and when m increases. This, in addition to the ability to extract denser communities, can also be exploited to reduce computation time.

5   Discussion

In this paper we have extended the CPM method to identify overlapping communities in multiplex networks. We have first focused on the formal definition of the method, discussing how to extend existing concepts to the multiplex context, defined an algorithm and studied its empirical behavior on real datasets. Some interesting aspects emerge from the formal definition of the method and from our experiments.

The attempt to keep communities homogeneous results in a phenomenon not visible when single graphs and the original method are used. While in CPM the same vertex can belong to multiple communities, in CPM^M whole cliques can belong to different communities, as demonstrated in our working example. This suggests that the type of overlapping produced using our approach enables the identification of some kind of hierarchical community structures.

As a final consideration, if some edge types are denser than others they may end up appearing more often in the found communities. A possible way to reduce the prominence of some edge types is to then remove these edge types and run the method again for decreased k and m, to find more communities on other edge types. However, evaluating this approach requires a more extensive qualitative analysis than the one fitting this paper, and we leave it to future work.

Acknowledgments. This work was partially funded by the European Union's Horizon 2020 research and innovation program under grant agreement No. 732027.

A Algorithm

The algorithm is divided into three parts, as in the original method: finding cliques, building the adjacency graph, and extracting communities.

A.1 Finding Cliques

Our algorithms starts by locating all maximal k-m-AND-cliques. Algorithm 1 is an extension of Bron–Kerbosch's algorithm. It is a recursive algorithm where the recursive step takes a clique A as input and returns all maximal k-m-AND-cliques containing A that can be constructed using vertices in B, with $k \geq \overline{k}$ and $m \geq \overline{m}$. In this way, given a multiplex network $M = (V, E, \mathcal{L})$, a call to find-cliques($\{\}, V, \{\}, \overline{k}, \overline{m}$) with $\overline{k} > 1$ and $\overline{m} > 0$ returns all maximal cliques in M with $k \geq \overline{k}$ and $m \geq \overline{m}$.

The algorithm works by updating two sets: one containing vertices that can be used to extend the currently processed clique, and one to keep track of already examined cliques. More precisely, the parameter B is a set of vertices such that, for every vertex $n \in B$, $A \cup \{n\}$ is a previously unseen clique on at least $\overline{m}$ edge types. Whenever a vertex from B is used to extend the clique A, then B is updated by removing those vertices that are no longer connected to all vertices in the new clique A'. C is the same as B, but containing those vertices that have already been examined by the algorithm during some previous iteration, so that no duplicates are produced. Given a set of vertices A we notate the set of edge types where the vertices in A form a clique as $L(A)$, and the number of vertices in A as $S(A)$. Therefore, if $|L(A)| = 0$ then A is not a clique on any edge type. We also define $\max(\emptyset) = 0$.

As an example, assume we call find-cliques($\{\}, \{0, 1, \ldots, 9\}, \{\}, 3, 1$) on the network in Fig. 3. The algorithm would then start exploring one of the vertices in B, let us say 5. The new call will thus include in B only those vertices that can still form a clique on at least one edge type when joined with 5: find-cliques($\{5\}, \{2, 3, 4, 6, 8\}, \{\}, 3, 1$). Let us now assume that at the next iteration 3 is added to the current clique: find-cliques($\{3, 5\}, \{2, 6\}, \{\}, 3, 1$), and then 6: find-cliques($\{3, 5, 6\}, \{2\}, \{\}, 3, 1$). At this point $S(A)$ is 3, satisfying the minimum clique size, and $|L(\{3, 5, 6\})| = 2 > \max(\{|L(A \cup \{b\})| : b \in B\}) = \max(\{|L(\{2, 3, 5, 6\})|\}) = 1$. In fact, $\{3, 5, 6\}$ is a clique on two edge types, while $\{2, 3, 5, 6\}$ is a clique on only one edge type. Therefore, the current clique is returned as a maximal one (c4 in Fig. 3). At the next iteration, find-cliques($\{2, 3, 5, 6\}, \{\}, \{\}, 3, 1$) is called and clique c3 is returned. At some later point, the algorithm would call find-cliques($\{2, 3, 5\}, \{\}, \{6\}, 3, 1$), not returning any clique because $C = \{6\}$ indicates that this path has already been explored, and find-cliques($\{4, 5\}, \{2\}, \{3\}, 3, 1$), ultimately leading to the discovery of clique c1, and so on.

Algorithm 1. find-cliques($A, B, C, \overline{k}, \overline{m}$) returns all maximal k-m-AND-cliques containing A that can be constructed using vertices in B, with $k \geq \overline{k}$ and $m \geq \overline{m}$

Input: A a clique
Input: B a set of vertices n such that $A \cup \{n\}$ is also a clique
Input: C a set of vertices n such that $A \cup \{n\}$ has already been processed by the algorithm before
Input: $\overline{k}$ minimum number of vertices to output a clique
Input: $\overline{m}$ minimum number of layers to output a clique
  1: **if** $S(A) \geq \overline{k} \wedge \max(\{|L(A \cup \{b\})| : b \in B\}) < |L(A)| \wedge \max(\{|L(A \cup \{c\})| : c \in C\}) < |L(A)|$ **then**
  2:     OUTPUT A
  3: **end if**
  4: **for** $b \in B$ **do**
  5:     $A' = A \cup \{b\}$
  6:     $B = B \setminus \{b\}$
  7:     $B' = \{b' \in B : |L(A' \cup \{b'\})| \geq \overline{m}\}$
  8:     $C' = \{c' \in C : |L(A' \cup \{c'\})| \geq \overline{m}\}$
  9:     find-cliques($A', B', C', \overline{k}, \overline{m}$)
 10:     $C = C \cup \{b\}$
 11: **end for**

A.2 Clique-Adjacency Graph

In a simple graph, each clique is included in exactly one community, therefore, communities can be identified from a clique-clique overlap matrix (see [3] for the details). However, this statement is not necessarily true for k-m-AND-cliques and the corresponding communities. Because of the more complicated relations between cliques, instead of the overlap matrix used in the original method we generate an adjacency graph as the one represented in Fig. 3, where each vertex of the graph corresponds to a maximal clique and an edge between two vertices indicates that the corresponding cliques share at least k vertices and at least m edge types on all of their pairs of vertices. In the graph we have indicated for each vertex the edge types where the corresponding clique is defined. In the following we refer to this graph as clique-adjacency graph.

A.3 From the Clique-Adjacency Graph to Communities

As previously mentioned, each clique can be included in different communities with different combinations of its adjacent cliques. Here our objective is using the adjacency graph and the information regarding the edge labels simultaneously to find communities in the Multiplex network. Two cliques can be included in at least one community if: (1) there exists a path between the corresponding vertices in the clique-adjacency graph, and (2) for all vertices in the path the corresponding cliques share at least m edge types on all of their pairs. We call the latter rule the *cliques' constraint*, and we call a tree *maximal* if no other adjacent clique can be added without reducing the maximal m for which the cliques' constraint is satisfied. Therefore, each community in the original network corresponds to a maximal tree in the clique-adjacency graph where the cliques' constraint holds for all vertices in the tree. So the problem is equivalent to recognizing all such maximal trees in the graph.

Algorithm 3 takes a community A as input and returns all maximal communities containing A. In this algorithm, given a set of cliques (that is, a community) A we notate the set of edge types we are currently considering to find a maximal community as $\Lambda(A)$. Notice that $\Lambda(A) \subseteq L(A)$: we are going to run this algorithm multiple times starting from the same clique with different $\Lambda(A)$'s, that is, looking for communities in different sets of edge types. We also define $N(c)$ as the neighbors of c in the adjacency graph, as before.

Algorithm 3 consists of two phases. First, it finds a maximal community on $\Lambda(A)$ (lines 1–15). Then, it recursively does the same for all subsets of $\Lambda(A)$ for which larger communities can be found (lines 17–20). B contains the set of cliques that may be used to extend the community A.

To understand the algorithm we invite the reader to start inspecting lines 1–3, 7–8, and 13–15: this is just a simple depth-first visit of the adjacency matrix, finding the largest connected component containing A only traversing cliques that exist on all the edge types in $\Lambda(A)$ (line 3). This visit, that finds the maximal community containing A on $\Lambda(A)$, is extended in two ways. First, lines 4–6 make sure that we do not produce communities that have already been found starting from another clique: if we encounter an already processed clique containing all the edge types in $L(A)$, then this community must have been found while processing it. Second, lines 9–12 cover the case when during the visit we encounter a neighboring clique that only contains a subset L' of $\Lambda(A)$. This means that there is a community containing A that is maximal on L'. Consequently, for each L' we encounter during the process we will later call Algorithm 3 again to extract a maximal community containing A on those edge types (line 17–19). Line 16 makes sure that we do not process the same set L' more then once (notice that the elements of D are sets of edge types). The fact that the different L''s correspond to cliques that we have encountered while visiting the adjacency matrix guarantees that we are not running the algorithm for all the subsets of $L(A)$ but only for those for which a community exists.

Algorithm 2. find-communities(Cliques, $\overline{m}$)

Input: Cliques is the set of cliques produced by the previous step
Input: $\overline{m}$ is the minimum number of edge types to output a community
  1: $C = \emptyset$
  2: **for** $c \in$ Cliques **do**
  3:     $A = \{c\}$
  4:     $\Lambda(A) = L(\{c\})$
  5:     find-communities($A, N(\{c\}), C, \emptyset, \overline{m}$)
  6:     $C = C \cup \{c\}$
  7: **end for**

Algorithm 2 uses Algorithm 3 to iterate over all cliques and finds all maximal communities containing the clique under examination for any $m \geq \overline{m}$. Therefore, at the end it outputs all maximal communities.

A.4   Time Complexity

Finding maximal cliques is an NP-hard problem, that is, one for which even small datasets can take too long to be processed. In practice, as for its simple-graph version, the execution time of the multiplex clique percolation algorithm depends on the input data and in particular on the number and size of cliques.

Table 3 shows the algorithm's execution time for real multiplex social networks of increasing size from an online repository (http://multilayer.it.uu.se), on a 2,4 GHz Intel Core i7 desktop computer with 16 GB RAM. We have repeated each execution 5 times, observing similar results (the mode is indicated in the table) and we have stopped the computation after 10 min. The drastic drop in execution time for the dkpol dataset (including follow, mention and retweet edge types from Twitter) when stricter constraints are used, and the execution times on the ff-tw-yt data, representing common users from three online social

---

Algorithm 3. find-communities($A, B, C, D, \overline{m}$) returns all maximal communities containing A.

Input: A is a set of cliques (partial community)
Input: B is the set of cliques that can be used to extend the community A
Input: C contains the vertices already processed by the algorithm
Input: D is a set of sets of edge types, not to process the same set of edges again
Input: $\overline{m}$ is the minimum number of edge types to output a community
1: **while** $B \neq \emptyset$ **do**
2:     $c = B.pop()$
3:     **if** $\Lambda(A) \subseteq L(\{c\})$ **then**
4:         **if** $c \in C$ **then**
5:             **return**
6:         **end if**
7:         $A = A \cup \{c\}$
8:         $B = B \cup N(c) \setminus A$
9:     **else if** $|\Lambda(A) \cap L(\{c\})| \geq \overline{m}$ **then**
10:         **if** $L(\{c\}) \notin D$ **then**
11:             $S = S \cup \{c\}$
12:         **end if**
13:     **end if**
14: **end while**
15: OUTPUT A
16: $D = D \cup \Lambda(A)$
17: **for** $L' \in \{L(c) : c \in S\}$ **do**
18:     $\Lambda(A) = L'$
19:     find-communities($A, S, C, D, \overline{m}$)
20: **end for**

Table 3. Execution time (s)

Data	#edges	$k = 3, m = 1$	$k = 4, m = 2$
aucs	620	0	0
dkpol	20226	>600	1
arxiv	59026	569	547
ff-tw-yt	74862	>600	106
dblp	222510	>600	>600

networks, highlight how the computation time strongly depends on the data structure and is not linearly dependent on the network size. At the same time, these experiments show the effect of the constraints on execution time.

References

1. Fortunato, S.: Community detection in graphs. Phys. Rep. **486**(3–5), 75–174 (2010)
2. Coscia, M., Giannotti, F., Pedreschi, D.: A classification for community discovery methods in complex networks. Stat. Anal. Data Min. **4**(5), 512–546 (2011)
3. Palla, G., Derényi, I., Farkas, I., Vicsek, T.: Uncovering the overlapping community structure of complex networks in nature and society. Nature **435**(7043), 814–818 (2005)
4. Kivelä, M., Arenas, A., Barthelemy, M., Gleeson, J.P., Moreno, Y., Porter, M.A.: Multiplex Networks. J. Complex Netw. **2**(3), 203–271 (2014)
5. Dickison, M.E., Magnani, M., Rossi, L.: Multiplex Social Networks. Cambridge University Press, Cambridge (2016)
6. Sun, Y., Han, J.: Mining Heterogeneous Information Networks: Principles and Methodologies. Synthesis Lectures on Data Mining and Knowledge Discovery. Morgan & Claypool Publishers, San Rafael (2012)
7. Bott, H.: Observation of play activities in a nursery school. Genet. Psychol. Monogr. **4**, 44–88 (1928)
8. Moreno, J.L.: Who Shall Survive? A New Approach to the Problem of Human Interrelations. Nervous and Mental Disease Publishing Co., Washington, D. C. (1934)
9. Xie, J., Kelley, S., Szymanski, B.K.: overlapping community detection in networks: the state-of-the-art and comparative study. ACM Comput. Surv. (CSUR) **45**(4) (2013)
10. Kumpula, J.M., Kivelä, M., Kaski, K., Saramäki, J.: Sequential algorithm for fast clique percolation. Phys. Rev. **78**(2), 026109 (2008)
11. Yan, B., Gregory, S.: Detecting communities in networks by merging cliques. In: IEEE International Conference on Intelligent Computing and Intelligent Systems, ICIS 2009, vol. 1, pp. 832–836. IEEE (2009)
12. Nepusz, T., Petróczi, A., Négyessy, L., Bazsó, F.: Fuzzy communities and the concept of bridgeness in complex networks. Phys. Rev. E **77**(1), 016107 (2008)
13. Zhang, S., Wang, R.-S., Zhang, X.-S.: Identification of overlapping community structure in complex networks using fuzzy c-means clustering. Phys. A Stat. Mech. Its Appl. **374**(1), 483–490 (2007)

14. Ahn, Y.-Y., Bagrow, J.P., Lehmann, S.: Link communities reveal multiscale complexity in networks. Nature **466**(7307), 761–764 (2010)
15. Evans, T.S., Lambiotte, R.: Line graphs, link partitions, and overlapping communities. Phys. Rev. E **80**(1), 016105 (2009)
16. Bothorel, C., Cruz, J.D., Magnani, M., Micenkova, B.: Clustering attributed graphs: models, measures and methods. Netw. Sci. **3**(3), 408–444 (2015)
17. Berlingerio, M., Coscia, M., Giannotti, F.: Finding and characterizing communities in multidimensional networks. In: International Conference on Advances in Social Networks Analysis and Mining (ASONAM), pp. 490–494 (2011)
18. Cai, D., Shao, Z., He, X., Yan, X., Han, J.: Community mining from multi-relational networks. In: Jorge, A.M., Torgo, L., Brazdil, P., Camacho, R., Gama, J. (eds.) PKDD 2005. LNCS (LNAI), vol. 3721, pp. 445–452. Springer, Heidelberg (2005). https://doi.org/10.1007/11564126_44
19. Rodriguez, M.A., Shinavier, J.: Exposing multi-relational networks to single-relational network analysis algorithms. J. Inf. **4**(1), 29–41 (2010)
20. Tang, L., Wang, X., Liu, H.: Community detection via heterogeneous interaction analysis. Data Min. Knowl. Discov. **25**(1), 1–33 (2012)
21. Mucha, P.J., Richardson, T., Macon, K., Porter, M.A., Onnela, J.-P.: Community structure in time-dependent, multiscale, and multiplex networks. Science **328**(5980), 876–8 (2010)
22. Berlingerio, M., Pinelli, F., Calabrese, F.: ABACUS: frequent pAttern mining-BAsed Community discovery in mUltidimensional networkS. Data Min. Knowl. Discov. **27**(3), 294320 (2013)
23. De Domenico, M., Lancichinetti, A., Arenas, A., Rosvall, M.: Identifying modular flows on multilayer networks reveals highly overlapping organization in interconnected systems. Phys. Rev. X **5**(1), 11027 (2015)
24. Afsarmanesh, N., Magnani, M.: Finding overlapping communities in multiplex networks. https://arxiv.org/abs/1602.03746
25. Magnani, M., Rossi, L.: The ML-model for multi-edge type social networks. In: International Conference on Social Network Analysis and Mining (ASONAM), pp. 5–12. IEEE Computer Society (2011)
26. Newman, M.E.J., Girvan, M.: Finding and evaluating community structure in networks. Phys. Rev. E **69**(2), 026113 (2004)
27. Rossi, L., Magnani, M.: Towards effective visual analytics on multiplex and multi-layer networks. Chaos Solitons Fractals **72**, 68–76 (2015)
28. Leskovec, J., Lang, K.J., Mahoney, M.W., Dasgupta, A.: Statistical properties of community structure in large social and information networks. In: Proceeding of the 17th International Conference on World Wide Web - WWW 2008, p. 695 (2008)

Digitalized News on Non-communicable Diseases Coverage - What Are the Unhealthy Features of Media Content Induced for Chinese?

Angela Chang$^{(\boxtimes)}$

University of Macau, Taipa, Macau SAR
wychang@umac.mo

Abstract. As non-communicable diseases (NCDs) have become widespread and are now the leading cause of death among populations worldwide, they are also increasingly the focus of media attention. The objective of this study is to focus on NCDs from media coverage with an understanding that media say something about the society producing it and future effects. The data integrates various newspaper coverage on NCDs from China, Taiwan, Hong Kong, and Macao. Online news data and machine-aided content analysis were employed to examine disease topics, causes, and ultimately to allocate responsibility. The methodology used emerging big social data analytics for analysis. A total of 32,685 newspaper articles covering NCDs were identified from 2010–2017. The topics of metabolic diseases were covered more frequently in mainland China, while cardiovascular diseases were predominately covered in the neighbouring areas. The study highlights the difference between news frames of NCDs and NCDs cause was induced predominantly by a focus on the risk factor of alcohol consumption. The discussion attempts to explain causative agents of diseases covered while provides an example of big social data analytics in journalism for larger social forces. In conclusion, this study addresses challenges researchers face when analyzing big data.

Keywords: Social data · Automatic content analysis · Health

1 Introduction

A 2014 World Health Organization (WHO) report shows that non-communicable diseases (NCDs) are illnesses that are mostly caused by genetic, individual lifestyle, and/or environmental factors. Five NCDs – cardiovascular diseases, chronic respiratory disease, cancer, diabetes, and stroke – make up for the lion share of all deaths globally [1].

There are four categories of health-relevant behaviours that are considered risk factors for the development of most NCDs: unhealthy diet, lack of exercise, tobacco smoking, and alcohol consumption [2]. It is generally understood that reduction of these behaviours will result in a considerable decrease in the prevalence of the major NCDs [3].

© Springer Nature Switzerland AG 2018
S. Staab et al. (Eds.): SocInfo 2018, LNCS 11186, pp. 29–39, 2018.
https://doi.org/10.1007/978-3-030-01159-8_3

The Chinese population is experiencing a rapid increase in the prevalence of NCDs. The 2015 WHO report indicated that NCDs account for 8,577,000 deaths (approximately 87% of total deaths) in China [4]. NCDs in neighbouring areas of China, such as Taiwan, have also become a major health threat. The current NCD profile indicates that NCDs accounted for 110,720 deaths in 2009 (approximately 77% of total Taiwanese deaths) [5]. Another example is in Hong Kong (HK), where NCDs accounted for 35,365 deaths in 2015 (approximately 76.7% of total HK deaths). Additionally, NCDs in Macau have been the leading cause of death since the 1970's and current account for approximately 76% of total deaths [6].

Ideas about what NCDs news is and how it is selected have been important to researchers, journalists, and public health professionals. It is because certain coverages of the selected diseases and causal attributes will be emphasized, whilst others will be downplayed or excluded. Thus, this study attempts at presenting NCDs with news values and analyzing NCDs coverage selection from journalists and copy editors. The taxonomies of NCDs news and framing theory will be explored in the following section.

1.1 Framing Studies

Previous literature on framing studies shows that the news media serves as a major source of promoting public discourse by highlighting social reality and shaping public consciousness [7–9]. Media forms and frames impact the selection and presentation of reports. Although the framing theory has been used extensively in communication, there are still no settled and standardized rules for operationalizing the method [10].

Research on the media's framing of diseases for public health is limited, with a few exceptions. For instance, Shih, Wijaya, and Brossard [11] developed their framing typology by focusing on American newspapers' attention to three diseases. Their findings can be attributed to the event-oriented nature of coverage of epidemic hazards, with updates on consequences and actions taken by the local authorities. Another example was Whyte [12], who examined NCDs in Uganda and other African countries by proposing a way of framing NCDs within the general idea of chronic conditions to consider diseases within specific social and cultural conditions for better treatment. The above mentioned researchers contended that framing by population-level structure determinants assumes that knowledge of NCDs will motivate people to change their lifestyles. However, framing by environmental structure determinants emphasizes the negative effects of globalization, irresponsible marketing, rapid and unplanned urbanization, and environmental poverty.

Consistent with individual and environmental framing studies on diseases, several researchers evidenced that the American media is inclined to blame individuals for their own health afflictions, with little consideration of public health issues and governmental responsibility for solutions (e.g., [13–15]). Perhaps the clearest example of framing at the individual level is obesity. When the responsibility is assigned to individuals, solutions are targeted to an individual level too. The solutions of healthy eating habits and physical activity are often cited as individual ways to combat obesity. However, obesity is a result of not only personal factors, but also environmental, cultural, and socioeconomic conditions [13, 14, 16, 17].

Lay people usually seek health information from a range of sources, including the newspaper, which serves as an important source of information [16, 18, 19]. Newspapers are one of the most utilized sources of health information in Taiwan (e.g., [20]) and China (e.g., [21]). Most recently, online newspapers have become important and credible sources of health information, allowing readers to access unlimited information and understand more about cancer prevention [22]. Therefore, the dual purpose of this study was to understand how and which NCDs are covered in Chinese news media and what journalistic content says about NCDs issues and with what effects.

In this study, the framing media message is distinguished from other communication by its diachronic nature and by a computer-aided approach [10]. Therefore, we present a diachronic process model of disease framing by considering coverage in which news values may be perceived differently in different newspapers, in different geographical context, and over time. It also expands framing theory in analysing environmental and organizational perspective. Therefore, four research questions (RQ) were raised as follows:

RQ1. What is the amount of coverage of NCDs in Chinese newspapers?

RQ2. What is the general trend of newspaper coverage of diseases in mainland China, as compared with neighbouring areas?

RQ3. What diseases topics are covered more frequently in articles?

RQ4. Is there any difference in frame prominence of diseases causative agents covered?

2 Methodology

Content analysis has been the fastest growing method for studying media discourse [23–25]. Moreover, the recent developed method of computer-aided content analysis to identify communication issues has become a standard tool of methodology adopted by researchers in political communication, business management, computer sciences, and more [e.g., [26, 27]. In this study, a frame repeatedly invokes the same traits and the use of the diachronic approach on disease allows researchers to understand news coverages in time, and to reconstitute the sates of an evolving process [10, 28].

2.1 Sampling

The sampling criteria of mainland China newspapers followed a previous study by considering the highest circulation for Chinese and accessible with digital archives online [29]. A total of 10 newspapers were selected. Our next goal was to locate each article that contained an assertion about NCDs. The task was, therefore, to find a method that enabled the software to identify statements on the terms and causes of NCDs. A codebook was developed to collect the logic, definitions, and rules for registering media messages. Search terms were chosen from categories of NCDs in WHO documents [30], along with meeting the requirements for computer-aided machine scanning. This current study documents journalistic products of major news stories accumulating in digital archives from January 1, 2010 to June 15, 2017 for pragmatic research reasons.

2.2   Machine Coding Process

The procedure began with customized data storage, selection, screening, and analysis created for the special needs of this project. It was done with a tailored software, eMiner, a tool for computer-aided content analysis by e-RS in China. An exploratory test for validity and reliability was run several times for automatic content analysis. Figure 1 displays the conceptual map of the machine-aided content analysis in this study.

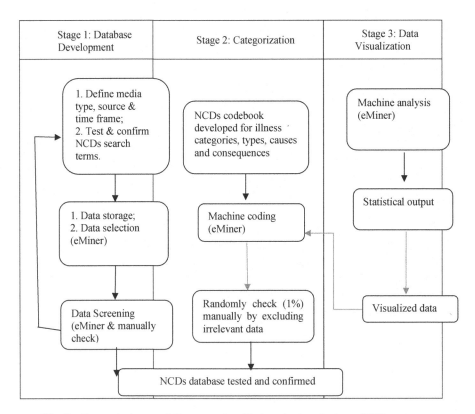

Fig. 1. Conceptual map of the computer-aided content analysis on NCDs coverage

3   Results

A total of 32,685 newspaper articles covering NCDs were identified. Overall, the NCDs coverage in Chinese newspapers has averaged about 4,358 stories every year. RQ1 focuses on the amount and prominent years(s) of NCDS coverage in Chinese newspapers. The highest surge of NCD-related articles was observed in 2012 (n = 5124), followed by 2016 (n = 4905) and 2011 (n = 4777). After a big drop to below-average reporting in 2014 (n = 2435) and 2015 (n = 3050), a renewed interest in covering NCDs was found in 2016 and 2017. Figure 2 displays the general trend of NCD coverage by displaying the number of articles in Chinese newspapers from January 2010 to June 2017.

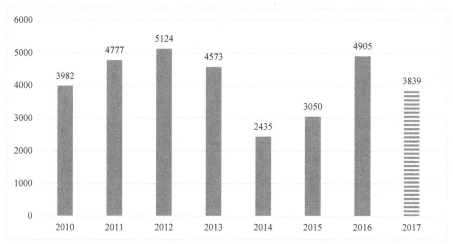

Note. Data was collected from January to June for the year of 2017.

Fig. 2. The number of NCDs articles in Chinese newspapers by year

RQ2 focuses on the general trend of Chinese newspaper coverage of NCDs in mainland China and its neighbouring areas. The highest surge of NCD-related coverage in mainland China was observed in 2016 and is likely to increase in 2017. China news reports about NCDs showed a big decrease of coverage in 2014 and 2015. A similar trend was observed in Hong Kong, as 2014 and 2015 had below-average reports. In comparison, there were above-average reports observed in Taiwan, with 564 articles on NCDs for every newspaper per year (x^2 = 153.46, df = 35, $p < .001$). Table 1 displays the distribution of NCD-related articles in mainland China, Taiwan, Hong Kong, and Macao from 2010-2017.

RQ3 focuses on the potential differences of NCDs topics covered in different areas. Among the six NCDs topics, a total of 19,043 articles were examined with significant difference in coverage (x^2 = 1534.03, df = 15, $p < .001$). Metabolic diseases (38.15%) in mainland China were covered the most, followed by cardiovascular (27.47%) and cancer diseases (23.81%). In the neighbouring areas, the coverage of cardiovascular diseases significantly outnumbered others disease types. Table 2 displays the comparison of the six top coverage of NCD topics in mainland China, Taiwan, HK and Macau.

RQ4 focuses on the causal attribution of NCDs covered in different areas. Overall, there was a substantially stronger focus on the risk factor of alcohol consumption than other causes of NCDs. However, the numbers and ranks of NCDs' shared causes were

Table 1. Number of NCD-related articles in Chinese newspapers from 2010 to 2017

	Mainland China 10931(%)	Taiwan 12690(%)	HK 7415(%)	Macao 1649(%)	All 32685(%)
2010	1028(9.4)	1538(12.1)	1179(15.9)	237(14.4)	3982(12.2)
2011	1555(14.2)	1829(14.4)	1150(15.5)	243(14.7)	4777(14.6)
2012	1712(15.7)	2012(15.9)	1171(15.8)	229(13.9)	5124(15.7)
2013	1798(16.4)	1277(10.1)	1294(17.5)	204(12.4)	4573(14.0)
2014	1123(10.3)	588(4.6)	539(7.3)	185(11.2)	2435(7.4)
2015	1592(14.6)	611(4.8)	641(8.6)	206(12.5)	3050(9.3)
2016	1296(11.9)	2543(20.0)	826(11.1)	240(14.6)	4905(15.0)
2017	827(7.6)	2292(18.1)	615(8.3)	105(6.4)	3839(11.7)

Note. Data was collected from January to June for the year of 2017.

Table 2. A comparison of coverage of six illnesses categories in mainland China and neighbouring areas

	Mainland China 6120(%)	Taiwan 7419(%)	Hong Kong 4625(%)	Macao 879(%)	All 19043(%)
Cardiovascular	1681(27.5)	3854(51.9)	2426(52.5)	372(42.3)	8333(43.8)
Metabolic	2335(38.2)	2093(28.2)	1158(25.0)	268(30.5)	5854(30.7)
Cancer	1457(23.8)	1192(16.1)	848(18.3)	186(21.2)	3683(19.3)
Autoimmune	353(5.8)	157(2.1)	52(1.1)	22(2.5)	584(3.1)
Musculoskeletal	278(4.5)	117(0.1)	75(1.6)	27(3.1)	497(2.6)
Neurological decline	16(0.3)	6(0.1)	66(1.4)	4(0.5)	92(0.5)

significantly different between mainland China and the neighbouring areas (x^2 = 1294.23, df = 30, p < .001). The causative agents of alcohol, tobacco, and stress were prominent in Taiwan, while alcohol, genetic predisposition, and stress received more media attention in mainland China. A similar trend of shared causes, such as alcohol, stress, and tobacco consumption, was observed frequently, but the causative agent of individual diet had no coverage in HK and Macau. The causes of social, personal, and diet attribution of NCDs were less covered in mainland China. Table 3 displays the causes of NCDs covered in mainland China and the neighbouring areas.

NCDs causes are presented in four newspapers in mainland China with a statistically significant difference (x^2 = 204.08, df = 27, p < .001). One of the nationwide newspapers, *People's Daily*, had the least NCDs coverage. Overall, the main shared cause was alcohol consumption and the least shared cause was poor diet. There was no coverage on two causes of social and environmental, and personality and psychological factors. Besides the main shared cause of alcohol, two causative agents such as stress and genetic were covered more frequently in *Southern Metropolis Daily* and *Guangzhou Daily News*. In addition, tobacco as a direct result of individual lifestyle was emphasized in *Beijing Evening News*. As links of causes at environmental level, the frame was prominent in displaying the risk factors of pollution and poverty

Table 3. Causal attributions of NCDs coverage in mainland China and Taiwan, HK and Macau

	Mainland China 7567(%)	Taiwan 5247(%)	HK 3990(%)	Macau 920(%)	All 17724(%)
Alcohol	1995(26.4)	2254(43.0)	1959(49.1)	327(35.5)	6535(36.9)
Stress	1419(18.8)	896(17.1)	655(16.4)	172(18.7)	3142(17.7)
Genetic predisposition	1494(19.7)	719(13.7)	525(13.2)	113(12.3)	2851(16.1)
Tobacco	1111(14.7)	937(17.9)	627(15.7)	172(18.7)	2847(16.1)
Pollution	647(8.6)	241(4.6)	157(3.9)	59(6.4)	1104(6.2)
Poverty	605(8.0)	148(2.8)	43(1.1)	58(6.3)	854(4.8)
Lack exercise	214(2.8)	1(0)	10(0.3)	10(1.1)	235(1.3)
Drugs	67(0.9)	38(0.7)	12(0.3)	5(0.5)	122(0.7)
Personal & family	7(0.1)	7(0.1)	1(0)	4(0.4)	19(0.1)
Poor diet	8(0.1)	5(0.1)	0(0)	0(0)	13(0.1)
Social & economic	0(0)	1(0)	1(0)	0(0)	2(0)

Table 4. Causal attribute of NCDs by four newspapers in mainland China

	People's Daily 336(%)	Southern Metropolis Daily 2985(%)	Guangzhou Daily 2991(%)	Beijing Evening 1255(%)
Alcohol	71(21.1)	680(22.8)	851(28.5)	393(31.3)
Stress	49(14.6)	620(20.8)	554(18.5)	196(15.6)
Genetic predisposition	60(17.9)	605(20.3)	625(20.9)	204(16.3)
Tobacco	58(17.3)	354(11.9)	454(15.2)	245(19.5)
Pollution	37(11.0)	292(9.8)	205(6.9)	113(9.0)
Poverty	47(14.0)	321(10.8)	182(6.1)	55(4.4)
Lack of exercise	12(3.6)	84(2.8)	82(2.7)	36(2.9)
Drugs	2(0.6)	20(0.7)	33(1.1)	12(1.0)
Personal/family	0(0.0)	5(0.2)	2(0.1)	0(0.0)
Wrong diet	0(0.0)	4(0.1)	3(0.1)	1(0.1)

implicitly in mainland China. Table 4 displays the causes of NCDs covered in four newspapers in mainland China.

NCDs causes are presented in seven newspapers in Taiwan, HK, and Macau respectively with statistical difference (x^2 = 403.86, df = 60, $p < .001$). Overall, the shared main cause of alcohol attribution outnumbered the other casual attributes and there was no coverage on one causation of personality and psychological agent. Besides the main shared cause of alcohol, two causative agent such as stress and tobacco were covered more frequently in all newspapers. As links of causes at environmental level, the least shared causes were on social level and diet risk factor in Taiwan and HK, respectively. As links of causes at environmental level, the frame was prominent in displaying the risk factors of pollution (2.5%–6.4% coverage). Table 5

Table 5. Causes of NCDs by seven newspapers in Taiwan, HK, and Macau

	United Daily News 1927(%)	Times Daily News 1590(%)	Liberty Times 1730(%)	Oriental Daily 1803(%)	Apple's Daily News 1264(%)	Ming Pao 923(%)	Macau Daily News 920(%)
Alcohol	708(36.7)	613(38.6)	933(53.9)	865(48.0)	695(55.0)	399(43.2)	327(35.5)
Stress	365(18.9)	302(19.0)	229(13.2)	293(16.3)	185(14.6)	177(19.2)	172(18.7)
Genetic	287(14.9)	242(15.2)	190(11.0)	242(13.4)	143(11.3)	140(15.2)	113(12.3)
Tobacco	378(19.6)	296(18.6)	263(15.2)	291(16.1)	187(14.8)	149(16.1)	172(18.7)
Pollution	101(5.2)	83(5.2)	57(3.3)	90(5.0)	31(2.5)	36(3.9)	59(6.4)
Poverty	64(3.3)	40(2.5)	44(2.5)	14(0.8)	16(1.3)	13(1.4)	58(6.3)
Lack of exercise	1(0.1)	0(0.0)	0(0.0)	3(0.2)	4(0.3)	3(0.3)	10(1.1)
Drugs	15(0.8)	11(0.7)	12(0.7)	4(0.2)	2(0.2)	6(0.7)	5(0.5)
Personal/family	5(0.3)	1(0.1)	1(0.1)	1(0.1)	0(0.0)	0(0.0)	4(0.4)
Poor diet	2(0.1)	2(0.1)	1(0.1)	0(0.0)	0(0.0)	0(0.0)	0(0.0)
Social	1(0.1)	0(0.0)	0(0.0)	0(0.0)	1(0.1)	0(0.0)	0(0.0)

displays the causes of NCDs covered in the seven newspapers in the neighbouring areas of mainland China.

4 Discussion and Conclusion

The way of overall framing NCDs within the idea of chronic conditions to consider diseases was significant in the years of 2012, 2016 and potentially in 2017. Two common causative agent – alcohol and psychological burden/stress – received a lot of media attention in most newspapers, which was unexpected. However, this finding of psychological burden/stress as causal attribution of NCDs is consistent with previous American studies (e.g., [13, 15]), which tend to blame individuals for their own health afflictions instead of considering non-individuals approach for solutions. The possible explanation are: (1) the news values changed from place to place and over time which is conditioned by editorial policy and politics; (2) the task of selecting NCDs news coverage and its causes was from limited supplies of information; and (3) journalists as gatekeepers in their occupational routines and ideology for coverage bias [10].

In addition, the risk factor of an unhealthy diet received no media coverage in one newspaper in mainland China and all newspapers in HK and Macau. The risk factor of lack of exercise also received no media coverage in two newspapers in Taiwan. These findings were in contrast to the previous studies from the WHO [30] and local government reports (e.g., [31]), which found that reduction of poor diet and lack of exercise will reduce the prevalence of NCDs. This is likely because each newspaper has a specific editorial policy and agenda in promoting public awareness of NCDs.

Several limitations should be noted to gain insights into the framing of journalism on NCDs. First, this study attempted to determine the news coverage of NCDs by presenting a diachronic process model of disease framing. The result of this study has shown the volume of the various diseases for the development of coverage through time. However, the coding of diseases was not time-sensitive which potential limited the diachronic process of disease analysis in exploring language use and development. Secondly, this study considers framing as a research paradigm for investigating news coverage and unhealthy behaviours in linking NCDs. Therefore, the measures in distinguishing issue-specific frames and thematic frames would support a desirable response, as suggested by Entman and others [10].

As one of the first comprehensive content analyses on the coverage of NCDs, this study provides a description of news information available to Chinese. It is concluded that Chinese people in mainland China, Taiwan, Hong Kong, and Macau are exposed to online news information which often covers various NCD topics with an emphasis on individual's causal attributes for solutions. Empirical research on public health and communication is facing fundamental challenges caused by the rapid diffusion and dynamic development of internet-based platforms and applications.

The concept of examining both individual's and populations' risks of getting the disease provide an insightful picture of how an epidemic outbreak might impact society [32]. Therefore, the future research building on our findings can further examine whether news framing affects the way the audience perceives what causes NCDs and how to prevent and treat them. Moreover, a comparison of NCDs news coverage in the result with the actual disease prevalence in those locales would enrich the analysis and also reflect the severity of the problem on the ground.

Acknowledgments. The views and opinions expressed in this article are from the individual author and not from sponsor organization. This study was funded by the University of Macau grant MYRG2015-0123-FSS & MYRG2018-0062-FSS. The author would like to thank Professor Peter J. Schulz and Professor Angus Cheong for their helpful comment and assistance and anonymous reviewers for their valuable comments.

Conflict of Interest. The authors declare no conflict of interest. The founding sponsor had no role in the design of the study; in the collection, analyses, or interpretation of data; in the writing of the manuscript, and in the decision to publish the results.

References

1. Beaglehole, R., et al.: Priority actions for the non-communicable disease crisis. Lancet **377** (9775), 1438–1447 (2011)
2. Harrison, O., Hajat, C., Cooper, C., Averbuj, G., Anderson, P.: Communicating health through health footprints. J. Health Commun. **16**(sup2), 158–174 (2011)
3. Waxman, A.: WHO's global strategy on diet, physical activity and health: response to a worldwide epidemic of non-communicable diseases. Scand. J. Nutr. **48**(2), 58–60 (2004)
4. Popkin, B.M., Kim, S., Rusev, E.R., Du, S., Zizza, C.: Measuring the full economic costs of diet, physical activity and obesity-related chronic diseases. Obes. Rev. **7**, 271–293 (2006)
5. Lo, W.C., et al.: Adult mortality of diseases and injuries attributable to selected metabolic, lifestyle, environmental, and infectious risk factors in Taiwan: a comparative risk assessment. Popul. Health Metr. **15**(1), 17 (2017)

6. Taskforce for Annual Report of Macao Cancer Registry. 2015 annual report of Macao cancer registry. Health Bureau of the Government of Macao Special Administrative Region. http://www.ssm.gov.mo/docs/12572/12572_0e75eb1483fc45669758f417942b00dc_000.pdf. Last accessed 21 Nov 2017

7. Altheide, D.L.: The news media, the problem frame, and the production of fear. Sociol. Q. **38**(4), 647–668 (1997)

8. Entman, R.M.: Framing: Toward clarification of a fractured paradigm. J. Commun. **43**(4), 51–58 (1993)

9. Wallington, S.F., Blake, K., Taylor-Clark, K., Viswanath, K.: Antecedents to agenda setting and framing in health news: An examination of priority, angle, source, and resource usage from a national survey of US health reporters and editors. J. Health Commun. **15**(1), 76–94 (2010)

10. Entman, R.M., Matthes, J., Pellicano, L.: Nature, sources, and effects of news framing. In: Wahl-Jorgensen, K., Hanitzsch, T. (eds.) The Handbook of Journalism Studies, pp. 175–190. Springer, Heidelberg (2009)

11. Shih, T.J., Wijaya, R., Brossard, D.: Media coverage of public health epidemics: linking framing and issue attention cycle toward an integrated theory of print news coverage of epidemics. Mass Commun. Soc. **11**(2), 141–160 (2008)

12. Whyte, S.R.: Chronicity and control: framing 'noncommunicable diseases' in Africa. Anthropol. Med. **19**(1), 63–74 (2012)

13. Hawkins, K.W., Linvill, D.L.: Public health framing of news regarding childhood obesity in the United States. Health Commun. **25**(8), 709–717 (2010)

14. Kim, S.H., Anne Willis, L.: Talking about obesity: news framing of who is responsible for causing and fixing the problem. J. Health Commun. **12**(4), 359–376 (2007)

15. Lawrence, R.G.: Framing obesity: the evolution of news discourse on a public health issue. Harv. Intl. J. Press Polit. **9**(3), 56–75 (2004)

16. Shen, F.Y., Yen, C.M.Y.: Causal attributions and frames: an examination of media coverage of obesity among adults and children. Commun. Soc. **31**, 45–64 (2015)

17. Yoo, J.H., Kim, J.: Obesity in the new media: a content analysis of obesity videos on YouTube. Health Commun. **27**(1), 86–97 (2012)

18. Schulz, P.J., Hartung, U.: What to eat in the land of cheese and chocolate: a content analysis of Swiss print media messages on a healthy diet. Commun. Med. **8**(1), 99–110 (2011)

19. Zhang, Y., Jin, Y., Stewart, S., Porter, J.: Framing responsibility for depression: how US news media attribute causal and problem-solving responsibilities when covering a major public health problem. J. Appl. Commun. Res. **44**(2), 118–135 (2016)

20. Hsu, L.L.: An exploratory study of Taiwanese consumers' experiences of using health-related websites. J. Nurs. Res. **13**(2), 129–140 (2005)

21. Gao, L.L., Larsson, M., Luo, S.Y.: Internet use by Chinese women seeking pregnancy-related information. Midwifery **29**(7), 730–735 (2013)

22. Nan, X., Verrill, L., Kim, J.: Mapping sources of food safety information for US consumers: findings from a national survey. Health Commun. **32**(3), 356–365 (2017)

23. Hopkins, D.J., King, G.: A method of automated nonparametric content analysis for social science. Am. J. Polit. Sci. **54**(1), 229–247 (2010)

24. Macnamara, J.: Media content analysis: its uses, benefits and best practice methodology. Asia Pac. Public Relat. J. **6**(1), 1–34 (2005)

25. Matthes, J.: What's in a frame? A content analysis of media framing studies in the world's leading communication journals, 1990–2005. J. Mass Commun. Q. **86**(2), 349–367 (2009)

26. Guo, L., Vargo, C., Pan, Z., Ding, W., Ishwar, P.: Big social data analytics in journalism and mass communication: comparing dictionary-based text analysis and unsupervised topic modeling. J. Mass Commun. Q, **93**(2), 332–359 (2016)

27. Grimmer, J., Stewart, B.M.: Text as data: the promise and pitfalls of automatic content analysis methods for political texts. Polit. Anal. **21**(3), 267–297 (2013)

28. Maurice-Naville, D., Jacques, M.: The development of diachronic thinking: 8–12-year-old children's understanding of the evolution of forest disease. Br. J. Dev. Psychol. **10**(4), 365–383 (1992)

29. Peng, W., Tang, L.: Health content in Chinese newspapers. J. Health Commun. **15**(7), 695–711 (2010)

30. Noncommunicable diseases country profiles 2014. World Health Organization. http://www.who.int/nmh/publications/ncd-profiles-2014/en/. Accessed 21 Dec 2017

31. NCDs preventive committee. http://www.ssm.gov.mo/cpc/zh/download/reportAccessed 20 Jan 2017

32. Massaro, E., Ganin, A., Perra, N., Linkov, I., Vespignani, A.: Resilience management during large-scale epidemic outbreaks. Sci. Rep. **8**(1), 1859–1868 (2018). https://www.nature.com/articles/s41598-018-19706-2.pdf. Accessed 4 July 2018

Network Structure of e-Shops Profile
as Factor of Its Success: Case of VK.com

Olga Dornostup[1](✉) and Alena Suvorova[1,2]

[1] National Research University Higher School of Economics, Saint Petersburg, Russia
o.dornostup@gmail.com
[2] SPIIRAS, St. Petersburg, Russia

Abstract. Modern internet technologies open a wide range of opportunities for enterprises: keeping accounts online, connecting with customers from different locations, collecting and analyzing data about their target audience and other advantages. One of the actively explored factors related to the potential success is using the Internet tools for projects presentation. The aim of this study is to identify the network distinctive patterns forming the strategies for running and maintaining an online shop's profile on Russian social networking site vk.com. We collected data about 706 e-shops profiles on vk.com including their descriptions, information about the communities followers and posts on profile wall. For each profile we built an ego graph of followers network and calculated its centrality measures which were further used to run the k-means clustering algorithm. As a result, we identified six distinct clusters which we assume will approximate different strategies of maintaining an e-shop. These clusters differed in terms of important profile features such as community's audience size, posting activity, followers network connectivity, the presence of "hubs", e-shops operating mostly on vk.com or having an external head website. Considering the network-structure patterns as a result of an online shop's formed strategy, the potential success can be estimated. Taking a monthly number of visits to a website from vk.com as a success metrics, it turns out that the centrality's indicators themselves and generalized clusters have associations with a site-visiting frequency.

Keywords: Social media · e-Commerce · Network analysis
Clustering

1 Introduction

Modern internet technologies open a wide range of opportunities for newborn firms: keeping accounts online, connecting with customers from different locations, collecting and analyzing data about their target audience and other advantages.

Nowadays most of the new business digitize and move online because it meets customers need of being mobile and it is cheaper for maintaining. Along with the specialized "independent" websites, one type of the actively used Internet-tools

© Springer Nature Switzerland AG 2018
S. Staab et al. (Eds.): SocInfo 2018, LNCS 11186, pp. 40–50, 2018.
https://doi.org/10.1007/978-3-030-01159-8_4

for running an e-commerce is social networking site (SNS). They attract a target audience (young and middle-aged population) of online shops, and therefore, are a good source for advertisement and presentation. Taking this into consideration, the social media platforms can be seen as the ground for two-sided markets. Generally, the two-sided market (or a two-sided network) is a place of meeting for two sets of agents, interacting via some intermediary (in our case SNS) [12,15].

The so-called network externalities are the benefits that an additional user of goods (potential consumer) add to others' value of this product. An illustration of such a relation is the telephone communication services, where an increasing number of users raises its value to all the agents [7,8]. Applying this to the SNS, the principle is expected to be working in a similar way: more members join the platform, the higher network effects and value for each agent are. Therefore, the network externalities from using the networking sites can be engaged by e-shops in different ways depending on their commercial purpose or trading strategies.

For example, Swomynathan with co-authors [18] have studied an auction site called Overstock Auctions, which forms an online user's profile based on her/his connections with other users. They performed a network analysis to show how social contacts affect business transactions. The obtained results prove that through communication customers became loyal and trust more to sellers, what eventually increases buyer's satisfaction. Moreover, more recent study [3] of three Czech online shops also shows the significance of communication between two parties.

There are many possible strategies for maintaining an e-commerce store. Spiller and Lohse [17] classify Internet retail sites into five distinct Web groups, basing on their characteristics and activity patterns, while Lim, Sia, Lee and Ben-basat [9] focus on the trust-building strategies in online shopping environments. Reviews of other users and information provided by the profile administrator both influence the customer choice. Previous studies show that the structure of the group members friendship network is associated with the general aim of the group [14] as well as a strategy of inviting new members [10]. The latter is even more important for e-shops and includes advertising strategy, anticipated target audience, and profile activity.

However, there is the lack of studies focusing on the role of networks in e-shop success in the Russian context. The current study is the first step of the large research and it aims to explore the network structures of online-shop profiles on the social networking site and to estimate their relations to the e-shop's potential success. We hypothesize that (1) structure characteristics of friendship networks among the followers of e-shop profile form distinct patterns; (2) these patterns are associated with e-shop success measures.

2   Methodology

2.1   Data

The study combines two data sources. All the data related to activity at the electronics e-shops' profiles on the two-sided platform are collected from vk.com.

We focus our study on social networking site VKontakte (VK, vk.com) since VK is the most popular online social media and the most used social networking service in Russia according to the Russian Public Opinion Research Center[1]. To exclude the confounding effect of the type of selling products we selected only the online shops, specializing in electronics since they represented homogeneous selling products.

Another source of data is SimilarWeb.com, which provides the approximations for some online-success metrics of maintaining the shops' websites.

The dataset with structural patterns of online shops consists of two subsets depending on the way the information has been found on vk.com. The smaller one contains data of 57 vk-communities, which have indicated the goods they sell and, therefore, belong to the formal category "Shop". Particularly, these e-shops specialize in electronics and clearly state their products into the formal market section (called "Products") in the profile.

Since the most part of the online shops' vk-pages do not formally specify the selling goods, these profiles cannot be collected by filtering the category "Shop". To address that we added into analysis all the communities' profiles which can be found by search query "shop of electronics" (in Russian). It turns out that the number of such e-shops is several times higher compared to the number of shops found earlier in "Shop" category, and accounts to 649 vk-profiles. Overall, our data include information from the profiles of 706 e-shops, selling electronic goods online by using vk.com as a platform for meeting the audience. We examined all the profiles manually and ascertain that the dataset does not include any false positives, i.e. all profiles are electronics e-shops. At the same time, data collection procedure can miss the profiles without "electronics" in title or description.

For each selected profile on vk.com we collected data that included profile's description (textual description, website if mentioned, contacts), "wall" statistics (posts, published by profile moderator, comments, likes, reposts), information about community's followers, and the graph-structured data with the friendship (i.e. formal connection between users on vk.com) between their followers.

The second data source is SimilarWeb.com, which collects site-related statistics for the shops operating on the Internet. These statistics include a total number of visits per day and a proportion of indirect visits to an e-shop's site through vk.com.

2.2 Procedures and Design

Since the current study is focused on the online shops operating on a platform regarded as a two-sided market, the features related to some personal connections between users are about to be considered. First, we identified several groups of e-shops' vk-profiles formed on a basis of their follower's friendship network

---

[1] https://wciom.ru.

structures. Then we compared these clusters and described them in terms of general[2], content-related[3] and network-related[4] features.

On the first step we constructed the ego graphs of followers for each e-commerce vk-community; the nodes represent the followers and the edges are the existing vk-friendship between them. For each network normalized centrality measures such as degree, betweenness, closeness and eigen centrality have been calculated. Normalization with centering here allows eliminating an impact of the network size while keeping only the structural differences. Besides, the share of isolated nodes has been calculated for controlling on the network connectivity.

Next, we divided all vk-profiles into several clusters according to their structural patterns. For this purpose, the popular k-means clustering algorithm [5] has been chosen and run to the network-related variables. According to the Elbow method an optimal number of clusters was equal to six. The averaged network and content-related measures for each cluster are presented in the Table 1.

A further analysis was concentrated on comparing these clusters (distinct patterns) in terms of the e-shops' success. There are many ways of measuring this e-commerce success, including the shop's revenue or profit. However, these data are not publicly available for most of the considered shops, therefore, in this study, we are going to look at the shop's potential success expressed in their audience performance. For all the vk-profiles of electronics' online shops, the meaningful determinant of popularity and visitability is a number of activated (not banned/deleted) followers.

Another success indicator is a frequency of visiting the shop's external website following the link mentioned on vk.com. This mean number of visits per month (SimilarWeb.com data) is only applicable to the online shops using vk.com mostly for advertisement and reaching the target audience because they have a separate online source for selling their products. Not all the e-shops on vk.com have a website, thereby, the data subset is limited to 216 observations. It has also turned out that 3 popular shops, specializing in electronic goods, have different vk-pages depending on a location, but a unified link to the head site. For dealing with this issue, we spread the number of visits to the main sites between vk-groups proportionally to their numbers of followers. Moreover, in the subset of 216 vk-pages with a link, we identified three small "fake" vk-profiles of leading electronics shop and removed them from the analysis, because these communities are mostly "dead" and do not reflect the real activity.

The next part of the analysis was about finding the relations between the raw e-shops' network-structure features or expressed in a cluster form (calculated before) and the metrics of potential success. Particularly, we explore the set of variables including network-related indicators (centrality measures themselves or cluster), content-related statistics (number of posts per day, proportion of reposted post to own ones, share of posts having audio/photo/video and others)

---

[2] Profile's description and demographic information of the community's followers.

[3] Information published on the community's wall.

[4] Structure and centrality measures of the graph-organized data with the online-relations between the followers.

and control variables (gender and mean age of followers, by category/search found).

The regression models illustrate the contribution of different patterns of within profile's activity and some general characteristics of the communities and their audience. Through the Box-Cox [2] transformation of the success-variables we determine the optimal models' specification.

All statistical analysis are performed using R version 3.3.2 [21] with RStudio IDE [22].

3   Results

As mentioned above, the initial data are presented by two types of e-shops: having vs not having a formal attribute "Products" as a separate section in a vk-profile. Formal "Shop" vk-profiles have a greater number of followers, the active (not deactivated or banned) ones, in particular. These groups are, generally, "younger" comparing to pages found by the search query, but they have more published posts and more actively used "attention grabbers" such as photo, video or audio files supporting the publication. Moreover, these e-shops are more likely to have a link to an external e-shop's website. It can mean that the possibility to sell goods on vk-page does not guarantee that a particular shop is using the social networking site as the main platform for trading. The comparison of the e-shops with and without an external website link shows the same associations. Generally speaking, keeping for analysis only the e-shops having both vk-profile and a head site allows exploring the ways of using the social network site as a platform mostly for indirect selling, through meeting the target audience, spreading information about the products and using advantages of "word-of-mouth" phenomenon. This point will be taken into account later for the case of predicting an average monthly site-visiting level.

To explore the network structure effects we control for the members count by calculating the scaled and normalized centrality measures of followers' ego graphs. The results of k-means clustering division performed only on these centralized network-based features (degree, closeness, betweenness, eigen centrality) and the proportion of isolates can be found in the Table 1.

The clusters can be characterized in the following way: the biggest (V) and smallest ones (IV) (in terms of the cluster size) combine weakly connected large-sized and tiny-sized groups (in terms of followers count), respectively. Other two small-sized clusters (I and II) contain communities having a little audience as well, but in the first cluster there are weakly-connected groups with some "bridges"[5] (high betweenness) and "hubs"[6] (high degree), while in the second cluster the networks are well-connected enough.

Almost a half of followers from the III cluster are isolated, but there are some nodes with high centrality measures, however, the general network connectivity

---

[5] An edge (or a node) is called a "bridge" if it connects several relatively big network components.

[6] A node is called "hub" if it has relatively high number of connections to other nodes.

Table 1. K-means clusters comparison

Network-related variables							
Variable/Cluster	I	II	III	IV	V	VI	F-value
Number of edges	15.42	883.21	1084.66	64.65	1905.11	19446.64	5.091***
Share of isolates	0.300	0.740	0.587	0.238	0.179	0.586	216***
Degree centrality	0.399	0.672	0.458	0.139	0.150	0.183	314.7***
Betweenness centrality	0.720	0.741	0.447	0.127	0.129	0.189	323.4***
Closeness centrality	0.727	0.793	0.196	0.178	0.023	0.041	613***
Eigen centrality	0.570	0.737	0.776	0.298	0.899	0.880	269.9***
Content-related variables							
Proportion with site	0.457	0.459	0.364	0.371	0.6325	0.5812	6.04***
Proportion of men	0.603	0.608	0.563	0.581	0.592	0.507	5.755***
Age of followers	29.07	30.55	29.65	29.27	29.85	30.19	1.355
Proportion of deactivated foll.	0.267	0.132	0.161	0.310	0.314	0.138	39.56***
Total number of posts	33.94	37.84	77.38	29.32	256.52	532.82	12.05***
Posts per day	3.003	3.354	2.324	3.076	3.646	2.888	0.588
Days from first post	1602.1	851.5	1148.7	1362.5	1218.3	1027.9	7.296***
Proportion of reposted posts	0.057	0.138	0.151	0.086	0.083	0.095	0.002
Proportion of posts having text	0.743	0.748	0.809	0.810	0.874	0.851	3.655**
Proportion of posts with audio	0.002	0.024	0.015	0.002	0.016	0.012	0.967
Proportion of posts with photo	0.804	0.892	0.824	0.814	0.897	0.924	4.09**
Proportion of posts with video	0.082	0.059	0.051	0.043	0.079	0.089	1.28
Comments per post (mean)	0.478	0.123	0.238	0.302	1.000	1.109	0.974
Likes per post (mean)	1.164	1.836	2.666	2.179	11.235	12.172	3.892***
Likes per post (median)	0.630	1.598	1.368	1.500	5.585	6.957	2.747*
Reposts per post (mean)	0.161	0.471	0.489	0.153	1.090	1.470	4.425***
Reposts per post (median)	0.050	0.384	0.222	0.060	0.335	0.457	2.118
Cluster size	59	61	118	35	215	117	–

Note: *$p<0.05$, **$p<0.01$, ***$p<0.001$.
F-values from ANOVA.

is low. And the last VI cluster combines many large-sized groups, but their average size is similar to the one in V cluster. The clusters V and VI mostly differ by the nature of their weak connectivity: vk-groups in cluster V have less edges (connections) than nodes (followers), while vk-profiles from a cluster VI are likely to have many connections per node. Such a difference in a number of edges along with the similar in normalized centrality measures leads to the idea that the connections in VI cluster's groups are quite evenly distributed over the networks, while in cluster V there are groups having some small tight communities of highly centralized nodes.

To sum up, operating only by the followers' network-based features, we can distinguish groups (clusters) of online shops with the relatively different audience structures. It can be understood as a result or a sided effect of following some strategies for maintaining an e-shop's vk-page.

In terms of "external" features, not used for clustering, the gender distribution in our data is generally biased towards the male audience, because of an e-shops' specialization on electronic goods, but in small-size groups from clusters I and II this bias is even stronger and men proportion is 60%. We may assume that unpopular communities can be too narrow-focused and attract the special audience. However, one of the main differences between these two clusters (I and II) is the mean age: groups with more tight networks (II) are twice as "younger" as communities having low centrality measures.

Comparing two large-audience clusters (V and VI) the main difference is in total publication frequency. It can be seen that the vk-profiles belong to the cluster VI are "younger" and have more publications than those from cluster V, in general. This is an evidence of higher publication activity along with the lower proportion of deactivated followers, in addition.

As mentioned above, we use two success measures to evaluate the impact of network structure: the number of visits to a website from vk.com per month normalized to the followers' count (profiles with a website only) and number of followers (all profiles). We used log-transformation for response variables (optimal according to Box-Cox transformation) and three blocks of predictors: controls, wall-related and strategy-related. Control variables include follower's age and gender, a proportion of deactivated users, having a site (for the model explaining the followers count) and being included to formal "Shop" category. The wall-based statistics includes the profile's moderator activity only because all the patterns generated by followers (likes, comments, reposts) are strongly associated with a community size. Finally, the structure predictors are expressed in two forms: in clusters generalizing the networks' centrality measures and in these centrality measures themselves as the separate variables.

Therefore, four regression models have been built (see Table 2, here a first capital letter in the variables' names refers to a particular block of predictors: wall, controls or strategy). Starting with comparing two models explaining monthly site-visiting level corrected on a group size (first 2 columns in output), the following pattern can be noticed: being formal "Shop" on vk.com matters in both models. It means that external sites associated with vk-page, which have not been indicated as the formal vk-shops, are more visited, on average. From the set of strategy-related determinants, clusters III, V and VI significantly differ from the referent cluster IV (small groups with weak follower's network connectivity). It means that e-shops, which have the network from one of these three clusters have fewer visits on site from vk.com, comparing to the cluster IV. Maybe these groups are selling their products directly from the vk-page, and followers have no need to go on a website. Moreover, looking "inside the clusters (at the second model), the most powerful centrality measure relates to the "clicking on website link is eigen centrality. Its value is high if nodes are connected to many nodes whom themselves have the high scores. So, the coefficient's negative sign for this network measure represents the similar trend less connected networks provide greater attendance.

The next models with the number of "active" followers as success metric perform more significant results (see Table 2, columns 3–4). These models are built

Table 2. Linear regressions results

	Dependent variable:			
	log(Visits from vk.com per month)		log(Active members count)	
	(clusters)	(centrality)	(clusters)	(centrality)
W.Posts per day	−0.070 (0.103)	0.011 (0.103)	0.004 (0.006)	0.004 (0.005)
W.Days from first post	−0.0003 (0.0003)	−0.0002(0.0003)	−0.0001 (0.0001)	−0.00003 (0.0001)
W.Proportion of reposts	2.631** (1.248)	1.684 (1.231)	−0.369 (0.282)	−0.256 (0.251)
W.Proportion with text	−1.828* (0.998)	−0.778 (0.999)	0.626*** (0.241)	0.322 (0.211)
W.Proportion with audio	−2.212 (5.167)	−1.650 (5.072)	2.149** (1.015)	1.509* (0.871)
W.Proportion with video	1.819 (1.394)	1.575 (1.374)	0.148 (0.464)	0.058 (0.386)
W.Proportion with photo	−0.643 (1.346)	1.051 (1.342)	1.171*** (0.252)	0.916*** (0.227)
C.Proportion of men	−0.309 (1.503)	−0.215 (1.456)	−1.088*** (0.383)	−0.687** (0.322)
C.Age of followers	−0.130 (0.721)	0.703 (0.778)	0.691*** (0.135)	0.344*** (0.123)
C.Age of followers (sqr)	0.004 (0.012)	−0.010 (0.013)	−0.011*** (0.002)	−0.005*** (0.002)
C.Proportion of deactivated foll.	−1.909 (1.617)	−2.436 (1.691)		
C.Proportion with site			0.428*** (0.125)	0.312*** (0.108)
C.Proportion by "category"	−1.348** (0.551)	−1.013* (0.546)	2.466*** (0.223)	2.175*** (0.193)
S.Cluster I	0.747 (1.620)		−0.084 (0.221)	
S.Cluster II	−1.467 (1.578)		0.157 (0.238)	
S.Cluster III	−2.329* (1.322)		1.002*** (0.207)	
S.Cluster V	−3.720*** (1.267)		2.122*** (0.218)	
S.Cluster VI	−2.840** (1.290)		1.954*** (0.264)	
S.Closeness centrality		0.433 (1.496)		−0.775*** (0.280)
S.Betweenness centrality		1.102(1.196)		−0.932*** (0.298)
S.Eigen centrality		−9.610*** (2.244)		4.892*** (0.454)
S.Proportion of isolates		0.123 (0.983)		−0.186 (0.223)
Constant	3.771 (10.928)	−5.467 (11.319)	−9.072*** (2.119)	−5.240*** (1.903)
Observations	143	143	523	523
R²	0.401	0.417	0.627	0.711
Adjusted R²	0.319	0.343	0.615	0.702
Residual Std. Error	2.174 (df = 125)	2.135 (df = 126)	1.278 (df = 505)	1.125 (df = 506)
F Statistic	4.920** (df = 17;125)	5.639** (df = 16;126)	50.021*** (df = 17;505)	77.756*** (df = 16;506)

Note: *p<0.05, **p<0.01, ***p<0.001.
Robust standard errors are in the parenthesis.

on a wider set of observations because this time our focus is on a vk-profile's determinant (not an external source). For both ways of presenting the strategy-related patterns, most of the coefficients with controls and wall-indicators are highly significant, apart from the strategy-features themselves. In particular, vk-groups having a greater proportion of publications with some visuals and audio files are more likely to have a larger audience, along with a relatively higher number of female followers. Controlling for having a site or a "Products" section (category) in a vk-profile allows seeing a significant difference in averages for these subsets of e-shops. Simply speaking, more vk-users are following an e-shop's profile if it has a website link or presents the goods in a separate section. However, we found no significant difference in publication activity during last 3 month before data collecting (March 2018) neither between clusters (see Table 1), nor for posting frequency in the model and even on single profile basis (Pearson's product-moment correlation between number of active users member and number of posts per day $r = 0.019$, $t = 0.476$, p-value $= 0.633$). In other words, the popularity of profiles cannot be explained just by the speed of wall's updating.

Considering a contribution of network-related features to the follower number, all the clusters, except first two with the small-sized communities, are significantly different from the referent one. Belonging to these clusters (or following these strategies) positively relates to the audience size of e-shop, which is quite expected because these are middle- and big-sized vk-groups (see Table 2, column 3). As for the last model with the initial centrality measures (see Table 2, column 4), the signs of significant coefficients make possible to assume, that the large-audience communities have more homogeneous networks in terms of connections distribution, without big outliers, since the high betweenness and closeness are associated with fewer level of active followers. To sum up, we have tested the idea that e-shops following different strategies vary in audience size, and that the structural patterns of their members' network also relate to the absolute size activated audience.

Overall, the potential success and sided positive effects of maintaining a vk-page of some e-shop vary depending on the cluster. The network externality expressed in site-visiting rating presents in the small poor-connected networks probably because their followers are really interested in the certain selling products. At the same time, communities benefiting from the large audience size more frequently use the features provided by the social network.

4   Conclusion

Not only nascent entrepreneurs need to implement an optimal development strategy from the very beginning, but also larger firms have to know how to attract and keep their customers. Using the newest tools of information technologies makes a huge contribution to solving this issue by introducing plenty of Internet platforms for running and developing business, such as online social networking sites. While the influence of Facebook has already been studied in different ways, including an e-commerce approach, the most used in Russia vk.com has not been fully explored before.

Defining the structure of social networking communities is an important step for understanding a target audience formation processes and further information spreading. Depending on the motives and understanding of success, the different behavioral patterns should be applied for maintaining an account on the two-sided platform. For example, in case of getting a network effect formed in target audience attraction, the certain activities are about to be done on the community's wall, while to induce people going on a website, the structural features can better work.

Since the current research was focused only on the vk-profiles of e-shop specializing on the particular products (electronic goods), the possible further development of the study is to include other shops from different sectors for comparing with their structures and characteristics. Moreover, it would be interesting to compare the identified e-shop's strategies formed on vk.com with those existing on foreign networking sites such as Xing.com in Germany or Qzone.com in China.

The fact that some success metrics can be evaluated only having the determinants calculated on open public data, means that it is possible to plan large-scale research for exploring the socio-economical effect of SNS without access to the firm's inside information. It is obvious that such indicators as profits, return on an advertisement or a monthly cash flow made on the SNS would be the better approximations of successful functioning. However, the relations between the network-behavioral patterns make possible for future research to deepen into inventing some new success assessments relying on the bigger open data.

Acknowledgements. The article was prepared within the framework of the Academic Fund Program at the National Research University Higher School of Economics (HSE) in 2017 2019 (grant No. 17-05-0024).

References

1. Baron, R.A.: Psychological perspectives on entrepreneurship: cognitive and social factors in entrepreneurs' success. Curr. Dir. Psychol. Sci. **9**(1), 15–18 (2000)
2. Box, G.E., Cox, D.R.: An analysis of transformations. J. R. Stat. Society. Ser. B (Methodol.) 211–252 (1964)
3. Cenek, J., Smolk, J., Svatosovd, V.: Marketing on social networks: content analysis of Facebook profiles of selected Czech e-shops. Trendy Ekonomiky a Managementu **10**(26), 9 (2016)
4. Edmiston, K.: The role of small and large businesses in economic development (2007)
5. Hartigan, J.A., Wong, M.A.: Algorithm AS 136: a k-means clustering algorithm. J. R. Stat. Soc. Ser. C (Appl. Stat.) **28**(1), 100–108 (1979)
6. Hopkins, J.L.: Can Facebook be an effective mechanism for generating growth and value in small businesses? J. Syst. Inf. Technol. **14**(2), 131–141 (2012)
7. Katz, M.L., Shapiro, C.: Network externalities, competition, and compatibility. Am. Econ. Rev. **75**(3), 424–440 (1985)

8. Katz, M.L., Shapiro, C.: Product introduction with network externalities. J. Ind. Econ., 55–83 (1992)
9. Lim, K.H., Sia, C.L., Lee, M.K., Benbasat, I.: Do I trust you online, and if so, will I buy? An empirical study of two trust-building strategies. J. Manag. Inf. Syst. **23**(2), 233–266 (2006)
10. Meylakhs, P., Rykov, Y., Koltsova, O., Koltsov, S.: An AIDS-denialist online community on a Russian social networking service: patterns of interactions with newcomers and rhetorical strategies of persuasion. J. Med. Internet Res. **16**(11) (2014)
11. Quan, X.: Prior experience, social network, and levels of entrepreneurial intentions. Manag. Res. Rev. **35**(10), 945–957 (2012)
12. Rochet, J.C., Tirole, J.: Defining two-sided markets. mimeo, IDEI, Toulouse, France, January 2004
13. Rochet, J.C., Tirole, J.: Two sided markets: a progress report. RAND J. Econ. **37**(3), 645–667 (2006)
14. Rykov, Y., Koltsova, O., Meylakhs, P.: Structure and functions of online communities network mapping of HIV-relevant groups in VK.com SNS. Sotsiologicheskie Issledovaniia, **8** (2016)
15. Rysman, M.: The economics of two-sided markets. J. Econ. Perspect. **23**(3), 125–143 (2009)
16. Song, Y.: From offline social networks to online social networks: changes in entrepreneurship. Informatica Economica **19**(2), 120 (2015)
17. Spiller, P., Lohse, G.L.: A classification of Internet retail stores. Int. J. Electron. Commer. **2**(2), 29–56 (1997)
18. Swamynathan, G., Wilson, C., Boe, B., Almeroth, K., Zhao, B.Y.: Do social networks improve e-commerce? A study on social marketplaces. In: Proceedings of the First Workshop on Online Social Networks, pp. 1–6. ACM, August 2008
19. Wennekers, S., Thurik, R.: Linking entrepreneurship and economic growth. Small Bus. Econ. **13**(1), 27–56 (1999)
20. Wong, P.K., Ho, Y.P., Autio, E.: Entrepreneurship, innovation and economic growth: evidence from GEM data. Small Bus. Econ. **24**(3), 335–350 (2005)
21. R Core Team: R: A language and environment for statistical computing. R Foundation for Statistical Computing, Vienna. https://www.R-project.org/
22. RStudio Team: RStudio: Integrated Development for R. RStudio Inc., Boston. http://www.rstudio.com/

Studying Migrant Assimilation Through Facebook Interests

Antoine Dubois[1], Emilio Zagheni[2], Kiran Garimella[3](✉), and Ingmar Weber[4]

[1] Aalto University, Helsinki, Finland
antoine-dubois@hotmail.com
[2] Max Planck Institute for Demographic Research, Rostock, Germany
emilioz@uw.edu
[3] EPFL, Lausanne, Switzerland
kiran.garimella@epfl.ch
[4] Qatar Computing Research Institute, Doha, Qatar
iweber@hbku.edu.qa

Abstract. Migrant assimilation is a major challenge for European societies, in part because of the sudden surge of refugees in recent years and in part because of long-term demographic trends. In this paper, we use Facebook data for advertisers to study the levels of assimilation of Arabic-speaking migrants in Germany, as seen through the interests they express online. Our results indicate a gradient of assimilation along demographic lines, language spoken and country of origin. Given the difficulty to collect timely migration data, in particular for traits related to cultural assimilation, the methods that we develop and the results that we provide open new lines of research that computational social scientists are well-positioned to address.

1 Introduction

Managing migration flows and the integration of migrants is a major challenge for our societies. Recent crises and conflicts have led to large flows of refugees. For example, in 2015 alone, more than one million refugees arrived in Germany, largely from Syria.

In addition to the challenges of short-term crises, there are also long-term demographic changes that contribute to the migration debate. Longer lives and lower fertility levels mean that population aging is an inevitable consequence. Immigration is often seen as a stopgap measure to address population aging, which would otherwise strain the economy and public finances. In this context, immigration is expected to become a major driver of population dynamics.

Understanding the processes of assimilation and integration of migrants has become a priority for countries all over the world. Currently, United Nations member states are developing a global compact for safe, regular and orderly migration.[1] This is an inter-governmentally negotiated agreement to cover all

---

[1] http://refugeesmigrants.un.org/migration-compact.

© Springer Nature Switzerland AG 2018
S. Staab et al. (Eds.): SocInfo 2018, LNCS 11186, pp. 51–60, 2018.
https://doi.org/10.1007/978-3-030-01159-8_5

dimensions of migration. Policy action is informed by a number of indicators of integration that international organizations produce [8]. Traditional indicators include measures of education, language acquisition, poverty, intermarriage, and other aspects [11]. These indicators evaluate how opportunities and outcomes for migrants and their children differ from the ones of the host population.

Cultural assimilation is a more elusive quantity to measure with traditional methods. However, perceived cultural differences often fuel negative sentiments towards immigrants. At the same time, immigrants contribute to the cultural diversity of the host society. It is thus important to evaluate processes related to cultural assimilation.

In this paper, we use anonymized, aggregate data from Facebook users, available via Facebook's advertising platform, to evaluate cultural assimilation of Arabic-speaking migrants in Germany. Using this data, we compute an *assimilation score* and compare this score for different migrant populations in Germany, including migrants from Austria, Spain, France and Turkey. To the best of our knowledge, this paper is the first to make use of online advertising data from Facebook to show the feasibility of measuring migrant integration at scale.

2   Related Work

Understanding migrant integration and the effectiveness of policy measures to favor assimilation is a longstanding challenge. A wide range of aspects such as 'civic integration policies' [4] or multiculturalism [12] have been analyzed. These studies developed evaluation metrics based on concepts such as political trust [6] as well as lack of electoral participation or composite measures of civic integration [12]. For a review of empirical and theoretical challenges see [10] (2005).

New information, like Web and social media data, are a main source of innovation in the context of migration studies. Research in this area has focused on using online data to improve estimates of migration flows and stocks. After Zagheni and Weber used geo-located Yahoo! e-mail data to estimate international migration flows [14], several platforms have been used to understand the network structure of migration, including Facebook [5] and Google+ [7]. Geolocated Twitter data has proved useful for studying the relationship between internal and international migration [13], as well as short-term mobility versus long-term migration [1,3]. LinkedIn data has provided insights into global patterns of migration for professionals [9].

More recently, Facebook data for advertisers have been used to create estimates of stocks of international migrants [15]. These data are a promising source for generating timely migration statistics at different levels of spatial granularity. In this paper, we expand the use of these data to study cultural assimilation.

3   Data

Facebook's advertising platform allows advertisers to programmatically target their ads to a specific population, e.g. based on age, gender, country of residence, or spoken language.[2] Using the Marketing API, advertisers can obtain estimates of the number of people who belong to a certain demographic group and show certain *interests* (algorithmically generated) based on 'likes', pages that they visit and other signals.[3] As an illustrative example, consider *the number of Facebook users speaking Arabic, living in Germany, being in the age group 18–65 and interested in football.* As of May 3, 2018, Facebook Ads manager reports that there are 530k users matching these criteria. The complete list of available targeting options is available on the Facebook Ad API page.[4] We used an open source Python implementation to access the Facebook Marketing API and collect such audience estimates.[5]

We base our analysis on Facebook's interests. For each population, we obtain the audience size for each interest and we compare a measure of prevalence across populations. As an oversimplified example, we can compare the fraction of Arabic-speaking migrants in Germany who are interested in typically German interests such as Bundesliga – the German soccer league – to the same fraction of Germans in Germany interested in this topic. Arguably, if a migrant population has similar levels of interest as the host population, this is an indicator of assimilation in terms of cultural taste.

Facebook Marketing API has hundreds of thousands of interests to target ads. In this paper, we collected data for 2,907 interests[6] with the biggest global Facebook audiences. Our main criteria in selecting this subset is that their audiences should be sufficiently large so that the estimates are reliable. Then, we obtained the audience sizes for those interests for adults (aged 18–65) from different populations (e.g., non-expats living in Germany, or Arabic-speaking expats living in Germany).[7] In this paper, we focus mainly on the assimilation of Arabic-speaking migrants in Germany. To achieve this, we obtained data for (i) Arabic-speaking migrants living in Germany, and (ii) non-expats in Arab League countries.[8] Finally, for comparative purposes, we also collected audience estimates for the same set of interests and demographic groups for other migrant populations in Germany, from Austria, France, Spain and Turkey.

4   Methods: Quantifying Assimilation

Our goal is to obtain an assimilation score that could serve as a proxy for the assimilation of a group of migrants to a local population in terms of interests

---

[2] https://developers.facebook.com/docs/marketing-api/targeting-specs/.

[3] https://www.facebook.com/business/help/150756021661309.

[4] https://developers.facebook.com/docs/marketing-api/buying-api/targeting.

[5] https://github.com/maraujo/pySocialWatcher.

[6] We started with 3,000 interest IDs obtained in the summer of 2017, but 93 of those were subsequently removed by Facebook.

[7] We use the Facebook advertising platform terminology which does not refer to *migrants* but to *expats*, though we use migrant and expat interchangeably.

[8] A regional league of 22 Arabic-speaking countries https://en.wikipedia.org/wiki/Arab_League.

expressed by both groups. To reach this objective, for a given list of interests, we need the audience sizes of three groups: (i) the destination country (always Germany in our case), (ii) the target group in the destination country (i.e. Arabic-speaking migrants, French migrants, Turkish speakers, etc.), and (iii) the target group's home country (Arab League, France, Turkey, etc.). We will denote those groups as *Dest*, *Target* and *Home* respectively. We will focus on the case where *Dest* is German non-expats. We then proceed in two steps: (i) we identify 'distinctly German' interests – interests that are more popular in Germany (and more generally in *Dest*) compared to in *Home*; (ii) we use the audience sizes for those interests to compute the assimilation score. The selection of 'distinctly German' interests is a necessary preprocessing step to compute a meaningful score. If we were showing that migrants had the same level of interests as local people in generic interests that are prevalent across countries, like "Technology" or "Music", this would not necessarily be a sign of assimilation.

First we describe how, for each of the 2,907 initial interests, we evaluated if they are 'distinctly German'. Estimating how popular an interest is among a population could be simply done using the percentage of people in that population with the interest. However, this approach would be biased as a result of differential online activity level, since more active Facebook users also have more interests. Though the exact methods used by Facebook to calculate these interests is not disclosed, it is known to make use of a user's activity.[9]

To correct for this activity level bias, we can instead use the normalized audience percentage within each population given by

$$IR_p(i) = \frac{A_p(i)}{\sum_{i=1}^n A_p(i)}, \tag{1}$$

where $A_p(i)$ and $IR_p(i)$ denote, respectively, the audience size and what we call interest ratio for interest i in population p. Tables 1(a) and (b) show an example of the audiences for three populations and the corresponding interest ratios. IR can now be compared between populations to obtain typical interests.

We can identify 'distinctly German' interests by comparing the IRs for Germany and *Home*. 'Distinctly German' interests are defined as those that have a larger IR for Germany than for *Home* (shown in magenta and blue in Table 1(b)). For added numerical stability, we extract among those 'distinctly German' interests the ones that are the 'most German' (shown in blue in Table 1(b)). This is done by dividing the IRs for German interests by the ones for *Home*, for each of the 'distinctly German' interests, and keeping the top $k\%$ interests with highest value of the relative IRs.

After selecting the 'most German' interests, we compute the IRs for the target population only for these interests. Then, we define an assimilation score per interest i by dividing the IRs for *Target* by the ones of *Dest*.

$$AS_{Target}(i) = \frac{IR_{Target}(i)}{IR_{Dest}(i)} \tag{2}$$

---

[9] https://www.facebook.com/business/help/182371508761821.

Table 1. Numerical example of the whole process based on actual data for *Dest* as non-expats in Germany, *Home* as non-expats in Arab League countries and *Target* as Arabic-speaking migrants in Germany. (a) shows audience size for five interests. (b) shows the normalized interest ratios for those interests for *Dest* and *Home* and the selection of 'distinctly German' and 'most German' (top 50%) interests. (c) shows the subset of IR_{Target} interest ratios, as well as the assimilation score for the two selected interests. Typically German interests where IR_{Target} is close to IR_{Dest} correspond to a larger AS_{Target} score.

a)

Interests	A_{Dest}	A_{Home}	A_{Target}
Brewery	790k	260k	14k
Berlin	6200k	1500k	320k
Technology	1200k	12,000k	120k
Music	1600k	6400k	690k
God in Islam	14k	21,000k	170k
Total	9804k	41,160k	1314k

b)

Interests	IR_{Dest}	IR_{Home}	IR_{Dest}/IR_{Home}
Brewery	0.081	0.006	13.5
Berlin	0.632	0.036	17.6
Technology	0.122	0.292	0.42
Music	0.163	0.156	1.04
God in Islam	0.002	0.510	0.004

c)

Interests	IR_{Target}	AS_{Target}
Brewery	0.011	0.14
Berlin	0.244	0.39

where $AS_{Target}(i)$ is the assimilation score of *Target* for interest i.

For instance, for the interest 'Brewery' in the example in Table 1(c), the assimilation score for the target group is $0.011/0.081=0.14$. A specific interest i is considered to be fully assimilated by the migrant population if $AS_{Target}(i) \geq 1.0$.

Finally, to have a single score for the target population, we aggregate the per-interest scores by taking the median across all the 'most German' interests.

5 Results

We start by validating some of the assumptions in our data collection. Although Facebook identifies expats of some countries of origin, such as Spain, most Arab League countries cannot be targeted individually this way, though there is a catch-all "Expats (all)". Thus we use a proxy for this group by instead obtaining estimates for the Arabic-speaking residents in this "Expats (all)" group. To test if it is indeed a good approximation for expats from Arab League countries, we compared the number (per square km) of migrants in the 16 German states from a recent report by the Brookings Institute[10] with the estimated number of migrants per state using the data from Facebook ads manager. We find that there is a near perfect correlation between the two sets of values (Pearson's $r = 0.99$).

Then, we evaluate the selection of 'distinctly German' interests. Table 2 shows the top and bottom of the list of interests sorted in descending order according to $IR_{Germany}/IR_{Arab\ League\ countries}$. Note that the top of the list showing some

---

[10] https://www.brookings.edu/research/cities-and-refugees-the-german-experience/.

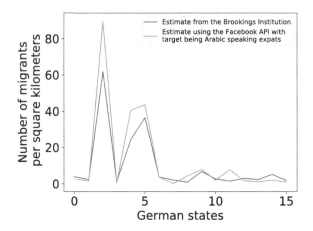

Fig. 1. The number of migrants per square kilometers in each German state according to two sources; in blue, from a study of the number of refugees by the Brookings institution; in orange, from the estimated audiences by the Facebook ads manager using the Arabic-speaking expats as target population. (Color figure online)

'distinctly German' interests is obtained when using the set of the 2,907 interests that are most popular worldwide. This is why even more typically German interests such as Oktoberfest do not show up. Similar lists were computed to validate this process when using a different *Home* but are not shown here due to space constraints.

In the remainder of this section, we evaluate our assimilation score. We set the 'most German' parameter k to 50% and we recall that this list of interest is always computed using the *Home* corresponding to the *Target* being analyzed.[11] Our first line of analysis compares *Targets* coming from different countries – Austria, France, Spain and Turkey. Since there is a sizable minority of Turkish-speaking non-expats in Germany[12], we divide the Turkish population into two: (i) All Turkish speakers in Germany, and (ii) Turkish-speaking non-expats in Germany (this is a subset of (i) containing residents of Germany who speak Turkish). The assimilation scores for different sub-populations from these countries is shown in the first part of Table 3 in comparison to Arabic-speaking migrants in Germany. The results show that European migrants have a higher assimilation score than Arabic-speaking migrants and Turkish speakers.

Next, we compared the assimilation scores for different sub-groups among the Arabic-speaking migrants. More precisely, we divided this population according to gender, age and education level. The results for those sub-groups are shown in the rest of Table 3. We explored all attribute combinations to see if there were

---

[11] We also tested for other values of k, 10–50 in intervals of 10, and the trends in the results remain consistent. So we only report results for $k = 50$.
[12] http://bit.ly/2E4UqpD.

any additive effects. Due to space constraints, assimilation scores for only a small selection of attribute combinations are included.

Women appear to be less assimilated in terms of their Facebook interests than men. We also observe that the assimilation score for university graduates is slightly higher than that for non-graduates. Note that for both educational levels, the scores are lower than the one for the whole Arabic-speaking migrant group. This statistical phenomenon, akin to Simpson's Paradox, is due to the aggregation process of the per-interest scores. Finally, in our analysis, young people between 18–24 are the most assimilated.

Table 2. The top and bottom of the list of 2,907 Facebook interests sorted by descending order according to $IR_{Germany}/IR_{Arab\ League\ countries}$.

Top German Interests	Bottom German Interests
British rock	CCTV News
Die (musician)	Carrefour
Psychedelic pop	Kuwait
Space age pop	Egyptian Arabic
Western music (N-A)	God in Islam
Fifty Shades of Grey	Munhwa Broadcasting Corporation
Sophisti-pop	Insha'Allah
Berlin	Prophets and messengers in Islam
Premiere	China Central Television
Warner Bros.	Arab League
Brewery	Algeria

Table 3. Assimilation score (*AS*) for different choice of *Target* in Germany using the top 50% distinctly German interests of 2,907 interests. Lines 1–5 of the first column correspond to non-Arab populations. The remaining cells, all with the "A:" prefix, correspond to Arabic-speaking migrants and sub-groups of this population.

Target	AS	Target	AS
Austrian Migrants	.900	A: Men	.648
French Migrants	.803	A: Women	.503
Spanish Migrants	.864	A: Uni. Grad.	.637
Turkish-Sp. Non-Expats	.922	A: Not Uni.	.626
Turkish Speakers	.746	A: <18	.590
A: Arabic-Sp. Migrants	.643	A: 18–24	.665
A: Men, Uni. Grad., 18–24	.677	A: 25–44	.603
A: Men, Uni. Grad., 25–44	.620	A: 45–64	.504
A: Women, Not Uni., 45–64	.461	A: >64	.553

6   Discussion

The work that we presented in this article has important limitations that we would like to acknowledge. At the same time, we also want to emphasize the potential for further research that computational social scientists can perform in this area.

Some limitations are related to our methods. For example, the results may be sensitive to the total number of interests that we consider, currently 2,907. To check the robustness of our approach, we computed the assimilation scores using random subsets of sizes varying from 100 to 2,900, in steps of 100 within our chosen subset. Figure 2 shows the variation in assimilation score. The figure shows that for any subset of size 500 or bigger, the assimilation score becomes stable. The maximum relative change from the average score across all considered populations was 10.4%, and the average relative change was 4.7%. This indicates that our results are relatively stable with respect to the number of interests being used.

Some limitations are related to the type of data. Our work relies on audience estimates produced by Facebook. The procedures used to infer users' interests are not well documented. For example, there could be differences in how well content in the Arabic or German language is processed, leading to artificial differences in interest profiles. Additionally, Facebook data do not provide information about the number of years that people have spent in the country, a key variable for the study of assimilation processes.

In our analysis, we grouped together arabic speaking migrants from all 22 countries of the Arab league into a single group, which might introduce biases. Though the arabic speaking countries typically share a lot of cultural similarities, different confounding factors (e.g. colonial history) can create differences.

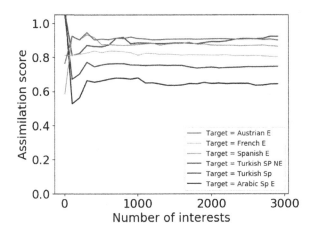

Fig. 2. Variation of the assimilation score for different Arab and non-Arab populations in Germany using the top 50% distinctly German interests when changing the size of the set of interests. 'E' denotes expats and 'NE' non-expats.

Our choice to group these users was because of a limitation by the Facebook Marketing API which does not allow us to target individuals from specific arabic speaking countries (e.g. Syria). Also, since a majority (around 75%) of Arab migrants in Germany are from Iraq and Syria [2], we think this bias would highly influence our results.

Despite these limitations, this article opens important lines of research that computational social scientists are well-positioned to address with Facebook data for advertisers. First, migration affects the host society and these data can be used to evaluate the extent to which the host society absorbs and embraces exposure to diversity. Second, assimilation processes can be studied at different levels of geographic granularity and in relation to contextual variables like political orientation of various sub-regions. Third, the idea that we presented for the specific case of Germany can be scaled to many countries of the world and used to study macro-regional processes like integration in the European Union.

7   Conclusion

We presented a methodology that uses anonymized, aggregate data from Facebook's advertising platform to compare the interest profiles of different migrant groups to that of the German host population. Based on the interest similarities, we derive an *assimiliation score* and observe that this score is lower for Arabic-speaking migrants compared to several European reference groups. We also show that the score varies among sub groups with younger and more educated men scoring highest.

References

1. Blanford, J.I., Huang, Z., Savelyev, A., MacEachren, A.M.: Geo-located tweets. Enhancing mobility maps and capturing cross-border movement. PloS One **10**(6), e0129202 (2015)
2. Deutschland, S.: Bevölkerung und erwerbstätigkeit (2011)
3. Fiorio, L., Abel, G., Cai, J., Zagheni, E., Weber, I., Vinué, G.: Using Twitter data to estimate the relationship between short-term mobility and long-term migration. In: WebSci (2017)
4. Goodman, S.W.: Integration requirements for integration's sake? Identifying, categorising and comparing civic integration policies. J. Ethn. Migr. Stud. **36**(5), 753–772 (2010)
5. Herdagdelen, A., State, B., Adamic, L.A., Mason, W.A.: The social ties of immigrant communities in the United States. In: WebSci (2016)
6. Maxwell, R.: Evaluating migrant integration: political attitudes across generations in europe1. Int. Migr. Rev. **44**(1), 25–52 (2010)
7. Messias, J., Benevenuto, F., Weber, I., Zagheni, E.: From migration corridors to clusters: the value of Google+ data for migration studies. In: ASONAM (2016)
8. OECD: Indicators of immigrant integration 2015 (2015). https://doi.org/10.1787/9789264234024-en

9. State, B., Rodriguez, M., Helbing, D., Zagheni, E.: Migration of professionals to the U.S. In: Aiello, L.M., McFarland, D. (eds.) SocInfo 2014. LNCS, vol. 8851, pp. 531–543. Springer, Cham (2014). https://doi.org/10.1007/978-3-319-13734-6_37

10. Waters, M.C., Jiménez, T.R.: Assessing immigrant assimilation: new empirical and theoretical challenges. Annu. Rev. Sociol. **31**, 105–125 (2005)

11. Waters, M.C., Pineau, M.G. (eds.): The Integration of Immigrants into American Society. The National Academies Press, Washington, D.C. (2015). https://doi.org/10.17226/21746. https://www.nap.edu/catalog/21746/the-integration-of-immigrants-into-american-society

12. Wright, M., Bloemraad, I.: Is there a trade-off between multiculturalism and sociopolitical integration? Policy regimes and immigrant incorporation in comparative perspective. Perspect. Polit. **10**(1), 77–95 (2012)

13. Zagheni, E., Garimella, K., Weber, I., et al.: Inferring international and internal migration patterns from Twitter data. In: WWW (2014)

14. Zagheni, E., Weber, I.: You are where you e-mail: using e-mail data to estimate international migration rates. In: WebSci (2012)

15. Zagheni, E., Weber, I., Gummadi, K.: Leveraging Facebook's advertising platform to monitor stocks of migrants. Popul. Dev. Rev. **43**(4), 721–734 (2017)

Access-Control Prediction in Social Network Sites: Examining the Role of Homophily

Nicolás E. Díaz Ferreyra$^{(\boxtimes)}$, Tobias Hecking, H. Ulrich Hoppe,
and Maritta Heisel

RTG User-Centred Social Media, University of Duisburg Essen, Duisburg, Germany
{nicolas.diaz-ferreyra,maritta.heisel}@uni-due.de,
{hecking,hoppe}@collide.info
https://www.ucsm.info/

Abstract. Often, users of Social Network Sites (SNSs) like Facebook or Twitter have issues when controlling the access to their content. Access-control predictive models are used to recommend access-control configurations which are aligned with the users' individual privacy preferences. One basic strategy for the prediction of access-control configurations is to generate access-control lists out of the emerging communities inside the user's ego-network. That is, in a *community-based* fashion. Homophily, which is the tendency of individuals to bond with others who hold similar characteristics, can influence the network structure of SNSs and bias the users' privacy preferences. Consequently, it can also impact the quality of the configurations generated by access-control predictive models that follow a community-based approach. In this work, we use a simulation model to evaluate the effect of homophily when predicting access-control lists in SNSs. We generate networks with different levels of homophily and analyse thereby its impact on access-control recommendations.

Keywords: Homophily · Preferential attachment · Adaptive privacy
Access-control prediction · Social Network Sites

1 Introduction

Users of Social Network Sites (SNSs) like Facebook or Twitter interact with a vast network of people who often represent various facets of their life. Like in the real world, similarities in gender, age, race, nationality or education level gather together people in online communities. This basic organization principle, in which people with similar characteristics tend to create connections with each other inside a network, is called *homophily* or *assortative mixing* [13]. In terms of structural properties, homophily translates into attribute similarity (i.e. "closeness" in terms of profile attributes) between the actors inside a network [16,18]. Consequently, it affects the type and strength of online relationships, and the formation of communities or clusters in a SNS.

© Springer Nature Switzerland AG 2018
S. Staab et al. (Eds.): SocInfo 2018, LNCS 11186, pp. 61–74, 2018.
https://doi.org/10.1007/978-3-030-01159-8_6

The type and strength of online social relationships are considered important factors which influence users' access-control decisions inside SNSs [15]. For instance, a user Alice can choose to exclude her work colleagues from a negative post she writes about her workplace in order to avoid future problems with her employer. As one can see in this example, feature similarity (in this case "workplace") is used by the user as an access-control *rule of thumb* in order to protect her privacy. Although this is a good and common privacy strategy, creating and maintaining access-control lists or circles can generate a high cognitive burden on the users. In consequence, users do not employ these privacy-preserving features, leaving their private information accessible to unintended audiences.

Privacy scholars have engineered different Access-control Predictive Models (ACPMs) in order to relieve the users from the burden of creating and maintaining lists of information recipients [6,7,14]. These models generate and recommend Access-control Lists (ACLs) based on the users' previous *privacy decisions* (i.e. with whom they have shared private information in the past), or their *privacy preferences* (i.e. asking them to assign *allow/deny* labels to a representative sample of friends). In other words, they predict *black lists* of information recipients using the user's privacy preferences or past decisions as predictor *variables*, and particular *instances* of these predictors as training examples. One basic strategy is to map these examples to emerging communities inside the user's *ego-network* (i.e. the network of connections between his/her friends) [15]. For instance, if a user Alice has excluded her friends Bob, John and Bill from the audience of a particular post, then it is to expect that she will exclude them again in the future together with other friends with similar characteristics. Let us assume that Alice's ego network can be clustered into three communities $C1$, $C2$ and $C3$, where Bob, John and Bill are grouped together in $C1$ (as illustrated in Fig. 1). Since community membership often indicates similarity between people, then one could expect that the rest of friends inside community $C1$ are also ought to be excluded by Alice from the audience of her future posts. Hence, an ACL consisting of all members of $C1$ is generated and recommended to Alice.

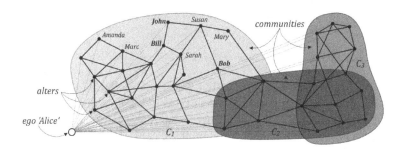

Fig. 1. Guilt-by-association approach for access-control prediction in SNSs.

Community-based ACPMs like the one just mentioned follow a *guilt-by-association* approach [4,15]. This is, all members inside a community are classified as untrusted recipients of a particular post because one fraction of its members were previously classified as untrusted (e.g. in Fig. 1 Amanda, Marc, Susan, Sarah and Mary are guilty-by-association). Although this approach is a good starting point for recommending personalized access-control lists, its accuracy depends largely on the semantics of these untrusted communities. For instance, if Alice excludes Bob, John and Bill from a post because they are her work colleagues, then Alice would expect an access-control recommendation containing a high number of work colleagues. However, algorithms used to identify communities inside a network do not take into account attribute similarity between individuals (i.e. homophily) and therefore do not provide cues about the semantic of emerging communities. In other words, for the example of Fig. 1 it is not possible to determine whether $C1$ gathers people working in the same company, people living in the same city, or people who share the same music taste. Therefore, it is hard to guarantee that the recommended access-control list will contain a large number of Alice's work colleagues. Consequently, there is a probability for Amanda, Marc, Susan, Sarah and Mary to be unfairly guilty-by-association.

As it is shown in the previous example, homophily between individuals can influence the structural properties of ego-networks and impact the performance of access-control predictions. In this work we examine the role of homophily when predicting ACLs in SNSs though a simulation model. Using this model, we generate (i) ego-networks out of different homophily scenarios, (ii) user-centred privacy preferences, and (iii) ACLs following the guilt-by-association approach. We show that community-based ACPMs can lead to unfair predictions under particular homophily scenarios, and that ACLs require validation from the user to ensure that they are aligned with his/her privacy preferences.

The rest of this paper is organized as follows. In the next section we briefly outline the simulation methodology used to analyse the impact of homophily when predicting ACLs in SNSs. The simulation of ego networks, which is an important part of our approach, is fully explained in the Appendix. In Sect. 3, we use our methodology to generate ACLs under different homophily scenarios and evaluate their performance against user-centred privacy preferences. For this, we propose a fairness metric and compare the results of each simulation execution. In Sect. 4 we analyse the strengths and limitations of our method. Finally, in Sect. 5 we conclude and discuss future work.

2   Methodology

As it is shown in Fig. 2, an ACPM requires (i) the user's ego-network and (ii) his/her privacy preferences in order to generate a personalized ACL. To simulate the user's ego-network, we developed a preferential-attachment model for generating scale-free networks. In this model, the ego and its alters are characterized with the attributes *gender*, *workplace* and *location* where gender can take the values *male* or *female*, workplace the values *Starbucks*, *Google* or *Ikea*, and location the values *Leeds* or *York*. The preferential attachment rule takes into account an openness matrix Λ to compute the linking probability between two nodes. The values inside Λ can range from 0 to 1 and describe how strong/weak attribute similarity is for this linking process (e.g. a value Λ_{York}^{Leeds} closer to zero describes a setting in which users located in *York* are less likely to connect with users living in *Leeds*). In this work, we have analysed the role of homophily in community-based ACPMs through different configurations of Λ which represent different homophily scenarios. A full description of this model can be found in the Appendix.

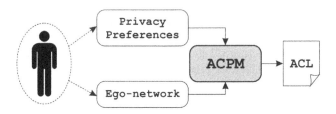

Fig. 2. Simulation pipeline.

In addition to an ego-network, a community-based ACPM requires the user's privacy preferences to generate a personalized ACL. In the practice, such preferences are elicited by asking the user to assign *allow/deny* labels to a reduced sample of friends. That is, the user is asked to provide examples of contacts that should be excluded/included from the audience of a particular piece of private information (e.g. a post or profile attributes). Basically, this kind of access-control decisions are influenced by two factors (i) the homophily degree between the user and his/her contacts, and (ii) the type of information to be disclosed. For instance, a user who posts a negative comment about his/her workplace is likely to assign *deny* labels to a sample of work colleagues inside his/her network. Then, using the emerging communities inside the user's network, the ACPM takes this set of examples and generates a larger customized ACL.

In order to simulate the user's privacy preferences, we must introduce a *selection criterion* of nodes inside the simulated ego-network. Given a *self-disclosure scenario* (i.e. a *user profile* and a piece of *private information* to be disclosed), such criterion consists of selecting nodes that hold a *critical attribute*. For instance, let us assume that our user is *male*, works at *Ikea* and lives in *York*, and the information to be disclosed is a post containing a negative comment about the user's workplace. If this post is seen by a colleague from *Ikea* the user might suffer an unwanted incident such a reputation damage, wake-up call from a superior or even job loss. Therefore, the attribute *Ikea* is *critical* for the user's privacy under this scenario. We can simulate the privacy preferences for this scenario by selecting n nodes from the simulated ego-network that hold the critical attribute *Ikea*. In order to choose the most influential nodes among these ones, we will select the n nodes with the highest degree.

3   Simulation Execution

In order to analyse the role of homophily in community-based ACPMs we put our methodology into practice. For this, we simulate ego-networks with different homophily configurations and use them to generate ACLs. Thereafter, we analyse the accuracy of these ACLs through the privacy preferences derived from a particular self-disclosure scenario.

3.1   Homophily Scenarios

As mentioned previously, each homophily scenario is described using a Λ matrix (refer to Appendix B for details). In our case, we have chosen similarity in *location* and *workplace* as the homophily aspects to control in our simulations. Therefore, the Λ of these scenarios differ only in the values assigned to Λ_{York}^{Leeds}, $\Lambda_{Google}^{Starbucks}$, $\Lambda_{Starbucks}^{Ikea}$ and Λ_{Google}^{Ikea} while the rest of the group-openness factors are set to one. The homophily scenarios used to execute our model were the following:

- $S_1 : \{\Lambda_{Google}^{Starbucks} = \Lambda_{Starbucks}^{Ikea} = \Lambda_{Google}^{Ikea} = 0.7\}$
- $S_2 : \{\Lambda_{Google}^{Starbucks} = \Lambda_{Starbucks}^{Ikea} = \Lambda_{Google}^{Ikea} = 0.3\}$
- $S_3 : \{\Lambda_{Google}^{Starbucks} = \Lambda_{Starbucks}^{Ikea} = \Lambda_{Google}^{Ikea} = 0.01\}$
- $S_4 : \{\Lambda_{York}^{Leeds} = 0.7\}$
- $S_5 : \{\Lambda_{York}^{Leeds} = 0.3\}$
- $S_6 : \{\Lambda_{York}^{Leeds} = 0.01\}$

As it can be observed, we have varied the openness values between the groups corresponding to *workplace* in scenarios S_1, S_2 and S_3. This set of scenarios represent different levels of users' openness/closeness when creating ties with individuals from other workplaces. Likewise, for scenarios S_4, S_5 and S_6 we have varied the openness values between the groups corresponding to *location*. In this case, these scenarios describe different levels of openness/closeness when users bind with individuals from another location.

3.2   Execution and Analysis

We have implemented our simulation model using iGraph [5], a library for network analysis and visualization for R^1. The model was initialized and executed according to the set-up parameters described in Sect. B.2 of the Appendix and the homophily scenarios introduced previously. We have simulated 6 topologies of ego-networks corresponding to the scenarios S_1, S_2, S_3, S_4, S_5, and S_6. Additionally, we have introduced a control scenario S_0 in which homophily does not influence the preferential attachment rule (i.e $\Lambda = 1$, an all-ones matrix). This scenario was also simulated, giving a total of 7 simulated ego-networks.

---

[1] The scripts can be found in the following repository: https://bit.ly/2Nth7HE.

As we described in Sect. 2, one must define a *self-disclosure scenario* in order simulate the user's privacy preferences. For our simulations, we have proposed a scenario in which a user (i.e. the ego of the simulated ego-network) who is *male*, works in *Ikea* and lives in *York*, posts a *negative comment* about his employer on a SNS. Based on this scenario, we have simulated the privacy preferences of this user by selecting 10 nodes from each simulated network that hold the critical attribute *Ikea*. This selection was made so that the nodes with the highest degree were chosen. The column *Preferences* of Table 1 shows the privacy preferences generated for each simulated scenario. We can observe for instance, that for scenario S_0 the 10 nodes with highest degree that hold the attribute *Ikea* are P_0: $\{4,6,2,3,28,20,44,65,88,17\}$. Hence, these nodes are defined as the user's privacy preferences in S_0.

Table 1. Simulation results for scenarios S_0, S_1, S_2, S_3, S_4, S_5 and S_6.

Scn.	Preferences	Method	N° Communities	Size of best-fit community	Nodes with critical attribute	Fairness
S_0	P_0:\{4,6,2,3,28,20, 44,65,88,17\}	MC	15	51	19	37.25%
		LE	11	225	82	36.44%
S_1	P_1:\{2,6,4,30,32, 15,75,35,40,25\}	MC	15	53	16	31.19%
		LE	28	49	24	48.98%
S_2	P_2:\{1,4,11,3,75, 27,13,14,81,10\}	MC	15	67	34	50.75%
		LE	16	40	30	75.00%
S_3	P_3:\{1,6,16,17,28, 2,54,72,120,78\}	MC	6	141	140	99.29%
		LE	6	172	168	97.67%
S_4	P_4:\{7,3,8,19,24, 2,14,5,39,55\}	MC	15	41	18	43.90%
		LE	18	62	20	32.26%
S_5	P_5:\{2,8,5,30,9, 82,18,39,50,23\}	MC	15	71	26	36.62%
		LE	20	96	35	36.46%
S_6	P_6:\{4,1,28,7,29, 8,18,49,41,5\}	MC	9	117	35	29.91%
		LE	9	145	57	39.31%

In order to predict the corresponding ACLs, preferences (i.e. the selected nodes) are mapped to the emerging communities inside the ego-network of each scenario. For each scenario, the community that best-fits the preferences (i.e. the one that covers the majority of the nodes) is then chosen as ACL. To identify communities inside networks we have applied two different community-detection algorithms: Leading Eigenvector (LE) [17] and Multilevel Community (MC) [3]. Both methods generate a hierarchy of nested communities in which nodes belong to at most one community. In the case of LE, this process is done following a top-down approach (i.e. starting with the entire network and iteratively splitting it into partitions), whereas in the case of MC, this is done in a bottom-up fashion (i.e. starting with single nodes and iteratively merging them into communities). Both algorithms are part of the iGraph package.

As described in Sect. 2, the community that best-fits the user's privacy preferences becomes the personalized ACL. In order to determine if such ACL is indeed aligned with the user's privacy preferences, we have defined a *fairness* metric. In this case, fairness is computed as the percentage of nodes that hold the critical attribute inside the predicted ACL. For instance, when using MC the community that best-fits P_0 has 19 out of 51 nodes with the attribute *Ikea*. Therefore, the fairness of the corresponding ACL is $19/51 * 100 = 37.25\%$. Low levels of fairness like this one indicate that the predicted ACL is not reflecting the privacy expectations of the user. That is, instead of generating a list of contacts mainly composed by work colleagues from *Ikea*, the ACPM generates a list mostly composed of contacts who do not work there. Hence, the ACL will not cover the privacy expectations and needs of the user, and most of the contacts inside the ACL will be unfairly guilty-by association.

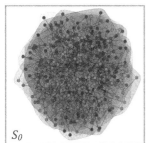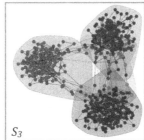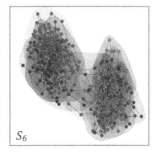

Fig. 3. Emerging communities for scenarios S_0, S_3 and S_6 using MC.

Table 1 shows that the highest and lowest levels of fairness correspond to scenarios S_3 and S_6, respectively. The emerging communities for these configurations together with the ones of S_0 are shown in Fig. 3. As it can be observed, the plot corresponding to S_3 has three highly dense areas and the one from S_6 has two. This is due to the Λ assigned to each scenario: in S_3 nodes with *workplace* similarity were more likely to connect to each other, whereas in S_6 this was the case for nodes with the same *location*. Consequently, in S_3 nodes are condensed in areas corresponding to the values *Ikea*, *Starbucks* and *Google* whereas nodes in S_6 are condensed in areas corresponding to *Leeds* and *York*. Therefore, since emerging communities in S_3 reflect *workplace* similarity, the fairness of its corresponding ACL is much higher than in S_6 where communities reflect *location* similarity. Consequently, in S_3 the effect of homophily contributes positively to the fairness of the predicted ACL, whereas in S_6 such effect has a negative impact.

4   Discussion

From the execution of our model, we can conclude that community-based ACPMs can lead to unfair predictions under certain homophily scenarios. Basically, we have observed that this happens when the semantic of the best-fit community is not aligned with the user's privacy preferences. However, one should take into account that in a controlled simulation environment (like the one used for this study) assumptions and parameters can influence the results of our experiments. One of the assumptions that should be closely analysed is the distribution of attributes proposed in Sect. B.1 of the Appendix. For our experiments, we have proposed three attributes and distributed their values uniformly. However, this is not always the case and often some values tend to prevail over others. For instance, Volkovich et al. [19] suggest that online ties preferentially connect closer people. For the self-disclosure scenario that we have proposed, this suggest that nodes with $location = York$ should prevail over nodes with $location = Leeds$. Consequently, the distribution of attributes should be characterized in a way that resembles a more realistic set-up.

Another aspect to be considered is related to the homophily scenarios proposed to generate the ego-networks. We have considered basically two homophily factors in our simulations: (i) similarity in workplace and (ii) similarity in location. The scenarios proposed in Sect. 3.1 consider homophily as an *attribute-specific* phenomenon and not as a *cross-attribute* phenomenon. That is, group-openness factors were specified only among the groups corresponding to a particular attribute and not between groups from different attributes. For instance, scenarios S_1, S_2 and S_3 define values (different to one) for Λ_{York}^{Leeds}, $\Lambda_{Google}^{Starbucks}$ and $\Lambda_{Starbucks}^{Ikea}$, but do not define values for Λ_{York}^{Ikea} or $\Lambda_{Leeds}^{Starbucks}$. Therefore, the influence of homophily across the attributes *workplace* and *location* is ignored in our simulations. It is necessary to take a closer look at the predominant homophily scenarios in SNSs and incorporate this information to the model. Empirical evidence can be a vehicle to cope with this task.

5   Conclusions and Future Work

The limitations of community-based ACPMs that we have exposed in this work suggest that users should take a more active role in the automatic generation of ACLs. Basically, ACPMs should include a validation stage in which the user can provide feedback on the composition of the resulting ACL. Strategies to incorporate users into the information flow of recommender systems is one of the main challenges of human-computer interaction [8]. Our future work will focus on exploring different alternatives to include the user's feedback into ACPMs for SNSs. Likewise, we will investigate the predominant homophily processes that take place on SNSs in order to improve the efficiency of our model.

The community-detection algorithms used for the simulation are also a matter of future research. Basically, the two approaches used in this work identify non-overlapping communities based solely on the network structure. Approaches like the one of Leskovec et al. [11] generate overlapping communities combining network structure with attribute similarity. We believe this can help to discover communities that adjust better to the user's privacy preferences and improve thereby the fairness of the generated ACLs. This aspect will be analysed and discussed in future publications.

Acknowledgments. This work was supported by the Deutsche Forschungsgemein- schaft (DFG) under grant No. GRK 2167, Research Training Group "User-Centred Social Media".

Appendix

In this Appendix we introduce the theoretical foundations used for the definition and implementation of our simulation model of ego-networks.

A   Network Evolution with Homophily

Up to now, scholars have proposed several evolution models for constructing scale-free networks. Among them, the *prefferential attachment* mechanism intro- duced by Barabassi and Albert [2] is one of the most prominent ones. However, this model does not consider attribute similarity when computing the linking probability between two nodes. Following, we introduce an approach for the simulation of ego-networks that takes homophily explicitly into account.

A.1   Group-Openness

Many empirical and theoretical studies have shown that people prefer to link to those people with whom they share certain characteristics [13]. Moreover, these studies have also shown that homophily can lead to the emergence of clusters inside a social network in which similar people are linked more densely with each other [9]. In order to study the role of homophily in the evolution of scale- free networks, Kim et al. [10] introduced *group-openness* characteristics to the preferential attachment mechanism of Barabasi and Albert [1]. In this approach, nodes which share a particular characteristic s belong to group s. Consequently, the group-openness factor Λ_s^t between two groups s and t is defined as:

$$\Lambda_s^t = \begin{cases} \Lambda, & \text{if } s \neq t \\ 1, & \text{if } s = t \end{cases} \qquad 0 \leq \Lambda \leq 1 \qquad (1)$$

where the homophily index Λ is a real number between 0 and 1 [9]. If $\Lambda = 0$, nodes in group s do not link with nodes in group t $(t \neq s)$ but link only with those nodes in the same group. This state describes completely *closed* groups, in which members prefer to link only with those who hold their same charac- teristics. Conversely, if $\Lambda = 1$ homophily does not affect the linkage between nodes, independently of whether they belong to the same group or not. This state describes completely *open* groups that show neutrality when linking to others [10].

A.2   Preferential Attachment with Homophily

The preferential attachment mechanism introduced by Barabasi and Albert [1] describes the process by which new nodes prefer to link to the more connected nodes in a network (i.e. the hubs). Hence, the probability Π_i that a new node connects to node i is proportional to the degree k_i of node i:

$$\Pi_i = \frac{k_i}{\sum_j k_j}.m \qquad \begin{aligned} m &= \text{number of new links} \\ k_i &= \text{degree of node } i \end{aligned} \tag{2}$$

Using the group-openness mechanism defined in Eq. 1, Kim et al. [10] introduced homophily to the preferential attachment model of Eq. 2. As result, the probability Π_i^{pq} that a new node of group q is linked to node i of group p is defined as:

$$\Pi_i^{pq} = \frac{k_i^p.\Lambda_p^q}{\sum_j k_j^\mu.\Lambda_\mu^q} \qquad \begin{aligned} k_i^p &= \text{degree of node } i \text{ from group } p \\ \Lambda_p^q &= \text{openess of group } p \text{ with group } q \end{aligned} \tag{3}$$

where k_i^p is the degree of node i of group p, and Λ_p^q represents the homophily between the group of the new node q and the group of node i. As one can observe, in Eq. 2 the probability that a new node connects to an existing node i is normalized by the sum of degrees of all existing nodes in the network. This is also the case for Eq. 3, only that this time the group-openness factor of each node is considered for the normalization. In other words, if all groups are completely open (i.e. $\Lambda = 1$), Eq. 3 is identical to Eq. 2. On the other hand, if the groups are completely open (i.e. $\Lambda = 0$), Eq. 3 is reduced to Eq. 2 for each particular group [10].

In order to explain the evolution of nodes who are active inside a network for a long period of time, Kim et al. [9] introduced an additional rule which describes the creation of links between existing nodes. This is, the probability Π_{ij}^{pq} that node i of group p links to node j of group q is defined as:

$$\Pi_{ij}^{pq} = \frac{k_i^p.k_j^q.\Lambda_p^q}{\sum_l \sum_{m>l} k_l^\mu.k_m^\nu.\Lambda_\mu^\nu} \tag{4}$$

where k_i^p and k_j^q are the degrees of node i and of node j respectively [10]. Nodes i and j belong to groups p and q respectively, and Λ_p^q is the group-openness between these two groups. Like in Eqs. 2 and 3, Eq. 4 is normalized by the sum of all possible combinations of links between existing nodes in the network [10]. In this case, k_l^μ and k_m^ν are the degrees of nodes l and m which belong to groups μ and ν, respectively. Likewise, Λ_μ^ν refers to the group-openness between groups μ and ν [10].

B   Simulation Model

The model introduced in Sect. A.2 of this Appendix generates a network in which nodes link with each other according to attribute similarity. Therefore, it assumes that the values of these attributes have been assigned to the nodes prior to the attachment phase. Following, we define the attributes used to characterise the nodes of our simulated networks and the distribution of their respective values. Likewise, we define the parameters used to set-up the simulation.

B.1   Node-Attributed Ego-Networks

In our model, the ego and its alters are characterized with the attributes *gender*, *workplace* and *location* where gender can take the values *male* or *female*, workplace the values *Starbucks*, *Google* or *Ikea*, and location the values *Leeds* or *York*. These attributes and their respective values are conditionally distributed following the probability tree of Fig. 4. According to this distribution, a node in the network is generated with 50% chance of being female and 50% chance of being male (i.e. $P(male) = P(female) = 0.5$). Then, the values for workplace are assigned with 33% chance according to the gender value of the node. For instance, if $gender = female$, then $P(Starbucks|female) = P(Google|female) = P(Ikea|female) = 0.33$. Likewise, the values for location are assigned with 50% chance given the gender and workplace values of the node. This means that in the case of a node whose gender and location attributes are *female* and *Ikea*, then $P(York|female \cap Ikea) = P(Leeds|female \cap Ikea) = 0.5$.

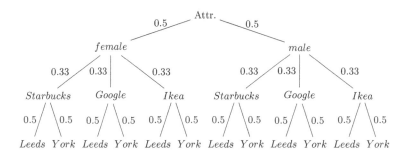

Fig. 4. Attributes probability distribution.

Each attribute value represents a group. Therefore, our model consists of 7 groups (i.e. *male*, *female*, *Starbucks*, *Google*, *Ikea*, *Leeds* and *York*) together with the corresponding group-openness factors between them. If we consider group-openness a symmetric relation between two groups s and t, then $\Lambda_s^t = \Lambda_t^s$. This means that for 7 groups one must define $C_{7,2} = \frac{7!}{2!(7-2)!} = 21$ different group-openness factors. This information can be expressed through a group-openness matrix $\Lambda_{7 \times 7}$ in which each cell represents a factor Λ_s^t as shown in Fig. 5. As one can observe, this matrix is symmetric and contains ones on its main diagonal. This is because $\Lambda_s^t = \Lambda_t^s$ and, according to Eq. 1, the group-openness factor Λ_s^t is 1 when $s = t$.

$$\Lambda = \begin{bmatrix} \Lambda_{male}^{male} & \Lambda_{male}^{female} & \cdots & \Lambda_{male}^{York} \\ \Lambda_{female}^{male} & \Lambda_{female}^{female} & \cdots & \Lambda_{female}^{York} \\ \vdots & \vdots & \ddots & \vdots \\ \Lambda_{York}^{male} & \Lambda_{York}^{female} & \cdots & \Lambda_{York}^{York} \end{bmatrix} = \begin{bmatrix} 1 & 0.7 & \cdots & 0.3 \\ 0.7 & 1 & \cdots & 0.5 \\ \vdots & \vdots & \ddots & \vdots \\ 0.3 & 0.5 & \cdots & 1 \end{bmatrix}$$

Fig. 5. Group-openness matrix.

Nodes are described in terms of one value per attribute and, consequently, belong to more than one group at the same time (e.g. a node whose gender is *female*, works in *Ikea* and lives in *York*, belongs to the groups *female*, *Ikea* and *York* respectively). Therefore, the *total* homophily factor between two nodes i and j depends on more than one group-openness factor. In other words, one should compute the homophily between i and j considering the group-openness factors of all possible combinations among the groups to which i and j belong. For instance, if i belongs to the group-set *male*, *Starbucks* and *York*, and j to the group-set *female*, *Google* and *York*, then one should consider Λ_{female}^{male}, Λ_{Google}^{male}, Λ_{York}^{male}, $\Lambda_{female}^{Starbucks}$, $\Lambda_{Google}^{Starbucks}$, $\Lambda_{York}^{Starbucks}$, Λ_{female}^{York}, Λ_{Google}^{York}, and Λ_{York}^{York}. Consequently, the total homophily factor between two group-sets P and Q is defined as:

$$\mathcal{H}_P^Q = \prod_{\substack{p \in P \\ q \in Q}} \Lambda_{p,q} \qquad \begin{array}{l} P = \text{groups to which node } i \text{ belongs} \\ Q = \text{groups to which node } j \text{ belongs} \end{array} \tag{5}$$

where P and Q are the groups to which nodes i and j belong, respectively. According to the definition above, the preferential attachment model described in Eqs. 3 and 4 can be re-defined. That is, the probability Π_i^{PQ} that a new node of group-set Q is linked to node i of group-set P is defined as:

$$\Pi_i^{PQ} = \frac{k_i^P . \mathcal{H}_P^Q}{\sum_j k_j^M . \mathcal{H}_M^Q} \qquad \begin{array}{l} k_i^P = \text{degree of node } i \text{ from group-set } P \\ \mathcal{H}_P^Q = \text{total homophily factor between} \\ \text{group-set } P \text{ and group-set } Q \end{array} \tag{6}$$

where k_i^P is the degree of node i from group-set P, and $\mathcal{H}_P^Q$ represents the total homophily factor between the group-set of the new node Q and the group-set of node i. Likewise, the probability Π_{ij}^{PQ} that node i of group-set P links to node j of group-set Q is defined as:

$$\Pi_{ij}^{PQ} = \frac{k_i^P . k_j^Q . \mathcal{H}_P^Q}{\sum_l \sum_{m>l} k_l^M . k_m^N . \mathcal{H}_M^N} \tag{7}$$

where k_i^P and k_j^Q are the degrees of node i and of node j respectively and $\mathcal{H}_P^Q$ is the total homophily factor between group-sets P and Q.

B.2   Simulation Set-up

Our simulation model for ego-networks comprises Eqs. 6 and 7 together with the attribute probability distribution introduced in Appendix B. According to the Pew Research Center, the average size of an ego-network in Facebook was of 338 friends/nodes in 2014[2] (this number scaled up to 425 in a study focused on adolescents and online privacy in 2013 [12]). Therefore, we will consider an average ego-network consisting of 500 nodes and execute our simulation for $F = 500$ time units. The initial set-up for all simulations consists of an network of two nodes ($N(0) = 2$) and one link ($K = 1$). It is also assumed that only one node enters the network at time t ($b = 2$) and generates only one link ($\beta = 1$). On the other hand, the number of new links between existing nodes at time t is given by $\lfloor N(t) \cdot \alpha \rfloor$ where $0 \leq \alpha < 1$ and $N(t)$ is the number of links at t. In order to preserve the degree distribution in our simulated networks we adopt $\alpha = 0.001$ as suggested by Kim et al. [9].

References

1. Barabási, A.L.: Network Science. Cambridge University Press, Cambridge (2016)
2. Barabási, A.L., Albert, R.: Emergence of scaling in random networks. Science **286**(5439), 509–512 (1999). https://doi.org/10.1126/science.286.5439.509, http://science.sciencemag.org/content/286/5439/509
3. Blondel, V.D., Guillaume, J.L., Lambiotte, R., Lefebvre, E.: Fast unfolding of communities in large networks. J. Stat. Mech. Theory Exper. **2008**(10), P10008 (2008)
4. Boyd, D., Levy, K., Marwick, A.: The networked nature of algorithmic discrimination. In: Data and Discrimination: Collected Essays. Open Technology Institute, New America Washington, DC (2014)
5. Csardi, G., Nepusz, T.: The igraph software package for complex network research. InterJournal Complex Syst. **1695**(5), 1–9 (2006). http://igraph.org
6. Díaz Ferreyra, N.E., Meis, R., Heisel, M.: At your own risk: shaping privacy heuristics for online self-disclosure. In: Proceedings of the 16th Annual Conference on Privacy, Security and Trust, August 2018
7. Fang, L., LeFevre, K.: Privacy wizards for social networking sites. In: Proceedings of the 19th International Conference on World Wide Web, pp. 351–360, WWW 2010. ACM, New York (2010). https://doi.org/10.1145/1772690.1772727
8. Gil, M., Pelechano, V., Fons, J., Albert, M.: Designing the human in the loop of self-adaptive systems. In: García, C.R., Caballero-Gil, P., Burmester, M., Quesada-Arencibia, A. (eds.) UCAmI 2016. LNCS, vol. 10069, pp. 437–449. Springer, Cham (2016). https://doi.org/10.1007/978-3-319-48746-5_45
9. Kim, K., Altmann, J., Hwang, J.: The impact of the subgroup structure on the evolution of networks: an economic model of network evolution. In: 2010 INFOCOM IEEE Conference on Computer Communications Workshops, pp. 1–9, March 2010. https://doi.org/10.1109/infocomw.2010.5466705
10. Kim, K., Altmann, J.: Effect of homophily on network formation. Commun. Nonlinear Sci. Numer. Simul. **44**, 482–494 (2017)

---

[2] http://www.pewresearch.org/fact-tank/2014/02/03/what-people-like-dislike-about-facebook/.

11. Leskovec, J., McAuley, J.: Learning to discover social circles in ego networks. In: Pereira, F., Burges, C.J.C., Bottou, L., Weinberger, K.Q. (eds.) Advances in Neural Information Processing Systems, vol. 25, pp. 539–547. Curran Associates, Inc. (2012)
12. Madden, M., et al.: Teens, social media, and privacy. Pew Res. Cent. **21**, 2–86 (2013)
13. McPherson, M., Smith-Lovin, L., Cook, J.M.: Birds of a feather: homophily in social networks. Annu. Rev. Sociol. **27**(1), 415–444 (2001)
14. Misra, G., Such, J.M.: REACT: recommending access control decisions to social media users. In: Proceedings of the 2017 IEEE/ACM International Conference on Advances in Social Networks Analysis and Mining 2017, pp. 421–426, ASONAM 2017. ACM, New York (2017). https://doi.org/10.1145/3110025.3110073
15. Misra, G., Such, J.M., Balogun, H.: Non-sharing communities? An empirical study of community detection for access control decisions. In: IEEE/ACM International Conference on Advances in Social Networks Analysis and Mining (ASONAM), pp. 49–56 (2016)
16. Newman, M.E.J.: Mixing patterns in networks. Phys. Rev. E **67**, 026126 (2003). https://doi.org/10.1103/PhysRevE.67.026126
17. Newman, M.E.J.: Finding community structure in networks using the eigenvectors of matrices. Phys. Rev. E **74**, 036104 (2006). https://doi.org/10.1103/PhysRevE.74.036104
18. Thedchanamoorthy, G., Piraveenan, M., Kasthuriratna, D., Senanayake, U.: Node assortativity in complex networks: an alternative approach. Procedia Comput. Sci. **29**, 2449–2461 (2014)
19. Volkovich, Y., Scellato, S., Laniado, D., Mascolo, C., Kaltenbrunner, A.: The length of bridge ties: structural and geographic properties of online social interactions. In: Proceedings of the 6th International AAAI Conference on Weblogs and Social Media (2012)

Mobile Applications as Tools of Alternative Communication, Diagnostics and Language Development for Children with Language Disorders

Liudmila Mozheikina[1,3] and Pavel Emelyanov[2,3(✉)]

[1] Novosibirsk State Technical University,
20 pr. K. Marksa, Novosibirsk 630073, Russia
mozhejkina@mail.ru
[2] A.P. Ershov Institute of Informatics Systems,
6 pr. Lavrentiev, Novosibirsk 630090, Russia
[3] Novosibirsk State University, 1 ul. Pirogova, Novosibirsk 630090, Russia
emelyanov@mmf.nsu.ru

Abstract. In this paper, we present several software tools to diagnose and correct child language disorders. These tools implement a playing strategy to decrease stress and improve effectiveness. In addition, we describe a tool for an alternative communication via pictograms.

Keywords: Language disorders · Diagnostics · Alternative communication
Language development · Mobile applications

1 Introduction

Language communication is an essential part of an individual's private and social life. Thus, it has a significant impact on life quality. Language disorders of different kinds may cause personal issues and prevent the successful development of an individual. Early diagnostics and precise correctional recommendations enable such issues to be resolved efficiently in childhood; postponing corrective efforts to later stages can have serious adverse effects. Indeed, it is vital for children to have convenient and expressive ways to communicate even if they are currently struggling with language problems.

Several common manifestations appear in children with language disorders, and indicate a systematic pathology of language activity [1]. These include a range of disorders, from specific language impairment (incoherent speech; a sequential, lexical, and grammatical construction of speech; and a phonetical and phonematical understanding and verbalization of concepts in general) to disorders that can be placed on the autism spectrum (from limited communication with the external world to the complete rejection of social interaction). The systematic nature of speech disorders manifests in

---

This work is supported by the Ministry of Science and Education of the Russian Federation under the 5–100 Excellence Programme.

S. Staab et al. (Eds.): SocInfo 2018, LNCS 11186, pp. 75–84, 2018.
https://doi.org/10.1007/978-3-030-01159-8_7

the following ways: children begin to speak later, their speech is devoid of grammar, and their insufficiently phonetically framed speech activity is reduced and with age, if not corrected, declines sharply. Such incomplete speech activity also has an effect on other areas of a child's mental development. Children with such disorders may have unstable attention and not know how to distribute it. Their verbal memory may be deficient. They may not develop verbal and logical thinking as quickly. In addition, they may lag behind their peers in the reproduction of motive assignments, in terms of space-time parameters and tasks that involve fine motor skills. There are data to support that such children have difficulty learning the Russian language in a comprehensive school environment [2]. Our experience reveals that language disorders can be an obstacle to academic success, even if the university does its best to remedy the situation.

We are interested in developing software tools designed for the diagnostic and correction of language development in children with special health disabilities. Creating software tools is quite important, especially when dealing with children. The peak of prophylactic and therapeutic activities occurs in pre- and primary school age.

Duenser et al. [3] have found that, in Australia, 20% of children at the age of 4 years has a language disorder that hinders their development and understanding of the English language. Of the total number of children who undergo special logopedic examinations, 25% wait approximately six months for the preliminary results, while 15% of children wait for more than a year. After receiving the preliminary results, 18% of children wait an entire year before the speech therapy sessions begin. In remote areas, this issue is exacerbated by the shortage of specialists. Lack of diagnosis or additional training can lead to a sharp decline in the progress and literacy of children, increasing the likelihood of problems in social interactions, which can negatively affect a child's emotional state. The authors affirm the need to create a mobile application that can diagnose and correct language disorders, and that would allow parents to help their children without requiring them to obtain special knowledge in the field of language disorders. According to data gathered between 2011 and 2014, in Russia about 40% of pre- and primary school children have language development issues, and this number is only growing.

When comparing the traditional "paper" approach to the modern mobile-based one, the authors [4, 5] have determined that the traditional approach has significant short-comings: a small number of therapists, a large number of children for whom testing is necessary, in addition to planning, a large amount of preparatory work, processing of the results, monitoring, *inter alia*. Nevertheless, in language therapy practices, paper carriers are still widely used, both in Russia and abroad. One disadvantage is that they are voluminous and take up much of a therapist's office space. An experimental evaluation of mobile applications' effect on children with specific language impairments (32 and 26 children, respectively) has found that the amount of time needed to achieve an appropriate level of the language development is substantially reduced, compared to the traditional approach. The difficulties in using paper methods are evident in the time-consuming diagnostics of language development:

- the diagnostic material is selected manually by examining several collections of illustrations;
- the results are recorded in a special form;
- the results are then transferred into electronic tables for processing;
- decisions are subsequently made and recommendations given.

The personal experience of one of the authors reveals that the traditional "paper" method for testing a group of 20–25 preschool children requires up to three weeks to accomplish.

Hence there are at least three reasons to involve modern information technologies:

- the diagnostics methods should be applicable on a mass scale;
- they should be attractive and non-disturbing for a child;
- they should be easily reconfigurable and tunable.

Using mobile applications is also highly beneficial for therapists. First, it cuts the amount of time required for preparatory procedures, as well as the time needed for processing all of the data received during a child's diagnostics. In Russia, therapists spend one-third of their working time preparing and processing paper carriers. Thus, if they spend less time on these tasks, they can devote more time to face-to-face communication with children. Secondly, the therapy process becomes universal: the electronic form allows a specialist to work with a child at any convenient location. Thirdly, the work of the speech therapist is automated: the program records the intermediate and final results, visualizes the results in the form of tables and graphs, and saves them.

Children with developmental challenges, including language disorders, require a special learning environment that should meet educational needs and create comfortable conditions for development. For modern children, mobile applications are a natural part of their daily lives. Thus, the use of mobile applications can make receiving help more interesting, more comfortable and more productive. Preparing for the implementation of mobile applications, the authors used an eye-tracking technique to compare the effectiveness of diagnostics when using paper carriers and when using a portable device. Although the authors cannot insist on the completeness of this study, it nevertheless demonstrated that the electronic approach aided the child in focusing on the test for a longer period of time than did the paper approach.

Among the substantial number of children's applications (entertainment, gaming, regulating activities, developing) there are various training programs that allow children to navigate a studied topic independently, or in tandem with an adult. Using these programs, children can be in charge of their own educational trajectory and the application will monitor its own effectiveness in the training process. In addition, mobile applications help to maintain children's attention on the therapeutic process and motivate young patients to actively participate.

Moreover, software tools reduce the cost of therapy, making it more affordable. For example, the price of printed sets of testing and training papers can be as high as several hundred dollars in the US market. In contrast with the printed version, software errors can easily be corrected and therapeutic methods can be updated intermittently.

Recently, the Department of Fundamental and Applied Linguistics of the Humanitarian Institute of the Novosibirsk State University initiated an interdisciplinary project that integrates fundamental and applied research in applied linguistics, computer linguistics, psycholinguistics, speech therapy and cognitive psychology. The practical result of this project was the creation of software tools for the diagnosis and development of speech disorders in children with special health abilities. To date, we have developed and tested three programs for the language therapy practice:

- LogoBall diagnostic program;
- Piktobschenie (the Russian for 'Communicate through pictures'), a mobile application for the development of coherent speech and alternative communication;
- Razvivaem rech' (the Russian for 'Develop speech'), a mobile application for the development of impressive speech.

The game-based diagnostic tool, Logokvest, is currently being tested. Our approach to developing a mobile application conforms to the modern concept of the universal (inclusive) design [6]: i.e. suitable for both children with disabilities and children without.

Lorusso et al. [7] have stated that, at the moment, software tools for aiding in language disorder therapy are not well characterized with regard to therapeutic effectiveness. However, since this is not within the scope of the present study, it is not possible to further review existing solutions, of which there are many. In addition, there is scarce information about the clinical testing of such solutions, which makes it difficult to assess their effectiveness.

2 Tools Developed

2.1 LogoBall

The LogoBall diagnostic program was designed to automate the process of detecting a child's speech pathology: create tables and graphs, compare the results of diagnostics at different stages of training, and save the list of errors made by the child during the diagnosis. It is beginning to be introduced into logopedic practices.

The application for diagnosing children's speech has a diagnostic structure, according to N.V. Nishchevoy [8], that consists of 9 series and 33 groups. Each diagnostic criterion is subdivided according to the age gradation (4, 5, and 6 years). The diagnostic series are as follows: (1) sound-syllabic structure of the word; (2) phonemic perception; (3) phonemic analysis and synthesis; (4) understanding of speech; (5) understanding of word combinations and simple sentences; (6) lexical and grammatical structure of the child's speech; (7) inflection, (8) word formation; (9) coherent speech. Thus, it is further necessary to examine the application from two perspectives: that of the speech therapist and that of the child. The directly stimulated diagnostic material is divided into two types: with and without illustrative support.

If the task on the screen does not provide illustrative support, the child can only see buttons with words, phrases or sentences, with which he/she must perform the task. If the child's answer is wrong, then the app saves information about the mistake.

Recording the child's errors is integral for further constructing the individual trajectory of the developmental work for each child by the speech therapist. If the task on the screen does provide illustrative support, then the child must perform the tasks specified by the illustrations. The child's errors are also recorded for these tasks. On the right side of the screen, there are buttons numbered from 0 to 3, which represent an evaluation of the child's performance. The specialist can move to the next task but it is not possible to go back. However, there is no time limit to perform a task.

The principal functionality of LogoBall is to record and synchronize the scores set by the language therapist for each task; record the errors made by a child when pressing the incorrect button that corresponds to the incorrect word; provide a simple interface to make the application easy to use; implement an illustrative series to help children concentrate.

A session consists of a series of tasks. For example, one task tests the ability of a child to match adjectives with nouns in the singular (e.g. a green bucket, a red flag, a blue pencil, etc.). The therapist shows a picture on the screen and asks questions so that the child can demonstrate his ability to match the adjectives with the nouns: "What color is the bucket? Which bucket will we take to fetch water? Which bucket can we fill with water? To which bucket can we attach a rope?", etc.

After the child has completed a task, the therapist assigns a corresponding score according to the rating system to which he adheres. We recommend using the following system, although we do not insist upon it: "0" means that the child has absolutely failed the job; "1" means that the child has performed less than 30% of the task; "2" means that the task has been partially performed correctly (no more than 70%); "3" means the task has been performed completely, or almost completely. We deliberately do not prescribe clear criteria for scoring, because in Russian language therapy there are controversial ways of evaluating the results. Thus, the program is purposefully flexible to allow the specialist to choose the criteria independently.

To receive feedback on the quality of the developed application, 22 experts, teachers, and language therapists were questioned. We developed a questionnaire, which includes nine evaluation criteria. All of the questions aim at identifying issues with the program. In order to improve the functionality of the application, each criterion is assessed on a five-point scale, where 1 is very poor, 2 is poor, 3 is satisfactory, 4 is good, and 5 is excellent. The open questions asked encouraged respondents to express their desires for the application and specify its shortcomings. Based on the results of the questionnaire, we calculated the results (average score for each criterion of the questionnaire).

The most successful aspect of the application is its stability, with a rating of 4.93. The second best was the speed of the application, at 4.86. Subsequently, how well the diagnostic material corresponds to the original received a rating of 4.71. The average scores obtained for the rest of the criteria are as follows: application design - 4; navigation - 4.23; color solution - 4.05; correspondence between illustrations and tasks - 4.1; and application functionality - 4.47. The criterion with the lowest score is the quality of visualization, which received an average score of 3.84.

Taking into account the results of the experts' evaluation, the following conclusions are drawn with regard to improvements that need to be made to the application LogoBall. The first improvement relates to the illustrative series. Illustrations are perceived by the children better if they are decorated in the same style and presented against a white background, without any additional background (context). Second, it is reasonable to place no more than three or four pictures on one slide. This allows the therapist to improve the child's concentration on a specific task. Third, to work with pre-school-age children, it is necessary to include "step back" and "pause" handles because such young children are unable to concentrate on any task for more than 20 min and therefore, speech therapists and teachers must conduct diagnostics in two or even three stages. Fourth, the program should contain extensive instructions and explanations for each diagnostic task so that it can be used by anyone, and not just specialists.

We believe that the following suggestions will greatly improve the application. To facilitate the child's perception of the interface, we should continue improving the illustrative application series. This is a challenging task, which involves an examination of complex cognitive problems relating to human-computer interactions. Moreover, tasks should be arranged with respect to their complexity level to allow the therapist to distinguish among children with different levels of language development and thus, differentiate their tasks. Finally, adding several game elements may increase a child's motivation to undergo diagnostics.

2.2 Piktobschenie

Piktobschenie is a mobile application for portable computers which was designed to improve children's coherent speech and alternative communication. This application allows an individual to communicate using the language of the icons and their color scheme. The same pictogram can denote an action (if it is red), an object (if it is blue), or a sign (if it is green). Examples are homonyms like *to smile* and *a smile*. The color black is used for service words. Color indication helps to construct phrases more correctly. Children can make both simple and complex sentences by placing the pictograms in a certain order, which is the most important stage of learning cohesion.

The application was developed for pictogram-based communication, which is an interactive version of the learning exercises from speech therapy workbooks. Our experience demonstrates that pictograms enable speech-impaired and/or non-speaking children to satisfy their need to communicate.

The program consists of two modules: a trainer and a communicator. Before undertaking software implementation, ontological modelling was accomplished.

- The training module serves to familiarize the child with a symbol-meaning relationship; the module trains the child to associate the images of objects with their functions, and teaches the principles of the logical construction of a phrase by encouraging the child to choose the right symbols.
- The communicator module is an alternative means of communication and a tool for the development of coherent speech. The main sections of this module are as follows:
  - Specials: The section is designed so that at one touch of a button the child can quickly report a situation that requires immediate resolution (for example, "I have a headache", "I want to go to the toilet").

- • I want: The section enables a child to ask quickly for a certain thing, simply by clicking on the object icon. It consists of a limited number of pictographs most needed by the child.
- • Phrases: In this section, the child can put pictograms together to make phrases.

The users tested the developed application to assess its perception. We registered a developer account on GooglePlay, where the mobile application was hosted. Subsequently, a test group of 50 people – specifically, parents of children with speech disorders – was recruited. A questionnaire was compiled to assess the level of the children's familiarization with the language of pictograms, effectiveness of the mobile application as a means of alternative communication, and its influence on the development of coherent speech. The parents' responses indicate that, in general, the idea of such an application is interesting and in high demand, but there are also some issues; for example, the quality of the pictures. The application is currently being improved and refined to address these issues.

Of the 50 people who enrolled, only 40 passed the test; several refused, either for no apparent reason or under the pretext that, for example, the children would find the application boring. Judging by the feedback and the results, the icons initially seemed somewhat scaring, but after a short interaction with the training module, the users' attitudes changed. It should be mentioned that in contrast with the initial testing where average number of errors (their range is from 8 to 26) was 18 per test after training average number (their range is from 1 to 9) of errors was 5 per test.

Overall, the application demonstrates significant potential for speech development, in particular, for the development of coherent speech. Currently, we are working on improving the following areas:

- – The quality of the graphics of the pictogram base: creating animated pictograms (instead of using the originals [9]);
- – The communicator module: in particular, adding assignments directly aimed at developing the coherence of speech as a key parameter of speech development;
- – application testing: to not only include children who are on the autistic spectrum, but also children who suffer from various manifestations of language underdevelopment.

2.3   Rasvivaem Rech'

It is not always possible for parents to consult a speech therapist; In this case, they can benefit from speech therapy games and tasks, as well as applications for mobile devices, which are currently being developed. A mobile application has a greater effect than its paper counterpart because, due to its interactive nature, it increases the child's involvement in speech therapy. This idea is the basis of our interactive mobile application for children who exhibit a general language underdevelopment at the 1st, 2nd, and 3rd level. The app is intended to develop impressive speech. It allows children to perform various speech therapy exercises independently. There are 10 tasks at each level; the approximate time for executing tasks on the same level is 5 min. The application uses sound effects for the text and users' actions. After completing the tasks, the user can see the result.

When the application starts, the user can choose a task level. At each level, the user is asked to complete 10 tasks, one by one. Each task is a new window in the program. In the center of each screen is the text of the task. Above the text is the button for playing the text of the task, i.e. the sound effects of the task. This button can be clicked an unlimited number of times, so the child can listen to the task as many times as s/he needs. A typical job screen offers a choice of 1 to 4 answer options. There is no time limit for each task. Moreover, you can skip tasks and proceed to the following task in the same level. In this case, the results of the missed exercises are not taken into account.

The mobile application Rasvivaem rech' was evaluated for quality, functionality, stability, reliability and accessibility on a five-point scale by 20 speech therapy teachers who work at several children institutions. The testers left comments regarding their opinions of the application. The criteria chosen fully describe the idea of the mobile application, and the five-point grading system is the same as what is used in Russian schools, so the expert group felt comfortable with it.

The experts' opinions about the appearance of the program were split evenly between the scores of 4 and 5. The location of the buttons and availability scored the highest. The experts found the interface convenient and not too overloaded with unnecessary elements. Some experts noted that the soundtrack should be finalized: the synthesized voice must be replaced with a live one, the tempo of speech should be slower, pauses and intonation should be added. Moreover, they noted that, at times, the synthesized speech was inaudible, making it difficult to understand the tasks. For this reason, the average soundtrack scores ranged between 3 and 5. The scores given to the size of the images and their readability were either 4 or 5. However, many experts remarked that the pictures in the tasks to build a story based on a fairy tale plot are too small. In addition, the order of these pictures can be optionally broken to increase the task's complexity. All speech-therapy teachers agreed that the application should be of great interest to the children since, in their experience, children spend a substantial amount of time on phones and other portable devices. The item "interest to the children" received a rating of 5. Functionality, stability and speed of the program scored between 4 and 5. Moreover, the experts noted that the option to rotate the screen needs to be improved, as the application crashes after the screen automatically turns off, and that it subsequently takes about 30 s to start up again. Such shortcomings can affect a child's concentration and thus, his or her involvement in the gameplay. The correspondence of the tasks presented in this mobile application to the typical speech therapy exercises used in practice received an average rating of 4.

In general, the application received positive feedback from professional teachers and speech therapists. Nevertheless, criticisms include: improving audio tracks, enlarging some images, increasing the variety of tasks and developing an incentive system. The interface and tasks, however, have been sufficiently developed. The use of such mobile applications can be of great help to speech therapists, as they allow children to improve their own speech more efficiently.

The potential of the application is that it can be used for various speech disorders. We are planning to develop several levels of complexity, and to specify tasks depending on the kind of verbal violation.

2.4   Logokvest

This application implements game-based diagnostics to test a child's level of lexical and grammatical proficiency. It is a set of mini-games grouped into five thematic complexes depending on the game story. The results can be recorded in the program memory.

In the first complex, the child is invited to select items belonging to a certain group from presented shelves and collect whole things from pieces, thus allowing them to improve the lexical level of their language. The second complex is a journey through a zoo, during which the child must identify the sounds produced by the animals, give the correct names of the offspring of various animals and match the animals and parts of their bodies, composing the forms of possessive adjectives. The third complex encourages the child to assume the identity of an artist. Here, the lexical and grammatical aspects of speech are tested. The child is asked to assemble a palette of certain colors, draw geometric figures and paint objects; all of which is accomplished by composing a word combination in the correct form. In the fourth complex, the child is tasked with "creating" several items from one, dividing them into groups of two and five, and verifying the presence or absence of certain objects; this tests the child's knowledge of plural forms, and determines whether s/he can use numerals with them, etc. The fifth complex, which is set in the wilderness, tests the child's ability to form prepositional-case constructions with prepositions and create verbs of the perfective aspect.

For each correctly classified object, the child receives one point; errors do not affect the diagnosis, which helps reduce the level of stress. Each mini-game has four levels. The number of points received for each mini-game and each complex is entered into a table, after which the total number of points is counted. The more points a child gets, the less serious is his or her language development problem. The illustrative material is created in a uniform style to ensure that the external component of the program appears attractive, and that the game process is fascinating.

References

1. Levina, R.E.: Pedagogical questions of pathology of the speech at children. Spec. Sch. **2**, 121–130 (1967)
2. Zaidan, I.N.: Therapeutic Didactics in Teaching the Russian Language: Development of Communicative and Social Competencies. NGPU, Novosibirsk (2013)
3. Duenser, A., et al.: Feasibility of technology enabled speech disorder screening. Stud. Health Technol. Inform. **227**, 21–27 (2016). https://doi.org/10.3233/978-1-61499-666-8-21
4. Robles-Bykbaev, V., López-Nores, M., García-Duque, J., Pazos-Arias, J.J., Guillermo-Anguisaca, J.C.: A multilayer mobile ecosystem to support the assessment and treatment of patients with communication disorders. In: IADIS International Conference e-Health, pp. 35–42. IADIS (2015)

5. Robles-Bykbaev, V., López-Nores, M., Ochoa-Zambrano, J., García-Duque, J., Pazos-Arias, J.J.: SPELTRA: a robotic assistant for speech-and-language therapy. In: Antona, M., Stephanidis, C. (eds.) UAHCI 2015. LNCS, vol. 9177, pp. 525–534. Springer, Cham (2015). https://doi.org/10.1007/978-3-319-20684-4_51

6. Burgstahler, S. (ed.): Universal design in higher education: promising practices. DO-IT, University of Washington, Seattle (2013). http://www.uw.edu/doit/UDHEpromising-practices/

7. Lorusso, M.L., Biffi, E., Molteni, M., Reni, G.: Exploring the learnability and usability of a near field communication-based application for semantic enrichment in children with language disorders. Assist. Technol. **30**(1), 39–50 (2018). https://doi.org/10.1080/10400435.2016.1253046

8. Chirkova, G.V. (ed.): Methods of Examining Children's Language: Manual for the Diagnostics of Language Disorders, 3rd edn. ARKTI, Moscow (2003)

9. Baryaeva, L.B., Loginova, E.T., Lopatina, L.V.: I Speak! Child in the Family. Exercises with Pictograms: Workbook for Lessons with Children. Drofa, Moscow (2007)

Studying the Impact of Trained Staff on Evacuation Scenarios by Agent-Based Simulation

Daniel Formolo[1](✉) , Tibor Bosse[2] , and Natalie van der Wal[3]

[1] Department of Computer Science, Vrije Universiteit,
1081 HV Amsterdam, The Netherlands
d.formolo@vu.nl
[2] Behavioural Science Institute, Radboud University,
6500 HE Nijmegen, The Netherlands
t.bosse@ru.nl
[3] Centre for Decision Research, Leeds University Business School, Leeds, UK
C.N.VanderWal@leeds.ac.uk

Abstract. Human evacuation experiments can trigger distress, be unethical and present high costs. As a solution, computer simulations can predict the effectiveness of new emergency management procedures. This paper applies multi-agent simulation to measure the influence of staff members with diverse training levels on evacuation time. A previously developed and validated model was extended with explicit mechanisms to simulate staff members helping people to egress. The majority of parameter settings have been based on empirical data acquired in earlier studies. Therefore, simulation results are expected to be realistic. Results show that staff are more effective in complex environments, especially when trained. Not only specialised security professionals but, especially, regular workers of shopping facilities and offices play a significant role in evacuation processes when adequately trained. These results can inform policy makers and crowd managers on new emergency management procedures.

Keywords: Crowd management · Evacuation · Agent-based model
Staff

1 Introduction

Crowd incidents show the importance of well trained staff being present during evacuations. From past incidents it becomes clear that staff members need to communicate to the crowd what is happening as well as manage the directions and density of the crowd. The 1968 crowd crush disaster in Buenos Aires[1] was mainly due to the absence of clear exit signage and stewards to guide the public to the correct exit. It was unclear for people where the entry and exit points were. People moved towards exit gates that were closed, leading to 74 fatalities and 150 injured. In 1999, 54 people died,

---

[1] https://www.cbsnews.com/news/major-soccer-stadium-disasters/.

© Springer Nature Switzerland AG 2018
S. Staab et al. (Eds.): SocInfo 2018, LNCS 11186, pp. 85–96, 2018.
https://doi.org/10.1007/978-3-030-01159-8_8

and 150 people injured in a crowd crush in a station in Minsk, Belarus[2]. More than 1000 people rushed inside the station tunnel to find cover from a thunderstorm. There was not enough staff present to manage the people entering the station. They had no information on what was happening further down the tunnel, where people had been trampled. Two policemen that tried to manage the crowd died. The 2003 tragedy in the Station Nightclub in Rhode Island, USA, is also partly due to untrained staff[3]. Bar staff or managers should have stopped the band playing during the fireworks. Most people taking the familiar route to the entrance, this resulted in people getting stuck in the entrance. 100 people died in the fire.

As illustrated by these scenarios, staff members play a critical role in successfully evacuating a crowd during incidents. Moreover, in addition to regular security personnel and crowd managers, also other staff members such as bartenders, hostesses and food sellers may be crucial. In different environments, the same person can show different behaviours during a fire [1]. For example, when a fire in one's own house appears, the person most likely evacuates immediately or tries to stop the fire. When this person is in a shop or other public building, the person will expect the management of this building to be responsible for evacuation and initiating it [2]. Another explanation is that these non-security staff members know the environment, and most likely know what to do [3]. Be it security personnel or other staff, the fact is that staff members are not always well trained for evacuation and crowd management. This is partly because of responsibility, but also because of the excessive costs and practical difficulties associated with evacuation training.

In [4, 5] the authors analyse the regular staff behaviour (workers of stores) in five unannounced evacuations of Marks and Spencer retail stores. The client's store started to evacuate on average 30.3 s after the alarm and the call to evacuate had been activated. The most notable of this case are the standard deviations ranging from 1 to 100 s among the population to start to evacuate. Results showed that regular staff behaviour is crucial to start the evacuation and inappropriate staff response could even induce long evacuation delays. A further study inspected the pre-movement times across 4 of the same stores [3]. It found a mean pre-movement time range from 25 to 37 s with standard deviations ranging from 13 to 19 s. Still, that time range is considerably less than the recognition times quoted in the British fire safety norm BSI DD240. The paper concludes that training staff should not be underestimated. Different incidents are reviewed and compared in [5]. In one of the cases, a fire in Japan took only 10 min to cover an entire floor, which indicates the importance of a fast evacuation. According to [6], the staff have a flagrant influence on the dynamics of an evacuation in many cases, as they have the power to calm down the population. Similarly, de Vries et al. [7] suggest that the words said, attitude, and behaviour of employees transmit a sense of safety to a crowd.

As human evacuation experiments can trigger distress, be unethical and present high costs, computer simulations can be a solution to determine the effectiveness of new emergency management procedures. Few evacuation models consider social

---

[2] http://news.bbc.co.uk/1/hi/world/europe/356828.stm.

[3] https://en.wikipedia.org/wiki/The_Station_nightclub_fire.

aspects in evacuations and almost none include staff members instructing evacuees. The ASCRIBE model [8] represents crowd members as agents that possess a number of static personality characteristics (openness and expressiveness) as well as dynamic mental states (beliefs, intentions and emotions). The ESCAPES model [9] also features mechanisms to represent the mental states of agents, as well as their interactions. In contrast to ASCRIBE, the authors in [22] do study the role of security personnel. Their agents are modelled by giving them a low 'FearFactor' and a high 'calming effect' on other agents. A similar, but slightly different system for crowd simulation is MACES [10]. Within MACES, agents have different stress levels, where high levels of stress may result in more difficulty to orient oneself quickly. Different agent roles are explored, such as trained leaders, untrained leaders and untrained non-leaders. The authors conclude that communication is a key factor to a success evacuation.

In this research, we build upon the results discussed in these papers by studying the effect of *communication skills* of security personnel on evacuation time. The presence of calm authorities in the environment has a contagious effect on the population, and it is well known that not running reduces the evacuation time due to fewer falls and less congestion at the exits [11, 12]. As perceived in the situations described above, we observe relevant aspects shared by incidents that are (1) Every minute is important to a successful evacuation; (2) The staff influences the decision to start to evacuate; (3) Even with most people evacuating voluntarily in a brief period of time, part of them still remain in the environment, delaying the decision to evacuate. Those people should be the target to an efficient evacuation.

Indeed, the current paper is part of a larger project that aims to develop a simulation-based system to train staff members in how to act in stressful circumstances [13]. The emphasis is on adequate communicative skills, e.g., how to quickly convince passers-by that (and how) they have to evacuate from a burning building without making them more stressed. Our expectation is that having more and better trained personnel generally results in more efficient evacuation procedures. However, the extent to which this will be the case and the precise circumstances in which trained staff members are beneficial are hard to predict without actually testing this in real scenarios. As a solution, *agent-based simulation* is used in this research to better understand the impact of trained staff on evacuation scenarios.

The main research question is what is the effect of the level of training of staff members on the evacuation time in environments that differ in complexity? To answer this question, we chose an existing crowd simulation model[4] [14–16] and extended it by explicitly incorporating the role of staff members with different levels of training. By systematically varying the model's parameters and running simulations, the impact of staff training on evacuation time can be determined. The remainder of this paper is structured as follows. Section 2 describes the used model while Sect. 3 presents results of the simulations. Section 4 concludes the paper with a discussion.

---

[4] Source code available to download in: (https://formolo.wixsite.com/impact-project).

2 Model Description

The evacuation dynamics were modelled using an agent-based model with the beliefs-desires-intentions paradigm [17] and a temporal-causal network modelling approach [18]. Figure 8 of Appendix shows a representation of the internal decision process of an individual, his (or her) actions and the external factors that influence his beliefs, desires and intentions. Each node has a value between 0 and 1 and represents a characteristic, action or external stimulus. The oriented arrows indicate how one or several nodes influence other nodes at each simulation step. Each arrow has a weight that regulates its contribution in a node input. Some nodes have fixed values e.g.: 'Gender' is 0 or 1, indicating the gender of the agent. Others have formulas which combine the input signals to generate a new node output transmitted to following nodes. Details of connection weights and node formulas are described in our previous work [14]. The model was validated against a complex benchmark named Exodus[5].

The results are close to expected by the benchmark, see [19] for more details. The actions of the agents are described in Table 1 of Appendix. The internal states can be divided in beliefs, intents and intermediate states among beliefs, intentions and actions. The familiarity node represents the agent's beliefs about the environment. It is binary, either the agent knows the environment or not. If it is familiar with the environment, then it always takes the nearest exit. If it is not familiar, it will trace a route to the main exit after it decides to evacuate. In the midway of its position and the main exit, it can be convinced by a staff agent to follow him to the nearest exit. The intention to evacuate depends on the *belief of danger*, which is directly linked to observations from the external world. The *fear belief* is a combination between external stimuli and feedback loops of *desire to evacuate* and *desire to walk randomly*. These last two states compete with each other. They inversely drive the two intention states. Other cultural factors like nationality, compliance, age and gender impacts on several internal nodes and they define the individual personality of each agent. Observation states link external events with the internal model and they are part of the personality. The weights of the links connecting these states give more importance to external events when they are set close to 1 or less importance when set close to 0. All these factors are considered because of their importance in the incident scenarios. Parameters like speed range of males, females, children and elders; nationality, compliance and fall rate are set according to technical specifications, see [14] for more details. The external stimuli of each agent are described in Table 2 of Appendix.

An agent can observe the instructions of one or more staff members several times, as described at the end of this section. It always has the option to either accept the staff suggestion or not. Together with other nodes, the *obs_staff_instr* node is directly linked to the *action_movetoexit* node. The *action_movetoexit* is a combination of the speed of the passenger and his target: one of the exits. The value of the intention to evacuate influences the speed of moving to the exit. The familiarity, observation of staff instructions, and the public announcement influences the choice of exit [20]. The *obs_staff_instr* is either 0 or 1. If the agent observes a staff agent, then it has a chance of

---

[5] http://fseg.gre.ac.uk/exodus/index.html.

accepting the staff instruction, activating the *obs_staff_instr* node. As described in Sect. 1, staff members influence the decision of customers or visitors on delaying their evacuation or not. In [3, 4], the authors refer to regular workers of stores and how their posture is reflected in the clients' attitudes during emergency scenarios. In terms of modelling, we consider two staff types: Authorities specialised in security (Staff$_{sec}$), which have at least some training on how to manage incidents. In the most cases, they are in lower quantity, not sufficient to cover all areas. On the other hand, store, service and office workers (Staff$_{wor}$) are present in most parts of an environment but, in general, do not are regularly training to deal with incidents. Both walk randomly and have the same effect on the agents (people), which is to convince them to evacuate. The only differences between them are the quantity and ability to convince people to evacuate. We consider Staff$_{sec}$ agents with initial training skills of between 0.5 and a maximum of 1, while Staff$_{wor}$ training skills range from 0 to a maximum of 0.5. The relation among normal agents (clients, audience, passengers, etc.) and staff agents is modelled into the connection between *staff_instr* and *obs_staff_instr* nodes. It considers the quantity of staff agents in the observable distance of a regular agent and the ability of a staff agent to convince regular agents to evacuate. If a regular agent is convinced, then it keeps the desire to evacuate until the end of the simulation.

3 Experiments

3.1 Methodology

With the use of a validated evacuation model that includes social elements, our experiments aim to determine the effect of the number and type of staff members on the evacuation process and time.

Measurements: The average evacuation time and the assembly area rate will be measured as indications of the effect of the staff members. The average evacuation time refers to the average egress time of the agents since the incident has started until the last agent has egressed. The assembly area rate is the measurement of agents that reach one of the zones close to the exits. This measurement is a complement measurement to avoid distortions injected by the limited egress capacity of the exit doors.

Environment: In order to isolate the social effect of staff on the population, we selected two variations of neutral scenarios already used in our previous works [14–16]. The first is a square room without walls. The second environment adds two barriers separating the room in 3 parts, occulting the incident of people placed on 2 of the 3 areas of the room. Both rooms are 400 m^2 and have one main exit that everybody knows and one secondary exit that only the agents familiar with the environment know. The doors are 4 m wide. The incident is randomly placed around the centre of the room, between the walls and the assembly areas and has a fixed size of 8 m^2 (2% of the room size). Figure 1 shows the two environments.

Variables: The density varies in 2 and 4 people per square metres. Both staff and people are randomly distributed. The Staff$_{wor}$ skills in managing incidents varies in steps of 25% from 0% to 50%, while, Staff$_{sec}$ varies in steps of 25% from 50% to 100%.

These values come from an existing paper on the use of serious games for training [21]. The incident is identified as a red square of fixed size randomly placed on the middle of the room and between the assembly areas.

All other parameters remain fixed: (a) contagion model, public announcement, fire alarm, helping and falling behaviours are enabled, (b) the percentage of males and females is 50%, percentage of children and elderly is 15%, percentage of people alone is 50%, while the other half of the population is divided in groups of 2, 3 and 4 people and divided in 33%, 33% and 34% respectively of the people who are in groups, (c) the cultural distributions are divided evenly. For more details about these social parameters, see Sect. 1.3 of [14].

Quantity of Simulations. For each experiment, the minimum number of repetitions is defined by the equation $n \geq [(100 \cdot Z \cdot s)/(r \cdot \bar{x})]^2 = 63.70$. This number is rounded up to 65 in order to guarantee that the error in each outcome result is within 5% of the maximum error with 95% of confidence. Z = confidence interval of 95% $\rightarrow$ 1.96; s = standard deviation = 63.55; r = max. error of 5%; $\bar{x}$ = avg. evacuation time of 100 samples = 312.11. The results represent the average of these runs [22].

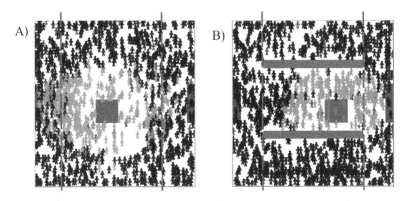

Fig. 1. Layout of rooms. Figure A without walls and Figure B with 2 walls in grey. The assembly areas are between the dashed lines and the exit doors in blue. The incident is in red; agents in pink are evacuating; in black are those still not aware; grey are casualties and staff is green. (Color figure online)

3.2 Experiment A – Effect of Staff$_{wor}$ in a Square Room Without Walls

The experimental design to determine the effect of Staff$_{wor}$ in a neutral scenario varies the following parameters: Crowd Density = 2, 4; Number of staff$_{wor}$ = 0, 8, 16, 32, 64 and staff$_{sec}$ = 0; Skills ability of staff$_{wor}$ = 0%, 25%, 50%.

The graphs A and B of Fig. 2 show the influence of Staff$_{wor}$ on evacuation time in an open room. While, there is no influence of Staff$_{wor}$ on the time to reach the assembly area, the final evacuation time is significantly reduced (more than 1 min) when #staff$_{wor}$ $\geq$ 32. The reason for a low influence of Staff$_{wor}$ on reaching the assembly areas is that in an open space it is easy and fast for regular agents to see the incident and

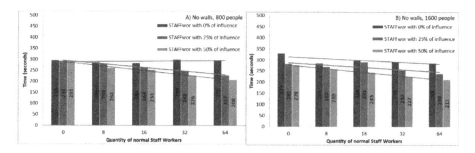

Fig. 2. Average evacuation time of agents and trend lines. No Walls room with Staff$_{wor}$

affect others with their fear. As many regular agents are observing the incident, the social influence is big and the impact of Staff$_{wor}$ is only a small added factor.

Nevertheless, the Staff$_{wor}$ still play a role, guiding other agents to the nearest exit, reducing the bottleneck of the main exit door and influencing the final evacuation time. As shown in Fig. 2, the more Staff$_{wor}$, the better the results. Furthermore, when there is almost no one in the room, but only a few regular agents, the Staff$_{wor}$ speed up the evacuation of those last agents, convincing them to escape. That is not the case in simulations without the intervention of Staff$_{wor}$. Those few regular agents take more time to evacuate because they do not have many more agents to share information (fear) with and, in most cases, the only possibility of evacuating is when they observe the incident by themselves. This behaviour matches with what is summarized in item (3) of Sect. 1. Another important pattern is the regularity in the evacuation time injected by Staff$_{wor}$. In all cases and subsequent experiments, increasing the number of staff and their skills leads to a lower standard deviation (σ), for the average evacuation times. To cite an example, in the experiment of Fig. 2, from #Staff$_{wor}$ = 0 to #Staff$_{wor}$ = 64, σ is respectively 42, 38, 30, 22 and 17. Hence, staff promotes order, and predictability on results, even with variations on agents and incident positions.

3.3   Experiment B – Effect of Staff$_{sec}$ in a Square Room Without Walls

The experimental design to determine the effect of Staff$_{sec}$ in a neutral scenario varies the following parameters: Crowd Density = 2, 4; Number of staff$_{wor}$ = 0 and staff$_{sec}$ = 0, 2, 4, 8, 16; Skills ability of staff$_{sec}$ = 50%, 75%, 100%. The results in Fig. 3 reflect the

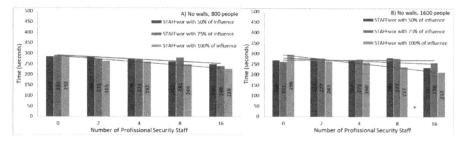

Fig. 3. Average evacuation time of agents and trend lines. No Walls room with Staff$_{sec}$

same behaviours of Sect. 3.2 with less intensity, mostly because of the number of Staff$_{sec}$. Apparently, the number of Staff$_{sec}$ is insufficient to deal with the quantity of agents. The effect of the Staff$_{sec}$ is surrounded by the amount of social influence among the regular agents.

3.4   Experiment C – Effect of Staff$_{wor}$ in a Square Room with Division Walls

Experiment C follows the design of Experiment A. It measures the effect of Staff$_{wor}$ in a neutral scenario with barriers dividing the environment in 3 parts. The walls make the environment more complex, the social influence among the regular agents reduces. In this scenario, 2/3 of them cannot easily see the incident and get in contact with others beyond the wall. Assembly area rates and evacuation times increase comparing to the results with and without Staff$_{wor}$. Increasing the quantity of Staff$_{wor}$ results in a reduction of the evacuation time and assembly area time. Moreover, the effects are clear when skills are set to 50%. Comparing Fig. 4A with Fig. 4B and Fig. 5A with Fig. 5B, the number of staff per people also has a significant impact on reducing the evacuation and assembly area times. That fact indicates again that the quantity of staff influences the results, which also occurred in Experiment B (Sect. 3.3). According to Fig. 4, 32 or more Staff$_{wor}$ reduce the final evacuation time by more than a minute, which is a significant achievement for managing incidents, as cited in item (1) of Sect. 1.

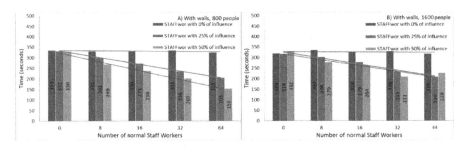

Fig. 4. Average evacuation time of agents and trend lines. No Walls room with Staff$_{wor}$.

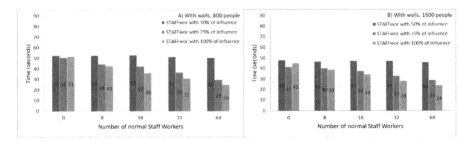

Fig. 5. Average assembly area time of agents. No Walls room with Staff$_{wor}$.

3.5   Experiment D – Effect of Staff_sec in a Square Room with Division Walls

Experiment D follows the design of Experiment B. It measures the effect of Staff$_{sec}$ in a neutral scenario. Similar to Experiment B, Figs. 6 and 7 show a clear influence of Staff$_{sec}$ in reducing the average evacuation time. The same effect is observed to egress time when comparing the results to the room without walls in the same conditions, despite the lower effect when compared with Experiment C. Again, the quantity of Staff$_{sec}$ is a dominant factor to limit the influence of Staff$_{sec}$.

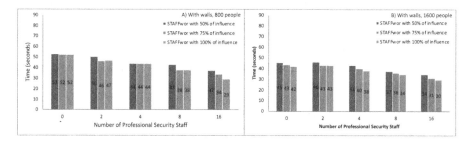

Fig. 6. Average evacuation time of agents and trend lines. No Walls room with Staff$_{sec}$

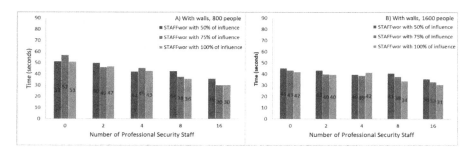

Fig. 7. Average assembly area time of agents. No Walls room with Staff$_{sec}$

4   Discussion

In this paper, multi-agent based simulation was applied to study the effect of different training levels of staff members on the evacuation time in environments that differ in complexity. To this end, a previously developed (and validated) crowd simulation model was taken as point of departure [14–16], and was extended with explicit mechanisms to simulate staff members that guide passers-by to the nearest exit. By manipulating a parameter for 'skills', we could simulate a range of different types of staff members, varying from 'regular' staff members that have not received much training to well-trained security personnel or staff members.

The simulations results showed several interesting findings. For instance, presence of staff has more effect in more complex environments. The average evacuation time and average assembly area time could be reduced mainly by increasing the number of staff placed at strategic locations in the environment, but also by using (a smaller number of) better trained staff members. Although these findings may not be extremely surprising by themselves, the added value of the current simulation model is that we are now able to explain in more detail why they occur and predict in which hypothetical circumstances they occur. Since the majority of parameter settings have been based on empirical data acquired in an earlier study, the resulting simulations are expected to be reasonably realistic. If the model is applied to real-life scenarios, it can provide rough indications of the added value of training staff member, thus serving as a decision support tool for investments in training staff.

Nevertheless, there is room for a more extensive validation of the simulation model. As soon as more empirical data about evacuation scenarios and the role of staff members becomes available, such a validation could be performed. Another interesting direction for future research is to conduct an experiment to explicitly test the impact of staff members who have worked with our training system [13] in the context of an evacuation experiment or drill in a controlled environment.

Acknowledgments. This project has received funding from the European Union's Horizon 2020; innovation programme under the Marie Skłodowska-Curie grant agreement No. 748647 and Brazilian government - Science without Borders – CNPq (No: 233883/2014-2). We would like to thank our Consortium Partners and stakeholders for their input.

Appendix

Table 1. Description of individual actions of each agent in a simulation.

Action	Description
Fall (enabled)	The agent falls and remains stopped for a certain amount of time. Falls are a consequence of speed, age and crowd congestion
Die	If the agent is at the same place where the incident occurs, it dies
Express belief of danger	The agent expresses its dangerous belief level to other agents
Express fear	The agent shows its fear level to other agents around him
Walk	Agent strolls randomly in the environment until it decides to evacuate
Help	An agent can help other fallen agents. The decision depends on its own gender, age and that of the fallen person, and if the agent is part of a group
Evacuate	Evacuation is directly related with the intention to evacuate which is influence by its fear level and belief of danger

Table 2. Description of external stimuli of each agent.

Input	Description
Crowd congestion location	The number of agents and their speed depending on the number of agents within the same square metre: ≤ 4 people (no speed reduction), 5 people 62.5%, 6 people 75%, 7 people 82.5%, 8 people 95% [23]
Fire location	If the agent observes the incident it changes its belief of dangerous
Alarm	Is 'on' after three minutes of the simulation. Then all agents are aware that something unusual is happening. Some agents start to evacuate immediately, others take more time to be convinced about the danger
Others belief dangerous	The beliefs of danger of all agents in the vision range
Others fear	The fear sensations of all agents in the vision range
Public announcement	Is 'on' one minute after the alarm is 'on'
Staff instructions	Agent receives instructions from staff member in its observable range

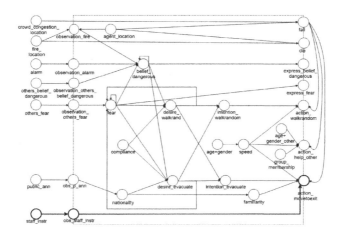

Fig. 8. Graphical conceptual representation of the internal model of a regular agent

References

1. Canter, D.V.: Fires and Human Behaviour. Wiley, New York (1980)
2. Proulx, G.: How to initiate evacuation movement in public buildings. Facilities **17**, 331–335 (1999)
3. Samochine, D., Boyce, K., Shields, T.: An investigation into staff behaviour in unannounced evacuations of retail stores - implications for training and fire safety engineering. Fire Saf. Sci. **8**, 519–530 (2005). https://doi.org/10.3801/IAFSS.FSS.8-519
4. Shields, T., Boyce, K.: A study of evacuation from large retail stores. Fire Saf. J. **35**, 25–49 (2000). https://doi.org/10.1016/S0379-7112(00)00013-8
5. Gwynne, S.M.V., Purser, D., Boswell, D.L.: Pre-warning staff delay: a forgotten component in ASET/RSET calculations. In: Peacock, R.D., Kuligowski, E.D., Averill, J. (eds.) Pedestrian and Evacuation Dynamics, pp. 243–253. Springer, Boston (2011). https://doi.org/10.1007/978-1-4419-9725-8_22

6. Smith, C.A., Ellsworth, P.C.: Patterns of cognitive appraisal in emotion. J. Pers. Soc. Psychol. **48**, 813 (1985)
7. de Vries, P.W., Galetzka, M., Gutteling, J.M.: Inzet communicatie bij crowd management en crowd control. Universiteit Twente-Faculteit Gedragswetenschappen (2013)
8. Bosse, T., Hoogendoorn, M., Klein, M.C.A., Treur, J., van der Wal, C.N., van Wissen, A.: Modelling collective decision making in groups and crowds: integrating social contagion and interacting emotions, beliefs and intentions. Auton. Agent. Multi-Agent Syst. **27**, 52–84 (2013). https://doi.org/10.1007/s10458-012-9201-1
9. Tsai, J., et al.: ESCAPES—Evacuation Simulation with Children, Authorities, Parents, Emotions, and Social comparison, p. 8 (2011)
10. Pelechano, N., O'Brien, K., Silverman, B., Badler, N.: Crowd simulation incorporating agent psychological models, roles and communication. In: First International Workshop on Crowd Simulation, pp. 21–30 (2005)
11. Helbing, D., Johansson, A.: Pedestrian, crowd and evacuation dynamics. In: Meyers, R.A. (ed.) Encyclopedia of Complexity and Systems Science, pp. 6476–6495. Springer, New York (2009). https://doi.org/10.1007/978-1-4419-7695-6
12. Santos, G., Aguirre, B.E.: A critical review of emergency evacuation simulation models. (2004)
13. Bosse, T., Gerritsen, C., de Man, J.: An intelligent system for aggression de-escalation training. In: ECAI, pp. 1805–1811 (2016)
14. van der Wal, C.N., Formolo, D., Robinson, M.A., Minkov, M., Bosse, T.: Simulating crowd evacuation with socio-cultural, cognitive, and emotional elements. In: Mercik, J. (ed.) Transactions on Computational Collective Intelligence XXVII. LNCS, vol. 10480, pp. 139–177. Springer, Cham (2017). https://doi.org/10.1007/978-3-319-70647-4_11
15. Formolo, D., van der Wal, C.N.: An adaptive simulation tool for evacuation scenarios. In: Oliveira, E., Gama, J., Vale, Z., Lopes Cardoso, H. (eds.) EPIA 2017. LNCS (LNAI), vol. 10423, pp. 766–777. Springer, Cham (2017). https://doi.org/10.1007/978-3-319-65340-2_62
16. van der Wal, C.N., Formolo, D., Bosse, T.: An agent-based evacuation model with social contagion mechanisms and cultural factors. In: Benferhat, S., Tabia, K., Ali, M. (eds.) IEA/AIE 2017. LNCS (LNAI), vol. 10350, pp. 620–627. Springer, Cham (2017). https://doi.org/10.1007/978-3-319-60042-0_68
17. Rao, A.S., Georgeff, M.P., et al.: BDI agents: from theory to practice. In: ICMAS, pp. 312–319 (1995)
18. Treur, J.: Network-Oriented Modeling. Springer, Cham (2016). https://doi.org/10.1007/978-3-319-45213-5
19. Formolo, D., van der Wal, C.N.: Simulating collective evacuations with social elements. In: Nguyen, N.T., Papadopoulos, G.A., Jędrzejowicz, P., Trawiński, B., Vossen, G. (eds.) ICCCI 2017. LNCS (LNAI), vol. 10448, pp. 160–171. Springer, Cham (2017). https://doi.org/10.1007/978-3-319-67074-4_16
20. Challenger, R., Clegg, C.W., Robinson, M.: Understanding crowd behaviours: practical guidance and lessons identified. TSO (2010)
21. Bosse, T., Gerritsen, C., de Man, J.: Evaluation of a virtual training environment for aggression de-escalation. In: Proceedings of Game-On, pp. 48–58 (2015)
22. Kotrlik, J., Higgins, C.: Organizational research: determining appropriate sample size in survey research appropriate sample size in survey research. Inf. Technol. Learn. Perform. J. **19**, 43 (2001)
23. Still, G.K.: Introduction to Crowd Science. CRC Press, Boca Raton (2014)

Towards Understanding Communication Behavior Changes During Floods Using Cell Phone Data

Lingzi Hong[1] , Myeong Lee[1(✉)] , Afra Mashhadi[2],
and Vanessa Frias-Martinez[1]

[1] University of Maryland, College Park, USA
{lzhong,myeong,vfrias}@umd.edu
[2] University of Washington, Seattle, USA
mashhadi@uw.edu

Abstract. Natural disasters such as hurricanes, floods or tornadoes affect millions of individuals every year. As a result, governments spend millions of dollars in emergency response allocating resources to mitigate the damages. Effective resource allocation requires a deep understanding of how humans react when a disaster takes place. Due to the multiplicity of human behavior, however, it is not trivial to understand human behaviors at large scale during and after the disaster. In this paper, we explore the use of Call Detail Records (CDR) data to model people's responses to flooding events from the communication perspective in Senegal. Specifically, we examine how different levels of flooding affect call volumes and communication network features. Our results show that individuals are more active in calling behaviors during flooding events than under normal conditions, which might imply their support-seeking behavior. Regressions on network features indicate that people in a large city in Senegal might have less access to resources outside of their neighborhoods and require better infrastructures.

Keywords: Behavior modeling · Disaster managment · CDR

1 Introduction

Natural disasters such as hurricanes, floods, and tornadoes affect millions of individuals every year. As a result, governments spend millions of dollars in emergency response allocating resources to mitigate the damages. Effective resource allocation and relief efforts usually require an understanding of how people react to the disasters. However, gathering this information at large scale during a disaster is not trivial, especially when it comes to human behaviors under different contextual information. While, understanding human behaviors such as mobility and communication patterns during and after disasters is critical in evaluating the situation and spotting the geospatial locations that need appropriate actions.

© Springer Nature Switzerland AG 2018
S. Staab et al. (Eds.): SocInfo 2018, LNCS 11186, pp. 97–107, 2018.
https://doi.org/10.1007/978-3-030-01159-8_9

They not only represent the effects of disasters on the community, but also provide evidence on which governments and international organizations should put resources.

Many researches in the crisis management literature studied this topic by conducting interviews and field studies [1,6]. While these studies provide in-depth understanding of the affected population and their psychological and behavioral factors, these approaches could have limitations in its scalability, thus, potentially miss important patterns that can be found only in certain areas. Also, the data acquisition process for survey studies is usually complex and expensive, which makes it hard to expand the scope of study subjects. Fortunately, the widespread use of cell phones worldwide has allowed to model human behaviors at large scale through the use of Call Detail Records (CDR) or mobile apps [13,22]. Given the potentials of the CDR data, previous studies about disasters mainly focused on unrevealing the common behavior patterns of human movement activities in situations where a one-time, large-scale disaster took place [16,27,30]. However, few has studied disaster-related human behavior using longitudinal CDR data for long-standing and regular disasters when the levels of their intensity vary.

In this paper, we explore the use of CDR data as proxies to evaluate human behavioral changes in communication during and after the recurring floods in Senegal. Specifically, we use call volumes to evaluate the city-level communication activities with respect to the levels of flooding in a 10-month period. Communication network features are also computed per tower coverage based on the calling records between towers. These CDR-based features inform how recurring floods can affect the communication behaviors of a specific area. The longitudinal nature of the CDR data enables us to examine communication behavior changes with floods that have different contextual information. This approach would be useful particularly for countries with very few resources where manpower or sensor networks for evaluating population behaviors in disasters are hardly available. The resulting analyses are expected to provide, in addition to existing methods, clues for allocating resources when a disaster happens and enhancing emergency planning and prevention.

The rest of the paper is organized as follows. Following the reviews on related work, we first describe the dataset used as proxies to understand human behavior and that used to measure the level of flooding. Section 4 presents models that evaluate the human behavior change relates to different floods separately for four cities in Senegal, in terms of call volumes and social network features. We find that (1) individuals are more active in calling behaviors during flooding events than under normal conditions, which might imply their support-seeking behavior, and (2) areas with more recurring floods tend to have more introversion communication, although this phenomenon is mainly observed in large cities.

2   Related Work

Using human generated data to understand collective human behaviors after disasters has been extensively studied. Many studies focused on anomalies of human activities *after* disasters by analyzing social media data, such as tweets [3,19]. Volunteered geographic information, news, and reports have also been used to create maps that visualize people's responses to disasters to support decision making for crisis management [21,29]. Meanwhile, some other researchers aimed to model the common patterns of individuals' movement or communications *during* natural disasters using geo-referenced Twitter data [11,12,30], mobile GPS data [27,28] or CDR data [9,14,20]. While these studies provide in-depth analyses on human behavior at large scale, they often characterize human behaviors under a unique instance of a disaster without considering diverse contexts of the disasters such as the level, the affected area, or the dynamics of the recurring floods, which in turn limit the scope of the study to a particular situation.

Another stream of the work used agent-based models to simulate the human reactions during and after disasters. For example, Grinberger *et al.* developed an agent-based model to evaluate the aftermath of a hypothetical earthquake in an urban area, specifically the residential location preferences and land use change [10]. Schoenharl *et al.* utilized the cell phone activities per tower region to detect the potential anomalies caused by crisis events and evaluated the mitigation strategies based on simulation of evacuation routes [24]. Solmaz and Turgut proposed the simulation model of human movement activities during anomalous events [26]; and Frias-Martinez *et al.* [7,8] presented an agent-based model to evaluate human movement during an epidemic. Building these simulation models, however, usually lacks verifications with real-world cases.

The most similar work to this paper examined the human behavior response to different types of events; it shows that behavioral responses can be complex and multidimensional where call behaviors or movement behaviors increase in some cases, but decrease in others [4]. However, the study does not reveal a clear relationship between factors. In this study, we examine the large scale human behaviors in various disaster events, which targets similar types of behaviors but with regards to different levels of intensity, providing implications on how human communication behavior changes during disasters.

3   Data Description

3.1   Cell Phone Data

Cell phone networks are formed based on a set of towers that are responsible for communicating cell phone devices within the network. Each cellular tower is identified by the latitude and longitude of its geographical location. The coverage of each tower ranges from less than $1\,km^2$ in dense urban areas to more than $4\,km^2$ in rural areas. For simplicity, it is common in the literature to assume that the cell of each tower is a 2-dimensional non-overlapping polygon, which is typically approximated using Voronoi diagrams. Whenever any type of cell phone connected to the network makes or receives a phone call or uses a service, the tower in charge generates a record, which gives an indication of the geographical position of the cell phone at the time of the call. The CDR data we use is aggregated data in tower-level provided by Senegal Orange [15]. The dataset contains records of calls from one tower to another throughout Senegal's territory in 2013.

3.2 Flood Maps of Senegal

To identify flooded areas, we used the real-time global flood maps provided by NASA Goddard's Hydrology Laboratory [17]. The flood maps are created using the Dartmouth Flood Observatory algorithm to detect water areas from MODIS imagery at approximately 250 m resolutions [23]. The water areas outside of the normal water extent are marked as flood. To avoid the false detection caused by shadows such as cloud and terrain, a water area is defined only if there is water in 2 consecutive days.

Floods might happen (or not) in rainy seasons from June till September-October with different intensities. Since our objective is to identify behavioral changes during floods using CDR, we select regions in Senegal that often suffer from floods in the June-October period. There are four flooding regions identified: Dakar, Kaolack, Matam and St. Louis. Figure 1 shows the geographical areas covered in detail.

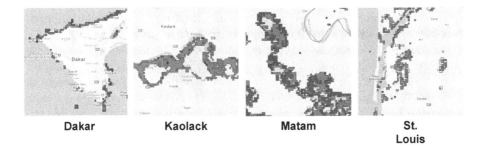

Dakar　　　　**Kaolack**　　　　**Matam**　　　　**St. Louis**

Fig. 1. Flooded Areas of Dakar, Kaolack, Matam and St. Louis from June to October in 2013. Each color indicates a specific biweekly time period.

4   Modeling Behavioral Changes

In this section, we use the features extracted from CDR data to evaluate the communication behavior changes regarding different flooding events. Specifically, we evaluate how the flooding intensity can affect communication activities in terms of call volumes and social networks.

4.1   Change of Call Volumes

We first identify the towers that serve each city, so the data recorded by these towers reflect the communication behavior of each city. For these towers, we compute the sum number of calls every two days during the dry and rainy seasons, aligned with the two-day window of the flood maps. For each two-day window, we calculate the total amount of floods in each area as an indication of the flooding intensity. Then, we run regressions to compare the communication behavior signatures against the flooding levels where the unit of analysis is a two-day time-stamp, and report standardized coefficients β and R-squared values. The purpose of the regression analyses is to evaluate how well the changes in flooding levels can explain changes in calling behaviors (computed using CDR data) in a temporal manner. By regressing the flooding levels over the CDR features, we explore how well the independent variable (flooding levels) explains the dependent variable (CDR volumes).

We compute the R-squared statistics between the two time series for different time lags to identify potential situations where the calling behaviors might change either in advance or a little bit later than the flood events. We repeat this process for the four urban regions: Dakar, Kaolack, Matam, and St. Louis. It is important to note that we separate incoming from outgoing calls to disentangle situations where, for example, outgoing signatures might decrease in volumes due to people's displacements while incoming signatures might increase due to others trying to reach the flooded region.

We ran both the region-level (including suburban areas) and urban-level (focusing on population-dense regions) analyses, and report only the region-level analyses which give more significant results. The region-level results are not significant probably due to the averaging effect of the communication behaviors over large regions. The results were adjusted with the Bonferroni correction since there are multiple tests.

Table 1. Regression results for region-level regions with time lag of $+2$ days (IV: sum of flooding area in a given time frame, DV: call volumes, R: Rainy season, NR: Non-rainy season.)

	Dakar	Kaolack	St. Louis	Matam
Number of incoming calls	$\beta = .40^{**}, R^2 = .16(R)$ $N.S.(NR)$	$\beta = .47^{**}, R^2 = .22(R)$ $N.S.(NR)$	$\beta = .32^{*}, R^2 = .10(R)$ $N.S.(NR)$	$\beta = .33^{*}, R^2 = .11(R)$ $N.S.(NR)$
Number of outgoing calls	$\beta = .39^{**}, R^2 = .15(R)$ $N.S.(NR)$	$\beta = .50^{**}, R^2 = .25(R)$ $N.S.(NR)$	$\beta = .33^{*}, R^2 = .11(R)$ $N.S.(NR)$	$\beta = .36^{**}, R^2 = .13(R)$ $\beta = .25^{\dagger}, R^2 = .06(NR)$

($\dagger p < 0.10$, $*p < 0.05$, $**p < 0.01$, $N.S.$: not significant)

Table 1 shows a summary of the regression analyses. Specifically, we focus on the results for regressions between CDR volume and flood level in time series with a time-lag of two days, i.e., call changes that took place (DV) after changes in flooding levels (IV), since these were the best results obtained. We distinguish regressions between rainy and non-rainy seasons for making sure that the behavioral changes are detected only during the rainy season; this allows us to hypothesize a correlation between the behavioral changes and the floods.

We observe that the volumes of incoming and outgoing calls are correlated with flooding level for all the four cities. Different slopes and R^2 may reflect that the resilience to flooding is different, or the proportion of affected population is small. One notable pattern is that few regions showed any significant relationships between calling behavior and flood levels during non-rainy seasons (only marginal ones with the exception of outgoing calls for Matam). These results highlight that users change their calling behaviors during floods and that communication patterns (volumes of incoming and outgoing calls) could be partially explained through changes in flooding levels. In other words, flooding appears to be one of the potential causes of the behavioral changes observed in the calling activities of the affected population. Furthermore, the regressions reveal that the higher the flooding intensity, the larger the increase in calling volumes by users ($0.35 < \beta < 0.37$).

Communication behavior is usually the precursor of other resilience behaviors such as help-seeking behavior and mobility changes. This means that it might be possible to interpret communication behaviors as an indicator for the community resilience. Follow-up studies that identify the relationships between communication behaviors and other resilience-related behaviors are needed to confirm this possibility.

4.2   Change of Regional Social Network Features

Unlike the city-level call volumes, social network features in the tower level measure how individuals in the specific region communicate with people in other regions, which can reflect how information flows and whether one place is more isolated than others in communication during a disaster. Also, they can indicate the accessibility to social capitals and resources outside of their neighborhoods [25]. In this section, we aim to find how the severity of recurring flooding relates to the communication behaviors of a specific area. Social network features are computed per tower coverage area based on people's calling patterns among towers. Specifically, Voronoi diagrams were generated based on the cellphone tower locations, and a region-to-region network was created based on tower-to-tower calling data. The data was aggregated across different time periods. Network features extracted from the communication network are as follows:

Introversion. It is calculated by the proportion of calls made inside of a region to the number of outgoing calls. It quantifies the extent to which individuals in a region reach out to those who are in the same region, compared to people in other regions, indicating people's access to social capitals and resources outside of their neighborhoods [25].

Entropy. Entropy quantifies the diversity of a node (i.e., tower) in the communication network: the extend to which a focus tower communicates with diverse towers [5]. This can imply the potential capability to reach diverse resources.

PageRank. The PageRank value focuses on the importance and popularity of a region in terms of communication, maybe due to its role as support provider or support requester [18].

Eigenvector Centrality. Similarly to PageRank, it also quantifies the importance and popularity of a region, but focuses more on the communication networks formed with nearest neighborhoods, rather than towers in distance.

We conducted regressions where each feature (normalized) is the dependent variable (DV) while the sum of flooded areas in each polygon is the independent variable (IV). The results are presented in Table 2.

Table 2. Regressions between flooding intensity and network features for four cities. All the regressions are OLS except for the one against Dakar's introversion, which exhibited heteroskedasticity. It was adjusted using the Box-Cox transformation [2]. Also, the results were adjusted using the Bonferroni correction.

	Introversion	PageRank	Centrality	Entropy	In-Calls	Out-Calls
Dakar	$\beta = 1.78^*$ $R^2 = 0.02$	$\beta = -2.20^{**}$ $R^2 = 0.04$	$\beta = -3.21^{**}$ $R^2 = 0.05$	N.S.	$\beta = -2.75^{**}$ $R^2 = 0.04$	$\beta = -2.73^{**}$ $R^2 = 0.04$
Kaolack	N.S.	N.S.	N.S.	N.S.	N.S.	N.S.
St. Louis	N.S.	N.S.	N.S.	N.S.	N.S.	N.S.
Matam	N.S.	$\beta = 0.11*$ $R^2 = 0.10$	N.S.	N.S.	$\beta = 0.15^*$ $R^2 = 0.10$	$\beta = 0.15^*$ $R^2 = 0.10$

($\dagger p < 0.10, *p < 0.05, **p < 0.01,$ N.S.: not significant)

The results show that flooding events in urban regions are partially related to people's communication behavior patterns in a long term (1-year in the dataset). The communication network features in Dakar, the biggest city in Senegal, are mostly correlated with flooding intensity indicating some useful insights about communication patterns. Inconsistency between the results of Dakar and other cities poses needs for further research.

Introversion is positively correlated with the flooding intensity in Dakar. Since introversion indicates people's accessibility to resources and social capitals outside of their regions, a positive relationship implies that local neighborhoods are less likely to have access to resources outside of their communities when a flooding happens. This information can be helpful for decision makers in crisis management. Figure 2 in Appendix shows the map of Dakar, where flooded areas are colored blue (the darker the color is, the more the flooding intensity is), and the dark color of dots represent the high introversion value in this region. For zoomed area A and B, it is possible to observe that these areas are heavily flooded, and have a high level of introversion. It indicates that residents in these two regions might have less access to outside resources and rely on local communications more. This communication pattern shows that these areas may require more attention from decision makers.

There are consistent findings on the negative relationships between flooding intensity and the PageRank/eigenvector centrality. It indicates that in more affected areas, the popularity or importance of these areas in terms of communication becomes less significant (results of call volumes also support this). Meanwhile, less affected areas might become more important either as service provider or as service requester during disaster. If some regions that have low PageRank scores provide services during disasters, communication infrastructures could be enhanced to better serve other regions in the city; conversely, if some regions are popular in the communication network due to the high demands for help, policy-makers and service providers can take this into account for keeping track of dynamically-changing needs. To better understand the roles of each region in terms of communication, further studies need to be designed; questions to be answered include how the network advantage of each region is determined and what socio-economic factors could affect them.

Inconsistency between the results of Dakar and other cities also provides some evidence of urban dynamics and suggests further research questions. Since Dakar is a big city with high population density, it is possible that other cities have insufficient data points, or the urban dynamics such as mobility patterns and structure of local communities are different. The positive relationship between PageRank and flooding intensity in Matam, for example, indicates that highly affected regions might also play an important role in terms of communication within the city. It could be either due to the separation between areas with high population and low population or due to the concentration of important infrastructures in flooded regions. Thus, this observation raises questions as to how the communication infrastructure is related to disaster and how the urban-rural segregation could impact the behavior changes during disaster.

5   Conclusion and Limitations

In this paper, we explored the use of CDR data to model human communication responses to flooding events regarding call volumes and social networks for four cities in Senegal. While the analyses were conducted in a high level, the results provide useful implications. It was possible to show that people tend to call more during flooding events than under normal conditions, and its volumes is positively related to the intensity of flooding. Network features provided more subtle communication changes than call volumes such as people's access to resources outside of their neighborhood during disasters. While these analyses provide implications on possible dimensions of human behavior changes during disasters, they raise further questions on the urban structure, crisis policies, and communities to unveil the urban dynamics during disasters.

This paper has several limitations where one of which is at data sources. We rely on the flooding maps to identify floods. Flooding levels are computed using data gathered over 2-day periods and based on cleaning algorithms to eliminate elements in the image, e.g., clouds, that could be confused with water areas. This approach is not perfect and might suffer from false positives or erroneous calculations of flooding levels. Moreover, it is impossible for us to acquire detailed information about floods such the reasons of flooding and its cumulative impact over time (e.g., whether it was regular or unexpected), while these anomalies can also affect communication behaviors in different ways. In addition, the CDR data is aggregated in the cellular tower level which can show only the communication patterns in a region basis; this aggregation makes it hard to build computational models that operationalize individual-level behavioral changes. In this sense, this paper should be seen as preliminary results of how the high-level communication behavior changes when flooding level varies. Our focus is to provide an overall pattern change during flooding and list future research questions of why behavior changes in specific regions. We hope this paper can help researchers identify important questions regarding flooding in the era of climate change.

Appendix: Example of the Interface of a Decision-Making Map

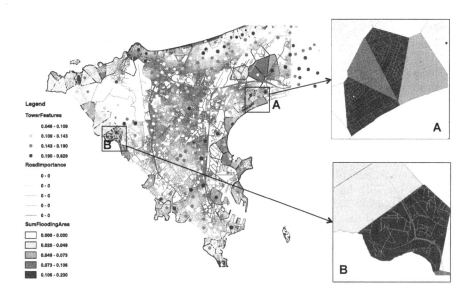

Fig. 2. Example of the interface of a decision-making tool (Color figure online)

References

1. Bardsley, D.K., Hugo, G.J.: Migration and climate change: examining thresholds of change to guide effective adaptation decision-making. Popul. Environ. **32**(2–3), 238–262 (2010)
2. Box, G.E., Cox, D.R.: An analysis of transformations. J. R. Stat. Soc. Ser. B (Methodol.) **26**, 211–252 (1964)

3. Candia, J., González, M.C., Wang, P., Schoenharl, T., Madey, G., Barabási, A.L.: Uncovering individual and collective human dynamics from mobile phone records. J. Phys. A Math. Theor. **41**(22), 224015 (2008)
4. Dobra, A., Williams, N.E., Eagle, N.: Spatiotemporal detection of unusual human population behavior using mobile phone data. PloS One **10**(3), e0120449 (2015)
5. Eagle, N., Macy, M., Claxton, R.: Network diversity and economic development. Science **328**(5981), 1029–1031 (2010)
6. Elliott, J.R., Pais, J.: Race, class, and hurricane Katrina: social differences in human responses to disaster. Soc. Sci. Res. **35**(2), 295–321 (2006)
7. Frias-Martinez, E., Williamson, G., Frias-Martinez, V.: An agent-based model of epidemic spread using human mobility and social network information. In: IEEE Third International Conference on Social Computing (SocialCom), pp. 57–64. IEEE (2011)
8. Frias-Martinez, V., Rubio, A., Frias-Martinez, E.: Measuring the impact of epidemic alerts on human mobility using cell-phone network data. In: Second Workshop on Pervasive Urban Applications@ Pervasive, vol. 12 (2012)
9. Ghurye, J., Krings, G., Frias-Martinez, V.: A framework to model human behavior at large scale during natural disasters. In: 2016 17th IEEE International Conference on Mobile Data Management (MDM), vol. 1, pp. 18–27. IEEE (2016)
10. Grinberger, A.Y., Lichter, M., Felsenstein, D.: Dynamic agent based simulation of an urban disaster using synthetic big data. In: Thakuriah, P.V., Tilahun, N., Zellner, M. (eds.) Seeing Cities Through Big Data. SG, pp. 349–382. Springer, Cham (2017). https://doi.org/10.1007/978-3-319-40902-3_20
11. Hong, L., Fu, C., Torrens, P., Frias-Martinez, V.: Understanding citizens' and local governments' digital communications during natural disasters: the case of snowstorms. In: Proceedings of the 2017 ACM on Web Science Conference, pp. 141–150. ACM (2017)
12. Hong, L., Fu, C., Wu, J., Frias-Martinez, V.: Information needs and communication gaps between citizens and local governments online during natural disasters. Inf. Syst. Front. 1–13 (2018, in press)
13. Isaacman, S., et al.: Human mobility modeling at metropolitan scales. In: Proceedings of the 10th International Conference on Mobile Systems, Applications, and Services, pp. 239–252. ACM (2012)
14. Isaacman, S., Frias-Martinez, V., Frias-Martinez, E.: Modeling human migration patterns during drought conditions in La Guajira, Colombia. In: Proceedings of the ACM First Conference on Computing and Sustainable Societies (2018)
15. de Montjoye, Y.A., Smoreda, Z., Trinquart, R., Ziemlicki, C., Blondel, V.D.: D4D-Senegal: the second mobile phone data for development challenge. arXiv preprint arXiv:1407.4885 (2014)
16. Moumni, B., Frias-Martinez, V., Frias-Martinez, E.: Characterizing social response to urban earthquakes using cell-phone network data: the 2012 Oaxaca earthquake. In: Proceedings of the 2013 ACM Conference on Pervasive and Ubiquitous Computing Adjunct Publication, pp. 1199–1208. ACM (2013)
17. NASA: NRT global flood mapping. https://floodmap.modaps.eosdis.nasa.gov (2017). Accessed 25 July 2017
18. Page, L., Brin, S., Motwani, R., Winograd, T.: The pagerank citation ranking: bringing order to the web. Technical report, Stanford InfoLab (1999)
19. Palen, L., Starbird, K., Vieweg, S., Hughes, A.: Twitter-based information distribution during the 2009 red river valley flood threat. Bull. Assoc. Inf. Sci. Technol. **36**(5), 13–17 (2010)

20. Pastor-Escuredo, D., et al.: Flooding through the lens of mobile phone activity. In: 2014 IEEE Global Humanitarian Technology Conference (GHTC), pp. 279–286. IEEE (2014)
21. Roche, S., Propeck-Zimmermann, E., Mericskay, B.: Geoweb and crisis management: issues and perspectives of volunteered geographic information. GeoJournal **78**(1), 21–40 (2013)
22. Rubio, A., Frias-Martinez, V., Frias-Martinez, E., Oliver, N.: Human mobility in advanced and developing economies: a comparative analysis. In: AAAI Spring Symposium: Artificial Intelligence for Development (2010)
23. Sakamoto, T., Van Nguyen, N., Kotera, A., Ohno, H., Ishitsuka, N., Yokozawa, M.: Detecting temporal changes in the extent of annual flooding within the Cambodia and the Vietnamese Mekong Delta from MODIS time-series imagery. Remote Sens. Environ. **109**(3), 295–313 (2007)
24. Schoenharl, T., Bravo, R., Madey, G.: WIPER: leveraging the cell phone network for emergency response. Int. J. Intell. Control. Syst. **11**(4), 209–216 (2006)
25. Smith-Clarke, C., Mashhadi, A., Capra, L.: Poverty on the cheap: estimating poverty maps using aggregated mobile communication networks. In: Proceedings of the SIGCHI Conference on Human Factors in Computing Systems, pp. 511–520. ACM (2014)
26. Solmaz, G., Turgut, D.: Theme park mobility in disaster scenarios. In: 2013 IEEE Global Communications Conference (GLOBECOM), pp. 377–382. IEEE (2013)
27. Song, X., Zhang, Q., Sekimoto, Y., Shibasaki, R.: Prediction of human emergency behavior and their mobility following large-scale disaster. In: Proceedings of the 20th ACM SIGKDD International Conference on Knowledge Discovery and Data Mining, pp. 5–14. ACM (2014)
28. Song, X., et al.: A simulator of human emergency mobility following disasters: knowledge transfer from big disaster data. In: AAAI, pp. 730–736 (2015)
29. Tomaszewski, B.M., Robinson, A.C., Weaver, C., Stryker, M., MacEachren, A.M.: Geovisual analytics and crisis management. In: Proceedings of the 4th International ISCRAM Conference, pp. 173–179, Delft, The Netherlands (2007)
30. Wang, Q., Taylor, J.E.: Patterns and limitations of urban human mobility resilience under the influence of multiple types of natural disaster. PLoS One **11**(1), e0147299 (2016)

How Happy You Are: A Computational Study of Social Impact on Self-esteem

Fakhra Jabeen[1,2(✉)]

[1] Department of Information Technology,
The Punjab University, Lahore, Pakistan
[2] Behavioural Informatics Group,
Vrije Universiteit Amsterdam, Amsterdam, The Netherlands
f.jabeen@vu.nl

Abstract. People take the opportunity from social-networking sites like Facebook, to express themselves in various communities. Various studies address that it has influence over self-esteem of its users. In this paper, we analyse how the self-esteem of a person is affected in the computational world. To accomplish this, we built a computational model of esteem. A questionnaire-based survey was conducted to collect data for model verification. Different simulation experiments were conducted to compare and evaluate the model concerning findings from the literature and data. This model can be used as a useful input to provide support to people who are influenced by negative feedback.

Keywords: Self-esteem · Computational model · Social pain

1 Introduction

Social networking in the era of digital technology, provide a platform extensively used for self-expression and gives a good opportunity to get feedback from society. Positive feedback helps in improving oneself. However, negative feedback may become expensive, as it may not positively affect the self-assessment and thus esteem of a person [1, 2]. Esteem is an attitude which determines the positive and negative features or feelings of oneself [3]. These feelings of worthiness can be a cumulative effect of self-evaluations or an immediate effect of opinions from others [4].

Rise and fall of esteem of a person is being studied in various aspects. For example, famous people have higher esteem than the lonely people [5]. Another study indicates that when esteem reaches a certain level, individuals do not further engage themselves in self-presentation for any feedback [6]. People having high esteem have a sociable and healthier lifestyle [7], than the people with low esteem who feel lonely and rejected [2, 8, 9]. Although esteem was studied in numerous contexts [6, 10], however, no effort was seen to assess computationally how feedback of others influences esteem.

To address the influence of a feedback over the esteem of a person, we present a temporal-causal network model. This model provides an essence of how a certain type of feedback is translated in the human mind to influence the esteem of a person. It is based upon the concepts derived from cogntive and social neuroscientific literature.

© Springer Nature Switzerland AG 2018
S. Staab et al. (Eds.): SocInfo 2018, LNCS 11186, pp. 108–117, 2018.
https://doi.org/10.1007/978-3-030-01159-8_10

It presents and models the activations of mental states inspired by the human brain along with the feedback translation and assessment. For verification of our model, we performed mathematical analysis and survey analysis of a Likert scale based questionnaire.

The remainder of the paper is organized by six sections. Section 2 discusses state of the art. Section 3 presents the temporal-causal network model and its analysis in detail. Section 4 discusses the experimental setup and simulations of esteem with respect to neuroscience. Lastly, Sects. 5 and 6 verifies the model and concludes the paper respectively.

2 State of the Art

Social networking sites provide abundant opportunities for social comparison, however, this comparison influences a human's brain and psychology. Therefore, this section addresses both the neurological and social or psychological aspects of esteem.

Viewed from a cognitive neurological perspective, various parts of the human mind are involved during esteem analysis on a feedback. A fMRI study indicated that dACC; vmPFC; right insula; precuneus; hippocampus; and few other parts are more activated during social exclusion for a person with low esteem [4]. dACC and lingual gyrus detect the fear of rejection while *vm*PFC acts as a valuation system to assign personal value thus suppressing negative self-view [11]. According to psychologists and neuroscientists, the hippocampus is responsible for storing the experiences for future decision making, and along with precuneus it also plays a vital role in evaluations of self-view [11, 12], resulting the interpretation of esteem of a person [13]. dACC and right insula are more active in the people being rejected than the people who are treated equally [2], causing body awareness or chemical sensations or focal attention [14].

According to sociometry theory, various studies show that feedback from others influence esteem of a person. For example, a questionnaire-based study indicated that person's esteem increases if he received more likes and comments [15]. Another related study concluded that people who mostly use Facebook have lower esteem. When participants were given an exposure to the profiles of Facebook profiles the participants observed the targets with higher lifestyle than theirs [16, 17]. Moreover, it was studied that when esteem reaches to a certain level then people do not engage themselves further in self-presentation for any feedback [6].

In research esteem acts as a variable in few models [10], however, no one has computationally looked how esteem works with self-evaluation and feedback from others. Esteem is a mental process which is related to feelings and evaluations related to oneself. It considers prediction effects by feeling and valuing (Chap. 6 [18]). Moreover, strong fears in a person should be regulated in an adaptive manner so that he can learn to cope with his experiences (Chap. 5 [18]).

Esteem can be a cumulative effect of self-evaluations or an immediate effect of opinion from others [4]. Therefore, we build a model in Sect. 3, based on the literature mentioned above, to see how feedback influences esteem of a person.

3   The Temporal-Causal Network Model

In this section, we present a computational model for esteem (Fig. 1), which explains how a human mind works as he receives feedback from his social circle.

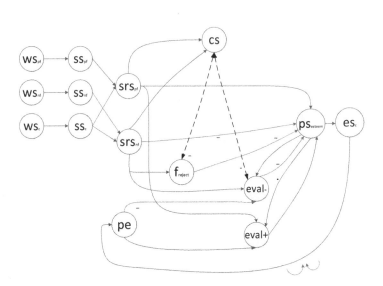

Fig. 1. Temporal-causal network model of self-esteem of a person

To design our model we used a temporal-causal modeling approach, in which model is specified by causal relationships between two states such that $X \rightarrow Y$. Here Y follows after the occurrence of state X. The future values of each state Y after some time Δt (i.e. $Y(t+\Delta t)$) is computed by value at current time t (i.e. $Y(t)$). This relationship is mathematically expressed by Eq. 1 as [18]:

$$Y(t + \Delta t) = Y(t) + \eta_Y[c_Y(\omega_{X_1,Y}X_1(t), , \ldots, \omega_{X_k,Y}X_k(t)) - Y(t)]\Delta t \qquad (1)$$

where $X_1, \ldots X_k$ are the states with outgoing connections to Y

η_Y = speed factor with which state Y changes its value.
c_Y = used to compute an aggregated impact of states X_i to Y.
$\omega_{X_i,Y}$ = connection weights indicating the impact of states X_i to Y.
Δt = step size of time for each interaction from states X_i to Y.

The temporal-causal model is designed on the background addressed in Sect. 2. Various parts of human mind play an essential role in measuring the esteem of a person over the course of time. For example, *vm*PFC is responsible for assigning significance to self-related content or self-worth, while hippocampus and precuneus acts as a part of the mentalizing system to interpret and evaluate feedback by others [13]. Similarly the dACC and few other parts like lingual gyrus and insula activate to detect threats related to esteem or social-rejection [2] and suppresses the negative self-view [11]. Figure 1 presents the conceptual representation of the model showing the influence of feedback over esteem of a person.

As figure illustrates, the possibility of getting a feedback acts as the primary stimulus for our model. The stimulus is conceptually represented by world states (ws_I); sensor (ss_I) states in the model. Here I indicates the context (c), positive (pf), and negative feedback (nf) in the model. Here context represents a situation in which esteem is computed, while feedback indicates the feedback received by a person most of the time. Positive feedback srs_{pf}, has a positive impact on positive self-evaluation eval+ as well as on esteem ps_{esteem}. However, the negative feedback srs_{nf} activates the fear of rejection (f_{reject}) and negative self-view (eval−) in a person lowering the esteem of the person. Nevertheless, pe acts as a mentalizing system which suppress the negative self-view and promotes the positive self-view (eval+) to escalate the esteem in a person. As a result execution state (es_c) expresses esteem of a person.

Moreover, control state (cs) is responsible for monitoring and regulating the negative feelings (f_{reject}, eval−), to improve esteem of a person. It is accomplished by monitoring of f_{reject} and eval− and suppression or regulation of these negative feelings. Besides, it can be observed that; there is an adaptive connection from es_c to pe; which indicates the learning process over time [13, 18]. Table 1 presents of each state with its meaning in the model respectively.

Table 1. Overview of state variables used (in Fig. 1)

State	Definition
ws_I	World state I: for the positive feedback; negative feedback and context in which esteem is measured
ss_I	Sensor state of I
srs_{pf}	Sensory representation of positive feedback
srs_{nf}	Sensory representation of negative feedback
cs	Control state
f_{reject}	The feeling of fear of rejection
pe	Predicted effect
eval−	Negative self-view
eval+	Positive self-view
ps_{esteem}	Preparation state for esteem
es_c	Communication of esteem to predicted effect

For activation level computation of each state, speed factors and connection weights are assumed in the range of 0–1. All connections are positive except the suppression connections, which are highlighted by red ($srs_{nf} \rightarrow ps_{esteem}$; $f_{fear} \rightarrow ps_{esteem}$; eval- $\rightarrow ps_{esteem}$; cs $\rightarrow f_{fear}$; and cs $\rightarrow$ eval− in Fig. 1). Aggregated impact of states is computed by Eq. 1, through two combination functions (c_Y). For states ws_I and ss_I we used the identity function id(V) = V, whereas rest of the states were computed by using advanced logistic function expressed as:

$$\textbf{alogistic}_{\sigma,\tau}(V_1,\ldots,V_k) = \left[\left(\frac{1}{1+e^{-\sigma(V_1+\cdots+V_{k-\tau})}}\right) - 1/(1+e^{\sigma\tau})\right](1+e^{-\sigma\tau}) \quad (2)$$

where σ = steepness of the curve, with range = 5–10, and

τ = threshold, with range = 0.2–1

These two functions were used as they are well-known to be non-negative and upward bounded by 1. Software environments are available in Matlab and Python to systematically simulate the designed models. These environments are inspired from theories presented for temporal-causal networks and are extensively used for adaptive and non-adaptive networks (Chap. 2 [18]).

4 Simulation Experiments

In this section we briefly discusses how we collected the data for the model and how simulation scenarios were performed

4.1 Data Collection

After designing the model, we conducted a survey inspired by a renown survey related to esteem [3]. 126 students (81 male; 45 female) from a Dutch university participated in the study with different ranges of their ages (4% in 35–44 ages, 30% in 16–24 years, 66% in 25–34). It was made compulsory to mention their reactions towards the feedback they receive from others.

After cleaning the collected data, we investigated 112 records by using boxplots. In Fig. 2a, we can see the whiskers boxplot concerning age groups, showing most of the participants has esteem in range of 20–25 (median = 22), for all the three age groups. For further analysis of fear of rejection, we extracted records of the persons, who experienced the fear of rejection (81 participants). Distribution of data of these participants was studied (Fig. 2b), which shows that 75% of both groups (a) a person agrees or (b) he strongly agrees have normal esteem in the range of 16–23.

Esteem scale is computed in range from 0 to 30, and it can be normal (15–25), or low (<15) [19]. Therefore, Table 2 shows the assumptions we made to compute esteem.

4.2 Simulation

This section presents the simulation experiments for the model designed in Sect. 3. As behavior dynamics faces the challenge of scarcity of numerical empirical data, therefore studied patterns and requirements through empirical literature for the purpose [20]. Table 3 shows the patterns derived from the literature discussed in Sect. 2. It will give an impression to the reader, how states in the human brain interact with each other when a person receives feedback.

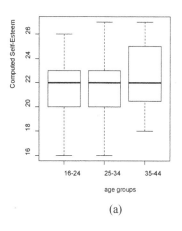
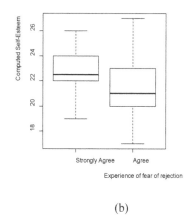

(a)   (b)

Fig. 2. Data insights: (a) Ratio of esteem regarding age groups, (b) People having a fear of rejection

Table 2. Self-esteem values [0–1] in accordance to self-esteem scale

Esteem level	Range in literature	Assumed values
Low	Less than 15	0 < 0.4
Normal	15–25	0.4–0.7
High	Greater than 25	0.7–1 ·

Table 3. Patterns derived from empirical literature

Empirical Literature	Pattern Deduced for states of model
People paying attention to negative feedback of others 'better than average effect' disappears and esteem decreases [11]	Based on ws_{nf}, srs_{nf} activates eval− and f_{reject}, loweing eval+ and ps_{esteem}
Self-evaluation is associated with neural activity of vmPFC and dACC [11]	cs activation along with the self-evaluation states (eval+; eval−)
Precuneus is part of mentalizing system helping in interpretation of reputation into state esteem [21]	eval− and eval+ are activated along with srs_l for interpretation of the feedbacks, into ps_{esteem}
Past experiences play an important role in guiding future choices, with the help of learning [12]	pe learns from experience and therefore is activated after establishment of ps_{esteem}, thus es_c
dACC and anterior insula are activated when a person experience rejection [2, 11]. Also dACC works with lingual gyrus to detect fears [11]	cs detect and monitors fears that is f_{reject} and eval− states. Therefore, it gets active on negative feedback
dACC is activated in conflict monitoring and PFC reduce the conflict [11]	cs tries to suppress the negative self-view (eval−; f_{reject})

From Table 3, patterns and requirements were deduced for simulations for resulting three levels of esteem expressed in Table 2 [20]. Any feedback stimulates control state (cs) and self-view of a person (eval+ and eval−) along with f_{reject}. A person receiving positive feedback occasionally, (s)he has stronger self-evaluations (both eval− and eval+ are high) along with fear of rejection (addressed in Fig. 3a); which results ps_{esteem} to be in the normal range (3a). Moreover, a person who receives positive feedback most of the time has low eval−, thus the cumulative esteem tends to be high, making the state pe higher as well to keep leaning from good experiences (Fig. 3b). Similarly, a victimized person receiving negative feedback tends to have elevated eval−, and f_{reject}, leading to low ps_{esteem} (3c). In all three cases, pe and es_c occurs after ps_{esteem} is triggered.

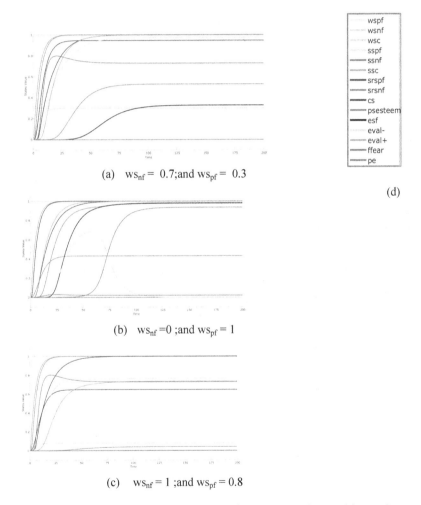

(a) $ws_{nf} = 0.7$; and $ws_{pf} = 0.3$

(d)

(b) $ws_{nf} = 0$; and $ws_{pf} = 1$

(c) $ws_{nf} = 1$; and $ws_{pf} = 0.8$

Fig. 3. Simulation results for esteem: (a) Normal: person receive positive and negative feedback.; (b) High: person mostly receives positive feedback; (c) Low: person is mostly victimized; and (d) Legend

5 Mathematical Analysis of the Model

In this section mathematical analysis of equilibria and analysis using statistical data are discussed.

5.1 Analysis of the Model in Equilibrium

Simulation experiments are helpful to study the dynamics of a model. However, other properties like equilibria, monotonicity can also be studied to verify a model mathematically. A model is in equilibrium at a certain time point t if the values for all the states are stationary, that is they remain the same from t to $t + \Delta t$ or $Y(t + \Delta t) = Y(t)$. This condition of equality infers that for equilibrium a model must satisfy the following condition for every state Y [18], expressed as:

$$\mathbf{aggimpact}_Y(t) = Y(t) \Leftrightarrow \mathbf{c}_Y\left(\omega_{X_1,Y}X_1(t),, \ldots, \omega_{X_k,Y}X_k(t)\right) = Y(t) \tag{3}$$

By using Eq. 3, we computed deviations for each state in the simulations (illustrated in Table 4). Considering Fig. 3a, it is observed that after time point $t > 35$ the model starts to converge, and ends up in equilibrium at $t = 136$, which gives evidence that model was implemented correctly.

Table 4. Computations of Stationary points for Fig. 3a.

State	srs_{pf}	srs_{nf}	cs	ps_{esteem}	es_c
Time t	40	40	93	105	126
$Y(t)$	0.9452	0.9789	0.9992	0.5504	0.3767
aggimpact$_Y(t)$	0.9461	0.9795	1.000	0.5512	0.3784
Deviation	0.0009	0.0006	0.0008	0.0008	0.0017

State	eval−	eval+	f_{reject}	p_{effect}
Time t	92	78	78	3
$Y(t)$	0.9712	0.9967	0.6970	$2.02e^{-11}$
aggimpact$_Y(t)$	0.9727	0.9980	0.6969	$4.04e^{-10}$
Deviation	0.0015	0.0013	0.0001	0

5.2 Analysis Using Statistics of Data

It is a challenge to collect numerical empirical data of mental states over time. As no perfect data was available, as a second-best option we used the collected empirical data in Sect. 4 for validation of the model. This data can used once model reaches to the equilibrium, i.e., when the behavior of the model ends up in a state that remains the same overtime.

Model at equilibrium is useful to deduce a causal relationship among its states. Therefore we computed Pearson Correlation, and a positive correlation with positive self-evaluation (value: 0.36), negative correlation with negative self-evaluation (value: −0.11) and fear of rejection (value: −0.22) was observed. This correlation is helpful to assess cumulative effects of esteem in a person [4], and can be studied in all simulations. It can be seen in Fig. 3b and c, that a negative correlation exists for negative self, that is f_{reject} and eval−. This implies that if esteem remains high than these two states will remain low. Similarly, there is a positive correlation between eval+ and ps_{esteem}, which indicates that both remain high if eval− and f_{reject} remains low or vice-versa. Therefore, the model is verified according to real world.

6 Conclusion and Future Work

This paper presents a temporal-causal network model which illustrates how feedback relates to the esteem of a person. This model was designed on the basis of different parts of brain like vmPFC, dACC, hippocampus and Precuneus to maintain self-worth or esteem of a person [2, 11, 13]. A Likert based survey was used to study influence of feedback on esteem of a person. The findings indicated that the participants with normal esteem have activated self-evaluations as well as they experience fear of rejection on negative feedback. This was also simulated in the designed model. For verification, we studied equilibria and Pearson's correlation, which showed that behaviour of model is same as it was intended. As the model is generic, therefore, it can be used as a basis for providing support for people who need improvement in their self-esteem. In future, we aim to extend our work by including different perspectives and traits of a human.

References

1. Sargeant, J., Mann, K., van der Vleuten, C., Metsemakers, J.: "Directed" self-assessment: practice and feedback within a social context. J. Contin. Educ. Health Prof. **28**, 47–54 (2008)
2. Kashdan, T.B., et al.: Who is most vulnerable to social rejection? The toxic combination of low self-esteem and lack of negative emotion differentiation on neural responses to rejection. PLoS ONE **9**, e90651 (2014)
3. Morris, R.: Conceiving the self. Am. J. Sociol. **86**, 907–909 (1979)
4. Onoda, K., et al.: Does low self-esteem enhance social pain? The relationship between trait self-esteem and anterior cingulate cortex activation induced by ostracism. Soc. Cognit. Affect. Neurosci. **5**, 385–391 (2010)
5. Manago, A.M., Taylor, T., Greenfield, P.M.: Me and my 400 friends: the anatomy of college students' Facebook networks, their communication patterns, and well-being. Dev. Psychol. **48**, 369–380 (2012)
6. Zywica, J., Danowski, J.: The faces of Facebookers: investigating social enhancement and social compensation hypotheses; predicting Facebook™ and offline popularity from sociability and self-esteem, and mapping the meanings of popularity with semantic networks. J. Comput. Med. Commun. **14**, 1–34 (2008)
7. Baumeister, R.F., Campbell, J.D., Krueger, J.I., Vohs, K.D.: Does high self-esteem cause better performance, interpersonal success, happiness, or healthier lifestyles? Psychol. Sci. Publ. Interest **4**, 1–44 (2003)
8. Sowislo, J.F., Orth, U.: Does low self-esteem predict depression and anxiety? A meta-analysis of longitudinal studies. Psychol. Bull. **139**, 213–240 (2013)

9. Merlo, E.M., Frisone, F., Settineri, S., Mento, C.: Depression signs, teasing and low self-esteem in female obese adolescents: a clinical evaluation, p. 16

10. Zarnaghash, M., Gholamrezai, S., Sadeghi, M.: Developing a model of loneliness on the basis of self efficacy, self esteem and life satisfaction of girl's veterans, p. 7 (2017)

11. Pan, W., Liu, C., Yang, Q., Gu, Y., Yin, S., Chen, A.: The neural basis of trait self-esteem revealed by the amplitude of low-frequency fluctuations and resting state functional connectivity. Soc. Cognit. Affect. Neurosci. **11**, 367–376 (2016)

12. Jai, Y.Y., Frank, L.M.: Hippocampal–cortical interaction in decision making. Neurobiol. Learn. Mem. **117**, 34–41 (2015)

13. Kawamichi, H., et al.: Neural correlates underlying change in state self-esteem. Sci. Rep. **8**, 1798 (2018)

14. Shura, R.D., Hurley, R.A., Taber, K.H.: The insular cortex: structure, function, and neuropsychiatric implications. In: Journal of Neuropsychiatry and Clinical Neurosciences, p. 14. Amer Psychiatric Publishing, Inc 1000 Wilson Boulevard, Ste 1825, Arlington, VA 22209-3901 USA (2014)

15. Zell, A.L., Moeller, L.: Are you happy for me… on Facebook? The potential importance of "likes" and comments. Comput. Hum. Behav. **78**, 26–33 (2018)

16. Vogel, E.A., Rose, J.P., Roberts, L.R., Eckles, K.: Social comparison, social media, and self-esteem. Psychol. Popul. Media Cult. **3**, 206 (2014)

17. Anthony, D.B., Wood, J.V., Holmes, J.G.: Testing sociometer theory: self-esteem and the importance of acceptance for social decision-making. J. Exp. Soc. Psychol. **43**, 425–432 (2007)

18. Treur, J.: Network-Oriented Modeling. Springer, Cham (2016). https://doi.org/10.1007/978-3-319-45213-5

19. Rosenberg Self-esteem scale. https://www.wwnorton.com/college/psych/psychsci/media/rosenberg.htm

20. Pohl, K., Rupp, C.: Requirements Engineering Fundamentals, 1st edn. Rocky Nook, San Rafael (2011)

21. Cabanis, M., et al.: The precuneus and the insula in self-attributional processes. Cognit. Affect. Behav. Neurosci. **13**, 330–345 (2013)

Influence of Temporal Aspects and Age-Correlations on the Process of Opinion Formation Based on Polish Contact Survey

Andrzej Jarynowski[1,2,3]([⊠]) and Andrzej Grabowski[3]

[1] Interdisciplinary Research Institute, Wroclaw, Poland
andrzej.jarynowski@sociology.su.se
[2] Smoluchowski Institute, Jagiellonian University, Cracow, Poland
[3] Central Institute for Labour Protection - National Research Institute, Warsaw, Poland

Abstract. On the basis of the experimental data concerning interactions between humans the process of Ising-based model of opinion formation in a social network was investigated. In the paper the data concerning human social activity, i.e. frequency and duration time of interpersonal interactions as well as age correlations - homophily are presented in comparison to base line homogeneous, static and uniform mixing. Recent research suggests that real (temporal and assortative) patterns can both speed up or slow down processes (like epidemic spread) on the networks. Also in our study, a real structure of contacts affects processes of opinion formation in various non-intuitive ways. The real patterns (correlation and dynamics) reduce 'freezing by heating' effect for small social temperature values. Moreover, our research shows that the cross interactions between contact frequency and its duration impose the significant increase in critical temperature.

Keywords: Dynamics of social systems · Propagation processes
Ising model of opinion formation · Physical contact networks

1 Introduction

The Ising-based model of opinion formation can be used to investigate various aspects of opinion formation, e.g. the process of the agents adopting new opinions or ideas [7]. The state of an individual takes a binary value (opinion) and can change according to neighbors and external field. The final opinion space can be uniform, fragmented or random, depending on many factors. Opinion formation (with the characteristic properties like longer time scale or consensus orientation) is an example of propagation process of many other kinds as: social norms change [15], diffusion of information [16], epidemic processes [17], spread of influence [14] or rumor spread [10]. Theoretical foundation of such social phenomenon

© Springer Nature Switzerland AG 2018
S. Staab et al. (Eds.): SocInfo 2018, LNCS 11186, pp. 118–128, 2018.
https://doi.org/10.1007/978-3-030-01159-8_11

have been still attracting the interest of the computational sciences [22]. A real structure of contacts affects processes in many various studies in different way causing many non-intuitive paradoxes (see Holme paradox of prostitution vs mobile phone in the shuffled-time-stamps scheme [12]).

The basic focus of this paper is the process of opinion formation in real social network of physical contacts [20] through:

(1) investigating the interactions between the duration and frequency of contacts (the temporal model);
(2) analyzing the influence of the age preference (homophily) in contacts on the structure of a social network (the age-correlated model).

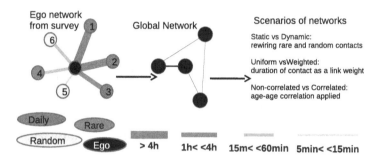

Fig. 1. Construction of the network from ego-networks with various scenarios. Illustrative diagram representing various type of links and neighbors with methodological differences between scenarios.

Physical Network and Survey Limitation to Ego-Network. Studying the statistical properties of real-world social networks (not only digitized fingerprints of human activities), e.g. contact networks, remains a challenge. To assess the basic properties of a network, e.g. the form of the degree distribution, a survey has to be conducted. However, there is still an unexplored area of research concerning human dynamics [1,2,21,25]. Using egocentric network dataset (which unfortunately contain only people's closest neighbors (Fig. 1)), we collect explicit connections (not implicit as digital) to understand how people manage their personal contact in real life. The two main new features of a social network in our model have been taken from empirical data (temporal aspects as well as the real age-age clustering).

Homophily - Age Correlations. The tendency of individuals to associate and bond with similar people is very often observed in many types of social networks. It is known from previous studies that number of contact and average age of nearest neighbors are highly correlated with age of an individual. This phenomenon is also known as homophily [3] and the characteristics of agents, such as age, have such a property in our dataset. The mean age of a contact is almost proportional to the age of a participant and most contacts take place within an equal age.

Temporal Aspects. Contact heterogeneity should be included in a realistic modelling of opinion formations. Moreover, individuals in real life interact with each other in a different time-scale and in different ways. Note that the model described below allows us to generate a network, of which the structure is based on experimental data, and to consider the real distribution of the duration and frequency of contacts. Temporal patterns exist in contact networks, because there are people we meet on a daily/weakly/yearly basis and other people we meet randomly. The recent research showed that the real distribution of time between contacts could both slow down or accelerate the spreading of the content, so it is hard to generalise on the relationship between the temporal process and the model behind it [12]. We observe many phenomena related to the temporal aspects, such as the burstiness [18] or fidelity [23]. Recently the availability of temporal contacts (mostly digitalized) is providing critical information to understanding propagation of information. To extract knowledge from this wealth of data an interdisciplinary approach is necessary, combining sophisticate computational modeling with network theory approaches [24]. Motivated by mentioned theoretical concepts of temporal networks (like loyalty), we addressed those issues in the model of opinion formation.

Information Propagation Issues on the Presented Network. The previous studies of the epidemic model showed that within the SIR model, age-correlations, as well as dynamic and weighed adjustments, may both increase and decrease the total size of outbreaks [6,9], but the impact on opinion formation is still unknown. To accomplish the mentioned task, numerical simulations were performed using the often applied toy-model: the Ising-based model of opinion formation. The results presented in this paper show the influence of human behaviour, which is the source of the correlations observed in the real world, on the above-mentioned dynamic phenomena. Using real data enables a qualitative and, more importantly, a quantitative assessment of the results. In this paper we present data collected in Poland (1012 participants recorded the characteristics of 16501 contacts with various individuals).

2   Data

To construct the model social network, we incorporated data from the contact survey conducted in Poland in the framework of POLYMOD [20]. Quota sampling was applied, taking into account the demographic variables, such as age, sex, region and type of residence. The participants were recruited by trained interviewers, visiting random households and each participant was randomly assigned one day, on which they had to record all their contacts. A contact was counted only in physical presence and the participants had to record all contact episodes with each contact person during the assigned day. Additionally, they filled the total duration, the location of the contacts and the usual frequency of the contacts with the given person. A detailed description of the study is provided elsewhere [20].

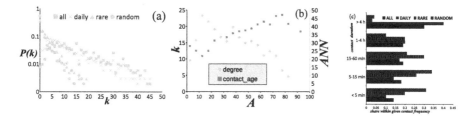

Fig. 2. (a) Empirical degree distribution: all contacts (squares), daily contacts (crosses), rare contacts (triangles), and random contacts (circles). (b) The relationship between the age and the degree and the relationship between the age and the average age of the nearest neighbours. (c) Weight distributions for various types (intensity) of contacts. Each element of the chart contains the percentage of contacts of a specific type (frequency) and weight (duration), e.g. 14% of all contacts are shorter than 5 min.

The temporal contact patterns under investigation had a three-level structure of interpersonal interactions (Fig. 2a, c). The intensity of contacts was measured as its duration (Fig. 2c), which allows us to calculate weights. The age A of each individual had a large influenced on the structure of the social network. The connectivity of an individual depended on their age (see Fig. 2b). Maximum connectivity was observed for teenagers and decreased (approximately linearly) with the age increasing. The average age of the nearest neighbours A_{NN} was highly correlated with the age of an individual (see Fig. 2b). For an age greater than 20 years, the A_{NN} increased approximately linearly with the age of an individual increasing. It should be noted that we found similar results in on-line social networks [8].

Next, the connections between individuals were created according to different scenarios. To investigate the influence of contact frequency, we made computations for two types of networks: static and dynamic. Additionally, link weight was taken into account, so that our network could be weighed or uniform. To investigate the influence of age-age and age-degree correlations, we distinguished another dimension: correlated and non-correlated. Non-correlated mode corresponds to static and uniform network from previous comparative descriptions.

The generic procedure of creating a network from ego-networks has been presented in Appendix A - network model and was the same as in our prvious papers on SIR spread with temporal - [9] and age-correlated - [6] as well as Rumor spread network models of Polish society [10].

3   Ising-Based Model of Opinion Formation

We study the evolution of opinions (opinion formation). We introduce the local field h_i for each individual, which is a function of interactions with k_i neighbours and the external field (stimulation) I:

$$h_i(t) = -S_i(t) \left(\sum_j^{k_i} w_{ij} S_j(t) + I \right) \qquad (1)$$

where $S_i = \pm 1$ - state of i-th individual, k_i - number of neighbors of i-th individual (in the case of dynamic network this value change in time), w_{ij} - weight of interaction between i-th and j-th individuals.

The external field I replaces the interaction with all other individuals and may be considered as the influence of mass media.

The opinions of the individuals change simultaneously, according to the probability corresponding to the local field and temperature T:

$$S_i(t+1) = \begin{cases} S_i(t) : & \frac{\exp(-h_i/T)}{\exp(-h_i/T)+\exp(h_i/T)} = \frac{1}{1+\exp(2h_i/T)} \\[2ex] -S_i(t) : & \frac{\exp(h_i/T)}{\exp(-h_i/T)+\exp(h_i/T)} = \frac{1}{1+\exp(-2h_i/T)} \end{cases} \qquad (2)$$

The parameter T may be interpreted as the *social temperature*. It describes the degree of randomness of the behaviour of individuals. If the temperature T increases, the probability that the individual will have a state opposite to the local field is higher [5]. Note that Eq. (2) is analogous to Glauber dynamics. The computations were performed for the initial conditions corresponding to the paramagnetic phase ($\langle S \rangle = \frac{1}{N} \sum_i S_i = 0$ for $t = 0$) using synchronous dynamics, while analysing the interdependence between time t and temperature T. We would like to find the critical value of temperature T_c and the time evolution of $\langle S \rangle$ in various settings. When external stimulation I is investigated, initially all individuals' states were opposite to external stimulation. The size of the network is always: 10^6 individuals.

4   Results: Age - Correlated (Homophily) vs Non-correlated

We investigate how the correlations between the age of the participants influence the process of opinion formation.

In the relation between $\langle S \rangle$ and temperature T, we observe 3 regimes, below, around and above the critical T_c (Fig. 3a). The trajectories of both scenarios (age-correlated homophily) vs the non-correlated do not vary at large temperatures. Due to the state transition formulation (2) if T goes to infinity, the opinion changes randomly and the average opinion is neutral $<S \approx 0>$. At low temperatures, the dominant opinion emerges in the community in all cases. When the temperature exceeds a certain critical value T_C there is an abrupt disappearance of the dominant opinion in the community - a phase transition is observed [13]. As we see in Fig. 3b, the dominant opinion emerges after approx. 100 time steps, even at temperatures close to the critical value. For all networks, the value of T_C is the same ($T_C \approx 1.85$). Discrepancies in results are observed at temperatures lower than critical, where homophily can both inhibit and catalyze process.

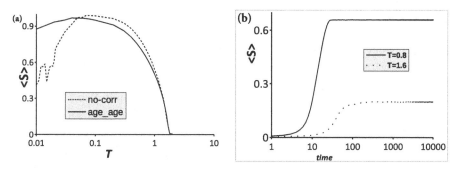

Fig. 3. (a) The relationship between $\langle S \rangle$ and the temperature T for different types of networks (with age-age correlations - solid line and without age-age correlations - dashed line). Simulation time is 1000 steps. (b) The relationship between $\langle S \rangle$ and time for different temperatures T (0.8 and 1.6 from top to down, respectively) for network without age-age correlations. Results were averaged over 10^2 independent simulations for both graphs.

In the case of network with age-age correlations the value of $\langle S \rangle$ is smaller for $T > 0.05$. Lower values of magnetisation in the case of a network with age-age correlations may be a result of sophisticated community structure (explained in Appendix A). Homophily over-perform presence of groups of individuals that are weekly connected with the rest of the individuals. An example of such group are the elderly and young, who have a lower number of connections in average (Fig. 2), and even the most of their connections are in the same age groups, the local clustering coefficient is also smaller. Thus, they could form the most resistant from propagation perspective chain-like structures, because such groups may have the opinion opposite to more central communities. Hence the value of $\langle S \rangle >$ is smaller.

We observe an interesting behaviour for a T slightly greater than zero. It is visible (Fig. 3a) that $\langle S \rangle$ initially increases with the temperature increasing. This behaviour is similar to the so-called "freezing by heating" phenomenon known also as "noise inducing/enhancing [4]" (in which the system reaches a ferromagnetic state for a high enough temperature).

5   Results: Temporal vs Static

Here, we investigate the effect of the temporal re-wiring of the network (the critical temperature T_c and time evolution). The non-monotonic relation between $\langle S \rangle$ and the temperature T close to zero as "freezing by heating" phenomenon appears for static scenarios, but is not observed at all in dynamic networks, because a random re-wiring of connections has a similar influence to an increase in temperature (the system is less prone to sticking at a local minimum). In real duration and dynamics case, the presence of the groups of nodes that are highly interconnected by connections with a high value of weights causes an increase in the critical value of the temperature (Fig. 4b). It turns out that the interactions of temporal aspects: the duration of the contact (the weight of the contacts) with its frequency shifting critical temperature, while one factor alone (duration or frequency) does not change it. The value of an average spin near the critical value of temperature is stable and does not change significantly for 10^5 time steps. Note that one time step corresponds to one day, hence the state of the network is stable for over three hundred years.

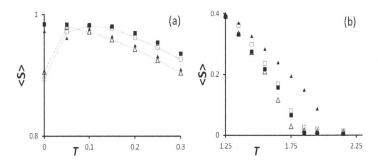

Fig. 4. The relationship between $\langle S \rangle$ and the temperature T for different types of networks (static - white markers, dynamic - black markers) and different distributions of weights (real - triangles, uniform - squares) and for low (a) and high (b) temperatures. The results were averaged over 10^3 independent simulations.

6   Conclusions

Opinion formation in a social network constructed on the basis of experimental contact data on interactions between humans is studied. In this paper, data on human social activity: temporal aspects of the duration (weight of contacts) with dynamics (frequency of contacts); as well as homophily (age-age correlation) of interpersonal interactions are presented. Investigated network scenarios seem to play only a little role in self-induced network (no external field), but there are significant insights when external field is turned on. Important changes in the behaviour of the system are observed at temperatures close to the critical value $T \approx T_C$ and at low temperatures (slightly greater than 0), at which the "freezing by heating" effect occurs only in static networks.

Age-Age Correlation. Our research shows that age-age correlations have a small influence on the process of opinion formation mostly for T approaching T_C. The results of numerical calculations indicate that the age structure does not influence T_C, but only the speed of the phase transition. In correlated networks the average spin is smaller than in non-correlated networks for $0.05 < T < T_c$. Age-correlations slow down critical processes, so such networks are less prone to abrupt changes [19]. It was showed before [6], that age-correlations in the same survey decrease the total size of an epidemic outbreak, which is not the case of opinion formation. Community structure could cause non-monotonic influence on $\langle S \rangle$.

Temporal Aspects: Dynamics and Weights. In epidemic model on the same survey data, real dynamics - speed up and real durations (weights) - slow down process [9] and in those aspects our current study gives different results. Only when **both real temporal aspects (weight and frequency) are considered, the critical value of the temperature T_C increases** significantly (Fig. 4b). Such a non trivial cross interaction could be the effect of competition within dynamic rewiring. Most of dynamic links are characterized by loyalty (Fig. 6b) and they catalyze transmitting opinion into other communities. However, totally random 'unique' are lost in Ising model from transmission perspective. Without help from external field, probability of transmitting opinion for a longer time is negligible through such a single rewiring. We suggest, that we could drop out such random links and while network is weighed, it cost almost nothing. In effect, only catalyzing part of dynamic links plays a role and whole process is catalyzed (T_C increases).

Contribution and Acknowledgments. AJ and AG designed study, AG run simulations, AJ analyzed data, AJ and AG wrote manuscript. Research was supported by NCBiR - Poland through grant no. IS-2/195/NCBR/2015. AJ received travel grant from COST Action IC1406.

A   Appendix: Network Model

In all scenarios degree distribution is fixed (to empirical one). However, by introducing temporal aspects or homophily other non-fixed structural properties as community structure may change.

The local clustering structure (with communities structure) change with modification of base static network (Fig. 5a). The most important difference cause age-correlations, which induce huge communities instead of many medium size communities (Fig. 6a). Thus, homophily decreases on average local clustering coefficient, so age-correlated network is less tided. Moreover, seniors and children (Fig. 5b) are places on periphery (far away form centers of the network), because of their small degree (Fig. 2b) as well as clustering (Fig. 5b).

The dynamic rewiring (corresponds to around 25% of the network) does not change clustering structure very much (Fig. 5a) because most of temporal links are sampled from local neighborhood. Links show very long memory.

Totally random links (which correspond to empirical 'random' contacts sampled from entire population) are in minority, because 'average of mass' is situated in loyal - repeatable links (corresponding to empirical 'rare' contacts sampled from bounded population). We define Loyalty as a measure of repeatability of the link. Loyalty of a single link occurrence takes the nominal value 'unique'.

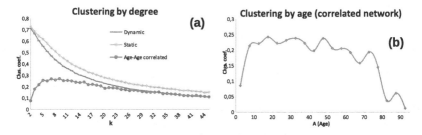

Fig. 5. The local clustering coefficient for given cohort of nodes: (a) in function of degree with various scenarios; (b) in function of age for the age-correlated network. Note that non-correlated and static networks are equivalent.

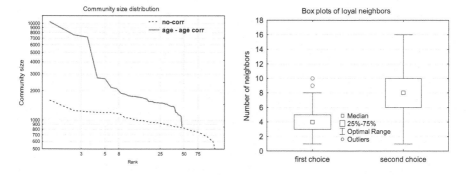

Fig. 6. (a) The Rank-size distribution of communities based on Louvain detection algorithm (with age-age correlations - solid line and without age-age correlations - dashed line). (b) Descriptive statistics for the number of loyal neighbors (first and second choice) of each node in the dynamic part of the network.

The range of variability in neighbors can be describes in terms of most frequent connections. Totally random re-wiring is not likely to form loyal connections (maximum Loyalty $\sim 4\%$). Thus most of temporal neighbors are limited to relatively small population. There are around 4 first choice neighbors (the most loyal neighbors appearing more than 40% of time) and around 8 second choice neighbors (neighbors appearing more less than 40% but more than 4% of time) (Fig. 6b). These second choice neighbors could be called 'weak' ties [11] between the communities that could have a different opinion.

References

1. Barabási, A.L.: The origin of bursts and heavy tails in human dynamics. Nature **435**, 207 (2005)
2. Barabási, A.L.: Bursts: The Hidden Pattern Behind Everything We Do. Penguin Group, New York (2010)
3. Christakis, N., Fowler, J.: The spread of obesity in a large social network over 32 years. N. Engl. J. Med. **357**, 370 (2007)
4. Czaplicka, A., Holyst, J.A., Sloot, P.M.: Noise enhances information transfer in hierarchical networks. Sci. Rep. **3**, 1223 (2013)
5. Grabowski, A.: Opinion formation in a social network: the role of human activity. Phys. A **388**, 961–966 (2009)
6. Grabowski, A.: The influence of age-age correlations on epidemic spreading in social network. Eur. Phys. J. B **87**, 146 (2014)
7. Grabowski, A., Kosiński, R.: Ising-based model of opinion formation in a complex network of interpersonal interactions. Phys. A **361**, 651–664 (2006)
8. Grabowski, A., Kosiński, R.: Mixing patterns in a large social network. Acta Phys. Polon. B **39**, 1291–1300 (2008)
9. Grabowski, A., Rosińska, M.: The relationship between human behavior and the process of epidemic spreading in a real social network. Eur. Phys. J. B **85**, 248 (2012)
10. Grabowski, A., Jarynowski, A.: Rumor propagation in temporal contact network from polish polls. In: 2016 Third European Network Intelligence Conference (ENIC), pp. 85–89. IEEE (2016)
11. Granovetter, M.: The strength of weak ties. Am. J. Sociol. **78**(6), 1360 (1973)
12. Holme, P.: Modern temporal network theory: a colloquium. Eur. Phys. J. B **88**, 1 (2015)
13. Hołyst, J., Kacperski, K., Schweitzer, F.: Phase transitions in social impact models of opinion formation. Phys. A **285**, 199–210 (2000)
14. Jarynowski, A., Buda, A.: Diffusion paths between product life-cycles in the European phonographic market. Control Cybern. **45**(2), 225–237 (2016)
15. Jarynowski, A., Gawroński, P., Kułakowski, K.: How the competitive altruism leads to bistable homogeneous states of cooperation or defection. In: Wyrzykowski, R., Dongarra, J., Karczewski, K., Waśniewski, J. (eds.) PPAM 2011. LNCS, vol. 7204, pp. 543–550. Springer, Heidelberg (2012). https://doi.org/10.1007/978-3-642-31500-8_56
16. Jarynowski, A., Jankowski, J., Zbieg, A.: Viral spread with or without emotions in online community. e.methodology **2**, 71 (2015). https://doi.org/10.15503/emet2015.71.78
17. Jarynowski, A., Liljeros, F.: Contact networks and the spread of MRSA in Stockholm hospitals. In: 2015 Second European Network Intelligence Conference (ENIC), pp. 150–154. IEEE (2015)
18. Laurent, G., Saramäki, J., Karsai, M.: From calls to communities: a model for time-varying social networks. Eur. Phys. J. B **88**, 301 (2015)
19. Michard, Q., Bouchaud, J.: Theory of collective opinion shifts: from smooth trends to abrupt swings. Eur. Phys. J. B **47**, 151 (2005)
20. Mossong, J., Hens, N., Jit, M., Beutels, P., et al.: Social contacts and mixing patterns relevant to the spread of infectious diseases. PLoS Med. **5**(3), e74 (2008). https://doi.org/10.1371/journal.pmed.0050074

21. Oliveira, J., Barabási, A.L.: Human dynamics: Darwin and Einstein correspondence patterns. Nature **437**, 1251 (2005)
22. Porter, M., Gleeson, J.: Dynamical Systems on Networks: A Tutorial, vol. 4. Springer, Cham (2016). https://doi.org/10.1007/978-3-319-26641-1
23. Stopczynski, A., Sapiezynski, P., Pentland, A., Lehmann, S.: Temporal fidelity in dynamic social networks. Eur. Phys. J. B **88**, 249 (2015)
24. Valdano, E., Poletto, C., Colizza, V.: Infection propagator approach to compute epidemic thresholds on temporal networks: impact of immunity and of limited temporal resolution. Eur. Phys. J. B **88**, 1 (2015)
25. Vázquez, A.: Exact results for the barabasi model of human dynamics. Phys. Rev. Lett. **95**, 248701 (2005)

Using Computer Vision to Study the Effects of BMI on Online Popularity and Weight-Based Homophily

Enes Kocabey[1], Ferda Ofli[2(✉)], Javier Marin[1], Antonio Torralba[1], and Ingmar Weber[2]

[1] Massachusetts Institute of Technology, Cambridge, MA, USA
kocabey@mit.edu, {jmarin,torralba}@csail.mit.edu
[2] Qatar Computing Research Institute, HBKU, Doha, Qatar
{fofli,iweber}@hbku.edu.qa

Abstract. Increasing prevalence of obesity has disconcerting implications for communities, for nations and, most importantly, for individuals in aspects ranging from quality of life, longevity and health, to social and financial prosperity. Therefore, researchers from a variety of backgrounds study obesity from all angles. In this paper, we use a state-of-the-art computer vision system to predict a person's body-mass index (BMI) from their social media profile picture and demonstrate the type of analyses this approach enables using data from two culturally diverse settings – the US and Qatar. Using large amounts of Instagram profile pictures, we show that (i) thinner profile pictures have more followers, and that (ii) there is weight-based network homophily in that users with a similar BMI tend to cluster together. To conclude, we also discuss the challenges and limitations related to inferring various user attributes from photos.

Keywords: Body-mass index · Computer vision · Social media

1 Introduction

Understanding social aspects surrounding obesity is of great interest to many stakeholders. However, studying the social context requires collecting data beyond the affected individual which can be challenging for standard approaches. At the same time, social media provide information on social context and are being increasingly used for studies in computational social sciences. Yet, these studies typically do not have access to an individual's weight information as this is rarely shared online. To tackle this challenge, [13] proposed a new system called Face-to-BMI to infer a person's BMI from their profile picture.

In this paper, we build an end-to-end data processing pipeline that first detects and localizes a user's face in their social media profile picture, and then, inputs the localized face region into the Face-to-BMI system to predict the user's BMI. We then apply this pipeline to hundreds of thousands of Instagram profile

© Springer Nature Switzerland AG 2018
S. Staab et al. (Eds.): SocInfo 2018, LNCS 11186, pp. 129–138, 2018.
https://doi.org/10.1007/978-3-030-01159-8_12

pictures to study population-level BMI from two angles. First, we investigate if there is a link between online popularity and weight status, showing a negative trend between BMI and the number of followers. Second, we investigate the existence of BMI-based homophily revealing that social connections on Instagram are linked to a smaller-than-expected difference in BMI values of the two connected users. All of these experiments are conducted in two diverse cultural contexts, the US and Qatar.

2   Related Work

Several studies have shown that being overweight can lead to a range of negative consequences in people's social interactions and health [5,15,19]. Some recent studies in the social sciences investigate how humans perceive health from profile pictures [7,12]. To scale the findings of these studies to larger populations, researchers have developed systems for predicting BMI from profile pictures using computational techniques [13,21,25].

As computer vision makes continuous advances, certain tasks are also fast becoming commodities with Google[1], Microsoft[2] and others offering cloud-based solutions. Among such tools, Face++[3] provides a service that, given a picture of a person, infers the position of the face and various demographic attributes of the person. Face++ has been successfully applied on social media profile pictures to study large-scale demographics [4] and the spread of happiness [2]. In our work, we use Face++ both to filter out non-faces and detect face bounding boxes, as well as to enrich our data with gender information.

Typically, existing studies on social media only analyze data from the Western world. Our work offers a cross-cultural perspective by juxtaposing results for the US with results from Qatar. In the context of Qatar, privacy plays a different role and Islamic religious values and cultural norms influence online behavior. An existing emphasis on gender roles has implications on the way social media users from different genders manage their online identities [3].

3   Social Media Profile Images

3.1   Data Collection

Our Instagram data comes from both the US and Qatar. The two data sets were obtained at different points in time following slightly different methodologies, though both were location-centric data collections.

---

[1] https://cloud.google.com/vision/.
[2] https://www.microsoft.com/cognitive-services/en-us/computer-vision-api.
[3] http://www.faceplusplus.com/api-overview/.

US Data. We started with a data set used in [16] that contained ~21M Instagram posts, from ~3.4M unique users across 316 US counties. For each unique user in this data set, we (i) identified the county that they resided in using the plurality or majority voting method over their Instagram posts, and (ii) crawled their Instagram profile pages to retrieve their *profile picture URL, follower count,* and *follow count.* After this, we were left with ~2.7M unique users with all the corresponding retrieved information.

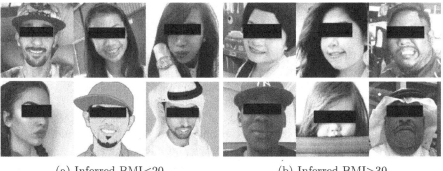

(a) Inferred-BMI<20   (b) Inferred-BMI>30

Fig. 1. Qualitative evaluation of the Face-to-BMI system on examples from our Instagram profile pictures data set, grouped by their predicted-BMI values. Black bars are added to respect user privacy in this paper, but they are not part of the input to the system.

Qatar Data. Following a two-step strategy, we first built a complete list of unique Instagram locations in Qatar. Then, for each retrieved location, we collected all the recent media data that were available via the Instagram Application Programming Interface (API) at the time of the collection. The resulting data set contained ~1.7M Instagram posts from ~137K unique users from ~38K unique locations across Qatar. We assumed all of these users live in Qatar and crawled their Instagram profile pages to extract the same user information as for the US data.

3.2   Face-to-BMI System

The Face-to-BMI system operates in two stages [13]. First, the system employs a deep neural network model trained for face recognition to extract features from a face image. Then, the system uses an epsilon support vector regression model over these features to predict a BMI value for the given image. According to the paper, the Face-to-BMI system achieved a Pearson correlation $r = 0.65$ on the held-out test set, and performed on par with humans for distinguishing the more overweight person when presented with a pair of profile images. Since we do not have ground truth BMI values for the Instagram profile pictures analyzed in this study, we cannot quantitatively validate the performance of the Face-to-BMI system. However, Fig. 1 illustrates qualitatively the performance of the system on our data set of Instagram profile pictures.

3.3   Data Processing Pipeline

Combining the Instagram data and the Face-to-BMI system, the whole pipeline then works as follows. As a pre-filter to remove images without any face, the downloaded profile images are fed into OpenCV Face Detection[4] and only images with at least one detected face are kept. These images are then passed through the Face++ API[5] to not only further refine the detection of faces, but also return their position in the image, as well as the predicted gender of the person. For the BMI prediction, the profile pictures with exactly one detected face were retained. Eventually, the detected face using the bounding box from Face++ was cropped and fed into the Face-to-BMI system to get a BMI estimation.

For the US data set, we first filtered out counties with less than 3,000 unique users. We then sampled 3,000 unique profiles from each of the remaining 130 counties, totaling $390K$ users. After running our data processing pipeline for this sample, we obtained $\sim149K$ individual visible faces with BMI estimations. For the Qatar data set, we simply ran the data processing pipeline for all the $\sim137K$ user set, and obtained $\sim48K$ users with BMI estimations.

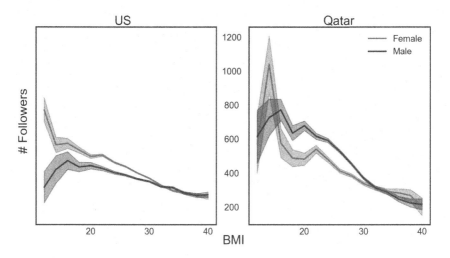

Fig. 2. Popularity vs. inferred-BMI, for both the US and Qatar. Each line curve represents the median number of followers for the set of users with a similar inferred-BMI value, broken down by gender. The shaded bands indicate the standard error bounds on the number of followers.

---

[4] https://opencv.org/.
[5] https://www.faceplusplus.com/face-detection/.

4   Experiments

4.1   BMI and Online Popularity

Previous work [24] had observed that Twitter users with a more obese-looking profile picture tend to have fewer followers. We tried to replicate their findings by analyzing the link between a person's inferred-BMI value and their number of Instagram followers. Figure 2 shows a consistent pattern, both for the US and Qatar, linking a higher inferred-BMI to a smaller followership. These plots also demonstrate a striking similarity to those presented in [22] for correlations between physical attractiveness and BMI.

Followership and online popularity are intrinsically linked to the online activity level as a user who never produces content is unlikely to attract a large audience. Hence the reason for the observed difference could simply lie in differences in activity levels. To both assess a potential mediation effect of the number of posts on the number of followers and to look more at the gender-specific link between BMI and number of followers, we conduct the following experiment: We measure the fitness of various linear models to our data each time using a different set of independent variables, i.e., (i) just the number of posts on Instagram, (ii) just the person's inferred-BMI, and (iii) both the number of posts and the inferred-BMI, to predict the number of followers (i.e., dependent variable). We compute the corresponding least squares linear model coefficients, p values, and adjusted-R^2. Users with more than 2,000 followers were ignored for this analysis as their large followership introduced model instability. Table 1 summarizes the results from the fitted models.

Table 1. Results for different linear model fits using (i) only the number of posts (β_1), (ii) only the inferred-BMI (β_2), and (iii) both, where β_0 indicates the model intercept. Results are broken down by country and by gender. All the corresponding p values are less than 10^{-10}.

	♀/♂	Model	β_0	β_1	β_2	adj. R^2
United States	Female	#posts (β_1)	318.2	.102	–	0.080
		BMI (β_2)	606.7	–	−8.26	0.026
		#posts & BMI	555.1	.103	−8.54	0.108
	Male	#posts (β_1)	295.9	.117	–	0.094
		BMI (β_2)	501.3	–	−5.28	0.011
		#posts & BMI	466.7	.119	−5.90	0.107
Qatar	Female	#posts (β_1)	361.2	.236	–	0.123
		BMI (β_2)	761.6	–	−11.25	0.013
		#posts & BMI	648.5	.234	−10.40	0.135
	Male	#posts (β_1)	426.4	.211	–	0.073
		BMI (β_2)	953.5	–	−16.63	0.027
		#posts & BMI	895.9	.212	−16.75	0.101

In all cases, the models were stable in that (i) the coefficients for the single variable case were close to the coefficients in the dual variable case, and (ii) the adjusted-R^2 roughly added up. Both of these indicate that the effect of the BMI on the size of the followership is *not* mediated by differences in the number of posts. Furthermore, looking at the value of the coefficients, we observe that the effect of BMI is stronger for women than for men in the US, whereas it is stronger for men than women in Qatar.

4.2 Social Network Analysis

The authors in [6] claim that obesity may spread through social networks as a "contagious" disease. However, others have questioned their results for methodological reasons [8].[6] Our data lacks the long-term temporal coverage to attempt to make such strong claims but online social networks can still be used to test the weaker hypothesis of weight-based homophily. For example, [1] observed that Twitter users tend to cluster based on their predicted obesity status.

To find evidence for BMI-based network assortativity, we start by constructing a social network for our data set. Both for the US and for Qatar, we create a bidirected edge between two users if the two users mutually commented on each others' pictures. As the Instagram API only provides the eight most recent comments left on a post, older comments could not be considered for the network construction.

After constructing the two social networks, one for the US and one for Qatar, we compared the average absolute BMI difference between two friends with what would be expected by random chance. This comparison was done by creating 10,000 permutations where the BMIs of the nodes were randomly shuffled among

Table 2. Significance test results for the absolute BMI difference in the US and Qatar social networks, broken down by gender.

	Category	Count	Empirical	Shuffled**	p
US	All	1,848	5.208	5.383	.006
	M-M	234	5.441	5.356	.671
	F-F	812	5.212	5.350	.084
	M-F	802	5.137	5.328	.029
Qatar	All	3,686	4.478	4.706	.000
	M-M	2,496	4.451	4.622	.001
	F-F	390	4.754	5.261	.001
	M-F	800	4.430	4.603	.028

* M – Male, F – Female.
** Mean of the distribution.

---

[6] See http://sociograph.blogspot.qa/2009/11/is-obesity-contagious-review-of-debate.html for an overview of the discussion around the said topic.

the edges. We then compared the observed, empirical difference with the distribution of the simulated, shuffled differences to obtain p values for testing the hypothesis that the average absolute BMI difference is not linked to the network structure. We perform this experiment for (i) all edges, (ii) same-gender edges and (iii) cross-gender edges. All the results are presented in Table 2.

We notice that in most cases the difference between the empirical and shuffled values is not large in absolute terms, though it is still statistically significant. Interestingly, for the US, there was more evidence for cross-gender BMI homophily than for within-gender BMI homophily. As friends might largely be chosen due to proximity, and as being in the same county already increases the probability of having a similar BMI, we also split the US friendship pairs into a within-county and an across-county set. The results were consistent in both cases though, due to the smaller number of instances, the statistical power was reduced.

5   Discussion

5.1   Algorithmic Bias

Our data processing pipeline relies on several technologies such as OpenCV Face Detection to detect faces, Face++ to refine the face detections and to predict the person's gender, and finally, Face-to-BMI tool to predict the person's BMI. Though each of these may introduce certain algorithmic biases[7], the authors of [13] found no evidence for bias in terms of race or gender. However, we could not test if there is any algorithmic bias affecting women with head cover as we did not have ground truth for this. Manual inspection of several cases did not reveal abnormal BMI predictions in these cases though.

5.2   Ethical Considerations

Before advances in computer vision, one could try to remain a "face in the crowd." Due to face recognition, that is becoming harder and our tool could be seen as contributing to this trend. For example, services such as FindFace[8] offer to find users on social media given just a picture of them. The not-so-thinly advertised use case is for finding contact details for attractive women. Similarly, there has been a growing body of work that successfully applies computer vision techniques on social media pictures to infer a person's personality [10,11,14,17]. Although most of these methods work "better than random guessing" at an aggregate level, they are highly unreliable at an individual level. Furthermore, even at the aggregate level, the observations should be taken with caution since the data sets collected from social media are not a uniform sample of the population. However, with proper weighting schemes [26], this concern can be reduced.

---

[7] https://www.theatlantic.com/technology/archive/2016/04/the-underlying-bias-of-facial-recognition-systems/476991/.

[8] https://findface.ru/.

5.3   Cultural Differences

Having collected data from both the US and Qatar allows us to look at cultural differences. For example, the fact that women in Qatar were less likely than their male counterparts to have a profile image with a face might be related to privacy concerns [3,23]. One observation from Fig. 2 worth investigating further in the future is the fact that for women in the US "the thinner the better" concerning the follower counts on Instagram, whereas for women in Qatar and for men in both the US and Qatar a very low BMI seems to also correspond to a lower number of followers.

6   Limitations

Our experiments are based on *observational data from social media*, enriched with outputs from computer vision technologies. Observational studies are limited concerning the causal claims they support. Findings need to be understood in the context of their limitations and we discuss some of these below.

The performance of the Face-to-BMI system is not perfect, despite being on par with humans for picking the more obese given a pair of profile pictures. However, our data processing pipeline for social media profile pictures can be used to detect relative trends at the *population* level unless the pipeline proves to be systematically biased. In other words, results of the form "the average BMI for group X is larger than for group Y" are far more robust than results of the form "this individual from group X has a higher BMI than this other individual from group Y". This distinction also applies to the BMI itself which is useful for studying population health but has shortcomings when used as a tool for individual health [9,18].

The fact that we detected BMI-based assortativity despite the noise in the BMI predictions strengthens our results. Given a noise-free inference mechanism we would expect the effect sizes to be larger than the ones currently observed. To exemplify this point, if we assume that the face-to-BMI measurement error is uncorrelated with its estimate, we can apply standard approaches for correcting for attenuation [20]. Such a correction leads to a roughly 50% increase in the adjusted-R^2 of the BMI-only models (see Table 1). However, as the underlying statistical assumptions do not hold in practice, it is not clear if the true increase in R^2 would be bigger or smaller in a noise-free setting.

Nevertheless, regarding BMI and online popularity, we may be observing a *reverse* causality. That is, as an Instagram user starts getting more followers, they in turn start paying more attention to their profile picture (e.g., post photoshopped selfie images that potentially look thinner and better). In our social network analysis, the observed homophily can be affected by unobserved confounding factors. For example, as an ethnic group, Asians tend to be less overweight. So if users choose their friends based on ethnicity, then this could induce BMI-based assortativity.

7   Conclusions

We built a data processing pipeline that enables analysis of social media profile pictures to study (i) the link between an Instagram profile picture's BMI and their number of followers, and (ii) the link between a person's BMI and that of their social connections. Both were studied in two culturally diverse contexts, the US and Qatar. In both countries we observed that (i) a lower inferred-BMI is linked to a larger number of followers, and that (ii) there is BMI-based network assortativity.

We hope this work will help advance understanding of the social aspects of obesity in an effort to reduce anti-social behavior such as fat shaming and increase population health.

References

1. Abbar, S., Mejova, Y., Weber, I.: You tweet what you eat: studying food consumption through Twitter. In: CHI (2015)
2. Abdullah, S., Murnane, E.L., Costa, J.M., Choudhury, T.: Collective smile: measuring societal happiness from geolocated images. In: CSCW (2015)
3. Abokhodair, N., Abbar, S., Vieweg, S., Mejova, Y.: Privacy and social media use in the Arabian Gulf: Saudi Arabian & Qatari traditional values in the digital world. J Web Sci. **3**(1) (2017)
4. An, J., Weber, I.: #greysanatomy vs. #yankees: demographics and hashtag use on Twitter. In: ICWSM (2016)
5. Brewis, A.A., Wutich, A., Falletta-Cowden, A., Rodriguez-Soto, I.: Body norms and fat stigma in global perspective. Curr. Anthropol. **52**(2), 269–276 (2011)
6. Christakis, N.A., Fowler, J.H.: The spread of obesity in a large social network over 32 years. N. Engl. J. Med. **357**(4), 370–379 (2007)
7. Coetzee, V., Perrett, D.I., Stephen, I.D.: Facial adiposity: a cue to health? Perception **38**(11), 1700–1711 (2009)
8. Cohen-Cole, E., Fletcher, J.M.: Detecting implausible social network effects in acne, height, and headaches: longitudinal analysis. BMJ **337**, a2533 (2008)
9. Daniels, S.R.: The use of BMI in the clinical setting. Pediatrics **124**(Supplement 1), S35–S41 (2009)
10. Dhall, A., Hoey, J.: *First Impressions* - predicting user personality from Twitter profile images. In: Chetouani, M., Cohn, J., Salah, A.A. (eds.) HBU 2016. LNCS, vol. 9997, pp. 148–158. Springer, Cham (2016). https://doi.org/10.1007/978-3-319-46843-3_10
11. Guntuku, S.C., Qiu, L., Roy, S., Lin, W., Jakhetiya, V.: Do others perceive you as you want them to?: modeling personality based on selfies. In: International Workshop on Affect & Sentiment in Multimedia (ASM) (2015)
12. Henderson, A.J., Holzleitner, I.J., Talamas, S.N., Perrett, D.I.: Perception of health from facial cues. Philos. Trans. R. Soc. Lond. B Biol. Sci. **371**(1693), 20150380 (2016)
13. Kocabey, E., et al.: Face-to-BMI: using computer vision to infer body mass index on social media. In: ICWSM (2017)
14. Liu, L., Preotiuc-Pietro, D., Samani, Z.R., Moghaddam, M.E., Ungar, L.: Analyzing personality through social media profile picture choice. In: ICWSM (2016)

15. Meigs, J.B., et al.: Body mass index, metabolic syndrome, and risk of type 2 diabetes or cardiovascular disease. JCEM **91**(8), 2906–2912 (2006)
16. Mejova, Y., Haddadi, H., Noulas, A., Weber, I.: #FoodPorn: obesity patterns in culinary interactions. In: DH (2015)
17. Nie, J., et al.: Social media profiler: inferring your social media personality from visual attributes in portrait. In: Chen, E., Gong, Y., Tie, Y. (eds.) PCM 2016. LNCS, vol. 9917, pp. 640–649. Springer, Cham (2016). https://doi.org/10.1007/978-3-319-48896-7_63
18. Prentice, A.M., Jebb, S.A.: Beyond body mass index. Obes. Rev. **2**(3), 141–147 (2001)
19. Puhl, R.M., Andreyeva, T., Brownell, K.D.: Perceptions of weight discrimination: prevalence and comparison to race and gender discrimination in america. Int. J. Obes. **32**, 992 (2008)
20. Spearman, C.: The proof and measurement of association between two things. Am. J. Psychol. **15**(1), 72–101 (1904)
21. Tai, C., Lin, D.: A framework for healthcare everywhere: BMI prediction using kinect and data mining techniques on mobiles. In: MDM (2015)
22. Tovee, M.J., Cornelissen, P.L.: Female and male perceptions of female physical attractiveness in front-view and profile. Br. J. Psychol. **92**, 391–402 (2001)
23. Vieweg, S., Hodges, A.: Surveillance & modesty on social media: how Qataris navigate modernity and maintain tradition. In: CSCW (2016)
24. Weber, I., Mejova, Y.: Crowdsourcing health labels: inferring body weight from profile pictures. In: DH (2016)
25. Wen, L., Guo, G.: A computational approach to body mass index prediction from face images. Image Vis. Comput. **31**(5), 392–400 (2013)
26. Zagheni, E., Weber, I.: Demographic research with non-representative internet data. Int. J. Manpow. **36**(1), 13–25 (2015)

News Headline as a Form of News Text Compression

Nataliya Kochetkova[1], Ekaterina Pronoza[2(✉)] [iD],
and Elena Yagunova[2]

[1] National Research University Higher School of Economics,
20 Myasnitskaya ul., Moscow, Russian Federation
natalia_k_ll@mail.ru
[2] St.-Petersburg State University,
7/9 Universitetskaya Nab., St.-Petersburg, Russian Federation
katpronoza@gmail.com, iagounova.elena@gmail.com

Abstract. In this paper we analyze news text collections (clusters) via extracting their paraphrase headlines into a paraphrase graph and working with this graph. Our aim is to test whether news headline is an appropriate form of news text compression. Different types of news collections: dynamic, static and combined (both dynamic and static) clusters are analyzed and it is shown that their respective paraphrase graphs reflect the characteristics of the texts. We also automatically extract the most informationally important linked fragments of news texts, and these fragments characterize news texts as either informative, conveying some information, or publicistic ones, trying to affect the readers emotionally. It is shown that news headlines of the informative type do represent their respective compressed news reports.

Keywords: News cluster · Paraphrase graph · Paraphrase extraction
Linked text segments · Text analysis

1 Introduction

Paraphrase extraction, identification and generation are increasingly popular topics of research in natural language processing nowadays. Paraphrase corpora can be helpful for various tasks like text summarization, text entailment recognition, information extraction, sentiment analysis, and many more. However, potential application of paraphrases is not limited to the mentioned tasks. We believe that paraphrases can help us to analyze the structure and other characteristics of text collections.

In this paper we work with news text collections (clusters). News clusters differ in style, themes and structure: they can be static or dynamic, informational or publicistic, conventional or unconventional, with different hierarchy and number of subtopics. We believe that news cluster can be considered a recognized object of text linguistics today. Indeed, modern media audience is often interested in a series of news on a given topic rather than in a single news report.

In this paper we propose a method of news cluster analysis via its paraphrase graph structure. A paraphrase graph is a graph where news headlines are vertices, and two

© Springer Nature Switzerland AG 2018
S. Staab et al. (Eds.): SocInfo 2018, LNCS 11186, pp. 139–147, 2018.
https://doi.org/10.1007/978-3-030-01159-8_13

vertices are connected by an edge if they are paraphrases. Such graph reflects the structure of the news cluster: for example, similar headlines tend to group into subgraphs which correspond to the subtopics in the news cluster.

Our aim is to test whether news headlines can be used to identify news clusters, i.e., that news headlines can be treated as a condensed representation of a news cluster. According to our results, it is not true for every news headline. Apart from the purely informational headlines, there are also publicistic ones which aim to affect the reader emotionally. That is why we also conduct experiments to identify informational and publicistic clusters. These experiments involve extraction of the most important linked text segments from headlines and bodies of the news reports, and their comparison.

2 Related Work

Clustering is a widely discussed problem in natural language processing, and there is a large number of papers on clustering news articles. To the best of our knowledge, most papers dealing with news clusters usually solve the problem of clustering news articles, however, in our case, the articles are already clustered and we work with the obtained clusters.

Some researchers propose methods of clustering news headlines, without considering the bodies of news reports. For example, in [3] news headlines are clustered using heuristic frequent term-based and frequent noun-based methods. These methods are reported to be as good as the traditional clustering methods, however, tested on scientific abstracts, the results are worse. In [8] the authors solve the problem of selecting appropriate labels for the clusters of news headlines. Some researchers work at the problem of online incremental clustering of news articles [2].

In our study, we focus on the analysis of the existing news clusters, and show that it can be conducted via the construction of paraphrase graphs based on the headlines of the clusters.

3 Data

Our data is represented by the news collections from Galaktika-Zoom news aggregator [1]. We work with 5 news clusters. They are extracted from various Russian media sources; each cluster consists of news reports about the same event. The clusters are about:

- the arrival of A. Schwarzenegger in Moscow (360 texts, about 110000 tokens);
- the appointment of S. Sobyanin as the Mayor of Moscow (660 texts, 170000 tokens);
- the predictions and the death of Paul the Octopus (310 texts, about 1 million tokens);
- the protests in Ecuador (569 texts, about 1 million tokens);
- the release of toxins in Hungary (346 texts, about 100000 tokens).

Our choice of clusters is dictated by several purposes:

- text should have more or less clear and simple syntactic and semantic structure (e.g., compared with fiction);
- clusters should be informationally important and of a large volume, with a clear plot, with only one main character;
- at least one of the clusters should be more dynamic (i.e., its texts are dynamic, with a chain of different situations [9]) – see the cluster about A. Schwarzenegger;
- at least one of the clusters should be more static (i.e., the texts are about one main event rather than a chain of situations [9]) – see the cluster about S. Sobyanin;
- at least one of the clusters should be mixed, with complex causal and temporal relationships inside – see the cluster about Paul the Octopus.

4   Method

4.1   Paraphrases Extraction

We propose a method of analyzing the structure of a news collection via its paraphrase graph. Paraphrase graph is a graph where headlines are vertices, and edges connect headlines if they are paraphrases. To decide whether two headlines are paraphrases, we calculate the matrix similarity value [6] which is actually an extended variant of soft cosine distance introduced by Sidorov et al. [7], or a matrix similarity metric described by Fernando and Stevenson [5], and establish a threshold so that two headlines are paraphrases if their similarity metric value is above the threshold value.

We experiment with various threshold values, from 0.1 to 0.9. Paraphrases form connected components in the graphs. For low threshold values (0.1, 0.2) there is a small amount of connected components in a graph, but for high threshold values the situation is quite the opposite. According to our previous experiments with paraphrases in the news collections, appropriate threshold values range from 0.4 to 0.6. We empirically selected a threshold equal to 0.5, and further in this paper all the graphs are constructed using this threshold value.

At this part of the research our hypothesis is that paraphrase graph of a news cluster reflects the compositional and linguistic characteristics of the cluster. We analyze such graph properties as density, the number of connected components, node degrees distribution and central nodes.

4.2   Extraction of Linked Text Segments

We extract linked text segments from the news collections using Dice coefficient. The experiment is conducted in several stages:

1. We calculate Dice coefficient for each pair of tokens from all text collections.
2. We link pairs of tokens together into text segments according to their Dice coefficient values and their context. As we move along the text, we decide whether current word should join the current text segment. We do not link the word to the preceding word if Dice coefficient for this pair is lower than the threshold value or if

it is lower than the average between the corresponding values for the left and the right pairs. As a result, we obtain a list of linked segments, calculated for each text independently and then united into a frequency list.[1] In other words, each text becomes annotated with linked segments (word sequences). As a result of such experiment, we obtain a list of linked segments describing a cluster, a list of linked segments describing each text of a cluster and a list of linked segments describing headlines inside a cluster.

5   Results

5.1   Results of the Experiment with Paraphrases

According to the algorithm described in Sect. 4.1, we have built a paraphrase graph for each news cluster in question. The graphs are presented in Figs. 1, 2, 3, 4 and 5. They were constructed using yEd graph editor.[2]

Fig. 1. News cluster about Ecuador   **Fig. 2.** News cluster about Paul the Octopus

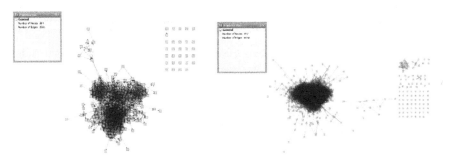

Fig. 3. News cluster about   **Fig. 4.** News cluster about S. Sobyanin
A. Schwarzenegger

---

[1] A program implementing the described algorithm is available at http://donelaitis.vdu.lt/ ~ vidas/tools. htm.

[2] https://www.yworks.com/products/yed .

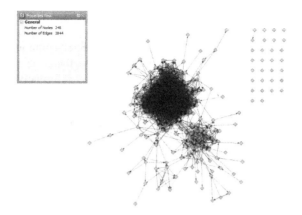

Fig. 5. News cluster about toxins

All the five graphs are similar to the social network graphs. There are communities with strong connections and a few vertices not connected to any community in each graph. We also calculated node degrees distribution for each of the graphs and it turned out that it follows power law, i.e., the graphs are scale-free networks (like social networks). Although, according to the illustrations, the graphs seem to be dense, especially the one corresponding to the cluster about S. Sobyanin (see Fig. 4), neither of them is truly dense. Density values of the five graphs sorted in descending order are shown in Table 1.

Table 1. Density values of the paraphrase graphs

Paul the Octopus	Toxins	Schwarzenegger	Sobyanin	Ecuador
0.181	0.093	0.069	0.065	0.035

It can be seen that the Paul the Octopus graph has the highest density compared to the other graphs. Thus, in such news cluster headlines tend to be paraphrases more than in other types of news clusters. Indeed, the Paul the Octopus cluster is the most complex one: although it is static, it is full of various details of the described event, and almost devoid of clichés. All the presented graphs have low density, and it gives us the intuition that they must contain several connected components. Thus, in each paraphrase graph we have also calculated the portions of their connected components (i.e., the number of connected components divided by the size of the graph). They are given in ascending order in Table 2.

Table 2. Percentage of connected components in paraphrase graphs

Schwarzenegger	Paul the Octopus	Toxins	Sobyanin	Ecuador
2.65	5.23	6.45	6.54	8.10

It can be noted that the graph corresponding to the most dynamic news cluster about A. Schwarzenegger has the lowest portion of the number of connected components. Most headlines tend to group into two large connected components. The cluster is evidently of a publicistic style, and, while the main theme is the arrival of A. Schwarzenegger in Moscow, the headlines are not purely informative: they are often humorous and trying to attract the reader's attention: "Schwarzenegger was hit by a turnstile in the Moscow metro", "Schwarzenegger has brought the spirit of the Silicon Valley", "Schwarzenegger has promised Russia a miracle", "Schwarzenegger showed Medvedev some exercises at the gym", etc.

The cluster about S. Sobyanin is an example of a static news cluster with several subtopics describing a single event. The headlines are informative, and each one describes exactly what is written in the body of a news report. It leads to the comparatively large number of connected components in a graph (i.e., subtopics in a cluster).

We also extracted central nodes of each graph (nodes with the largest centrality measure). They are presented in Table 3 (top 3 nodes per graph).

Table 3. Top-3 central nodes of the five graphs

Cluster	Top-3 central nodes
Ecuador	There is unrest in Ecuador A coup in Ecuador: police attacked the president A coup attempt in Ecuador
Paul the Octopus	Paul the Octopus died Died Paul the Octopus Died Paul the Octopus...
A. Schwarzenegger	Schwarzenegger in Moscow Medvedev took Schwarzenegger to Skolkovo in "Tchaika" Medvedev drove with Schwarzenegger to Skolkovo in "Tchaika"
S. Sobyanin	Sobyanin is the Mayor of Moscow Moscow City Duma approved Sobyanin as the new Mayor of Moscow Sergey Sobyanin is the new Mayor of Moscow
Toxins	In Hungary toxic waste fell into the Danube Toxic waste from Hungary fell into the Danube Hungary: toxic waste fell into the Danube river

It turned out that central nodes of the graphs correspond to the shortest headlines of the respective news clusters. For all the clusters (except for the Schwarzenegger one), central nodes are brief and informative and represent the compression of the news reports of the clusters. The Schwarzenegger headlines are also laconic, but not purely informative, in fact they are publicistic rather than informative.

5.2 Results of the Experiment with Linked Text Segments

All the linked text segments were extracted using a program by Daudaravičius [4]. The evaluation of the corresponding algorithm was conducted by its author and it was shown that in the task of keywords extraction it helps to increase F1 by 17–27% depending on the data.

Results of the experiment with linked text segments have proved our ideas about the differences in the style of the considered news clusters.

At this part of our research we only worked with the three news clusters out of five: the Schwarzenegger cluster, the S. Sobyanin cluster and the Paul the Octopus cluster as they cover all types of news clusters we consider in this paper, and are the most typical representatives of different style.

In the cluster about A. Schwarzenegger the theme of investment and innovations turned to be less important (according to headlines analysis) than the ride of A. Shwarzenegger on the Moscow subway and his posting about it in Twitter: «*шварценеггер_прокатился в московском_метро*»/Schwarzenegger took a ride in the Moscow metro/(8 occurrences), «*медведев_прокатил_шварценеггера_на "_чайке_"*»/Medvedev took Schwarzenegger for a ride in "Tchaika"/(6 occurrences), «*шварценеггер_гуляет в московском_метро и переписывается с_медведевым через_Twitter*»/Schwarzenegger takes a ride in metro and corresponds with Medvedev in Twitter/(3 occurrences), «*шварценеггер_хочет_вернуться в_кино*»/Schwarzenegger wants to return to acting/(3 occurrences). Dynamic sketchy style of the most texts about A. Schwarzenegger is similar to that of Twitter. It is characterized by short structures and thus has short linked segments. There is no strict compositional structure of a plot although the text is certainly close to the narrative. We believe that the cluster about A. Schwarzenegger most clearly reflects the differences between the data obtained from the headlines and from the bodies of the news reports: headlines are publicistic (trying to affect the addressee rather than share the information) while the bodies are informational.

Express analysis of the second cluster has shown that it has one main theme: the appointment of S. Sobyanin as the Mayor of Moscow. The second most important theme is about the retirement of Luzhkov. Such conclusions are proved by the frequency list of linked text segments obtained from the corresponding news cluster: «*новым_мэром москвы стал сергей_собянин*»/Sergey Sobyanin has become a new Mayor of Moscow/(7 occurrences), «*мосгордума_утвердила сергея_собянина на_пост мэра_москвы*»/Moscow City Duma has approved Sobyanin as the Mayor of Moscow/(4 occurrences), «*сергей_собянин - новый_мэр_москвы*»/Sergey Sobyanin as a new Mayor of Moscow/(4 occurrences), etc. There are much fewer news reports with headlines like «*лужков_не пойдет на инаугурацию_преемника*»/Luzhkov will not attend the inauguration of his successor/(2 occurrences). In the cluster about S. Sobyanin there is no striking contrast between the segments obtained from the headlines and the bodies of the news reports. Texts are static, they all tell about a single event and the main theme stands out very clearly. Linked segments derived from the headlines consist of informationally important fragments as well as the publicistic ones. Linked segments derived from the bodies of the news reports allow us to get an idea about important additional subtopics (e.g., the party path of Sobyanin, voting circumstances, etc.).

The main theme of the third cluster concerns the death of Paul the Octopus. Other less important themes are his predictions and other moments of his biography as well as the appointment of his successor. Few linked text segments some additional information, for example, «мемориал_осьминога_пауля установят в_его родном_не-мецком_океанариуме»/Paul the Octopus Memorial will be installed in his native German oceanarium/(5 occurrences). The intersection between the segments derived from the headlines and those from the bodies is minor. The texts in this cluster are static, they narrate about a single event and at the same time are full of various details and their compositional structure is not conventional. There could be two reasons for such disconformity: firstly, a bright publicistic style both in the headlines and the bodies of the texts (which forces to abandon clichés and use a variety of design options for the messages), and secondly, the abundance of details, i.e., topics and subtopics, which are difficult to attribute weights of informational importance. Thus, if we consider lists of linked segments as the compressed text of the cluster, then the cluster about Paul the Octopus is the most complex one among the three considered clusters.

6 Conclusion

This paper presents our results of the analysis of news clusters different in style, themes and structure. News clusters can be static or dynamic, informational or publicistic, conventional or unconventional, with different hierarchy and number of subtopics. We present a method of news cluster analysis via its paraphrase graph structure.

Our main idea is based on the idea of news cluster compression: we analyze news headlines as specific forms of compression. The specialty of headlines is that they are given by the journalists or editors and may be oriented mainly on information transmission function, or rather the function of the impact on the addressee.

We conduct two experiments. During the first experiment, we work with headlines inside each news cluster and extract paraphrase headlines. These paraphrase headlines, together with their similarity values, form a paraphrase graph which reflects the structure and the characteristics of the news cluster. During the second experiment, we work with linked text segments extracted from the headlines and the bodies of the news reports. It turns out that the characteristics of the derived lists of linked segments and the differences between the segments derived from headlines and bodies are closely related to the type of considered news cluster.

As a result of the experiments, we were able to confirm the following hypotheses:

– Paraphrase graph of a news cluster reflects the compositional and linguistic characteristics of the cluster.
– Headlines can be used as a traditional baseline for the analysis of the news clusters.
– The most frequent words from the headlines can be used for the express analysis of the news clusters.
– The comparison of the linked text segments obtained from the headlines and from the news reports themselves reveals the publicistic and the informational components in the headlines.

References

1. Antonov, A., Bagley, S., Meshkov, V., Sukhanov, A.: Documents clustering using metainformation. In: Proceedings of Dialog 2006, Moscow (2006)
2. Azzopardi, J., Staff, Ch.: Incremental clustering of news reports. Algorithms **5**, 364–378 (2012)
3. Bora, N.N., Mishra, B.S.P., Dehuri, S.: Heuristic frequent term-based clustering of news headlines. Proc. Technol. **6**, 436–443 (2012)
4. Daudaravičius, V., Marcinkevičienė, R.: Gravity counts for the boundaries of collocations. Int. J. Corpus Linguist. **9**(2), 321–348 (2004). John Benjamins Publishing Company, Amsterdam
5. Fernando, S., Stevenson, M.: A semantic similarity approach to paraphrase detection. In: Proceedings of Computational Linguistics UK (CLUK 2008) 11th Annual Research Colloqium (2008)
6. Pronoza, E., Yagunova, E., Pronoza, A.: Construction of a Russian paraphrase corpus: unsupervised paraphrase extraction. In: Proceedings of the 9th Summer School in Information Retrieval and Young Scientist Conference (2015)
7. Sidorov, G., Gelbukh, A., Gómez-Adorno, H., Pinto, D.: Soft similarity and soft cosine measure: similarity of features in vector space model. Computación y Sistemas **18**(3), 491–504 (2014)
8. Thirunarayan, K., Immaneni, T., Shaik, M.V.: Selecting labels for news document clusters. Lect. Notes Comput. Sci. **4592**, 119–130 (2007)
9. Yagunova, E.: Variations of speech perception (experimental study based on the Russian texts of different functional styles). Perm', St.-Petersburg (2008)

Designing a Smart Tourism Mobile Application: User Modelling Through Social Networks' User Implicit Data

Aristea Kontogianni[1]([⊠]), Katerina Kabassi[2], and Efthimios Alepis[1]

[1] University of Piraeus, Piraeus, Greece
{akontogianni,talepis}@unipi.gr
[2] TEI of Ionian Islands, Zakynthos, Greece
kkabassi@teiion.gr

Abstract. In an era facing data and information explosion, there is a demanding need to filter and adapt the content presented to users while interacting with mobile applications. Offering a personalized User Experience (UX) seems to be extremely important in a Smart Tourism-Destination App concept too, in order to enrich tourist experience and also to make a destination more competitive. The main objective of this paper is to present how user modeling could be accomplished via data originating from users' social networks, where various aspects of their personality are collected and profiled, as well as data collected from their smartphones implicitly, requiring no user interaction. The data collected by the user model are further processed using a multi-criteria decision making theory called Analytic Hierarchy Process (AHP) in order to select the touristic destination that seems to be the best for the user interacting with the mobile application.

Keywords: Social networks · User modeling
Personalized mobile applications · Smart tourism

1 Introduction

A key function in all User Modelling (UM) systems is "data gathering" in order to create the corresponding user models, whether this is accomplished explicitly or implicitly. A large number of recommendation and adaptation approaches coupled to user modelling, such as supervised machine learning, is depended on this data gathering process. To this end, crowdsourcing evolves a sourcing model where users as individuals may contribute to UM by providing their personal data to centralized software entities, utilizing mostly internet resources. Implicit data collection is considered as highly beneficial in UM since it requires minimum user interference and is considered as a key challenge of adaptive interactive systems in order to provide positive user experience [8].

This work has been partly supported by the University of Piraeus Research Center.

S. Staab et al. (Eds.): SocInfo 2018, LNCS 11186, pp. 148–158, 2018.
https://doi.org/10.1007/978-3-030-01159-8_14

Smartphone crowdsourcing enables real-time data gathering and gives UM software approaches greater reach and accessibility. Smartphones provide a surprisingly large number of modalities for interaction between them and their environment [2]. Combining all the available data from thousands or even myriads of users, big data gathering is realized. Deductively, this enormous database, properly handled and combined with another "huge" database, namely the Social Networks, can provide UM software with state-of-the-art user models in terms of completeness and data availability. Implicit information coming from smartphone crowdsourcing can be combined with location and time specific data and further utilize software adaptation, dynamic response, realizing smartphone context awareness [7].

Internet availability and smartphone connectivity is a necessary pre-condition for the aforementioned model. Each smartphone device may gather a sufficient amount of data regarding a specific user, nevertheless if only stored locally, can only serve the needs of a local and personal user model. Being able to anonymously, for privacy preserving purposes, transmit and communicate this data to a global software entity, e.g. a cloud-as-a-service infrastructure, can boost the ability to generate personalized advice and recommendations deriving from other user models, in a variety of ways, such as filling gaps of unavailable user data, and constructing user stereotypes.

This paper aims to present an innovative approach for achieving user modeling via implicitly gathered user data that can be exploited in a smart tourism application scenario. In particular, a native android application has been developed that collects user information via their social media channels, as well as their smartphones and processes it in order to build the user models required. The goal is to collect data not only for a particular user but also for a plethora of locations, Points of Interest (POIs) and other users, so as to form a database of destinations of touristic interest through crowdsourcing. Moreover, a multi-criteria decision making theory, Analytic Hierarchy Process (AHP) [10], is exploited for the evaluation of different alternative destinations that could be proposed to the user. The alternative destination that is selected by AHP is expected to be the most "appropriate" as the information of the particular user has been processed and evaluated. In this way, the resulting mobile system realizes personalized experience.

2   User Modeling

Using the term "user modelling", the related scientific literature is referring to the detailed recording and categorization of many aspects and characteristics of the interaction of human-users with electronic devices, e.g. computers. In this paper, we focus on user modeling aspects that are related to user data originating either from their social network interaction, or through their smartphones.

2.1   Social Networks and User Modeling

Research in the User Modeling field is an ongoing process during the last decades. In 1989 book [6] is published where twenty five prominent researchers analyze and present the developed user models at that time, mainly focusing on intelligent dialogue systems, and set the ground for future research. Since then, many different approaches regarding user modeling have been formulated with the simplest one statically storing user-related information [1].

In the last few years, web traffic reports reveal that the use of social networks is the most popular activity online [9] with the most recent statistics indicating that Facebook is counting 1,870 million users worldwide, Instagram 600 million, Twitter 317 million, while other social networks like LinkedIn and Pinterest have already established their presence in this thriving Market [19]. Another impressive fact is that by 2021 the number of monthly active social media users around the word is expected to be 3.02 billion, which is, actually, around one third of Earth's entire population [20]. That being the case, the growing interest in understanding users' behavior in social network as well as extracting and analyzing data from them is more than justifiable.

A key feature of all the aforementioned social networks is that they request and store a profile with information filled in directly by the user, as well as a plethora of other data that derive from all the activities users perform on a social media channel, like posting and checking into locations. Therefore, it comes as no surprise that social networks are considered to offer valuable resources for user modeling. For example, the authors of [3], focus on the dynamic user behavior modelling in social media systems as well as its' applications in temporal recommendations. They proposed a temporal context-aware mixture model, that aims to decide if users' choice is based on their personal interests or temporal ones and make a topic suggestion based on this decision, which then they extended to a dynamic one, which no longer assumes that users' personal interests remain unchanged through time. Another attempt to improve the quality of recommendations is made in paper [4], where a novel context-aware recommender system is proposed, namely SoCo, which exploits a combination of contextual information and social network ones so as to improve the quality of recommendations. An additional social regularization term is introduced here as user's preference for an item is determined by the tastes their friends with similar preferences have.

In contradiction to other user modeling techniques that request users answering a short questionnaire to gather some basic data, social networks offer loads of high quality information like user's age, places they have visited and what kind of pages they like, that can be accessed without user's intervention and derive from an interaction that takes place between the user and the social network for days, months or even years.

3   The Mobile Application

Within the scope of this research, a mobile application has been developed, namely ProfileMe, which aims to create a "profile" for its users in order to offer a personalized experience in a smart tourism application context. The information used for user modeling originates from a user's social media as well as his/her smartphone. Raw data is gathered implicitly from the aforementioned data sources and processed in order to build the user models required.

Based on the fact that the Android OS dominates the market share, we initially developed a native Android application as a test bed for our theory. The general architecture of the mobile application in question is presented in Fig. 1.

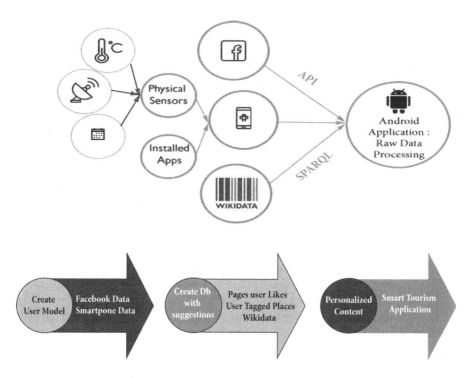

Fig. 1. ProfileMe general architecture

3.1   Data Gathered via Facebook

With Facebook currently being the most popular social network worldwide, the first step was to conduct a thorough research as to what data can be retrieved from this social media channel and how these data can be processed so as to effectively be exploited in user modeling. The part of the application that aims at collecting data that derives from Facebook and process it, consists of two basic Android components that are realized in terms of "Activities". In the Main Activity, the LoginManager class is used so as to manage login and permissions for Facebook [21,23]. The information accessed are users' profile, birthday, likes, hometown, current location as well as the places he/she has tagged themselves.

It is of great importance to note that the data gathered are anonymized, as there is no need to store the physical identity of a user (name, surname etc.). The information requested is strictly limited to the data required for users' personalized assistance in a smart tourism application. To that end, the application provides an easily accessed and understandable description of exactly what data is collected, processed and stored, as well as the reason why that kind of data is required.

3.2 Data Deriving from Users' Smartphones

In reality, being aware of the users' environment and current situation is crucial so as to offer personalized services that suit their needs at a particular time, event and location. Context awareness provided by smartphones offer significant consciousness of the environment and the condition the mobile device of a user is [14], which allows a smart tourism application to respond in a more intelligent manner than simply by using data gathered from a user's profile. Based on that assumption, the application developed utilizes smartphones physical sensors in order to dynamically obtain the data below:

- Current date, time and month: *Calendar* class
- Location updates: *GPS_PROVIDER*
- Environmental temperature: *SensorManager* class,
- Environmental luminosity: *SensorManager* class
- Users' current steps: *Sensor.TYPE_STEP_DETECTOR*

Along with the information mentioned above, another kind of data can be obtained through their smartphones, that can be used to serve as complement to the data deriving from Facebook. These information are the ones regarding the applications installed in user's smartphones and can be also used in user modeling. In particular, all apps installed in a mobile device can be parsed with the *PackageManager* class, which retrieves various kinds of information related to the application packages that are currently installed on the device. Thereinafter, a web service is used in order to retrieve the category of each application from Google Play.

4 Designing Personalization for a Smart Tourism Application

As mentioned in the above sections, information about the users can be collected. However, what is really important is the effective use of this information in order to successfully personalize the interaction of a user with the system. The system in the beginning does not adequate information about the user. Furthermore, there are the cases where the system does not have adequate information about the specific subject examined. This is a common problem of individual user modeling that acquires the information implicitly. A way to overcome the problem is to use the information the system can find in other users. Therefore, the system tries to collect this information by consulting the information that may find for other users with similar characteristics such as interests, likes, hometown etc.

In order to evaluate the different alternatives that could be proposed to the user and select the one that seems more appropriate for the specific user, we use a multi-criteria decision making theory. A multi-attribute decision problem is a situation in which, having defined a set A of actions and a consistent family F of n attributes on A, one wishes to rank the actions of A from best to worst and determine a subset of actions considered to be the best with respect to F [18]. Therefore, for every multi-criteria decision making theory, in order to be implemented the first two steps are:

- Finding the alternatives to be evaluated: In this step the system has to locate which are the alternatives that need to be evaluated. The alternatives that may be evaluated by the system are the possible destinations.
- Forming the set of criteria: The criteria for evaluating each alternative. Each alternative destination is evaluated in terms of some criteria.
  - Interests: information deriving by the pages a user likes as well as the interests of other individuals with similar preferences.
  - Distance
  - Weather: appropriateness of the weather conditions
  - Time schedule: working hours of a destination
  - Rating: if available
  - Touristic interest: tourist interest of a place within a distance of the destination in question
  - Accessibility: how accessible a place is, i.e. if a metro station is available

This information is further used by Analytic Hierarchy Process [10], a multi-criteria decision making theory to select the best alternative.

5   Applying Analytic Hierarchy Process

Analytic Hierarchy Process (AHP) [10] is one of the most popular Multi Criteria Decision Making (MCDM) theories. The choice of AHP amongst other MCDM theories is easily made as it presents a formal way of quantifying the qualitative criteria of the alternatives and in this way removes the subjectivity of the result [12]. The main steps of the AHP theory as these are proposed by [11] are: (1) Developing a goal hierarchy, (2) Setting up a pair-wise comparison matrix of criteria, (3) Ranking the relative importance between alternatives and (4) Calculating AHP values.

1. Developing a goal hierarchy: The hierarchical structure is formed as soon as the overall goal, the set of criteria and the alternative destinations are specified. The overall goal always is the specification of the most appropriate destination, the criteria are presented in the previous section and the possible destinations are dynamically generated by the system each time the user searches a new destination. The purpose of the hierarchical structure is to have the criteria and the alternative destinations combined to pairs.

2. Setting up a pair-wise comparison matrix of criteria
3. Ranking the relative importance between alternatives
4. Calculating AHP values

5.1   Setting up a Pair-Wise Comparison Matrix of Criteria

In this step a comparison matrix is formed so that the criteria of the same level are pair-wise compared. IV. In the comparison process, a V from the scale that is presented in Table 1 is assigned to the comparison result of two elements P and Q at first, then the value of comparison of Q and P is a reciprocal value of V, i.e. 1/V. The value of the comparison of P and P is 1.

Table 1. The comparison process

	P	Q
P	1	V
Q	1/V	1

The comparison process is performed by human experts as the proposed method is an inspection method. In order to overcome the problem of inspection methods that we have used a double system of experts that uses both computer and domain (tourism) experts. More specifically, each one of the five human experts that participated the experiment completes the pairwise comparison matrix of the criteria and each cell of the final matrix is calculated as a geometric mean of the values of the corresponding cells of the five matrixes collected by the human experts. As a result the final matrix is built, which is presented in Table 2.

Table 2. Pairwise comparison matrix of the criteria

	c1: Interest	c2: Distance	c3: Weather	c4: Time schedule	c5: Rating	c6: Touristic interest	c7: Accessibility
c1: Interest	1.00	5.43	5.26	5.00	2.55	4.79	3.00
c2: Distance	0.18	1.00	3.90	0.38	0.89	1.40	1.00
c3: Weather	0.19	0.26	1.00	0.19	0.17	0.92	1.15
c4: Time schedule	0.20	2.61	5.28	1.00	0.26	1.39	0.82
c5: Rating	0.39	1.12	6.00	3.78	1.00	2.77	2.56
c6: Touristic interest	0.21	0.72	1.09	0.72	0.36	1.00	0.49
c7: Accessibility	0.33	1.00	0.87	1.22	0.39	2.03	1.00

After making pair-wise comparisons, estimations are made that result in the final set of weights of the criteria. In this step, the principal eigenvalue and the corresponding normalized right eigenvector of the comparison matrix give the relative importance of the various criteria being compared. The elements of the normalized eigenvector are the weights of criteria. In terms of simplicity, we have use the 'Priority Estimation Tool' (PriEst) [17], an open-source decision-making software that implements the Analytic Hierarchy Process (AHP) method, for making the calculations of AHP. The weights of the criteria that have been resulted by this process are presented in Table 3.

Table 3. Final weights of the criteria

	Weight
c1: Interest	0.383
c2: Distance	0.097
c3: Weather	0.045
c4: Time schedule	0.110
c5: Rating	0.207
c6: Touristic interest	0.065
c7: Accessibility	0.094

5.2 Ranking the Relative Importance Between Alternatives

After calculating the weights of the criteria the alternative actions are evaluated. More specifically, the relative importance between each pair of destinations in terms of a criterion will be assessed in order to calculate a value for each one of the destination evaluated. Therefore, for each criterion a pair-wise comparison matrix is calculated for the alternatives distances that have been found by the system. The values of the cells of the matrix are completed by the system based on the information about the user that is acquired by the user model. All matrices are normalized and a weight of each alternative is also derived.

5.3 Calculating AHP Values

Finally, an AHP value is calculated for each destination and these values are used for ranking the possible destinations that may be proposed to the user. The destination that has the higher value is considered to be the best. The AHP value is computed using the following formula, where M is the number of alternatives and N is the number of criteria; denotes the score of the alternative related to the criterion; denotes the weight of the criterion:

$$AHP_i = \sum_{j=1}^{N} a_{ij} w_j, \quad for\ i = 1, 2, 3 ..., M \tag{1}$$

6   Conclusions

This paper focuses on how user modeling can be accomplished via implicitly collected user data, deriving from both users' social network as well as their smartphone and how the aforementioned user model can be of use in a smart tourism application scenario. Within the scope of this research a native android application has been developed that gathers data from the aforementioned sources regarding the user as well as loads of data about locations that can be of tourist interest. Wikidata knowledge base has also been exploited in order to enhance our knowledge about certain locations. With that being said, we came to the conclusion that data required for personalization and for recommendation purposes can indeed be collected.

Aiming to propose an effective way to use the aforementioned information so as to successfully achieve the personalized interaction of a user with the system we applied the Analytic Hierarchy Process, one of the most popular multi-criteria decision making theories. AHP is used to comprehend data from the user and process them to select the destination that seems to be the best for the particular user. It is among our future plans to distribute the application through the Google Play marketplace in order to further evaluate the effectiveness of the proposed approach. Users' feedback shall be collected both via a short questionnaire embedded in the application and Google Play's rating feature.

References

1. Fidas, C.A., Avouris, N.M.: Personalization of mobile applications in cultural heritage environments. In: 2015 6th International Conference on Information, Intelligence, Systems and Applications (IISA). https://doi.org/10.1109/IISA.2015.7388114
2. Bhargava, P., Agrawala, A.K.: Modeling users' behavior from large scale smartphone data collection. EAI Endorsed Trans. Context.-Aware Syst. Appl. **3**(10), e3 (2016). https://doi.org/10.4108/eai.12-9-2016.151677
3. Yin, H., Cui, B., Chen, L., Hu, Z., Zhou, X.: Dynamic user modeling in social media systems. ACM Trans. Inf. Syst. **33**(3), article 10, 44 pages (2015). https://doi.org/10.1145/2699670
4. Liu, X., Aberer, K.: SoCo: a social network aided context-aware recommender system. In: Proceedings of the 22nd International Conference on World Wide Web (WWW 2013), pp. 781–802. ACM, New York (2013). https://doi.org/10.1145/2488388.2488457
5. Yus, R., Pappachan, P.: Are apps going semantic? A systematic review of semantic mobile applications. In: Conference: 1st International Workshop on Mobile Deployment of Semantic Technologies (MoDeST 2015), Co-located with the 14th International Semantic Web Conference (ISWC 2015), Bethlehem, PA, USA (2015)
6. Kobsa, A., Wahlster, W.: User Models in Dialog Systems. Springer, Heidelberg (1989). https://doi.org/10.1007/978-3-642-83230-7
7. Otebolaku, A.M., Andrade, M.T.: User context recognition using smartphone sensors and classification models. J. Netw. Comput. Appl. **66**, 33–51 (2016). https://doi.org/10.1016/j.jnca.2016.03.013

8. Papatheocharous, E., Belk, M., Germanakos, P., Samaras, G.: Towards implicit user modeling based on artificial intelligence, cognitive styles and web interaction data. Int. J. Artif. Intell. Tools **23**(2) (2014). https://doi.org/10.1142/S0218213014400090
9. Fan, W., Gordon, M.D.: The power of social media analytics. Commun. ACM **57**(6), 74–81 (2014). https://doi.org/10.1145/2602574
10. Saaty, T.: The Analytic Hierarchy Process. McGraw-Hill, New York (1980)
11. Zhu, Y., Buchman, A.: Evaluating and selecting web sources as external information resources of a data warehouse. In: The Third International Conference on Web Information Systems Engineering (WISE 2000), pp. 149–160 (2000)
12. Tiwari, N.: Using the Analytic Hierarchy Process (AHP) to identify performance scenarios for enterprise application. Computer Measurement Group. Measure It, vol. 4(3) (2006)
13. Virvou, M., Alepis, E.: Mobile educational features in authoring tools for personalised tutoring. Comput. Educ. **44**(1), 53–68 (2005). https://doi.org/10.1016/j.compedu.2003.12.020
14. Yrr, O., Liu, C.H., Sheng, Z., Leung, V.C.M., Moreno, W., Leung, K.K.: Context-awareness for mobile sensing: a survey and future directions. IEEE Commun. Surv. Tutor. **18**(1), 68–93 (2016). https://doi.org/10.1109/COMST.2014.2381246
15. Hofer, T., Schwinger, W., Pichler, M., Leonhartsberger, G., Altmann, J., Retschitzegger, W.: Context-awareness on mobile devices - the hydrogen approach. In: Proceedings of the 36th Annual Hawaii International Conference on System Sciences, 10 pp. (2003). https://doi.org/10.1109/HICSS.2003.1174831
16. Kim, H.R., Chan, P.K.: Learning implicit user interest hierarchy for context in personalization. In: Proceedings of the 8th International Conference on Intelligent User Interfaces (IUI 2003), pp. 101–108. ACM, New York (2003). https://doi.org/10.1145/604045.604064
17. Siraj, S., Mikhailov, L., Keane, J.A.: PriEsT: an interactive decision support tool to estimate priorities from pairwise comparison judgments. Intl. Trans. Op. Res. **22**, 217–235 (2015). https://doi.org/10.1111/itor.12054
18. Vincke, P.: Multicriteria Decision-Aid. Wiley, Chichester (1992)
19. Global social media research summary (2018). https://www.smartinsights.com/social-media-marketing/social-media-strategy/new-global-social-media-research/. Accessed 30 Mar 2018
20. Social media - Statistics & Facts. https://www.statista.com/topics/1164/social-networks/. Accessed 30 Mar 2018
21. LoginManager class. https://developers.facebook.com/docs/reference/android/current/class/LoginManager/. Accessed 19 Apr 2018
22. Facebook SDK. https://developers.facebook.com/docs/android/getting-started/. Accessed 16 Apr 2018
23. Facebook Permissions. https://developers.facebook.com/docs/facebook-login/android/permissions. Accessed 18 Apr 2018
24. Facebook Graph Api Explorer. https://developers.facebook.com/tools/explorer/. Accessed 18 Apr 2018
25. https://developers.facebook.com/docs/graph-api/using-graph-api/#fieldexpansion. Accessed 20 Apr 2018
26. Graph Api Overview. https://developers.facebook.com/docs/graph-api/overview. Accessed 20 Apr 2018
27. All Facebook Categories. https://developers.facebook.com/tools/explorer/314199319068817?method=GET&path=fb_page_categories&version=v2.12. Accessed 20 Apr 2018

28. WikiData   overview.   https://www.wikidata.org/wiki/Wikidata:Main_Page. Accessed 20 Apr 2018
29. Wikidata Introduction. https://www.wikidata.org/wiki/Wikidata:Introduction. Accessed 20 Apr 2018
30. The Generation Z Study of Tech Intimates. https://www.commscope.com/Insights/. Accessed 23 Apr 2018

Monitoring and Counteraction to Malicious Influences in the Information Space of Social Networks

Igor Kotenko[1]([⊠]) [iD], Igor Saenko[1] [iD], Andrey Chechulin[1,2] [iD],
Vasily Desnitsky[1,2] [iD], Lidia Vitkova[1,2] [iD], and Anton Pronoza[1]

[1] St. Petersburg Institute for Informatics and Automation of the Russian
Academy of Sciences, 39, 14-th Liniya, St. Petersburg, Russia
{ivkote, ibsaen, chechulin, desnitsky}@comsec.spb.ru,
iskinlidia@gmail.com, pronoza@gmail.com
[2] The Bonch-Bruevich Saint-Petersburg State University of Telecommunications
(SPBGUT), Saint-Petersburg, Russia

Abstract. The paper considers an interdisciplinary problem of protecting the information space of social networks from unwanted and malicious information. One of the means for solving this problem is the development of an integrated system for monitoring and counteraction to malicious influences in social networks. The architecture of this system is proposed. The architecture includes components for collection, preprocessing and storage of information objects, semantic analysis of malicious information objects, identifying sources of attack and target audiences, analyzing the distribution channels of malicious information objects, and complex recognition of the impact elements. The issues of implementation and functioning of the components of the proposed system are discussed. The experimental evaluation showed high efficiency of the accepted architectural solutions.

Keywords: Information security · Protection from information
Data mining · Social networks · Classifier · Information retrieval

1 Introduction

The development of information technologies and social networks bring the scientific community to a fundamental revision of existing ideas about the methods of information confrontation. Not only in scientific circles, but also in the mass media, the interdisciplinary aspects related to national security, namely information and psychological security and information impacts are discussed.

The greatest severity of this problem is manifested when trying to recognize targeted information impacts (attacks) on social media users and counteracting these attacks. However, the issues of multi-level and multi-aspect management of the state information and psychological security for counteracting various types of targeted information impacts in the conditions of processing large volumes of heterogeneous data are currently researched insufficiently.

© Springer Nature Switzerland AG 2018
S. Staab et al. (Eds.): SocInfo 2018, LNCS 11186, pp. 159–167, 2018.
https://doi.org/10.1007/978-3-030-01159-8_15

The main shortcomings of the existing systems for managing the information space of social networks are: (1) absence of a comprehensive and detailed analysis of information security threats in the context of information confrontation in social networks; (2) insufficient completeness and adequacy of existing models for assessing the influence of the perpetrator on the state information sphere through social networks; (3) lack of the complete formalized representation for the process of automated situation assessment in social networks; (4) lack of adequate formalization of situational parameters and processes of forecasting, detection and evaluation of threats of malicious influence social networks; (5) focus on monitoring and blocking the channels for spreading the malicious information, but not on counteracting the perpetrators; (6) insufficient completeness and adequacy of existing models of information confrontation for social networks.

This causes the high urgency of creating an integrated system for monitoring and counteraction to malicious influences in the information space of social networks.

In this paper, we discuss the architecture and implementation of this system. A new approach to the management of the information space of social networks is proposed. It is based on the method of multi-level management of the state information-psychological security.

This method implements the so-called a posteriori protection of the target audience against information impacts, carried out on the assumption that the perpetrator has already had an impact (or may have an impact) to achieve his own goal. At the same time, this model is based on models of influences in social networks, the information conflict and the information confrontation.

The main tasks that will be solved by the integrated system for monitoring and counteraction to malicious influences in the information space include the tasks of counteracting the impact on the state information space by extremist organizations implementing their destructive program (including terrorist attacks and dissemination of false information). This information, as a rule, is aimed at forming attitudes and (or) stereotypes of behavior required by terrorists, or inducement to commit any actions or to refrain from committing them. This determines the theoretical contribution and novelty of the results considered in the paper.

The further structure of the paper is as follows. In Sect. 2, the relevant work is analyzed. Section 3 provides and justifies the overall architecture of the proposed system. Section 4 deals with issues related to the implementation of the components of the proposed system and their experimental evaluation. Section 5 contains conclusions and directions for further research.

2 Related Work

Today, the methods based on content analysis as well as approaches based on machine learning and social graphs are mainly offered. Research on the analysis of information in social networks is gaining popularity.

In [1] the possibility of using social networks for detecting influenza epidemics and predicting its spread has been shown. However, the drawback of this and many other modern systems and algorithms for monitoring social networks is that they are limited to the information that the user specified in the profile.

In [2] a system is proposed that allows one to determine the location of users of social networks through the social graph. Later, this method was improved in [3], where it was suggested to analyze not only the target audience, but also related users.

In [4], the "Social Tie Factor Graph (STFG)" method is presented. It uses the "What is Random Walk with Restart (RWR)" algorithm to sort friends according to the influence degree and evaluation of the users' similarity. This method allows one to calculate groups by users' interests and their interrelationships. It may be applicable to the analysis of extremist and terrorist communities, but previously it was not considered in the scientific community to achieve these goals.

In [5] the analytical systems "Tekstera" and "Talisman", intended for content analysis are considered. These systems realize the model and method for generating random graphs, possess the basic properties of social networks (degree distribution, diameter, clusterization coefficient, etc.) and a specified structure of user communities. The technologies and algorithms of Big data were used to implement these systems. These systems can calculate and forecast epidemics of influenza, and analyze demographic parameters of social networks. However, they were not designed to monitor the state information security, search for attack sources, repeaters and analysis of violations.

Studies on analyzing the emotional coloring of text messages are also of interest. Besides, in recent years, the techniques on automatic retrieval of comments were proposed [6, 7]. These techniques are not tied to specific web sites or commenting systems.

Separately it is worth mentioning the research on the methodology of information conflict in the psychological and socio-political spheres. The paper [8] considers an overview of the models of influences in social networks.

Thus, the analysis of related works shows that the content analysis systems are gaining increasing interest. However, known systems of this type do not provide the adequate capabilities of monitoring and counteraction to malicious influences in the information space of social networks.

3   General Architecture of the System

The architecture of the proposed system includes the following components:

(1)   collection, pre-processing and storage of information objects;
(2)   semantic analysis of malicious information objects;
(3)   identifying the sources of the attack and the target audience of the impact;
(4)   analysis of the channels for distribution of malicious information objects;
(5)   integrated recognition of the influence elements.

The relationships between these components are represented in Fig. 1.

The component of collection, pre-processing and storage of information objects performs procedures for searching and recognizing the structural elements of information objects of users, groups and messages of social networks and identifying

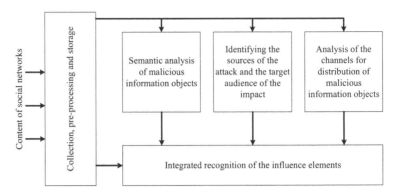

Fig. 1. The architecture of the system.

specific features according to available patterns as initial data of the algorithms for classification of malicious influences. Preliminary processing of information objects comprises procedures for filtering the redundant and doubled information in the source data stream as well as their aggregation within certain time gaps. This component allows taking into account the following aspects: poor structuring and heterogeneity of data; various ways of obtaining data (API, Streaming API, HTML parsing, etc.); restrictions on access to data (portioning of information delivery, restrictions on privacy settings, limits on data volumes, etc.); blocking by the server of the social network (by IP-address, by the called functions, by the account used, etc.); uploading the prohibited information or information which is limited to distribution by the legislation (personal data, prohibited literature, etc.).

The developed methods of data collection are characterized by an ability to load simultaneously disjoint portions of information. Thus, a comprehensive technique for data collection from social networks includes an algorithm for the operation of the control center of data collection and the distributed intelligent scanners of the social network under its control.

The component of the semantic analysis of malicious information objects performs classification according to the collected data on the analyzed information objects by specified groups using a hierarchically constructed system of binary, aspect and resultant classifiers. The architecture of the system is shown in Fig. 1. In particular the determination of the perpetrator's type and the countermeasures to it depends to a large extent on the type of information disseminated. The number of malicious influences include, for example, false reports that mislead public opinion under the guise of true ones; distortion/replacement of the official position by the perpetrator on socially significant events in the country and the world; publication through the opinion leaders in social networks of the materials containing a prejudiced assessment of the activities of the information exchange legitimate participants; discrimination and obstruction of reporting by mass news media. The detailed description of the web-pages classification prototype architecture and elements presented in earlier papers of the authors [9, 10].

The component of identifying the sources of the attack and the target audience of the impact is based on the generated perpetrator model and the perpetrator detection methods. The perpetrator model is based on formal features of a social network subject, such as disorderly friendships, round-the-clock activity time, static personal profile, etc. Fictitious pages can be referred to the implementation of this model, namely bots performing mass informational embedding.

The perpetrator model of a real person stands is described on the basis of the current legislation on the information that he (she) distributes. This model will be useful for producing countermeasures and statistical accounting of malicious influences in the social network. As a perpetrator detection method, the social profile is checked for compliance with a specific perpetrator model. Search for the perpetrator is fulfilled through the channels of dissemination of malicious information.

The component of analysis of the channels for distribution of malicious information objects allows searching for the perpetrator and his (her) target audience due to the structure of the social network itself as a platform for messaging. The analysis of information distribution channels includes tracking of thematic communities, highlighting of opinion leaders, identifying bot networks and building repost trees.

The most important aspect for this analysis is the development of a social network model that includes its subjects (users, communities, meetings, etc.), links between them and time intervals. The identification of appropriate channels is based on the application of methods for analyzing relationships within the model, clustering its elements, and information visualization.

Also, the methods of streaming contextual information retrieval can play a significant role in the search for malicious content and distribution chains. Thus, the identification of sources of attacks and target audiences of exposure and distribution channels in social networks together provide an integrated and interrelated system of fixing all stages of the work of the intruder.

It should also be noted that the revelation of the type of an perpetrator and countermeasures to his (her) actions largely depends on the type of information disseminated.

The component of integrated recognition of the influence elements is responsible for the performance of functions is a key component of monitoring. At the same time, the task to monitor the information which is circulating in the social network includes the allocation of content that carries out a malicious influence on its audience. In this case, we are talking about an information attack on the target audience in a social network, usually conducted in violation of the agreement about its resources using. To detect such an attack, an understanding, consistent with the legislation, is formed of what constitutes a harmful effect in social networks, as well as a method for identifying risk groups for subsequent monitoring, and continuous collection of data from the social network. To confirm the fact of the attack conducted in order to provide appropriate counteraction, four signs are established: the nature of the information transmitted, the source of the attack, the target audience and distribution channels.

Thus, to implement a subsystem for monitoring and counteraction to malicious influences in the information space of social networks, a comprehensive method for identifying the influence elements has been developed, including the analysis of malicious information objects, distribution channels, attack sources and target audiences.

4 Experiments and Discussion

A Python based software prototype of an integrated system for monitoring and counteraction to malicious influences in the information space of social networks for the purposes of proof-of-the-concept has been developed.

In particular as a part of the component of collection, pre-processing and storage of information objects, the functions for collecting the characteristics of users and communities, they are involved, have been implemented based on a given set of XML templates of social networking pages. It has been done without taking into account poorly structured and incompletely filled text fields, as well as the private and inaccessible publicly available data.

As part of the component of the semantic analysis of malicious information objects, the functions for verifying the collected data from a pattern of chains of "viral" distribution of small amounts of data between users were made with a link to the site of malicious content. Within the component of identifying the sources of the attack and the target audience of the impact, the processes of detecting software bots have been modeled. This modeling was based on statistical characteristics of the operation time, the periods of activity and the intensity of the outgoing information flow.

The following indicators, computed in the process of the experimental study of the prototype, were selected: the speed, recall and accuracy of the monitoring system. At the same time the problem of inconsistency of the initial data, collected during the analysis of information objects in the monitoring process, was revealed. The resolution of this problem will significantly improve the accuracy and completeness of the obtained monitoring process.

For experiments with the component, the semantic analysis of malicious information objects, a hierarchical system of the binary, aspect and resulting classifiers, based on the decision tree approach, was implemented. The choice of decision trees was determined by a number of earlier experiments, which showed that this approach enables us to obtain the best precision without a significant reduction of the overall accuracy. As information objects web pages were selected.

The following list of web-pages aspects was formed: whole text, text from tags (tags "title", "description", "keywords", "h1", "h2", "h3", "a", etc.), HTML structure, URL address, images. To form the training and testing sets, an open catalog of DMOZ was used. This catalog contains a large number of classified web pages. To make the task more complicated the following categories were added to the category list: chats, news and ecommerce. The features of these categories have volatile content. The final list of categories is as follows: adult; alcohol; chat; ecommerce; games online; hunting; medical; music; news; religion. Experiments have shown that web pages with adult, alcohol, games online, hunting, medical categories are recognized with more than 90% accuracy, but the categories chat (65%) and news (75%) can be recognized, but the accuracy of the result is significantly lower. In general, if except the web pages that were classified as Unknown, the accuracy of the classification was 90%. But it should be noted that about 20% of web pages contained almost no text (i.e. less than 100 bytes of text), and more than 40% of web pages did not contain images.

The social network VKontakte was used as the source for experiments with components for identifying attack sources, distribution channels and target audiences. The source of the attack was considered to be the user or the group that created is the original content containing inappropriate or malicious information. As distribution channels the repost of the records was used. To find the target audience, the number of record's views in groups and the number of "Like" marks were analyzed. It should be noted that the "number of views" indicator does not allow one to identify specific users who viewed the record, and repost analysis does not allow one to find records that were created manually by users and which are simultaneously appearing on different users' pages and groups. This way of disseminating information is much less convenient, but it allows users to be undetected. For the results analysis a graphic scheme for their representation was developed. As an example of visualization, the part of the "repost" relationship graph is shown in Fig. 2.

Fig. 2. Repost relations graph.

The presented graph gives an overview of information flows between users' pages and groups in the social network. The vertex color describes the uniqueness of the content created by the user or group member. If the vertex's color is closer to the green then the group or the user that is represented by this vertex has more unique records. Groups and user pages that contain mostly reposts of records from other sources are showed as red vertices. The same color scheme is used for links – the color of the edges repeats the color of the source vertex and indicates the uniqueness of the distributed content. The size of the vertex depends on the number of records in the group or in the user's page. The size of the edge depends on the number of reposts.

The experiments with the experts' involvement showed that a visual analysis based on the proposed models and data obtained from the social network allows to identify the general information flows and to find the important nodes in the information transfer network (sources, distribution channels and target audience).

In general the obtained experimental evaluation of the prototype showed the high efficiency of the adopted architectural solutions. In this case in view of the limitations imposed on the volumes of initial data within the framework of the experiments, the proposed solution is characterized by the acceptable time efficiency. At the same time, on the real data samples that should be used to monitor social networks in hundreds of millions of users and millions of communities, the problem of the speediness of their monitoring is extremely urgent.

5 Conclusion

The problem of protecting the information space of social networks from malicious information is formulated. One of the means for solving this problem is the development of the systems for monitoring and counteraction to malicious influences in the information space of social networks.

An architecture of this system is proposed, its software prototype is developed, and the results of experimental studies are obtained.

As areas of future research, it is planned to improve the developed monitoring components to increase the level of target indicators for time efficiency, completeness and accuracy, using large amounts of raw data comparable in size to existing large specialized social networks and networks of general purpose.

Acknowledgements. The work is performed by the grant of RSF #18-71-10094 in SPIIRAS.

References

1. Sadilek, A., Kautz, H.A., Silenzio, V.: Modeling spread of disease from social interactions. In: Proceedings of the Sixth International Conference on Weblogs and Social Media, Dublin, Ireland, 4–7 June 2012
2. Backstrom, L., Sun, E., Marlow, C.: Find me if you can: improving geographical prediction with social and spatial proximity. In: Proceedings of the 19th International Conference on World Wide Web, pp. 61–70. ACM (2010)
3. Jurgens, D.: That's what friends are for: inferring location in online social media platforms based on social relationships. ICWSM **13**, 273–282 (2013)
4. Chen, J., Liu, Y., Zou, M.: Home location profiling for users in social media. Inf. Manag. **53**(1), 135–143 (2016)
5. Trofimovich, U.S., Kozlov, I.S., Turdakov, D.Y.: Approaches to estimate location of social network users based on social graph. Inst. Syst. Program. Russ. Acad. Sci. Part **28**(6), 185–196 (2016)
6. Kao, H.A., Chen, H.H.: Comment extraction from blog posts and its applications to opinion mining. In: The Seventh International Conference on Language Resources and Evaluation (LREC) (2010)
7. Barua, J., Patel, D., Goyal, V.: TiDE: Template-independent Discourse data Extraction. In: Madria, S., Hara, T. (eds.) DaWaK 2015. LNCS, vol. 9263, pp. 149–162. Springer, Cham (2015). https://doi.org/10.1007/978-3-319-22729-0_12
8. Gubanov, D.A., Novikov, D.A., Chkhartishvili, A.G.: Social Networks: Models of Informational Influence, Control and Confrontation. FIZMATLIT, Moscow (2010)

9. Kotenko, I., Chechulin, A., Shorov, A., Komashinsky, D.: Analysis and evaluation of web pages classification techniques for inappropriate content blocking. In: Perner, P. (ed.) ICDM 2014. LNCS (LNAI), vol. 8557, pp. 39–54. Springer, Cham (2014). https://doi.org/10.1007/978-3-319-08976-8_4
10. Kotenko, I., Chechulin, A., Komashinsky, D.: Categorisation of web pages for protection against inappropriate content in the internet. Int. J. Internet Protoc. Technol. $1(10)$, 61–71 (2017)

Using Twitter Hashtags to Gauge Real-Time Changes in Public Opinion: An Examination of the 2016 US Presidential Election

Hannah W. Lee[(✉)]

University of Washington, Seattle, WA 98195, USA
hwlee23@uw.edu

Abstract. Polls have long been a tool for gauging public opinion, whether in general or in relation to specific events. Poll results, however, take a few days to be collected and published. Trending twitter hashtags, in contrast, are keywords that capture public sentiments about current events and could serve as a data source for gauging real-time changes in public opinion. This paper examines trending Twitter hashtags following the release of James Comey's letter to Congress shortly before the 2016 US presidential election day. I find that trending Twitter hashtags mirror and, more importantly, precede the poll results of the same period.

Keywords: Twitter hashtags · US presidential election · Sentiment analysis

1 Introduction

Election polling is a survey research method that examines opinions about political candidates, views of campaigns, and voter preferences. Polls have been used for decades during presidential elections to gauge public opinion. However, polls generally reflect public sentiment a few days after an event has occurred because it takes time to collect, weigh, adjust, and release data [7].

Trending Twitter hashtags, on the other hand, are an alternative tool that can be used to assess public opinion at any hour. Hashtags are a way to categorize tweets by a specific theme and to see "trending topics," which are topics that are popular in a given moment. They are keywords that capture the content or "sentiment" of an event. In comparison to polls, simple analysis of trending Twitter hashtags offers real-time data on public sentiments – including sudden shifts in views – about contemporaneous events. To assess the value of Twitter hashtag analysis, I will address the following question in this paper: Was there an increase in Twitter hashtags containing negative sentiments about Hillary Clinton immediately after James Comey's letter was released, which corresponded to, and preceded, a plunge in Clinton's popular vote margin as revealed by the polls in the 2016 US presidential election?

© Springer Nature Switzerland AG 2018
S. Staab et al. (Eds.): SocInfo 2018, LNCS 11186, pp. 168–175, 2018.
https://doi.org/10.1007/978-3-030-01159-8_16

2 Background

Throughout the 2016 US presidential campaign, national polls had Clinton ahead of Donald Trump [1] and indicated she had a decent chance of winning. Yet, on November 8th, Trump was elected the 45th President of the US.

A number of individuals, including FiveThirtyEight's Nate Silver and Clinton herself, believe Comey's letter to Congress played a significant role in influencing the election result [8]. At around 1 p.m. EST on October 28th, 2016, Comey, the FBI Director at the time, released a letter to Congress stating that the FBI had found additional emails showing Clinton had used her personal email server for official business when she was Secretary of State. The release of the letter so close to election day likely swayed voters who were on the fence.

In fact, Table 1 shows changes in Clinton's popular vote margin in three polls before and after Comey's letter was released. Clinton's margin declines at least +1 or +2 points after October 28th. The most dramatic drop is the ABC News/Washington Post poll, which fell from +6 to +1 percentage points after Comey's letter. This evidence lends support to Silver and Clinton's claim about the effect of Comey's letter. However, given the nature of polling, it took a few days for Clinton's popular vote margin to decline after Comey's letter was released. We might ask: Could we have known about the impact of Comey's letter on public opinion immediately, or at least much sooner?

Table 1. Clinton's vote margin from three polls leading up to the 2016 election day. *Source*: The New York Times

Dates of poll	Poll type	Number of respondents	Vote margin
ABC News/Washington Post			
11/3-11/6	Live Phone	2,220	Clinton +4
10/30-11/2	Live Phone	1,151	Clinton +3
10/26-10/29	Live phone	1,695	Clinton +1
10/22-10/25	Live Phone	1,135	Clinton +6
Politico/Morning Consult			
11/4-11/5	Online	1,482	Clinton +3
10/29-10/30	Online	1,772	Clinton +3
10/27-10/30	Live Phone	1,249	Clinton +5
10/19-10/20	Online	1,395	Clinton +6
Lucid/The Times-Picayune			
11/4-11/6	Online	931	Clinton +5
11/1-11/3	Online	873	Clinton +5
10/29-10/31	Online	866	Clinton +2
10/26-10/28	Online	865	Clinton +3
10/23-10/25	Online	875	Clinton +4
10/20-10/22	Online	884	Clinton +6

3 Related Work

Since Twitter was created in 2006, an increasing number of studies have found that Twitter data both complement election polling results and reflect public opinion [5]. Some studies show that number of mentions of political parties in Tweets correlate with vote share [10]. However, relying on the number of mentions is insufficient without examining the sentiment of the tweet [3]. Other studies have used lexicon-based sentiment analysis to illustrate how the reactions of Twitter users to exogenous events during a presidential election parallel the results of traditional surveys [2].

In the past year, the 2016 US presidential election has been of particular interest for social scientists. For example, Shaban et al. [6] used a weighted log frequency approach to capture Twitter keywords, and then mapped tweets to topics generated from event clustering on a news dataset. Their findings illustrate the impact of events, including the presidential debates and Comey's letter, during the 2016 US presidential election. Although their technique, as well as sentiment analysis approaches, have merits, I suggest that trending Twitter hashtags can similarly, and more efficiently, capture public opinion and measure the impact of an event on attitudes by the hour.

I follow Shaban et al.'s [6] study of examining the impact of events, but instead I use, for my study, trending Twitter hashtags, which (i) is a cleaner way to adjudicate sentiment because hashtags are designed to encapsulate attitudes about events, and (ii) does not rely on natural language processing or lexicon-based scoring methods.

4 Methodology

I downloaded tweets from the Twitter Archive for every hour of each day from October 21st to November 8th, 2016. Examining trending Twitter hashtags at least one week before Comey's letter was released provides a before-and-after snapshot of the effect of the letter. I removed URLs and characters that are not part of the natural language text, tokenized the tweets into words, and then filtered to just the hashtags. I was left with 8,962,650 hashtags. I then cleaned the hashtags to remove misspellings, such as changing #hillaryforprision to #hillaryforprison, and identified the 25 most common Twitter hashtags that explicitly referred to Clinton and Trump. I also removed hashtags that were not explicitly linked to Clinton and Trump, such as #wakeupamerica. My final sample size of hashtags used for my analysis was 298,002.

I categorized the 25 most common hashtags into the following sentiment categories: Positive Clinton; Positive Trump; Neutral; Negative Clinton; and Negative Trump. As shown in Table 2, the fact that one-third of the 25 most common Twitter hashtags were categorized as Negative Clinton is already telling of the general attitude among Twitter users in the weeks heading into election day. This outlook will be further detailed in this paper.

Table 2. Hashtag sentiment categories for the 25 most common Twitter hashtags, October 21st – November 8th, 2016.

Sentiment	Hashtag
Positive Clinton	#imwithher, #gohillary, #votehillary
Positive Trump	#maga, #trumptrain, #trumppence16, #trump2016, #votetrump, #makeamericagreatagain, #americafirst, #votetrumppence16
Neutral	#trump, #hillary, #hillaryclinton, #donaldtrump
Negative Clinton	#podestaemails, #draintheswamp, #hillarysemail, #crookedhillary, #neverhillary, #hillaryforprison, #hillaryindictment, #comey
Negative Trump	#nevertrump, #rememberwhentrump

5   Analysis

A number of interesting trends emerge from an examination of the most common Twitter hashtags relating to the 2016 US presidential election. Below is a summary of three key takeaways, which will be discussed in detail in this section:

1. There was an increase in the proportion of Negative Clinton hashtags from October 28th – November 4th;
2. There were two spikes in Positive Clinton hashtags, on October 30th and November 4th; and
3. Trending hashtags relating to Clinton's emails, specifically #podestaemails and #hillarysemail, were at the forefront of people's minds heading into the election.

5.1   An Increase in Negative Clinton Hashtags

The proportion of Negative Clinton hashtags increased between October 28th and November 4th (see Fig. 1). Specifically, it rose to a high of about 0.52 on November 3rd, which means around 52% of the most common Twitter hashtags relating to Clinton and Trump on that day were Negative Clinton hashtags. In contrast, for the same period, the proportion of Positive Trump hashtags declined, and the proportion of Positive Clinton hashtags remained flat except for on October 30th and November 4th. The increase in Negative Clinton hashtags following the release of Comey's letter suggests the letter had a large impact on Twitter discourse.

Furthermore, the precise turning point in Clinton's popular support can be identified by examining the change in the proportion of Negative Clinton hashtags on the day Comey released his letter. Around mid-day on October 28th, when Comey's letter was sent to Congress, the proportion of Negative Clinton hashtags increased substantially. Examining the specific hashtags used on October 28th, one can see a distinct increase in the proportion of #hillarysemail used in tweets at 12 p.m. CST, which is 1 p.m. EST (see Fig. 2). This analysis demonstrates the advantage of using real-time Twitter data; the rise in Negative Clinton hashtags immediately after Comey's letter precedes the drop in Clinton's polling margin, which we saw a few days after the fact.

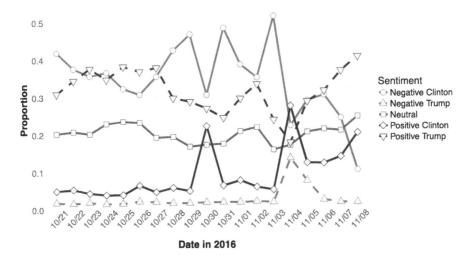

Fig. 1. Proportion of Twitter hashtag sentiments relating to 2016 US presidential election.

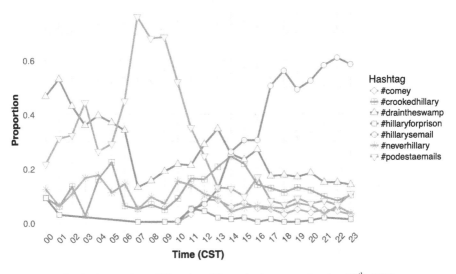

Fig. 2. Proportion of Negative Clinton hashtags on October 28th, 2016.

5.2   Spikes in Positive Clinton Hashtags

The data in Fig. 1 show two spikes in Positive Clinton hashtags on October 30th and November 4th. Part of the increase in Positive Clinton hashtags on October 30th appears to have been the result of a backlash against Comey's letter among Clinton supporters. There was an increase in the proportion of tweets using #gohillary hashtags on October 30th, such as "Democrats we need to go out and #vote …#GoHillary".

However, a few tweets also used the #gohillary hashtag negatively on October 30th, such as "I hope #GoHillary stays trending. Only then can people from all sides see how unfavorable @HillaryClinton is". Although #gohillary is an instinctively Positive Clinton hashtag, it appears to have been used in a negative way against Clinton too. Accordingly, the spike in Positive Clinton hashtags on October 30th appears to be an inflated figure.

Similarly, the spike in Positive Clinton hashtags on November 4th does not clearly represent an increased support for Clinton. There was a high proportion of #imwithher tweets at the beginning and end of the day. However, many tweets – mostly incomplete – looked similar to the following: "#smptweettest #ImWithHer RT : SONY SAYS IN STATEMENT - WE HAVE DECIDED NOT TO MOVE FORWARD W". A few bots appear to have generated automated tweets and were designed to support Clinton through the use of the #imwithher hashtag.

The two spikes in Positive Clinton hashtags shown in Fig. 1 therefore do not appear to be meaningful. The proportion of Negative Clinton hashtags on those two days should have been higher than what is shown in Fig. 1. This analysis further demonstrates the enduring and negative effect of Comey's letter on Twitter users' attitudes toward Clinton, which is also reflected in a drop in Clinton's popular vote margin as seen in the polls. It is also important to note that data shown in Fig. 1 are proportions. The two spikes in Positive Clinton hashtags drive the volatility in the proportion of Negative Clinton hashtags, which would otherwise have remained high, during the October 28th – November 4th period.

5.3   Clinton's Email Saga Was Top-of-Mind

Finally, examining the top three trending hashtags for each day for the short period leading up to the election suggests that Hilary's email saga was consistently lingering at the forefront of people's minds. #podestaemails was one of the top three hashtags used every day during the 19-day period, except on election day (see Fig. 3).

In addition, #hillarysemail was one of the top three hashtags used on both October 28th and 29th. Since Twitter users were already condemning Clinton about #podestaemails at least one week before Comey's letter, the news about additional emails linked to Clinton provided additional fodder to criticize her. The combined effects of #podestaemails and #hillarysemail on October 28th resulted in an increase in Negative Clinton hashtags, as mentioned earlier. This is consistent with a sudden drop in Clinton's popular vote margin, as reported in the polls.

Although trending Twitter hashtags could be a reflection of news media coverage, the amount of coverage about Clinton's emails is noteworthy in and of itself. Clinton's emails and Comey's letter were the headline stories between October 28th and November 4th [9], which supports Galtung and Ruge's [4] theory that the more negative an event, the higher likelihood that it will become a news item. Such extensive news coverage about Clinton generated and sustained a negative spotlight on her heading into election day. This observation lends further support to Clinton and Silver's claim that the Comey letter was a decisive factor in shaping the election outcome.

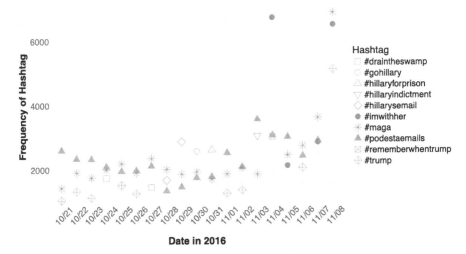

Fig. 3. Frequency of top 3 hashtags relating to the 2016 US presidential election, per day.

5.4 Limitation

A key limitation in this study is that Twitter accounts may be controlled by bots rather than humans. This issue becomes particularly pernicious if and when bots are designed to tweet hundreds of automated negative or positive messages about a candidate, which appears to be the case on November 4th. Twitter bots could thus either over- or under-estimate the sentiments of tweets, which could affect the accuracy of Twitter hashtag analysis, as well as general lexicon-based sentiment analysis. Therefore, there is a pressing need for future research to examine the effect of Twitter bots on sentiment analysis.

6 Conclusion

Overall, trending Twitter hashtags show generally similar patterns to trends revealed by the polls in the period leading up to the 2016 US presidential election. An analysis of hashtag sentiments, for the October 21st – November 8th period, suggests that Comey's letter had a significant negative effect on Twitter users' opinion of Clinton, which is consistent with a consequent drop in her polling margin. More importantly, making use of Twitter hashtags, we are able to pinpoint the precise moment on October 28th when the proportion of Negative Clinton hashtags started to increase. In comparison, polls took a few days to show a drop in Clinton's margin after Comey's letter was released.

Twitter hashtags offer a different means to gauge people's views on topics and issues. Although there are a few caveats in using Twitter to measure public opinion, Twitter hashtags provide real-time data about (i) changes in Twitter users' attitudes toward specific topics, and (ii) what lies at the forefront of people's minds. This analysis extends from previous studies by showing the extent to which Twitter hashtag analysis could be considered as a promising tool, in addition to polls, natural language processing or lexicon-based scoring methods, to monitor public sentiment.

References

1. Andrews, W., Katz, J., Patel, J.: Latest Election Polls 2016. The New York Times (2016). https://www.nytimes.com/interactive/2016/us/elections/polls.html?_r=0%29. Accessed 23 July 2018
2. Ceron, A., Curini, L., Lacus, S.M., Porro, G.: Every tweet counts? How sentiment analysis of social media can improve our knowledge of citizens' political preferences with an application to Italy and France. New Media Soc. **16**(2), 340–358 (2014)
3. Chung, J., Mustafaraj, E.: Can collective sentiment expressed on twitter predict political elections? In: Proceedings of the Twenty-Fifth AAAI Conference on Artificial Intelligence, pp. 1770–1771. AAAI Press, Menlo Park (2011)
4. Galtung, J., Ruge, M.H.: The structure of foreign news. J. Peace Res. **2**(1), 64–91 (1965)
5. O'Connor, B., Balasubramanyan R., Routledge, B.R., Smith N.A.: From tweets to polls: linking text sentiment to public opinion time series. In: Proceedings of the Fourth International AAAI Conference on Weblogs and Social Media, pp. 122–129. AAAI Press, Menlo Park (2010)
6. Shaban, T.A., Hexter, L., Choi, J.D.: Event analysis on the 2016 U.S. Presidential election using social media. In: Ciampaglia, G.L., Mashhadi, A., Yasseri, T. (eds.) SocInfo 2017. LNCS, vol. 10539, pp. 201–217. Springer, Cham (2017). https://doi.org/10.1007/978-3-319-67217-5_13
7. Silver, N.: Election update: the how-full-is-this-glass edition. FiveThirtyEight (2017). http://fivethirtyeight.com/features/election-update-the-how-full-is-this-glass-election/. Accessed 23 July 2018
8. Silver, N.: The real story of 2016. FiveThirtyEight (2017). http://fivethirtyeight.com/features/the-real-story-of-2016/. Accessed 23 July 2018
9. Silver, N.: The Comey letter probably cost clinton the election. FiveThirtyEight (2017). https://fivethirtyeight.com/features/the-comey-letter-probably-cost-clinton-the-election/. Accessed 23 July 2018
10. Tumasjan, A., Sprenger, T.O., Sandner, P.G., Welpe, I.M.: Predicting elections with Twitter: what 140 characters reveal about political sentiment. In: Proceedings of the Fourth International AAAI Conference on Weblogs and Social Media, pp. 178–185. AAAI Press, Menlo Park (2010)

Text-Based Detection and Understanding of Changes in Mental Health

Yaoyiran Li$^{(\boxtimes)}$ ⓘ, Rada Mihalcea$^{(\boxtimes)}$, and Steven R. Wilson

University of Michigan, Ann Arbor, MI, USA
{yaoyiran,mihalcea,steverw}@umich.edu

Abstract. Previous work has investigated the identification of mental health issues in social media users, yet the way that users' mental states and related behavior change over time remains relatively understudied. This paper focuses on online mental health communities and studies how users' contributions to these communities change over one year. We define a metric called the Mental Health Contribution Index (MHCI), which we use to measure the degree to which users' contributions to mental health topics change over a one-year period. In this work, we study the relationship between MHCI scores and the online expression of mental health symptoms by extracting relevant linguistic features from user-generated content and conducting statistical analyses. Additionally, we build a classifier to predict whether or not a user's contributions to mental health subreddits will increase or decrease. Finally, we employ propensity score matching to identify factors that correlate with an increase or a decrease in mental health forum contributions. Our work provides some of the first insights into detecting and understanding social media users' changes in mental health states over time.

Keywords: Natural language processing · Mental health
Social media

1 Introduction and Related Work

Mental health issues pose a major challenge for modern society [5,6,23] and early detection and intervention are fundamental to preventing the progression of mental illnesses [1,26,27,32,38,49,55]. To aid the work already being done by medical practitioners, social media data are increasingly being used to analyze and predict mental illnesses [3,14,15,22,28,31,39,42,43]. As much of the data shared by users on social media is unstructured text, language attributes have proven to be effective features for the analysis and prediction of mental health states of social media users [2,11,13,35,37,40,51]. In this paper, we focus on the discussion website, Reddit[1], where user-generated content is organized into topical, user-created boards called "subreddits". Previous work has studied

---

[1] http://www.reddit.com.

S. Staab et al. (Eds.): SocInfo 2018, LNCS 11186, pp. 176–188, 2018.
https://doi.org/10.1007/978-3-030-01159-8_17

mental health-related (MH) subreddits in terms of self-disclosure, social support and anonymity [22,43]. Prior work has also focused on both the detection and prediction of mental health problems using social media data [17,19,40,51]. Our work, however, focuses on the changes of individuals' mental states with the aim to address the following two tasks: (1) to build a classification system that is able to predict changes in the level of user interaction with online MH communities, and (2) to discover the underlying factors that correlate with those changes. While we would ideally like to track individuals' true mental states over time, this information is difficult to obtain directly. Therefore, in this work, we focus directly on the change in users' contributions to online MH communities as measured by the number of posts that these users contribute to MH subreddits. We show that this measure is, in fact, significantly related to different linguistic expressions of MH symptoms, and should serve as a beneficial index to consider in the study of MH discussions in online communities.

We collect users from MH subreddits and define a Mental Health Contribution Index (MHCI) to separate users into three categories: those who make more, less, or about the same number of contributions to MH subreddits in the second half of a given year (between 2017-03-01 and 2017-09-01) compared with those in the first half of that year (between 2016-09-01 and 2017-03-01). Here the term *contribution* means the number of posts contributed to target subreddits. When deciding the length of the time period, we follow the approach taken in previous work [18–21,35]. For the users in our study, we seek to address three research questions:

- **RQ1.** How do users, grouped by their MHCI scores, express different symptoms of MH problems throughout the year in general?
- **RQ2.** Can we build a classifier to predict if a user's contributions to MH subreddits will increase or decrease during the second half of the year?
- **RQ3.** What factors from the first six months correlate with either an increase or a decrease in MH contributions in the second half of the year?

2 Data Collection and Annotation

We crawl our data through the Python Reddit API PRAW[2] and annotate the data produced by a set of redditors (users of the Reddit site). The process consists of the following steps: (1) Identify MH subreddits and redditors; (2) Define a Mental Health Contribution Index (MHCI) based on posting and commenting actions; and (3) Filter target redditors according to their MHCI scores.

We start with fifteen well-studied MH subreddits reported in [21], from which we crawl posts and information about the users who wrote them. The subreddits used in our study are: r/depression, r/SuicideWatch, r/socialanxiety, r/mentalhealth, r/BPD, r/ptsd, r/bipolarreddit, r/rapecounseling, r/StopSelfHarm, r/survivorofabuse, r/EatingDisorders, r/hardshipmates, r/panicparty, r/psychoticreddit and r/traumatoolbox. As done in previous work [21,22,43],

---

[2] https://praw.readthedocs.io/en/latest/.

we do *not* assume that every user found on these subreddits is an active mental health patient. We conducted the crawl on 2017-09-01, collecting data from the past year, so that time span of our data is from 2016-09-01 to 2017-09-01. We crawl all the authors of posts found on these subreddits in the given time span. After removing moderators and suspended users, we are left with a final set of 53,416 unique users.

Next, we define the Mental Health Contribution Index (MHCI) which measures the change in contributions to MH subreddits against Non-MH subreddits for a given redditor between two 6-month time periods. The *contribution* to MH subreddits is defined as the total number of posts contributed in these subreddits, which is regarded as a reflection of the attention paid to MH topics, or the extent to which the user may resort to help and exchange ideas with others. First, we define t_1 as the time period between 2016-09-01 and 2017-03-01; t_2 as the time period between 2017-03-01 and 2017-09-01; m_i^r as the number of posts contributed to MH subreddits in $t_i, i = 1, 2$ for a redditor r; and n_i^r as the number of posts contributed to NonMH subreddits in $t_i, i = 1, 2$ for a redditor r. We then define the MHCI score for a redditor r as follows:

$$MHCI(r) = \alpha \frac{m_2^r + 1}{m_1^r + 1} + \beta \frac{(m_2^r + 1)(n_1^r + 1)}{(m_1^r + 1)(n_2^r + 1)} \tag{1}$$

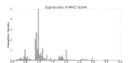

Fig. 1. Distribution of MHCI score in 53,416 redditors.

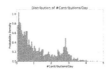

Fig. 2. Distribution of number of contributions per day over 1,767 redditors.

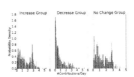

Fig. 3. Distribution of number of contributions per day over three types of users respectively.

The MHCI score is a weighted sum of the ratio between absolute MH contributions and the ratio between relative MH contributions in t_1 and t_2. We also introduce a score, $MHCI'(r)$, that is the same as $MHCI(r)$, but it includes the number of total posts *plus comments* (rather than only posts). The distribution of the MHCI score for all 53,416 redditors is shown in Fig. 1. The criteria we adopt to filter users with increased, decreased and no change in contributions to MH subreddits are as follows:

increase group: $MHCI(r) > 2.5, MHCI'(r) > 5$

decrease group: $MHCI(r) < 0.4, MHCI'(r) < 0.2$

no change group: $0.9 < MHCI(r) < 1.1, 0.75 < MHCI'(r) < 1.25$

We exclude all samples in "gray zones" (e.g. $0.4 < MHCI(r) < 0.9$) to reduce the risk of misclassification [16,19,33,47,52]. For filtered users, annotators are asked to manually look into all their posts and comments. Only users with self-reported diagnoses of MH problems are kept [12,13]. Other users who provide help, seek support for helping other people instead of themselves, distribute questionnaires for study and do not reveal their own MH states are ruled out. Based on the criteria above, we derive 641 redditors in the *increase* group, 758 redditors in the *decrease* group, and 368 redditors in the *no change* group; these 1,767 redditors form our final dataset which contains 113,630 posts and 692,203 comments where 13,162 posts and 66,961 comments are from MH subreddits and the rest are from Non-MH subreddits. Figures 2 and 3 show the activity of our redittors. We identify 703 subreddits that were contributed to by at least 12 of our 1,767 redditors in the first half-year, which we will use to answer RQ3. We anonymized our data and all individuals who participated in our project, including annotators, strictly follow the ethical guidelines as suggested in previous work [4,30].

3 RQ1: Changes of MH Symptoms

3.1 Method

In this section, we measure the differences in language use between the *increase* group and the *decrease* group over the time span of one year. We calculate the frequencies of using words belonging to different semantic categories in the Linguistic Inquiry and Word Count (LIWC) [45] lexicon during the year and conduct Welch's t-test to measure if there is a significant change in the usage of words from these categories. In our calculation, a positive t-stat represents the increased use of a semantic category, and a negative t-stat represents decreased use. We point out known MH symptoms as linguistic features and analyze the way that those symptoms change over the year.

3.2 Results and Analysis

Previous work suggests that some certain linguistic features extracted from social media users can be viewed as symptoms of mental disorders [18,19,24] and this fact is also supported by research in psychiatry [1,26,49]. Compared with control group, individuals with mental issues show more frequent use of categories such as 'negative emotion', '1st person singular pronouns', 'negate' and less frequent use of categories such as 'positive emotion', '3rd person singular pronouns' and '1st person plural pronouns'. Our results in Tables 1 and 2 show that, in general, high MHCI users express increased MH symptoms and low MHCI users express decreased MH symptoms in second half of the year:

Emotional Symptoms. High MHCI users show increased use of 'negative emotion', 'sad' and 'anxiety' categories and decreased use of 'leisure' and 'positive emotion' categories. However, low MHCI users exhibit the opposite trend.

Table 1. Welch's t-test results between contents of two six-month periods for *increase* group users (with high MHCI scores). The significance levels are $\alpha = 0.05/M(*)$, $0.01/M(**)$, $0.001/M(***)$. $M = 60$ is adopted for Bonferroni correction.

Category	Time period 1	Time period 2	t-stat	p
negate	0.0223	0.0242	21.569	***
death	0.0022	0.0024	6.420	***
health	0.0079	0.0100	39.353	***
affect	0.0633	0.0662	19.994	***
leisure	0.0128	0.0116	−18.577	***
interrogative	0.0174	0.0176	3.001	-
adverb	0.0618	0.0640	20.505	***
conjunction	0.0703	0.0721	11.791	***
pronoun	0.1685	0.1779	42.618	***
verb	0.1827	0.1901	32.261	***
1st person singular	0.0595	0.0651	39.597	***
1st person plural	0.0051	0.0047	−10.564	***
2nd person	0.0202	0.0217	17.077	***
3rd person singular	0.0131	0.0126	−7.080	***
positive emotion	0.0368	0.0365	−2.795	-
negative emotion	0.0258	0.0287	30.963	***
sad	0.0046	0.0058	28.839	***
anxiety	0.0037	0.0046	23.795	***

Table 2. Welch's t-test results between contents of two six-month periods for *decrease* group users (with low MHCI scores). The significance levels are $\alpha = 0.05/M(*)$, $0.01/M(**)$, $0.001/M(***)$. $M = 60$ is adopted for Bonferroni correction.

Category	Time period 1	Time period 2	t-stat	p
negate	0.0248	0.0231	−16.581	***
death	0.0027	0.0023	−9.489	***
health	0.0110	0.0081	−44.124	***
affect	0.0691	0.0623	−28.521	***
leisure	0.0103	0.0120	22.981	***
interrogative	0.0179	0.0177	−1.748	-
adverb	0.0658	0.0619	−23.448	***
conjunction	0.0735	0.0711	−13.696	***
pronoun	0.1873	0.1687	−71.382	***
verb	0.1944	0.1833	−41.384	***
1st person singular	0.0739	0.0573	−99.840	***
1st person plural	0.0047	0.0055	20.309	***
2nd person	0.0217	0.0197	−20.652	***
3rd person singular	0.0120	0.0123	3.634	**
positive emotion	0.0364	0.0366	1.747	-
negative emotion	0.0317	0.0269	−41.996	***
sad	0.0077	0.0049	−54.379	***
anxiety	0.0051	0.0039	−28.349	***

Linguistic Symptoms. High MHCI users show an increased use of verbs, which is considered to positively correlate with sensitivity [29]. Increased use of '1st person singular' and decreased use of '1st person plural' and '3rd person singular pronouns' indicates that high MHCI users become more socially isolated and self-attentional in the second half of the year [8]. The opposite trend is also true for the low MHCI users.

Subjectivity Symptoms. From the 'negate' category, we observe that high MHCI users tend to express more negative opinions in the second half of the year, while low MHCI users express fewer negative opinions during the same time period.

4   RQ2: A Classification Task

4.1   Method

In this section, we propose an initial framework for a classification task between high and low MHCI users based on only the texts that these users have written. The training and test data consists of all posts and comments contributed by the 641 users from the *increase* group and 758 users from the *decrease* group during t_1 and t_2. For each user, we extract features v_1 and v_2 from raw texts contributed during t_1 and t_2 respectively. Then, $v_2 - v_1$, which is expected to capture information on changes of language style for a user between the two halves of the year, serves as an input to a classifier. The output is binary variable representing whether or not a user's MH contributions increase or decrease in t_2 compared with t_1.

There are four types of features adopted in our work: Average Word2Vec, Average GloVe, Doc2Vec and LIWC. Although Word2Vec and GloVe provide pre-trained word embeddings, we train Word2Vec, GloVe and Doc2Vec embeddings from scratch on our data because of the uniqueness of our corpus. Here we introduce our features briefly:

Average Word2Vec. We use the Continuous Bag-of-Words Model (CBOW) to train 300-dimensional word embeddings which uses a neural network [36] with negative sampling [34]. We set the window size to 5 and the initial learning rate to 0.025. Then, for each user, we average together all word embeddings to produce a single feature vector for each of t_1 and t_2 to produce v_1 and v_2.

Average GloVe. We also train 300-dimensional GloVe word embeddings which are based on global word-word co-occurrence statistics [46]. The window size is set as 15 and the initial learning rate is set as 0.05. For each user, v_1 and v_2 are derived by averaging together all word embeddings in t_1 and t_2 respectively.

Doc2Vec. We implement Distributed Memory Model with Paragraph Vectors (PV-DM) [34] for training document embeddings with a window size of 10 and an initial learning rate of 0.025. For each user, the model will directly output 300-dimensional feature vectors, v_1 and v_2, that summarize all the user's posts and comments in t_1 and t_2, respectively.

LIWC. We use all semantic categories in the LIWC lexicon [45]. For each user, we count frequencies of use of those categories in t_1 and t_2 and derive v_1 and v_2.

We adopt Logistic Regression (LR), Support Vector Machine (SVM) and a custom Neural Network (NN) with two hidden layers of size 100 and 20 as our classifiers, and they are implemented through SciKit-learn package [44].

4.2 Results and Analysis

We evaluate our models with 10-fold cross validation, and report the average accuracy, precision, recall, f1-score and their 95% confidence interval of the score estimate (i.e. 2 times standard deviation) in Table 3. When using a single-source feature, we find that averaged word embeddings can capture the changes of mental states to some extent, but they are inferior to using LIWC categories. Doc2Vec, however, beats LIWC in accuracy, recall and f1-score. When we combine Doc2Vec with LIWC, however, the performance increases even further for all metrics when using the neural network classifier.

Table 3. Classification results with 10-fold cross-validation. We report here the average accuracy, precision, recall, f1-score and their 95% confidence interval of the score estimate (i.e. 2 times standard deviation).

Feature and classifier	Accuracy	Precision	Recall	F1-score
Word2Vec+LR	0.7713 (±0.0662)	0.7542 (±0.0758)	0.7442 (±0.0986)	0.7485 (±0.0760)
Word2Vec+SVM	0.7820 (±0.0688)	0.7521 (±0.0760)	0.7831 (±0.0911)	0.7668 (±0.0747)
Word2Vec+NN	0.7649 (±0.0842)	0.7454 (±0.0946)	0.7457 (±0.1500)	0.7395 (±0.1095)
GloVe+LR	0.7756 (±0.0672)	0.7638 (±0.1046)	0.7442 (±0.0584)	0.7530 (±0.0655)
GloVe+SVM	0.7692 (±0.0586)	0.7485 (±0.0822)	0.7505 (±0.0658)	0.7489 (±0.0608)
GloVe+NN	0.7527 (±0.0747)	0.7436 (±0.0907)	0.7209 (±0.1167)	0.7269 (±0.0877)
LIWC+LR	0.8142 (±0.0412)	0.7941 (±0.0605)	0.8066 (±0.1327)	0.7980 (±0.0574)
LIWC+SVM	0.8185 (±0.0491)	0.8052 (±0.0584)	0.7989 (±0.1219)	0.8004 (±0.0631)
LIWC+NN	0.8235 (±0.0419)	**0.8170 (±0.0639)**	0.8238 (±0.1066)	0.8143 (±0.0774)
Doc2Vec+LR	0.8234 (±0.0668)	0.8107 (±0.0610)	0.8019 (±0.1187)	0.8054 (±0.0803)
Doc2Vec+SVM	0.8113 (±0.0350)	0.7955 (±0.0399)	0.7925 (±0.0769)	0.7934 (±0.0446)
Doc2Vec+NN	**0.8241 (±0.0377)**	0.8088 (±0.0563)	**0.8268 (±0.0691)**	**0.8181 (±0.0342)**
Doc2Vec+LIWC+LR	0.8392 (±0.0610)	0.8284 (±0.0733)	0.8207 (±0.1025)	0.8235 (±0.0699)
Doc2Vec+LIWC+SVM	0.8306 (±0.0666)	0.8104 (±0.0689)	0.8238 (±0.1060)	0.8163 (±0.0758)
Doc2Vec+LIWC+NN	**0.8614 (±0.0535)**	**0.8587 (±0.0544)**	**0.8519 (±0.0763)**	**0.8558 (±0.0333)**

5   RQ3: Factors Correlate with Changes in MH Contributions

5.1   Method

In this section, we borrow the propensity score matching (PSM) method from the study of causal inference to find if contributions to certain subreddits in t_1 correlate with increased (high MHCI) or decreased (low MHCI) contributions to MH subreddits in t_2. PSM aims to isolate the effect of other observable covariates known as confounding variables [7,9,10] and thus PSM may be preferable to traditional statistical approaches like regression models which can give rise to confounding effects [20,21]. In our case, for each subreddit, we form pairs of users having similar *probabilities of contributing* to the subreddit, but *only one user in each pair actually contributed*. Then we conduct Welch's t-test to measure if the subreddit may have an effect on those users. Our dataset includes $n = 1,767$ users and $m = 703$ treatments (subreddits). Confounding variables are unigram features for every user, X_i, $i = 1$ to n. $T_{j,i}$, $j = 1$ to m (binary), represents if user i received treatment j. A Propensity Score is defined as the probability of receiving treatment j given a confounding variable, $P_j(X_i) = Prob(T_{j,i} = 1|X_i)$, $\forall i$, which is fitted with logistic regression model [44]. User labels are denoted as Y_i, $i = 1$ to n. Then our algorithm is summarized in Algorithm 1:

Algorithm 1. Measuring the effects of treatments on MHCI

Require: $X_i, Y_i, T_{j,i}, i = 1$ to $n, j = 1$ to m

   for $j = 1$ **to** m **do**

      step 1: Split data into a training set and a test set.

      step 2: Fit $model_j$ to the training data.

      step 3: Form treatment group and control group in test set based on Propensity Score Matching.

      step 4: Conduct Welch's t-test on treatment and control groups.

   end for

   return t-stats for all m treatments

5.2   Results and Analysis

Tables 4 and 5 show the top 15 treatments that correlate with an increase in MH contributions and ones that correlate with a decrease in MH contributions, respectively. Our analysis will pay more attention to treatments that correlate with decreased MH contributions since their t-stats are relatively higher. We then discuss the results in the following aspects:

Support Communities. Support communities are shown to correlate with decreased MH contributions in t_2 which are shown to be correlated with reduced MH symptoms in RQ1. MH support subreddits include 'r/depression', 'r/BipolarReddit', 'r/SuicideWatch', 'r/bipolar', 'r/mentalhealth',

Table 4. Top 15 treatments that correlate with an increase in MH contributions.

Treatment	t-stat
r/WikiLeaks	3.464
r/vancouver	3.464
r/trypophobia	2.752
r/Marijuana	2.738
r/Ask_Politics	2.449
r/cordcutters	2.449
r/piercing	2.291
r/cars	2.254
r/announcements	2.190
r/MeanJokes	2.038
r/AskUK	2.070
r/Bandnames	2.000
r/solotravel	2.000
r/whatisthisthing	1.981
r/Bitcoin	1.951

Table 5. Top 15 treatments that correlate with a decrease in MH contributions.

Treatment	t-stat
r/depression	14.191
r/BipolarReddit	5.740
r/SuicideWatch	5.554
r/StopGaming	4.472
r/bipolar	4.354
r/pics	4.157
r/mentalhealth	4.057
r/pornfree	3.464
r/rapecounseling	3.314
r/baseball	3.162
r/socialanxiety	3.004
r/comics	2.758
r/LongDistance	2.738
r/Rateme	2.662
r/BPD	2.660

'r/socialanxiety' and 'r/BPD' (Borderline Personality Disorder). Recent work shows the reciprocity between social media users who disclose their own MH issues and their online audience, which is consistent with our findings [25,53]. Other support communities include 'r/rapecounseling' (help with sexualized violence), 'r/StopGaming' (help with video game addiction) and 'r/pornfree' (help with addiction to porn).

Interesting Pictures, Comics and Memes. Some subreddits focus on sharing images, captioned photos etc. that are intended to be funny. This category includes 'r/pics' and 'r/comics' and both correlate with decreased MH contributions in t_2.

Story Sharing and Friend Making. These subreddits correlate with decreased MH contributions. 'r/LongDistance' is a subreddit to share stories about long-distance relationships and 'r/Rateme' for users to rate everyone else. As a support, psychological research shows that social interaction is helpful to reduce stress [41].

Politics. There are two subreddits related to politics in Tables 4 and 5. They are 'r/WikiLeaks' and 'r/Ask_Politics', and both correlate with increased MH contributions in t_2.

Other Subreddits. 'r/baseball' correlates with reduced MH contributions in t_2. 'r/Marijuana', 'r/trypophobia' (a community for those with a common fear of irregular clusters of holes or bumps found in the world) and 'r/piercing' (for discussion of various body piercings and jewelry) correlate with increased MH contributions. Some support for these findings can be found in psychological research on sports [48], drug use [50] and body piercing [54].

Our findings may provide some insights on what factors may influence individual's mental health. Those factors mainly include discussions in certain subreddits like 'r/Rateme'. Currently, we cannot make any claim on if engagement in a certain subeddit has a causal relationship with mental health, but we still deem it valuable for mental health researchers to investigate promising correlations such as those that we have discovered in this work.

6   Conclusion

This paper provides some insights into detecting and understanding changes in contributions to online mental health communities over time. We propose the MHCI index and filter users whose contributions to MH subreddits increase, decrease and stay about the same over two consecutive six-month periods. Our findings show that increased MH contributions correlate with increased MH linguistic symptoms while decreased MH contributions generally show the opposite trend. Further, we propose a framework for building classifiers to distinguish between high and low MHCI redditors and demonstrate the effectiveness of word embeddings and document embeddings in this task. Our work also reveals the underlying correlation between users' engagement in discussions in different subreddits and changes in those users' MH contributions over time.

Acknowledgement. We thank all anonymous reviewers for their constructive suggestions on our work. We also thank Dr. Márcio Duarte Albasini Mourão for helpful discussions with us on RQ1. This work is partly supported by the Michigan Institute for Data Science, by the National Science Foundation under grant #1344257 and by the John Templeton Foundation under grant #48503.

References

1. Abdel-Khalek, A.M.: Can somatic symptoms predict depression? Soc. Behav. Pers. Int. J. **32**(7), 657–666 (2004)
2. Amir, S., Coppersmith, G., Carvalho, P., et al.: Quantifying mental health from social media with neural user embeddings. In: Proceedings of Machine Learning for Healthcare 2017 (2017)
3. Benton, A., Mitchell, M., Harman, C.: Multitask learning for mental health conditions with limited social media data. In: Proceedings of the 15th Conference of the European Chapter of the Association for Computational Linguistics (2017)
4. Benton, A., Coppersmith, G., Dredze, M.: Ethical research protocols for social media health research. In: Proceedings of the First Workshop on Ethics in Natural Language Processing (2017)
5. Bijl, R., De Graaf, R., et al.: The prevalence of treated and untreated mental disorders in five countries. Health Aff. (Millwood) **22**, 122–133 (2003)
6. Bloom, D., et al.: The global economic burden of non-communicable diseases. In: Geneva: World Economic Forum, Geneva (2011)
7. Blundell, R., et al.: Alternative approaches to evaluation in empirical microeconomics. Port. Econ. J. **1**, 91–115 (2002)
8. Boals, A., Klein, K.: Word use in emotional narratives about failed romantic relationships and subsequent mental health. J. Lang. Soc. Psychol. **24**, 252–268 (2005)
9. Caliendo, M., Kopeinig, S.: Some practical guidance for the implementation of propensity score matching. J. Econ. Surv. **22**(1), 31–72 (2008)
10. Caliendo, M., et al.: The microeconometric estimation of treatment effects-an overview. Working Paper, J.W. Goethe University of Frankfurt (2005)
11. Chancellor, S., Lin, Z., Goodman, E.L., Zerwas, S., De Choudhury, M.: Quantifying and predicting mental illness severity in online pro-eating disorder communities. In: Proceedings of The 19th ACM Conference on Computer-Supported Cooperative Work and Social Computing (2016)
12. Coppersmith, G., Dredze, M., Harman, C., Hollingshead, K.: From ADHD to SAD: analyzing the language of mental health on Twitter through self-reported diagnoses. In: Proceedings of the 2nd Workshop on Computational Linguistics and Clinical Psychology: From Linguistic Signal to Clinical Reality (2015)
13. Coppersmith, G., Harman, C., Dredze, M.: Measuring post traumatic stress disorder in Twitter. In: Proceedings of the 8th International AAAI Conference on Weblogs and Social Media (ICWSM 2014) (2014)
14. Coppersmith, G., Dredze, M., Harman, C.: Quantifying mental health signals in Twitter. In: ACL Workshop on Computational Linguistics and Clinical Psychology (2014)
15. Corrigan, P.: How stigma interferes with mental health care. Am. Psychol. **59**(7), 614–625 (2004)
16. Coste, J., Pouchot, J.: A grey zone for quantitative diagnostic and screening tests. Int. J. Epidemiol. **32**(2), 304–13 (2003)

17. De Choudhury, M., Counts, S., Horvitz, E.: Predicting postpartum changes in emotion and behavior via social media. In: Proceedings of the 2013 ACM Annual Conference on Human Factors in Computing Systems (2013)

18. De Choudhury, M., Counts, S., Horvitz, E., Hoff, A.: Characterizing and predicting postpartum depression from Facebook data. In: Proceedings of the 17th ACM Conference on Computer Supported Cooperative Work and Social Computing (2014)

19. De Choudhury, M., Gamon, M., Counts, S., Horvitz, E.: Predicting depression via social media. In: AAAI Conference on Weblogs and Social Media (2013)

20. De Choudhury, M., Kiciman, E.: The language of social support in social media and its effect on suicidal ideation risk. In: Proceedings of the 11th International AAAI Conference on Web and Social Media (ICWSM 2017) (2017)

21. De Choudhury, M., Kiciman, E., Dredze, M., Coppersmith, G., Kumar, M.: Discovering shifts to suicidal ideation from mental health content in social media. In: Proceedings of the 2016 CHI Conference on Human Factors in Computing Systems, San Jose, California, USA, 07–12 May 2016 (2016)

22. De Choudury, M., De, S.: Mental health discourse on reddit: self-disclosure, social support, and anonymity. In: Proceedings of the 8th International AAAI Conference on Weblogs and Social Media (ICWSM 2014), Ann Arbor, MI, 2–4 June 2014 (2014)

23. Demyttenaere, K., Bruffaerts, R., Posada-Villa, J., et al.: Prevalence, severity, and unmet need for treatment of mental disorders in the world health organization world mental health surveys. J. Am. Med. Assoc. JAMA **291**(21), 2581–2590 (2004)

24. Ernala, S.K., Rizvi, A.F., et al.: Linguistic markers indicating therapeutic outcomes of social media disclosures of schizophrenia. In: Proceedings of the ACM Human-Computer Interaction, CSCW Online First (2018)

25. Ernala, S.K., Birnbaum, M., Rizvi, A., Kane, J., De Choudhury, M.: Characterizing audience engagement and assessing its impact on social media disclosures of mental illnesses. In: Proceedings of the 12th International AAAI Conference on Web and Social Media (2018)

26. Etkin, A., Wager, T.D.: Functional neuroimaging of anxiety: a meta-analysis of emotional processing in PTSD, social anxiety disorder, and specific phobia. Am. J. Psychiatry **164**(10), 1476–1488 (2007)

27. Field, T.A., Beeson, E., Jones, L.: The new ABCs: a practitioner's guide to neuroscience-informed cognitive-behavior therapy. J. Ment. Health Couns. **37**(3), 206220 (2015)

28. Goffman, E.: Stigma: Notes on the Management of Spoiled Identity. Prentice-Hall, Englewood Cliffs (1963)

29. Houghton, D., Joinson, A.: Linguistic markers of secrets and sensitive self-disclosure in Twitter. In: 2012 45th Hawaii International Conference on System Sciences (HICSS), pp. 3480–3489 (2012)

30. Hovy, D., Spruit, S.L.: The social impact of natural language processing. In: Proceedings of the 54th Annual Meeting of the Association for Computational Linguistics (2016)

31. Johnson, G., Ambrose, P.: Neo-tribes: the power and potential of online communities in health care. Commun. ACM **49**(1), 107–113 (2006)

32. Kessler, R., Price, R.: Primary prevention of secondary disorders: a proposal and agenda. Am. J. Community Psychol. **21**(5), 607–633 (1993)

33. Kroenke, K., Spitzer, R., Williams, J.: The PHQ-9: validity of a brief depression severity measure. J. Gen. Intern. Med. **16**(9), 606 (2001)

34. Le, Q., Mikolov, T.: Distributed representations of sentences and documents. In: Proceedings of the 31st International Conference on Machine Learning (2014)

35. Loveys, K., Crutchley, P., Wyatt, E., Coppersmith, G.: Small but mighty: affective micropatterns for quantifying mental health from social media language. In: Proceedings of the Fourth Workshop on Computational Linguistics and Clinical Psychology (2017)
36. Mikolov, T., Chen, K., Corrado, G., Dean, J.: Efficient estimation of word representations in vector space. In: ICLR Workshop Papers (2013)
37. Mitchell, M., Hollingshead, K., Coppersmith, G.: Quantifying the language of schizophrenia in social media. In: Proceedings of the 2nd Workshop on Computational Linguistics and Clinical Psychology: From Linguistic Signal to Clinical Reality (2015)
38. Mrazek, P., Haggerty, R.: Reducing Risks for Mental Disorders: Frontiers for Preventive Intervention Research. National Academies Press, Washington, DC (1994)
39. Nelson, B., McGorry, P.D., Wichers, M., Wigman, J.T.W., Hartmann, J.A.: Moving from static to dynamic models of the onset of mental disorder: a review. JAMA Psychiatry **74**(5), 528534 (2017)
40. Nguyen, T., Phung, D., Dao, B., Venkatesh, S., Berk, M.: Affective and content analysis of online depression communities. IEEE Trans. Affect. Comput. **5**(3), 217226 (2014)
41. Ono, E., et al.: Relationship between social interaction and mental health. In: IEEE/SICE International Symposium on System Integration (SII) (2011)
42. Park, M., McDonald, D.W., Cha, M.: Perception differences between the depressed and non-depressed users in Twitter. In: Proceedings of the 7th International AAAI Conference on Weblogs and Social Media (ICWSM 2013) (2013)
43. Pavalanathan, U., De Choudhury, M.: Identity management and mental health discourse on social media. In: Proceedings of WWW 2015 Companion: 24th International World Wide Web Conference, Web Science Track, Florence, Italy, 18–22 May 2015 (2015)
44. Pedregosa, F., Varoquaux, G., Gramfort, A., Michel, V., Thirion, B., et al.: Scikit-learn: machine learning in Python. J. Mach. Learn. Res. **12**, 2825–2830 (2011)
45. Pennebaker, J.W., Boyd, R.L., Jordan, K., Blackburn, K.: The development and psychometric properties of LIWC2015 (2015)
46. Pennington, J., Socher, R., Manning, C.D.: Glove: global vectors for word representation. In: Proceedings of the 2014 Conference on Empirical Methods in Natural Language Processing (EMNLP) (2014)
47. Radloff, L.: The ces-d scale: a self-report depression scale for research in the general population. Appl. Psychol. Meas. **1**, 385–401 (1977)
48. Raglin, J.: Exercise and mental health.beneficial and detrimental effects. Sport. Med. **9**, 323329 (1990)
49. Robinson, M.S., Alloy, L.B.: Negative cognitive styles and stress-reactive rumination interact to predict depression: a prospective study. Cogn. Ther. Res. **27**(3), 275–291 (2003)
50. Shedler, J., Block, J.: Adolescent drug use and psychological health: a longitudinal inquiry. Am. Psychol. **45**(5), 612–630 (1990)
51. Shen, J., Rudzicz, F.: Detecting anxiety on reddit. In: Proceedings of the Fourth Workshop on Computational Linguistics and Clinical Psychology (2017)
52. Sox, H., Blatt, M., Hinggins, M., Marton, K.: Medical Decision Making. Butterworth-Heinemann, Boston (1987)

53. Sprecher, S., Treger, S., Wondra, J.D., Hilaire, N., Wallpe, K.: Taking turns: reciprocal self-disclosure promotes liking in initial interactions. Cogn. Ther. Res. **49**(5), 860–866 (2003)
54. Stirn, A.: Body piercing: medical consequences and psychological motivations. Lancet **361**, 12051215 (2003)
55. Taylor, E.: Assessing, Diagnosing, and Treating Serious Mental Disorders: A Bioecological Approach for Social Workers. Oxford University Press, Oxford (2014)

Evaluating the Search and Rescue Strategies of Post Disaster

Qianqian Liu[1], Jianqiu Chen[2], Guoqing Peng[3(✉)],
Qian Wan[3,4], and Qiyu Liang[3,4]

[1] Guangxi University of Finance and Economics,
#100 West Mingxiu Road, Nanning, China
liuqq0312@foxmail.com
[2] Nanning University, #8 Longting Road, Yongning District, Nanning, China
[3] Guilin University of Electronic Technology,
#1 Jinji Road, Guilin 541004, China
243564846@qq.com
[4] Hualan Design and Consulting Group,
#39 Hua Dong Road, Nanning 530011, China

Abstract.

Introduction. Resource allocation is a challenging topic in the search and rescue (SAR) in post-disaster process, especially in situations with sparse infrastructure and dynamic demanding requirement. Previous studies have well demonstrated the need to improve the SAR decision-making process in these situations. However, a challenge that current models are facing is how to select target areas considering the random distribution of survivors with little information or coordination.

Method. This paper makes a first attempt to compare the different models in SAR process, where SAR teams are supposed to operate independently or are dispatched by a central system. The paper uses the dynamic network models, which can avoid the shortcoming of normal random search, for SAR strategy analyses.

Results. The numerical example shows that when information is uncertain, central dispatch easily leads to low efficiency in SAR management. Besides, quantity priority is proved to be more efficient than normal random search, especially when the distribution of survivors is not even.

Conclusion. The findings of this paper provide important information for selecting effective analytical models in SAR management to save survivors.

Keywords: Search and rescue · Strategy · Network model
Information requirement · Efficiency · Equity

© Springer Nature Switzerland AG 2018
S. Staab et al. (Eds.): SocInfo 2018, LNCS 11186, pp. 189–201, 2018.
https://doi.org/10.1007/978-3-030-01159-8_18

1   Introduction

The main objective of post-disaster search and rescue (SAR) is to "find, locate and rescue most survivors in shortest time". Instantaneous information with data analysis and processing can provide effective support for decision-making in SAR process. However, information in most cases is not timely and accurate enough to support the SAR efforts, and SAR teams have to cruise for searching survivors. Recent researches about SAR are mainly focusing on emergency decision making (Janis and Mann 1977; Danielsson and Ohlsson 1999; Kapucu and Garayev 2011), SAR resources allocation (Haghani and Oh 1996; Fiedrich et al. 2000; Sheu 2007), path selection (Yuan and Wang 2009; Batta et al. 2009), etc., while little attention has been devoted to evaluate how SAR strategies influence the SAR process and corresponding information demand.

Path selection and search work follow different behavior patterns, it is better to model the two kinds of behaviors separately. However, until now, little is known about the detailed depiction and modeling analysis of search patterns. The uncertainty of SAR was considered in the research by Waugh and Streib (2006), but the combination of planned SAR and randomness of disaster has not been studied continuously. As a result, making decisions through information and evaluating effects of decisions, especially evaluating equity and efficiency, become a worthy problem to study. In fact, considering the terrible power and communication conditions of the disaster area, available information that SAR teams can get is usually limited. They may need to search for survivors relatively independent in uncooperative way. Besides, in some developing countries or remote regions, there is no unified dispatching system due to lack of information management. Previous studies did not consider the dynamic independent search. It is important to explore how should SAR teams make decisions during independent search process and evaluate the effects of the search strategies.

The search strategies in this paper are limited to land SAR. Similarly, according to the former related research (Waugh and Streib 2006), we assume that SAR teams choose their target area and paths independently. Therefore, choosing a reasonable search strategy becomes very important. This study considers both simple intuitive strategy and complex strategy and analyzes their degree of demand for information. We not only compare different strategies considering search paths and area, but also helps to guide the analysis and simulation of SAR performance.

2   Problem Statement

2.1   Basic Condition

Consider a situation of rescue resource allocation problem after a disaster such as a rainstorm or an earthquake. The original roads and bridges are damaged during the disaster. Suppose the rest available roads in this region are passable and form a grid network $G(V, A)$, in which V is the set of nodes and A is the set of arcs (linked roads). There are a number of SAR teams in the road network, and the number is set to be fixed for simplicity. We suppose that survivors need be sent to the rescue center (node m) within the time period T to save their lives, and $t \in T$.

For the convenience of description, we divided the grid net G into several grids, and let g be one of them ($g \in G$). Assuming that there are some survivors in grid g at time t, let it be $S_g(t)$. Let S_g be the number of survivors in zone g at the initial time, and let S be the total number of survivors in the network, then the value of S is shown in Eq. (1)

$$S = \sum_{g \in G} S_g \qquad (1)$$

Assume that the remaining passable paths are not congested, and there is no delay because of traffic queue. Let c_{gm} be the travel time from m to grid g, and c_{mg} is constant. Suppose there are N SAR teams searching for survivors in the network, let $N_m(t)$ be the number of SAR teams in medical center at time t, then

$$N = N_m(1) \qquad (2)$$

According to Eq. (2), at the initial time ($t = 1$), all SAR teams gather in the rescue center, and let $N_g(t)$ be the number of SAR teams searching in zone g.

In order to describe SAR process correctly, the survival rate change should be taken into account. According to the previous research (Yuan et al. 2001; Kuwata 2000), the survival rate in our study is defined as follows:

$$r(t) = 100 \cdot e^{-\beta \cdot t} \qquad (3)$$

Where γ is survival rate, t is waiting time of survivors, and β is a positive parameter related to disaster types and can be obtained by statistical data. Equation (3) shows that survival rate is negatively correlated with waiting time of survivors.

2.2 General Time Cost of SAR

At the initial time, all SAR teams gathered at the rescue center. The scale of survivors in each grid is known, but their exact locations of survivors in the gird are not clear. When a SAR team chooses a target grid g and then go to the grid at time t, the SAR cost can be expressed as $C_{mg}(t)$.

The SAR work of the teams includes the following three steps, Step 1: According to instantaneous information, the SAR team chooses a target grid g and set off for the grid g from the rescue center m; Step 2: Arrive at target grid g and then search for survivors by cruising; Step 3: Send the survivors back to rescue center m after they find them. The motion trail of Step 1 and Step 3 is different from Step 2. In Step 1 and Step 3 the SAR teams select the shortest path between rescue center and target grids. But in Step 2, SAR teams have to search for survivors in the cruising way because they are not clear about the exact locations of survivors.

In order to discuss the strategy and motion trail of a single SAR team, we suppose each team works independently. Consider one SAR team arrives at grid g at time t and after time $c_g^s(t)$ the team finds a survivor. The SAR cost of each round $C_{mg}(t)$ is the sum of travel time c_{mg} (from rescue center m to target grid g), search time $c_g^s(t + c_{mg})$ and return time c_{gm} (from target grid g back to rescue center m).

$$C_{mg}(t) = c_{mg} + c_g^s \left(t + c_{mg} \right) + c_{gm} \tag{4}$$

In Eq. (4), $C_{mg}(t)$ is decision-making cost, which is the general time cost of a round of work of one SAR team.

2.3   Expected Search Time

In this section, we will derive the search time in step 2, which affects the decision-making cost. As mentioned above the expected search time in grid g is $c_g^s(t)$. Assuming that the number of survivors and SAR teams is $S_g(t)$ and $N_g(t)$ at time t.

Suppose the survivors in the grid network are uniformly distributed. Although the exact locations are not clear, we can obtain the distribution density. Let the total length of passable roads in the network be A_g and the distribution density of survivors be ρ_g at initial time, then

$$\rho_g = S_g / A_g \tag{5}$$

The survival rate reduces over time, so the distribution density of survivors will also reduce. At time t, for the affected area that have not been searched, the change of distribution density over time is

$$\rho_g(t) = \rho_g e^{-\beta(\cdot t - 1)} \tag{6}$$

Consider that there is a SAR team searching in grid g with speed v. After one unit time its search distance will be $v \cdot 1$ and the probability it finds a survivor will be $\left(\rho_g(t) \cdot v \right)$. At this moment the number of survivors is declining too, there is

$$\alpha_g(t) \cdot e^{-\beta \cdot 1} = \rho_g(t) \cdot v \cdot e^{-\beta \cdot 1} \tag{7}$$

In Eq. (7) $\alpha_g(t)$ is a search parameter indicates the search difficulty in remaining area. In addition, the smaller the value is, the sparser the survivors distribute and the higher the search difficulty. The total number of SAR teams in the network is $N_g(t)$, after a time unit the number of survivors has been found is $\alpha_g(t)e^{-\beta} \cdot N_g(t)$. After basic treatment, all the rescued survivors will be sent back to the rescue center m,

$$f_{gm}(t) = \alpha_g(t)e^{-\beta}N_g(t) \tag{8}$$

Where $f_{gm}(t)$ is the number of SAR teams from grid g to the rescue center m at time t, and the number of SAR teams in the network reduces $f_{gm}(t)$, which is

$$N_g(t+1) = N_g(t) - f_{gm}(t) = N_g(t)\left(1 - \alpha_g(t)e^{-\beta} \right) \tag{9}$$

Similarly, at time $(t + x)$, there is

$$N_g(t+x) = N_g(t)\big(1 - \alpha_g(t)e^{-\beta}\big)^x \tag{10}$$

Now $N_g(t+1) \sim N_g(t+x)$ form a geometric sequence. When the value of $N_g(t+x^*)$ equals 1, the value of x^* closes to the time that all survivors have been found. Based on the sequence,

$$x^* = lnN_g(t)/\ln(1 - \alpha_g(t)e^{-\beta})^{-1} \tag{11}$$

Then we can get the expected search time $(x^*/2)$, which is a SAR team reaches grid g and search in this grid at time t. The value of α_g can be obtained by the survey parameters, so

$$c_g^s(t) = lnN_g(t)/2\ln(1 - \alpha_g(t)e^{-\beta})^{-1} \tag{12}$$

3 SAR Strategies

3.1 Development of Strategies

In order to improve the success rate, each SAR team needs to find survivors as many as possible in the shortest time. The decision-makers will choose different strategies according to the difference of information. In this paper, we will discuss demands for information in different strategies. We assume that SAR teams can obtain continues and instantaneous information about the environment within the disaster region, so that they can learn the dynamic distribution of teams and make decision according to this information.

Based on different information demands, we discuss three kinds of SAR strategies which are shown in Fig. 1. ① Strategy 1. Approaching principle, the SAR teams prefer to select the nearest grid to be the target grid. If there is no survivor in the nearest grid, they will go to the second nearest grid. The rest grids are selected x in the same manner. ② Strategy 2. Quantity priority, the SAR teams prefer to the grid that has the most survivors. If there have been enough SAR teams in this grid or all survivors have been found, the grid with second most survivors will be the target. ③ Strategy 3. Minimum SAR cost, according to instantaneous information about the distribution of SAR teams and survivors, the SAR teams prefer to choose the grid with the minimum general time cost.

Among the three strategies, Strategy 1 only considers the distance information to select the path of SAR; Strategy 2 is based on the distribution information of survivors in the path selection decision; Strategy 3 takes use of the information about SAR teams' distribution in the decision making.

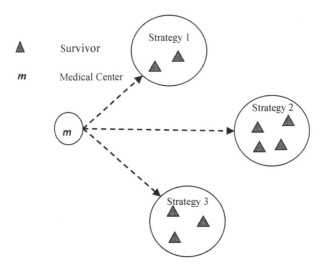

Fig. 1. Illustration graph of search strategies of SAR

3.2   Analysis of Strategies

Strategy 1 and Strategy 2 both conform to normal rules. In Strategy 1, SAR teams can arrive at the target grids in shortest time. Besides, they can return to the rescue center fastest. In a word, Strategy 1 is reasonable especially when available information is little.

Strategy 2 ensures the main rescue forces can be concentrated to key areas, in which there are most survivors. When the size of each grid is similar, this strategy may improve the success rate so that the dispute about this strategy will be less. But it also leads to unfairness for the survivors in the other grids.

Strategy 3 makes full use of the dynamic information of SAR teams' distribution and minimize the rescue cost so as to make optimal decision. It is worth noting that the strategy eventually achieves an optimal individual rescue status.

For example, there are $N_m(t)$ SAR teams in the rescue center waiting for searching survivors at time t. The SAR cost from rescue center m to grid g is $C_{mg}(t)$, and the cost is related to the number of SAR teams leaving for grid g. It means that if the number of SAR teams in one grid is excessive, the overall efficiency of SAR declines. Thus in Strategy 3 the costs of each SAR team to different grid should be equal, that is

$$C_{mg}(t) = C_{mg'}(t), \quad \forall g \neq g' \tag{13}$$

Now the problem transforms into a typical network distribution problem. In order to achieve efficiency maximization, the SAR teams need to minimize SAR cost of each round. With the change of disaster environment, $c_g^s(t)$ changes over time.

4   Team Distribution Model with Information

4.1   Movement of SAR Teams

In this section, we will analyze the motion model of SAR teams based on the process of SAR. At time t, the total number of SAR teams from m is $N_m(t)$. Let the number of teams from rescue center to each grid to be $f_{mg}(t)$, and similarly, we can get the number of teams back to rescue center from each grid. As the number of SAR teams at the initial time is known, so at time $t(t > 1)$ for grid g there is

$$N_g(t) = N_g(t-1) - f_{gm}(t) + f_{mg}\left(t - c_{mg}\right) \tag{14}$$

Note that the SAR teams spend time c_{mg} to reach grid g, so they begin to search at time $(t - c_{mg})$. The quantity of SAR teams at rescue center at time t is

$$N_m(t) = N_m(t-1) - \sum_{g \in G} f_{mg}(t) + \sum_{g \in G} f_{gm}\left(t - c_{mg}\right) \tag{15}$$

Equation (15) shows that subtracting the teams leaving for each grid $(\sum_{g \in G} f_{mg}(t))$ from the former number of teams at rescue center, and adding the teams back from each grid $(\sum_{g \in G} f_{gm}(t - c_{mg}))$, we can get the quantity of SAR teams at rescue center at time t. At that time the number of survivors is

$$S_g(t) = S_g(t-1) - f_{gm}(t-1) \tag{16}$$

4.2   The Decision Model

On the basis of the discussion in Sect. 3, we establish a decision model according to decision rules of different strategies respectively.

Model 1 (corresponding to Strategy 1): At time t, the SAR teams starting from the rescue center m choose the target grids according to the distance. For the SAR teams from the rescue center m to the grid g, there is

$$c_{mg} \le c_{mg'}, \ if \ f_{mg}(t) \ge 0 \tag{17}$$

Model 2 (corresponding to Strategy 2): At time t, the SAR teams choose the target grids according to the number of survivors in each grid. For the SAR teams to grid g,

$$N_g(t) \le N_{g'}(t), \ if \ f_{mg}(t) \ge 0 \tag{18}$$

Model 3 (corresponding to Strategy 3): At time t, the SAR teams starting from the rescue center m choose the target grids according to Strategy 3. The following conditions need to be satisfied: let $C_m^*(t)$ be the minimum SAR cost of the SAR team, $C_m^*(t) = \min\{C_{mg}(t), \forall g \in G\}$. For the SAR teams from rescue center m to grid g,

$$C_{mg}(t) \leq C_m^*(t), \quad f_{mg}(t) \geq 0 \tag{19}$$

Otherwise, when $C_{mg}(t) > C_m^*(t)$, it indicates that the SAR teams in grid g at this time is too intensive and the SAR costs will be high, so the SAR teams will prefer to other grids. Then the number of SAR teams from the rescue center m to each grid at time t can be obtained.

5 Numerical Example

A numerical example was considered in this study to evaluate the SAR effects. Suppose a region occurred by a flood disaster is divided into four grids which are labeled as 1, 2, 3 and 4. M is the rescue center and is mostly close to grid 4. At the initial time $t = 1$, there are M ($M = 100$) SAR teams which can get the latest distribution information of survivors. Each grid is connected by passable paths and every path is bidirectional. The travel time between each two grids is presented in Table 1.

Table 1. Link travel time (time unit period)

Link	1-2	2-1	2-3	3-2	3-4	4-3
Time	2	2	3	3	5	5
Link	1-4	4-1	1-m	m-1	4-m	m-4
Time	4	4	4	4	2	2

Each grid has a certain number of survivors S_g ($S_1 = 30, S_2 = 40, S_3 = 60$, $S_4 = 20$). Grid 1 and grid 4 is closer to the rescue center M than grid 2 and grid 3. SAR teams determine target grids based on different strategies and then choose the shortest paths. After arriving at the target grid, the basic rescue time c_g^r will be one-time unit. In this numerical example, three types of SAR strategies named Stategy 1, Strategy 2 and Stategy 3 are considered. The survival rate is described refer to Eq. (3).

As shown in Fig. 2, at time $t = 30$, if there are no SAR teams, the number of survivors in each grid decreases over time, the largest reduction of survivor number occurs in grid 2 and grid 3, it means that these two grids should be the primary rescue target areas.

Figure 3 shows the distribution of SAR teams at the initial time for Strategy 1 and Strategy 2. Based on the principle of Strategy 1, most SAR teams are dispatched to grid 2. While Strategy 2 gives priority to grid 2 and grid 3 where survivors are mostly concentrated.

Figure 4 shows the cumulative number of rescued survivors for Strategy 1 and Strategy 2 at time $t = 10$. The cumulative number of survivors rescued in each grid has a close relation with the SAR teams' initial distribution. For example, the rescued survivors for Strategy 1 mainly concentrate in grid 1 and grid 2, because they are closer to rescue center. For Strategy 2, most rescued survivors concentrate in grid 2 and grid 3, and in the first half of the time period, no survivor was rescued in grid 1 or grid 4.

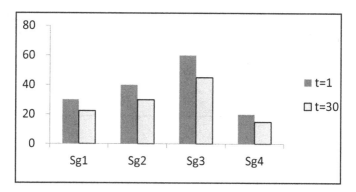

Fig. 2. Survivors' cumulative changes of each grid with the absence of SAR teams

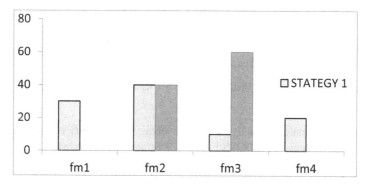

Fig. 3. Distribution of SAR teams at the initial time for Strategy 1 and Strategy 2 ($t = 1$)

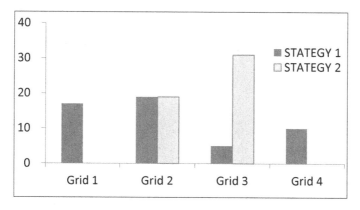

Fig. 4. The cumulative number of rescued survivors for Strategy 1 and Strategy 2

For Strategy 3, it takes the general cost to each grid into consideration and tries to balance it. It can be seen in Fig. 5 that for Strategy 3, the initial distribution of SAR teams is more adapted to the size of each grid, and distance is also taken into account. Compared with Strategy 1 and Strategy 2, the distribution of SAR teams with Strategy 3 is more homogeneous.

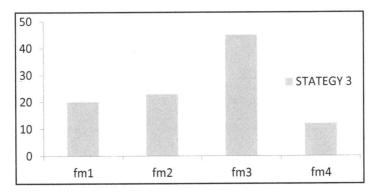

Fig. 5. The initial distribution of SAR teams for Strategy 3 ($t = 1$)

Through the simulation analysis, we can obtain the quantity of rescued survivors under different strategies (Fig. 6): Strategy 1 > Strategy 2 > Strategy 3. For Strategy 1, the most rescued survivors are from grid 4 which is nearest to the rescue center; for Strategy 2 the most rescued survivors are from grid 2. The above results suggest that the numerical example successfully reflects the basis objective of each SAR strategy, and the results of numerical study are reliable.

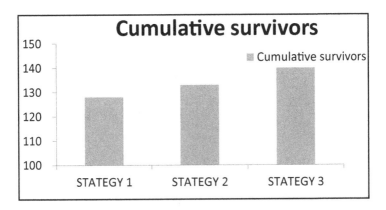

Fig. 6. The rescue time and cumulative number of rescued survivors for each strategy

Some other observations regarding the dynamic changes of each strategy are shown in Fig. 7. It can be found that in the first half of the time period, Strategy 3 rescued the largest number of survivors in the disaster region. The result suggests that Strategy 3 better considers the relationship between travel time and survivor distribution, and thus is more effective in optimizing the configuration of SAR teams.

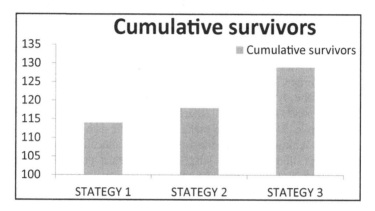

Fig. 7. The cumulative survivors of each strategy (considering survival rate)

Through the simulation analyses we found that when the survival rate changes, the degree of adaptation of each strategy changes as well. When survival rate falls over time, the number of rescued survivors changes. The number of Strategy 1 grows larger while Strategy 2 has a sharp drop. Comparatively, Strategy 3 has a better adaptability than the other two strategies. That may be because SAR teams need to take this change into their consideration, but Strategy 2 failed to adapt to this change. A lot of resources are still allocated into grid 3, resulting in too much time spent on traveling. Figure 7 shows the comparison of the quantity of rescued survivors with different strategies when survival rate changes. It is also found that under different survival rates, the independent SAR strategies are related to different adaptabilities. In general, the effect of Strategy 3 is the best because of its comprehensive consideration of the distribution changes of survivors and SAR teams. While the stabilities of the other two strategies are relatively poor and the number of rescued survivors fluctuates more obviously.

6   Conclusions

In order to improve the success rate of SAR, each SAR team needs to find survivors as many as possible within a limited time period. The main decision problem for SAR teams is how to select target grids. In this paper, we consider shortest path selection and target grid selection together. A network model is used to study SAR strategies, while the influence of survival rate is taken into account. We assume that the scale of survivors in each grid is known, but their locations are not clear. Thus, SAR teams can only learn about their fuzzy orientation. The assumptions are closer to the real scenario than simplified models developed previously. We discussed three strategies with different dependence on information. Strategy 1 only used distance information to make path selection, Strategy 2 requires distribution information of survivors, and Strategy 3 needs information about the distribution of SAR teams. The numerical example results showed that the effect of Strategy 3 is the best because it coordinated SAR needs in different regions.

Strategy 1 and Strategy 2 are consistent with the actual situations of SAR. At the beginning of SAR, the two strategies aim to search for survivors quickly. Strategy 1 chooses the nearest grid, which means the SAR teams can reach the target grid at the first time; while Strategy 2 ensures that the main rescue forces to be concentrated to the key regions. However, unfairness exists in these two strategies. Especially when information is uncertain, it is easy to lead to low rescue efficiency. While Strategy 3 makes full use of the dynamic distribution information of SAR teams and helps to achieve an optimal status of individual search which is defined in this paper for the first time. From the above discussion, we make the conclusion that the selection of SAR strategies can help improve the efficiency of SAR and allocate rescue resources more reasonably. Besides, findings of the study can also assist the design of emergency management systems and evaluation of SAR plans. We recommend that future studies could consider the uncertainty of shortest path selection and evaluate other cruising methods in the road network.

Acknowledgements. The authors appreciate the funding support from the National Natural Science Foundation of China (51508122), Guangxi science and technology projects (1524800210, AB16380280), Guangxi Natural Science Foundation (Grant No. 2015GXN SFBA139216), as well as The Scientific research project of National Ministry of Housing and Urban-Rural Construction (2017-K2-009). Scientific Research Project of Nanning University (2018XJ39).

References

Janis, I.L., Mann, L.: Emergency decision making: a theoretical analysis of responses to disaster warnings. J. Hum. Stress **3**, 35–45 (1977)

Danielsson, M., Ohlsson, K.: Decision making in emergency management: a survey study. Int. J. Cogn. Ergon. **3**(2), 91–99 (1999)

Kapucu, N., Garayev, V.: Collaborative decision-making in emergency and disaster management. Int. J. Public Adm. **34**(6), 366–375 (2011)

Haghani, A., Oh, S.C.: Formulation and solution of a multi-commodity multi-modal network flow model for disaster relief operations. Transp. Res. Part A **30**(3), 231–252 (1996)

Fiedrich, F., Gehbauer, F., Rickers, U.: Optimized resource allocation for emergency response after earthquake disasters. Saf. Sci. **35**(1–3), 41–57 (2000)

Sheu, J.B.: Challenges of emergency logistics management. Transp. Res. Part E **43**(6), 655–659 (2007)

Yuan, Y., Wang, D.W.: Path selection model and algorithm for emergency logistics management. Comput. Ind. Eng. **56**(3), 1081–1094 (2009)

Batta, R., Jotshi, A., Gong, Q.: Dispatching and routing of emergency vehicles in disaster mitigation using data fusion. Socio-Econ. Plan. Sci. **43**(1), 1–24 (2009)

Waugh, W.L., Streib, G.: Collaboration and leadership for effective emergency management. Public Adm. Rev. **66**(Suppl. 1), 131–140 (2006)

Liu, Q., Wang, Q.: A team distribution model of post-disaster search and rescue considering information accuracy difference. Chem. Eng. Trans. (2016). https://doi.org/10.3303/CET1651147

Bruycker, M., et al.: The 1980 earthquake in southern Italy: rescue of trapper victims and mortality. Bull. World Health Organ. **61**(6), 1021–1025 (1983)

Yuan, Y.F., Spencer, B.F., Hu, Y.X.: Assessing countermeasures to emergency response in earthquakes. In: Spencer, B.F., Hu, Y.X. (eds.) Earthquake Frontiers in the New Millennium. A.A. Balkema, Rotterdam (2001)

Simulating Mutual Support Networks
of Human and Artificial Agents

Lenin Medeiros[1]([✉])[iD], Tibor Bosse[2][iD], and Jan Treur[1][iD]

[1] Behavioural Informatics Group, Vrije Universiteit Amsterdam,
Amsterdam, The Netherlands
{l.medeiros,j.treur}@vu.nl
[2] Behavioural Science Institute, Radboud Universiteit, Nijmegen, The Netherlands
t.bosse@ru.nl

Abstract. In this paper, a multi-agent simulation model is presented to investigate the dynamics of 'mutual-support networks': online social networks consisting of both humans and artificial agents. Via such networks, human users who are coping with stress can share their problems, via text messages, with human peers as well as 'artificial friends'. Even though not everybody feels comfortable sharing personal problems with artificial agents, a bot is always available to help human users, and does not face any negative consequence of providing help to stressed peers. Using the simulation model, the dynamics of social networks consisting of an arbitrary combination of humans and agents have been explored under various circumstances. This exploration resulted in several insights that are useful for shaping our vision on artificial friends: (1) humans can provide less emotional support than artificial agents because they have limited emotional resources, (2) the type of support that is provided has a large impact on the human's stress level, and (3) the more open users are to receiving automated support, the more effective the support is in reducing their stress level. The model was internally validated by means of a mathematical verification.

Keywords: Computational model · Stress
Multi-agent based simulation
Computer-Generated Emotional Support

1 Introduction

This paper is part of a project that explores the potential of *Computer-Generated Emotional Support* [1,2] in the form of an online chatbot that helps people cope with everyday stress [3–5]. Although the chatbot is still under development, we are interested in studying its effect on group dynamics under different hypothetical circumstances. The current paper addresses this challenge by means of multi-agent based simulation [6].

Based on empirical data collected in a crowdsourcing study [7], a prototype version of our chatbot selects appropriate supportive strategies that fit with the

S. Staab et al. (Eds.): SocInfo 2018, LNCS 11186, pp. 202–214, 2018.
https://doi.org/10.1007/978-3-030-01159-8_19

types of stressful experiences that people share (cf. [8]). However, the effectiveness of such support is also expected to depend on some personal and network characteristics. Therefore, in this work, we use agent-based simulation to explore different scenarios in which the proposed chatbot could play a role. In particular, we explore the effect of (1) network topology, (2) different support strategies, and (3) how open human users are to receive support from a software agent.

In the next sections we present, respectively, our proposed simulation model (Sect. 2), a number of simulations under different parameter settings (Sect. 3) and a discussion about our findings (Sect. 4). In the Appendix a mathematical verification of the proposed model is provided.

2   Computational Model

The proposed model is an extension of an existing multi-agent simulation model about human agents within a mutual support social network [3]. The idea of that paper is that the users of such a network face stressful life situations from time to time and, depending on their emotional states, they take the decision of requesting online emotional support to their friends. One of the important conclusions of that work was the fact that, since the agents spend 'emotional resources' to provide support to others, they might face bad consequences as a collateral effect of helping stressed friends by sending supportive messages (i.e., they might become stressed themselves). Here, we propose a model of which the general idea is slightly different: we added the concept of *support agents* (or socialbots) to the network. As the behaviour of these agents is not dependent on their emotional resources, there is no limit to the amount of support they can provide to humans. Besides that, they always send responses 'immediately' (assuming there is an adequate Internet connection).

The model was developed in Python and can be accessed via a GitHub repository[1]. It uses the paradigm of network-oriented modelling, proposed by Treur [9]. The topology of the network can be defined by creating h human agents and b bot agents, and attaching them via arcs connecting any arbitrary pair of agents (i.e., humans can be connected to bots, but also to other humans). H_x is a human agent that belongs to the set of h humans, with $0 \leqslant x \leqslant h$. B_y is a bot agent that belongs to a set of b bots, with $0 \leqslant y \leqslant b$. If there is a connection between a pair of agents, then they will be able to request/send online emotional support to each other via text messages.

2.1   Model Overview

The process represented by the model is illustrated by the following scenario. At any point in time, a human agent faces some negative as well as positive events simultaneously. The stressful events lead to an increase of the human's stress level. On the other hand, the positive events increase the emotional resources that

---

[1] Available on https://github.com/leninmedeiros/modelmutualsupport.

the agent can use to provide support to his/her peers. As soon as the human's stress level exceeds a particular threshold, (s)he will share his/her problems with peers by sending messages to them. When a given agent, either bot or human, receives such a request for support from a peer, this agent sends back a supportive message, using one of the 5 emotional supportive strategies described in [8]. However, human agents will only send support if they have enough emotional resources.

Figure 1 provides an overview of one possible configuration for our proposed model, containing two human agents and one bot. Here, the nodes denote states of the world, and arrows denote causal-temporal relations between states. These effects can be either positive or negative. Input and output states are depicted on the boundaries of the agents, whereas internal mental states are depicted inside the agents. Table 1 explains what the labels for the nodes mean. The input states comprise positive and negative events (e^- and e^+), and reading messages. Output states refer to sending messages. Internal states include the agents' stress level and emotional resources.

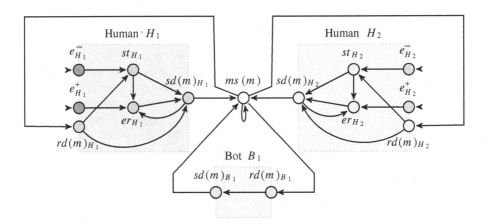

Fig. 1. Conceptual representation of the model for the topology consisting of 2 humans and 1 bot. The states e^- and e^+ refer to negative and positive life events, respectively. The network is fully connected (all the agents communicate with each other). A given message m can be either p, a description of a stressful situation (problem) or s, an emotionally supportive message (support).

It is important to state that not only the topology of the network is configurable. The model also contains a number of settable parameters. For instance, it is possible to adjust (1) how open a given human H_1 is to receive emotional support from a bot; and (2) how effective a particular supportive message is to reduce the given agent's stress level. To do so, one has to change the weight of the connection from $rd(m)_{H_1}$ to st_{H_1} (see Fig. 1), representing the effect of the support message s on H_1's stress level. In the model, this weight is equal to $-1 \cdot effectiveness \cdot openness$. In the simulations described in the next section,

Table 1. List of functions used per state in the model.

State	Label	Combination Function
Stress	st	scaled sum function
Emotional resources	er	scaled sum function
Sending problem	$sd(p)$	threshold function
Reading support	$rd(s)$	id function
Reading problem	$rd(p)$	id function
Sending support	$sd(s)$	support function 1, for humans
		support function 2, for bots
Problem Message	$ms(p)$	max function
Support Message	$ms(s)$	max function

the value of *openness* is varied. Instead, the value of *effectiveness* is fixed, based on the empirical results found in [7].

2.2   Model Formalization

Formally, the model consists of a set of formulae that represent the causal-temporal relationships between the various states. All states always have a value between 0 and 1. Every connection between two states has a weight factor ω_x, with $0 \leqslant x \leqslant j$, where j is the total number of connections present in the model. When the computational model is executed, for every time point t the value of a given state is updated via a combination function that takes into account the values at time point $t - \Delta t$ from all states that are connected to it as well as the respective weight factors.

Each human agent is provided with two inputs (also referred as stimuli) representing the negative and positive life events e^- and e^+, respectively. There is a positive effect of e^- on a human agent's stress level st: negative events lead to more stress. On the other hand, the agent's emotional resources er are positively affected by e^+: positive events increases emotional resources. The state st is negatively affected by $rd(s)$, since reading support messages helps to reduce stress, while $sd(s)$ exerts a negative influence on er, because a human spends his/her resources to support friends. Equations 1 and 2 show how the values for stress and emotional resources, respectively, are computed over time for the human H_x, who is connected to another given agent A_n.

$$st(t + \Delta t) = st(t) + \eta \cdot \left(\frac{\omega_j \cdot e^- - \omega_k \cdot rd(t)}{\omega_j} - st(t) \right) \cdot \Delta t \tag{1}$$

$$er(t + \Delta t) = er(t) + \eta \cdot \left(\frac{\omega_m \cdot e^+ - \omega_n \cdot sd(t)}{\omega_m} - er(t) \right) \cdot \Delta t \tag{2}$$

The function used in the previous equations is called *scaled sum function*, cf. [9]. Moreover, η is a *speed factor* parameter that tells how fast the effect from a state to another will take place.

Furthermore, if $st_{H_x} \geqslant th_1$ (i.e., the human's stress level exceeds a certain threshold th_1, which is set by default to 0.5), then H_x sends a message to all its peers. This is realised by making the value for $sd(p)_{H_x,A_n}$ equal to 1, where p is a text message describing the stressful situation. The state sd is updated via the following combination function, named *threshold function*.

$$sd(t + \Delta t) = \begin{cases} 1, & \text{if } w_o \cdot st(t) \geqslant 0.5 \\ 0, & \text{otherwise} \end{cases} \tag{3}$$

The state $ms(p)_{H_x,A_n}$, the (binary) environmental state representing the message sent from H_x to A_n, assumes the value 1 some time after H_x has shared message p. Once the message p appears in this process, it remains available for the recipients until the end of the simulation (representing the fact that the text message is readable on the reader's phone). The following function, named *max function*, is used to calculate $ms(p)$.

$$ms(t + \Delta t) = \begin{cases} w_p \cdot sd(t), & \text{if } w_p \cdot sd(t) \geqslant w_q \cdot ms(t) \\ w_q \cdot ms(t), & \text{otherwise} \end{cases} \tag{4}$$

Next, A_n reads the message describing the problem shared by H_x, which is represented formally by $rd(p)_{H_x,A_n} = 1$. This is as simple as an identity function, represented by the following equation, named *id function*.

$$rd(t + \Delta t) = w_r \cdot ms(t) \tag{5}$$

Consequently, A_n might send back a supportive response s, resulting in $sd(s)_{A_n,H_x} = 1$. However, if A_n is a human agent, it only occurs if $er_{A_n} \geqslant th_2$. Here, th_2 is another threshold (in our simulations set to 0.4) representing the minimal level of emotional resources a person requires to provide social support to others. The following two functions, named *support function 1* and *2*, are used to compute the values for sd regarding humans and bots, respectively.

$$sd(t + \Delta t) = \begin{cases} 1, & \text{if } w_s \cdot er(t) \geqslant 0.4 \text{ and } w_t \cdot rd(t) = 1 \text{ and } s = 0 \\ 0, & \text{otherwise} \end{cases} \tag{6}$$

$$sd(t + \Delta t) = \begin{cases} 1, & \text{if } w_u \cdot rd(t) = 1 \text{ and } s = 0 \\ 0, & \text{otherwise} \end{cases} \tag{7}$$

The environmental binary state $ms(s)_{A_n,H_x}$ is set to 1 when A_n sends a support message to H_x, and this value holds for the rest of the simulation. This state is also updated using the max function (Eq. 4). Consequently, also $rd(s)_{A_n,H_x}$ is set to 1, representing that H_x received an emotionally supportive text s from A_n, as a response to p. This is also done via the function defined in Eq. 5.

Table 1 contains a summary of the functions used by the model to calculate the values of all states over time.

Table 1 contains a summary of the combination functions used by the model. Note that some states share combination functions (the parameters differ, naturally).

3   Simulations

To explore the dynamics of humans and bots interacting within mutual support networks under different circumstances, a number of controlled simulations were conducted. In particular, we investigated the behaviour of our model using different settings for (1) network topology, (2) support strategies used and (3) openness to automated support. Topology stands for the distribution of humans and bots over the network and how they are connected to each other. The strategy used by the one who sends a supportive message is related to the strategies defined in [8]. Finally, the *openness* parameter is related to the extent to which human users accept emotional support that is automatically generated by a software agent.

The baseline situation we use here is a network containing one human and one bot. The human is considered relatively open to receiving support from an artificial peer. The openness value is 0.7 (on a scale from 0 and 1). The baseline scenario used is as follows: at the start of the simulation, the user faces a stressful situation at school (e.g., a bad grade for an exam), leading to stress. As a result, (s)he sends a text message to the bot asking for help. In response, the bot decides to send a supportive message following the so-called *Cognitive Change* (CC) approach. With this strategy, as explained in [8], supporters try to change the point of view of a peer related to a given problem, i.e. they typically send messages as "look at the positive side of it", "this is not that bad", etc. Previous results have shown that this is the most appropriate type of online emotional support for stressful situations related to school [7].

To analyse the effect of topology, we compared simulation results from two similar cases. In the first one, a bot provides emotional support to 4 human agents that face stressful situations (at school) in consecutive time steps; see Fig. 2.

As can be seen in the figure, as soon as any of the human users (H1–H4) starts to face a stressful situation, the respective stress level increases until it reaches the threshold 0.5. At this moment, the user decides to share this problem with the bot (B1). Because of that, the bot sends back a supportive message, leading to stabilization of the stress level. In this scenario, all humans face the same stressful situation ($e^- = 0.7$). Since the Internet connection is considered optimal (modelled by a maximal connection strength between the human and bot), the bot is able to provide effective support to all peers as soon as it receives a request to it.

In the second scenario, the network contains 5 human users. One of the users (H1) never faces a lot of stress (stress level does not reach the threshold

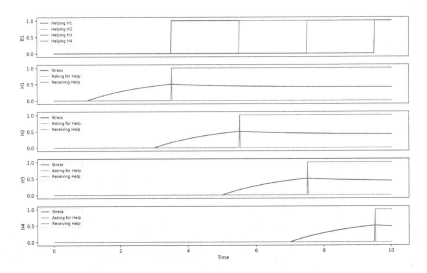

Fig. 2. Simulation scenario with 1 bot and 4 humans.

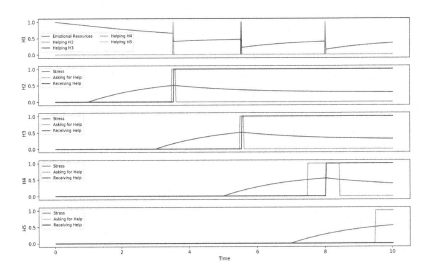

Fig. 3. Simulation scenario with 5 humans.

0.5) since the respective stimuli are set to $e^- = 0.3$ (negative event) and $e^+ = 0.7$ (positive event). However, the other humans consecutively receive the same stimuli: $e^- = 0.7$ and $e^+ = 0.3$. Therefore, only the first agent is able to provide emotional support to others due to his/her emotional resources. As can be seen in Fig. 3, the support provided by the human peer is in principle more effective than the support provided by a bot (Fig. 2), as it brings the stress level further down. However, since a human agent needs emotional resources, it takes some time until (s)he is sufficiently recovered to provide new supportive messages to peers. In fact, because of this phenomenon, the last human that faces a stressful situation (H5) never receives support.

Another set of simulations was performed to test the effectiveness of different support strategies. As briefly described earlier, the *effectiveness* parameter was based on results from a previous study to determine the effectiveness of 5 different support strategies [7]. To test the resulting patterns, we compared the cases of 5 humans with the same characteristics, facing exactly the same stressful situation (related to school). The bot agent sends them 5 different types of supportive message (one to each human). The results are presented in Fig. 4. It is clear that, indeed, CC is the most efficient support strategy in this case. This is the only strategy that reduces the stress of the user to the extent that (s)he does not require any more support. As mentioned earlier, the precise definitions of the support strategies can be consulted in [8].

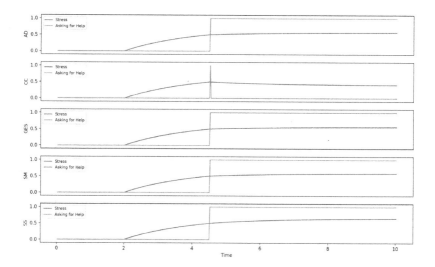

Fig. 4. Comparison between different types of emotional support strategies.

Finally, we checked results for different *openness* values. As explained earlier, this parameter tells how open a given human is to receive emotional support from bots, considering that the optimum value 1 is obtained when the agent that provides support is actually another human being. Again, we compare the results for 5 human users, each facing the same stressful situation at the same time and receiving the same type of support from a bot. The difference between the human agents is their value for openness. While the first agent is very reluctant to accept artificially generated support, the last one is almost as open to this as to receiving support from other humans. As Fig. 5 shows, the more close the openness value is to 1, the more effective is the automated support to reduce stress in humans.

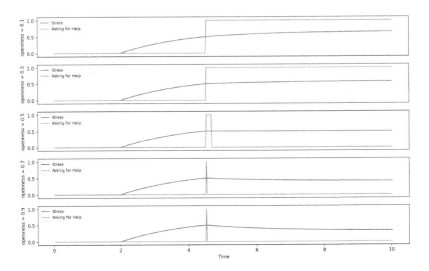

Fig. 5. Comparison between different values for openness to automated support.

4   Discussion

In this paper, multi-agent based simulation was applied to study the dynamics of mutual support networks of humans and artificial agents. The proposed model can be used to simulate a social network composed of m human users and n 'support agents' (or socialbots) that are connected according to any arbitrary topology. This way, the effect of introducing support agents as peers within online social media networks can be studied in a controlled environment. Indeed, the model was used to explore a number of hypothetical scenarios, by systematically varying model parameters such as the number of human and artificial agents, the topology of the network, and several personality characteristics of the agents.

The results of the simulations led to a number of relevant insights. First of all, certain situations were identified in which artificial support could be preferred over human support (even though emotional support provided by humans is in principle more effective than support provided by a chatbot). In particular, this holds for a case where one human user receives a number of consecutive requests for support (from different peers), which results in this user losing so many emotional resources that eventually (s)he is unable to provide support for another peer. Clearly, this is a problem from which the chatbot does not suffer, because it possesses 'unlimited emotional resources'. Secondly, it was shown that the type of support strategy that is selected by the (human or artificial) support agent has an impact on the extent to which the stress is reduced. For instance, when dealing with a user who is suffering from work-related stress, cognitive change works better than attentional deployment. Thirdly, the extent to which the stress is reduced is dependent on personal characteristics such as the person's openness to emotional support.

Although these findings (such as a chatbot being more effective than a human support agent) may not be extremely surprising by themselves, the added value of the current simulation model is that we are now able to explain in detail why they occur, and in which circumstances they occur. Since at least part of the parameter settings have been based on empirical data acquired in an earlier study, the resulting simulations are expected to be reasonably realistic.

Nevertheless, an obvious limitation of the current model is that the outcomes have not been validated against empirical data. Since the type of data required for this is currently lacking, empirical validation is simply not an option at this point. However, in future research we are planning to conduct an extensive study, in which we will actually create an online network consisting of human users and (several instances of) our chatbot, and acquire data about the development of users' stress via self-reports. By conducting such an experiment, we hope to not only evaluate the effectiveness of our chatbot, but also obtain the necessary empirical data to further fine-tune our model (using automated parameter tuning techniques). With the improved model, we expect to be able to make more precise predictions and gain further insight about how to exploit artificial support agents within online social networks.

Acknowledgements: The authors would like to thank the Brazilian government and to state that Lenin Medeiros' stay at VU Amsterdam was funded by Science without Borders/CNPq (reference number: 235134/2014-7).

Appendix

In order to verify our implementation, we performed a mathematical analysis of the equilibria of the model. Due to space limitations, we will not provide an exhaustive verification, but we limit the analysis to the following configuration:

- a given human H_1 faces a negative event e^- at time t (a problem at school);
- this leads to a stress value $st > 0$;
- consequently, the user sends a message p to bot B_1;
- as a response, the user receives a supportive message s, following the *cognitive change* strategy.

The purpose of this section is to illustrate that the model behaves as expected for this particular configuration.

A given state S has a *stationary point* at a time step t if $\frac{\partial S(t)}{\partial t} = 0$. Given that, the model is considered in *equilibrium* when each one of its states has a stationary point at a time step t. Therefore, for continuous stimuli over time (constant values for e^- and e^+), it is possible to verify that all the model's states reach a stationary point at a sufficiently large t within a given time window. One can check this behaviour via Fig. 6, which contains the results for two simulation cases considering a network with one human and one bot: the human faces negative situations at school equal to 0.3 and 0.7 in both cases, respectively. These values where chosen taking into account the fact that when a human agent's stress level exceeds the threshold 0.5, (s)he decides to ask for emotional support. As can be confirmed by checking the figure, the maximum stress level of a human agent is equal to e^- (value of the negative event). In other words, $\lim_{t \to \infty} st_{H_n} = e^-$. Therefore, it is expected that the human decides to send a request for support only with a stimulus $e^- > 0.5$.

After performing two simulations using the settings as described above, we substituted the states' final values in the equations used to define the model. This was done using an online linear solver tool[2].

For a stimulus $e^- < 0.5$, we have the following formulae for the states of the model:

$$X_1 = e^-_{H_1} = e \tag{8}$$

$$X_2 = st(t)_{H_1} = \frac{\omega_1 \cdot e - \omega_{10} \cdot rd(s,t)_{B_1,H_1}}{\omega_1} \tag{9}$$

$$X_3 = sd(t,p)_{H_1,B_1} = 0 \tag{10}$$

$$X_4 = ms(p,t)_{H_1,B_1} = \omega_3 \cdot sd(p,t)_{H_1,B_1} \tag{11}$$

$$X_5 = rd(p,t)_{H_1,B_1} = \omega_5 \cdot ms(p,t)_{H_1,B_1} \tag{12}$$

$$X_6 = sd(s,t)_{B_1,H_1} = \omega_6 \cdot rd(p,t)_{H_1,B_1} \tag{13}$$

$$X_7 = ms(s,t)_{B_1,H_1} = \omega_7 \cdot sd(s,t)_{B_1,H_1} \tag{14}$$

$$X_8 = rd(s,t)_{B_1,H_1} = \omega_9 \cdot ms(s,t)_{B_1,H_1} \tag{15}$$

The set that solves these eight equations is:

$$(X_1 = e, X_2 = e, X_3 = 0, X_4 = 0, X_5 = 0, X_6 = 0, X_7 = 0, X_8 = 0) \tag{16}$$

In contrast, for a stimulus $e^- > 0.5$, we have the following formulae for the states of the model:

$$X_1 = e^-_{H_1} = e \tag{17}$$

$$X_2 = st(t)_{H_1} = \frac{\omega_1 \cdot e - \omega_{10} \cdot rd(s,t)_{B_1,H_1}}{\omega_1} \tag{18}$$

$$X_3 = sd(p,t)_{H_1,B_1} = 0 \tag{19}$$

$$X_4 = ms(p,t)_{H_1,B_1} = 1 \tag{20}$$

$$X_5 = rd(p,t)_{H_1,B_1} = \omega_5 \cdot ms(p,t)_{H_1,B_1} \tag{21}$$

$$X_6 = sd(s,t)_{B_1,H_1} = \omega_6 \cdot rd(p,t)_{H_1,B_1} \tag{22}$$

$$X_7 = ms(s,t)_{B_1,H_1} = 1 \tag{23}$$

$$X_8 = rd(s,t)_{B_1,H_1} = \omega_9 \cdot ms(s,t)_{B_1,H_1} \tag{24}$$

The set that solves these eight equations is:

$$(X_1 = e, X_2 = \frac{(e \cdot \omega_1) + (\omega_{10} \cdot \omega_9)}{\omega_1}, X_3 = 0, X_4 = 1, X_5 = \omega_5, X_6 = \omega_5 \cdot \omega_6, X_7 = 1, X_8 = \omega_9) \tag{25}$$

---

[2] Available on: http://wims.unice.fr/wims/en_tool~linear~linsolver.en.html. Accessed on May 9, 2018.

The final results for the stress state (st) are, respectively, 0.298 and 0.407, for the first and the second case. As can be confirmed via Fig. 6, these results are satisfied by our implementation for the following set of parameters (besides the stimuli values stated above):

$$(\omega_1 = 1, \omega_2 = 1, \omega_3 = 1, \omega_3 = 1, \omega_3 = 1, \omega_3 = 1, \omega_3 = 1, \omega_3 = 1, \omega_3 = 1, \omega_{10} = -0.292) \qquad (26)$$

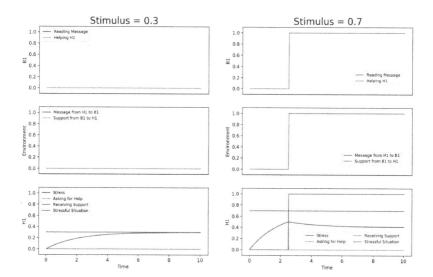

Fig. 6. Simulations of the verified cases. Note that some of the lines are overlapping.

Finally, another way of verification is to check to what extent the requirements of our model's description are satisfied. Some of the requirements are illustrated by Fig. 6: (1) a bot only sends support when a human has requested it; (2) there is an inhibiting effect of emotional support on stress level; (3) the maximum value for stress is equal to the negative event value used as stimulus; (4) a human only shares a problem seeking for emotional support when his/her stress level exceeds 0.5. All of these findings provide us confidence to state that the model is internally consistent.

References

1. van der Zwaan, J.M., Dignum, V., Jonker, C.M.: A conversation model enabling intelligent agents to give emotional support. In: Ding, W., Jiang, H., Ali, M., Li, M. (eds.) Modern Advances in Intelligent Systems and Tools. SCI, vol. 431, pp. 47–52. Springer, Heidelberg (2012). https://doi.org/10.1007/978-3-642-30732-4_6
2. DeVault, D., et al.: SimSensei kiosk: a virtual human interviewer for healthcare decision support. In: Proceedings of the 2014 International Conference on Autonomous Agents and Multi-agent Systems, pp. 1061–1068. International Foundation for Autonomous Agents and Multiagent Systems (2014)

3. Medeiros, L., Sikkes, R., Treur, J.: Modelling a mutual support network for coping with stress. In: Nguyen, N.-T., Manolopoulos, Y., Iliadis, L., Trawiński, B. (eds.) ICCCI 2016. LNCS (LNAI), vol. 9875, pp. 64–77. Springer, Cham (2016). https://doi.org/10.1007/978-3-319-45243-2_6

4. Medeiros, L., Bosse, T.: Empirical analysis of social support provided via social media. In: Spiro, E., Ahn, Y.-Y. (eds.) SocInfo 2016. LNCS, vol. 10047, pp. 439–453. Springer, Cham (2016). https://doi.org/10.1007/978-3-319-47874-6_30

5. Medeiros, L., Bosse, T.: An empathic agent that alleviates stress by providing support via social media. In: Proceedings of the 16th International Conference on Autonomous Agents and Multiagent Systems, AAMAS 2017, pp. 1634–1636. ACM Press (2017)

6. Davidsson, P.: Multi agent based simulation: beyond social simulation. In: Moss, S., Davidsson, P. (eds.) MABS 2000. LNCS (LNAI), vol. 1979, pp. 97–107. Springer, Heidelberg (2000). https://doi.org/10.1007/3-540-44561-7_7

7. Medeiros, L., Bosse, T.: Using crowdsourcing for the development of online emotional support agents. In: Bajo, J., et al. (eds.) PAAMS 2018. CCIS, vol. 887, pp. 196–209. Springer, Cham (2018). https://doi.org/10.1007/978-3-319-94779-2_18

8. Medeiros, L., Bosse, T.: Testing the acceptability of social support agents in online communities. In: Nguyen, N.T., Papadopoulos, G.A., Jędrzejowicz, P., Trawiński, B., Vossen, G. (eds.) ICCCI 2017. LNCS (LNAI), vol. 10448, pp. 125–136. Springer, Cham (2017). https://doi.org/10.1007/978-3-319-67074-4_13

9. Treur, J.: Network-Oriented Modeling: Addressing Complexity of Cognitive, Affective and Social Interactions. Understanding Complex Systems. Springer, Cham (2016). https://doi.org/10.1007/978-3-319-45213-5

Automatic Credibility Assessment of Popular Medical Articles Available Online

Aleksandra Nabożny$^{(\boxtimes)}$ (iD), Bartłomiej Balcerzak, and Adam Wierzbicki

Faculty of Information Technology, Polish-Japanese Academy
of Information Technology, Warsaw, Poland
aleksandra.nabozny@pja.edu.pl

Abstract. This paper presents the design concept of a credibility evaluation tool for medical web-documents and describes the implementation of its part. There have been numerous attempts to create such tool but most of them were strictly subject-specific. In this study, we aim to create a universal classifier for non-credible articles from the medical domain. Unlike most of the latest fact-checking solutions, it evaluates overall the credibility of the document instead of assessing separate claims. We collected a database of articles and sentences evaluated by experts, conducted the study of sentence's context in the task of credibility assessment, then performed statistical analysis in order to verify and fine-tune the design. The proposed scheme is constructed in such a way that it should be easy to update and has an easily interpretable output for Internet users with no expert knowledge about medicine.

Keywords: Automatic credibility assessment · Online credibility
Machine learning · Social informatics

1 Introduction

In the world where universal Internet access became a standard, a major fraction of literate human society turned to the Web as its main source of information. Since both publishing and accessing data is mostly unrestricted at this point, a large amount of unverified information has the ability of reaching out and having an impact. A great amount of this content pertains to vital aspects of people's lives, such as medicine and public health.

Recently, many efforts have been made to create tools for automatic credibility assessment. On the Internet information spreads very fast and people tend to form their opinion as soon as they read the heading of an article. That is why many existing solutions concentrate on claim detection and social media, like in [4] where Crowd Signals are used to track the spread of particular news. Other novel approaches include iFACT system, which gains accuracy with user's feedback [2], ClaimVerif that supports final score by the source credibility value of the article [5], as well as an earlier system proposed by [3] or ClaimBuster

© Springer Nature Switzerland AG 2018
S. Staab et al. (Eds.): SocInfo 2018, LNCS 11186, pp. 215–223, 2018.
https://doi.org/10.1007/978-3-030-01159-8_20

[1] including, among others, some tools to assist laypersons and professionals in understanding and vetting the claims.

It is assumed, however, that in medical domain the process of accessing and processing information by the user is quite different. When searching for medical advice online, people have a particular, pre-formulated problem about which they want to gain some knowledge. To attract user's attention the article has to be relevant and highly indexed by a certain search engine. Then, if the article has some features that elevate probability of a higher credibility assessment, or if misinformation is surrounded by true statements, users are put at risk of following advice that is contrary to the actual medical knowledge. That is why this paper focuses on overall web-documents credibility instead of assessing single truths. Single sentence evaluations are used in this solution, but as a tool to examine article's composition. The solution is constructed so that it could be easily implemented as a browser plug-in marking not credible articles with a warning, in an antivirus-like manner. The design proposal is shown in Fig. 1 and consists of two main parts: the classifier and the sentence comparison algorithm. This paper focuses on the first part, whereas the sentence comparison algorithm remains a concept.

In the course of work, the following research contributions were obtained:

1. The database of articles manually evaluated by experts, both overall and sentence by sentence. Additionally, sentences were evaluated both in and out of context.
2. The implementation of a classifier that filters out not credible medical web-documents. It is based on the aggregation of sentence evaluations made by experts in this field.
3. For the sake of this study, the following hypothesis was formulated: *Given the credibility evaluation of phrases and their position in space of the whole article, it is possible to create an effective classifier for credible and non-credible articles.* The hypothesis was confirmed throughout experiments.
4. Verification of the way in which context of the document affects expert assessment of individual sentence. By comparing contextual and non-contextual sentence evaluations, in a set of experiments it is shown that experts have difficulties when reviewing the credibility of a statement out of context.

In this study a following credibility definition was accepted: *a phrase/article is credible if an expert considered it so, his/her assessment being based on the current state of medical knowledge.*

2   Methods

2.1   Database Collection

The quantitative study was conducted to collect database for the study. However, a prior qualitative research on how experts read and process information from articles and phrases was necessary for designing indispensable tools better.

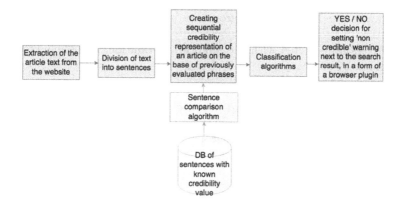

Fig. 1. Design concept of the final automatic credibility assessment tool.

Two medical doctors were asked to mark sentences with three colours, each corresponding with a value of credibility. There were three options available to choose from - a credible phrase, a not credible phrase and a neutral phrase. At the end they were asked to evaluate the whole article as credible or not credible. Think Aloud protocol was used throughout sessions. The records from those sessions were analysed and collected in a form of a report, which served as a base to prepare and refine final instructions for respondents of a quantitative study. They can be reviewed in the Appendix A.

The quantitative study was conducted on a group of 42 experts (mostly last year students of medical studies) through customized survey web service. It contained 247 articles that appeared on websites rated as the most relevant by Google search engine. Articles consisted of responses to short and simple queries (eg. "vaccinations", "child allergy", "prenatal testing", "HIV"). They were all saved manually to avoid gathering advertisement texts and other website artifacts, as well as to ensure reasonable distribution of various sources and leave the content uncontaminated. The publications focused on widely discussed and controversial topics ranging from public health domain such as obesity treatment and vaccines to prenatal testing, contraceptives, effects of vitamin D deficiency and more. The articles were automatically divided into phrases and saved in the database. Users assigned the labels to individual sentences, separated from each other by frames. Additionally, during the contextual round, sentences were ordered to form the article, which was to be labeled at the end of the survey. A single round of testing is described as follows:

1. A respondent reads the study instruction.
2. With 50% probability, contextual or non-contextual phrase evaluation survey round follows, offering respectively:
   (a) an evaluation of specific phrases that form the whole article visible to the respondent; at the end of the survey, there is a question concerning the article's credibility as a whole,

(b) phrases randomly selected from the initial database with their source article unknown to the respondent; only previously contextually evaluated phrases are selected with the uniform distribution of possible credibility values.

3. A respondent finishes the survey.

Instructions given to the respondent reflect the accepted definitions and evaluations structure. To encourage thoughtful assessments, all respondents received payment of approximately 15 USD per a completed round.

Database consists of:

- 11034 non-contextual phrase evaluations
- 11034 contextual phrase evaluations
- 247 article evaluations
- approximately 66% articles evaluated as credible and 33% as not credible.

2.2   Data Preparation

The representation of each article contains an ID, a vector representation of sentence credibility values distribution throughout the whole text, and its credibility value label. The sentence credibility distribution vector may contain one out of three values for each position - 0, 1 or 2 - where 0 stands for a not credible phrase, 1 for a neutral phrase and 2 for a credible phrase. Even though for non-contextual phrase evaluation respondents were left with additional -1 option that stood for "unable to evaluate without context", for final analysis those phrases were treated as neutral. A full exemplary representation is presented in Table 1.

Table 1. Digital representation of one input variable (article)

Article ID (**doc_id**)	eq. 1234
Article evaluation (**doc_eval**)	0 (not credible)/1 (credible)
Phrases credibility distribution vector (**phrase_vec**)	eq. [1 2 2 1 1 0 0 1]

Data exploration was conducted on the dataset that was divided into two parts, both prepared in two ways. Ultimately, four variants of the dataset presented below were constituted:

1. contextual sequential credibility model (CS) - an article is represented by contextual credibility vector with order of phrases preserved
2. non-contextual sequential credibility model (US) - an article is represented by non-contextual credibility vector with order of phrases preserved
3. contextual random credibility model (CR) - an article is represented by contextual credibility vector with phrases in a random order
4. non contextual random credibility model (UR) - an article is represented by non-contextual credibility vector with phrases in a random order

In CR and UR variants, phrase order randomization was performed independently for each input (article). For simplicity, in the following sections CS, US, CR and UR abbreviations will be used.

All credibility vectors were up-sampled to the length of the longest article, settling at 215.

2.3 Data Exploration

In order to check if the proposed representation allows for clear separation of the set into two classes, a clustering was performed. K-means algorithm was used for this purpose. After the analysis of cluster cohesion and intra-cluster distances, the parameter k was adjusted and set to 2 for all variants (CS, CR, US and UR).

Next, credible versus all phrases and not credible versus all phrases ratio for all data variants were examined.

Classification algorithm will play a vital role in the final software, as shown in Fig. 1. Random Forest algorithm was chosen, firstly, because of its ability to process ordinal data, secondly, because the order of features in input vector is irrelevant. The order of phrases' evaluations in the model does not influence classifier's output, as cluster and ratio analyses have shown, so the use of an algorithm that ignores it is justified. Just two variants of the dataset, CS and US, were used to build the classifiers. Their performance was measured and compared using F1 and recall metrics. Recall was chosen as the most important quality indicator because the main goal of the final software would be to filter out true negatives - not credible articles.

To check the importance for classification of the ratio of all phrases with specified credibility value (thus labeled 0 or 2) versus all phrases, another analysis was conducted. Upon CS and US variants of the dataset, related inputs were created with this ratio value decreasing by approximately 10% interval (at each iteration 0 and 2 evaluations were chosen randomly and converted to neutrals until desired ratio was reached). For all those inputs Random Forest classifiers were built and the same performance measures were calculated.

In order to understand the role of the context in credibility evaluation a pairwise comparison of the sentences evaluated by experts was conducted. The initial intention was to test whether any similarities between contextual and non-contextual can be attributed to anything else than random coincidence. In order to do so a two-tailed Chi-square test was conducted with a null hypothesis stating that the distribution of pairwise sentence evaluations is a result of random chance, and that contextual and non-contextual evaluations are stochastically independent. A p-value of 0.01 was chosen for significance testing, with the null hypothesis stating that contextual and non-contextual sentence evaluations are stochastically independent.

3 Results

Visualization was performed using the Multidimensional scaling (MDS) with Manhattan metric used for distance matrix creation. It can be explored in Fig. 2.

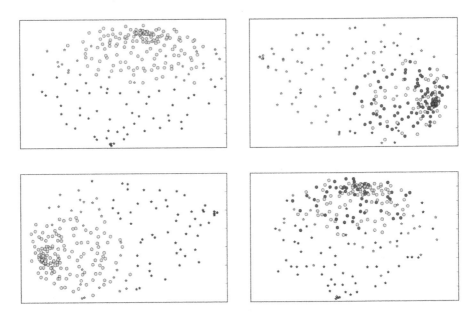

Fig. 2. Multidimensional scaling visualization. Circle - article evaluated as credible, asterisk - article evaluated as not credible. The color distinguishes the classes assigned by k-means. Performed on, from upper left to lower right: CS, US, CR and UR set types.

It appears that for a contextual dataset, clustering algorithms work sufficiently well as classifiers and there is no need to introduce more sophisticated methods. Classification works equally well for both CS and CR data sets. However, for non-contextual dataset there is much more randomness in the classification result that has to be examined further. Figure 2 illustrates well that expert knowledge (with medicine being a part of it) is based on a certain set of accepted truths. Credible articles have to contain mostly credible phrases. It is represented as a tight "credibility cluster" in each graph. Not credible articles, however, are not of such an obvious structure. They are far more diverse, and a simple not credible phrases versus all phrases ratio would not be enough to describe them. Nevertheless, to some extent, not credible article within this representation can be defined as the one that is located far enough from the credibility cluster.

As it was observed in K-means analysis, credible articles are well structured, with significantly higher credible to all phrases ratio than not credible to all. This is true for both models with phrases evaluated contextually and non-contextually. Not credible articles are much more diverse in their structure. Again, the above is true both in contextual and non-contextual model. This is because of expert knowledge, credibility appears to be much easier to define and evaluate than non-credibility.

The results from Table 2 present performance of Random Forest classifier built upon CS and US sets. The table contains mean and standard deviation

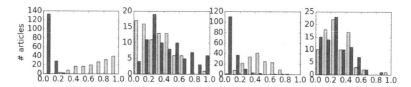

Fig. 3. Dark colour - noncredible phrases vs. all phrases ratio, light colour - credible phrases vs. all. From left to right: credible articles with sentences' evaluations performed with context, not credible articles with sentences' evaluations performed with context, credible articles with sentences' evaluations performed without context, not credible articles with sentences' evaluations performed without context.

of Recall and F1 measures for 10-fold cross-validation. Reasonable performance was achieved with the contextual input. For non-contextual data, however, recall measure is too close to 50% to prove classification usefulness (Fig. 3).

Table 2. Performance measures for Random Forest classifiers built upon two variants of the dataset.

	Recall [%]	F1 [%]
CS	87 (±13)	88 (±12)
US	65 (±7)	66 (±8)

The experiment of the reduction of specified credibility values of phrases in the input shows that the significant drop of classifier performance starts from approximately 40%, as is seen in Fig. 4. It means that we need only 40% of phrases from an article assessed to get a good classification result.

The pairwise comparison is shown in Table 3. The result of the Chi-squared test shows that the empirical distribution from the experiment is significantly different from the result expected from random probabilities. Therefore, it can be assumed that the similarities between pairwise sentence evaluations are not the results of random chance, and that contextual and non-contextual sentence evaluations are not stochastically independent. However, the observed relation is not a strong one, with only 60% agreement rate (among all the sentences only 60% have the same contextual and non-contextual evaluation). In order to understand better the difference between contextual and non-contextual evaluations, an analysis was conducted for a situation in which evaluations ranged from credible to not credible (i.e. sentence is contextually evaluated to be credible, but is non-contextually evaluated as not credible). The analysis has shown that there is a visible asymmetry in the way sentence evaluations differ. While it is quite improbable for a sentence that is non-contextually evaluated as credible to be contextually evaluated as not credible (9% probability), the opposite scenario occurs quite often (38% probability). This suggests that context can be used as a tool for 'hiding' not credible content in a document.

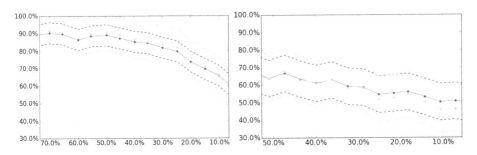

Fig. 4. Classifier's performance drop due to decrease of the number of phrases with specified credibility value. Light dots - mean recall, dark dots - mean F1, light dashed line - standard deviation boundary for mean recall, dark dashed line - standard deviation boundary for mean F1. From left to right: contextual model, non-contextual model.

Table 3. Pairwise comparison of contextual and non-contextual sentence evaluations

Contextual evaluation/Non-contextual evaluation	Not credible	Neutral	Credible
Not credible	878	543	469
Neutral	245	1711	811
Credible	702	2151	3373

4   Conclusions

The most important conclusion derived from the analysis is that it is not possible to build an efficient classifier based on a non-contextual model. The context of the whole article has to be considered while designing the core sentence comparison algorithm. The experiments conducted show that the classifier performs the task of filtering out not credible articles well if given the input that includes context. Even articles with only around 40% of phrases with a specified credibility value are labelled with sufficient recall. That is why, in further steps towards system implementation, focus shall be on developing an algorithm that creates a set of claims from sentences and their context, then automatically assesses claim credibility given the verified knowledge database. Aggregation of already existing frameworks for user aided claim verification systems and for the earlier solutions can result in an efficient and universal software for the automatic overall credibility assessment of medical articles.

In future work the goal will be to expand the database, as well as to develop more detailed analysis in relation to the role of the context in expert generated assessments. Proposed hypotheses include the use of semantic and lexical similarity of a single sentence and its context to predict the credibility of the new content. Other NLP-based approaches will include topic modelling in order to extract correlated themes with higher and lower credibility.

A   Quantitative Study Instruction

Phrases can be evaluated by using a three-degree scale:

CREDIBLE
- Is credible, does not raise any objections
- Contains information in the medical domain

NEUTRAL
- Contains worthless information or no information
- Is vague
- Is highly persuasive and remains consistent with the current medical knowledge

NOT CREDIBLE
- Is not credible
- Contains false or untested information
- Is highly persuasive, but is inconsistent with the current medical knowledge

Articles can be evaluated by using a two-degree scale:

CREDIBLE
- Does not raise any serious objections
- Does not call for actions inconsistent with the current medical knowledge
- Contains a fraction of specific medical knowledge

NOT CREDIBLE
- Does raise serious objections
- Calls for actions inconsistent with the current medical knowledge
- Does not contain any specific medical knowledge
- Contains false of untested information

References

1. Hassan, N., et al.: Claimbuster: the first-ever end-to-end fact-checking system. Proc. VLDB Endow. **10**(12), 1945–1948 (2017)
2. Lim, W.Y., Lee, M.L., Hsu, W.: iFACT: an interactive framework to assess claims from tweets. In: Proceedings of the 2017 ACM on Conference on Information and Knowledge Management, pp. 787–796. ACM (2017)
3. Popat, K., Mukherjee, S., Strötgen, J., Weikum, G.: Credibility assessment of textual claims on the web. In: Proceedings of the 25th ACM International on Conference on Information and Knowledge Management, pp. 2173–2178. ACM (2016)
4. Tschiatschek, S., Singla, A., Gomez Rodriguez, M., Merchant, A., Krause, A.: Fake news detection in social networks via crowd signals. In: Companion of the The Web Conference 2018 on The Web Conference 2018, pp. 517–524. International World Wide Web Conferences Steering Committee (2018)
5. Zhi, S., Sun, Y., Liu, J., Zhang, C., Han, J.: ClaimVerif: a real-time claim verification system using the web and fact databases. In: Proceedings of the 2017 ACM on Conference on Information and Knowledge Management, pp. 2555–2558. ACM (2017)

Urban Dynamics Simulation Considering Street Activeness and Transport Policies

Hideyuki Nagai[1(✉)] and Setsuya Kurahashi[2]

[1] Department of Risk Engineering, Graduate School of Systems and Information Engineering, University of Tsukuba, Tokyo, Japan
s1530156@u.tsukuba.ac.jp
[2] Graduate School of System Management, University of Tsukuba, Tokyo, Japan
kurahashi.setsuya.gf@u.tsukuba.ac.jp

Abstract. The purpose of this research is to verify the effectiveness of policies to control urban sprawl. By using an agent-based model (ABM), which was built for simulating urban structure changes through autonomous behavior of urban residents, this research clarified the following points and how they were. First, the combination of the proper location of a public facility for urban residents and the implementation of a policy to promote activeness around it was effective in maintaining a compact urban structure. Second, similarly, the synergistic effects of some transport policies and the above-mentioned policies could impact positively on urban environment generally.

Keywords: Agent-based model · Urban design · Urban sprawl
Compact City

1 Introduction

Along with the rapidly increase in the world population and urbanization during our current century along with the previous century, Urban sprawl has been criticized as an unsustainable form of urbanization [13]. Urban sprawl is defined by land-use characteristics such as expansion of urban area in outer fringe area, low-density development, scattered development, and leapfrog development [6, 8,11,16]. It also drives negative impact such as increase in traffic congestion and commuting time, air pollution, increase in energy consumption, increase in infrastructure maintenance and operation cost, hollowing out in an urban central area, and loss of agricultural and natural land [6,7,11,17]. In the future, Japan will definitely have a shrinking as well as ever-aging population. At the same time, the population has continued to concentrate in large city regions. These reasons have given rise especially to a concern about the serious negative impact caused by urban sprawl [1].

Researchers and experts have studied a shift into a sustainable urban form, "Compact City", as a countermeasure against urban sprawl that has driven such a multitude of negative impacts. It is commonly defined by the characteristics

S. Staab et al. (Eds.): SocInfo 2018, LNCS 11186, pp. 224–233, 2018.
https://doi.org/10.1007/978-3-030-01159-8_21

such as high-density, concentration of development, development in public transportation network, and monocentricity or polycentricity [3,5,8,18]. The compact city can overcome some of the negative impacts driven by urban sprawl. It also enhances the quality of life by offering a broad range of choices with regard to lifestyle and behavior including residences, travel modes, and shopping goods [5]. Considering the urban dynamics of a city including sprawl to be a complicated phenomenon of reciprocal interactions of a wide variety of autonomous entities, such as individuals, households, and firms [4,10,14], however, highlights the difficulty in direct control of the urban dynamics.

With these in mind, this research built an agent-based model (ABM) which can simulate urban structure changes. Then this research discussed the indirect improvement effect on urban structure by some policies, through the simulation experiments.

2   Related Works and Position of This Research

Urban sprawl is a special kind of land-use change, urban spatial expansion along a city boundary. And land-use changes come from its complex driving forces and their interactions [10,14]. Above all, the fundamental principle that land-use impacts transport and vice versa has been acknowledged by many scholars and supported by empirical findings [2]. Much research efforts based on this background have culminated in the development of operational urban LUTI models as decision support systems. Such models have subsequently continued to develop as hybrid agent-based urban models. And a series of these models have contributed to express complicated macro-level land-use patterns of cities including clusterization and sprawl as self-organization through micro-level adaptive behavior of agents, such as households and firms. Such models have served to explore urban growth scenarios [4,9,15].

And recently, revitalization of urban central areas that hollowed out along with urban sprawl has become a critically important issue. Along with this, researchers and experts have reevaluated the importance of informal public spaces for activities of local residents. The two factors are vital to forming such public space. First, such public space needs to serve as a hub for people in their daily. As for such urban hubs, public complexes based mainly on libraries have recently attracted much attention. The series of Idea Store in London, U.K. and several pioneering libraries built and put into operation recently in Japan are relevant to such cases. Second, such public space needs to generate "street activeness". Street activeness indicates a lively situation where individuals gather and stroll around downtown while enjoying exchanges [12]. It is a source of diversity and tolerance, therefore, it can bring about not only usefulness or efficiency, but also creative, cultural, or recreational benefits.

This research, by integrating the above-mentioned conceptual frameworks: urban LUTI model and revitalization of urban central area, built the agent-based model (ABM) to consider qualitative benefit obtained by using informal public space and being in such a place, along with the daily travel of urban residents.

Then this research verified the possibility that an urban environment can be controlled indirectly by locating of such a space, the policy to promote activeness in such a place, and some transport policies, through residents' selection of daily travel mode and where to live.

3   Simulation Model

Based on the modeling policy of abstraction as much as possible, this research focused especially on the daily travel and residential relocation of urban residents through their interactions, as well as the resulting change in land-use pattern, and simplify the other factors as far as possible. The overview of the experimental model was described below according to the ODD protocol.

Entities are a planar urban schematic and household agents who act in the urban schematic. Both are spatially-explicit. Figure 1 shows the urban schematic. The urban schematic is the abstracted expression of a part of a typical regional city in Japan, where a central business district (CBD) and bedroom towns connected by railway. This model simulates the behavior of 10,000 households. In the residence district, as the initial location, residences are located randomly based on normal distribution centering on the residence stations. Similarly, in CBD, job locations are also located centering on the central station. And one public facility such as a complex mentioned in the previous section is located in the central area or the suburb of CBD.

In the sub-model of daily travel, each household agent leaves the residence for the job location. And after all household agents arrive at each job location, they leave for the public facility. After arriving and staying there, finally they return to the residence. Then, the total travel cost is calculated. The total travel cost is the sum of cost time cost, charge cost, fatigue cost, and activeness value. According to this travel cost, the household agent changes the values of the selected linked trip. The following daily travel is done according to the linked trip selected by the ε-greedy method based on this value. And each household agent fixes their travel mode in one way through the learning period of repeating this daily travel 30 times. Around the public facility, a policy to promote activeness is implemented. Street activeness is generated when household agents, which travel on foot or by bicycle within this range, interact face-to-face, and relevant household agents gain benefit brought about by the street activeness as activeness value.

In the sub-model of residential relocation, after all household agents fix their travel mode in one way through the learning period, 1/10 of all household agents that are randomly chosen relocate their residences. The total living cost of these candidates is the sum of total travel cost and land rent. The total travel cost is calculated by conducting virtual daily travel from a candidate residence based on the fixed travel mode. The land rent at the candidate increases according to the agglomeration of neighboring residences and job locations. Each household agents relocate to the candidate residence of which the total living cost is the minimum out of 10 candidates. The change of land-use pattern is brought about through these residential relocations.

After the loop process of residential relocation is repeated 20 times, the simulation stops processing. The single simulation process corresponds to simulating 40 years in the real-world.

By observing the result of each experimental scenario according to the indicators, such as percentage of each representative travel mode, total CO_2 emission, average travel time, standard deviation of distribution of residences, and distribution map of residences, changes in the urban structure are evaluated.

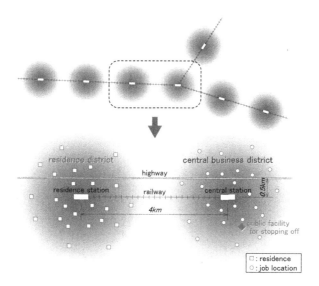

Fig. 1. Urban scheme

4   Experiment 1 - Public Facility for Stopping Off and Policy to Promote Activeness

This section verifies the change of the urban structure, which was formed according to the zoning with separation between residences and job locations, based on the introduction of a public facility for urban residents and the implementation of a policy to promote activeness around it. The simulation experiments were conducted while changing the location of the public facility and the implementation scale of the policy to promote activeness.

Table 1 and Fig. 2 show the results in this section.

In any cases when locating a public facility for stopping off (PFS) without implementing a policy to promote activeness around it, regardless of its location, the percentage of private automobile users increased, and their residences were distributed as sprawl, like the case when not introducing PFS.

In any cases except when introducing PFS at the same place as the central station, by advancing the policy to promote activeness and making it reach a certain scale, the percentage of private automobile users decreased, the total CO_2 emission reduced, and the sprawl was improved drastically - like "phase transition" took place. These suggest that the combination of the proper location of a public facility for urban residents and the implementation of a policy to promote activeness around it was effective in maintaining a compact urban structure. At the same time, this also suggests that such a policy is not effective unless implemented on a certain large scale.

Among these cases, in the cases when introducing PFS near the central station, the phase transition took place even though the policy to promote activeness was implemented on smaller scale. In contrast, in the cases when introducing PFS at the same place as the central station, the phase transition didn't take place. These suggest the possibility that the slight difference in the location of such a facility might bring about the significant difference in the future urban environment.

Table 1. Result of experiment 1

Scenario	Percentage of representative travel modes				CO_2 emission	Travel time	Standard deviation	
	Walk	Bicycle	Train	Automobile			x-cor	y-cor
A	1.3%	2.4%	7.3%	89.0%	100.0%	9.3 min	22.9	9.8
B0	1.2%	1.4%	3.9%	93.5%	159.7%	29.8 min	26.2	11.1
B10	1.4%	1.4%	4.0%	93.3%	161.5%	30.0 min	25.9	10.9
B20	1.2%	1.5%	4.1%	93.3%	175.3%	30.7 min	22.1	10.2
B30	2.6%	1.3%	47.7%	48.4%	102.3%	55.1 min	16.1	8.8
C0	1.1%	1.7%	3.9%	93.3%	158.7%	36.3 min	25.6	13.1
C10	0.9%	1.4%	4.2%	93.5%	163.8%	36.7 min	24.7	12.8
C20	1.2%	1.4%	5.1%	92.3%	177.9%	39.8 min	22.0	11.5
C30	2.7%	1.1%	48.9%	47.3%	98.1%	60.6 min	17.2	9.9
D0	1.2%	1.6%	9.8%	87.5%	120.5%	19.0 min	21.1	10.3
D10	1.1%	1.5%	10.3%	87.1%	119.5%	18.8 min	21.2	10.6
D20	1.2%	1.6%	10.4%	86.8%	119.5%	19.0 min	20.8	10.5
D30	1.3%	1.7%	12.2%	84.8%	117.8%	19.2 min	20.7	10.2
E0	1.0%	1.6%	5.6%	91.8%	129.4%	23.0 min	23.4	11.2
E10	1.1%	1.5%	9.3%	88.1%	133.7%	24.4 min	21.4	10.4
E20	1.7%	1.5%	47.6%	49.2%	84.9%	33.2 min	15.4	8.8
E30	2.3%	1.5%	66.8%	29.4%	58.3%	40.7 min	12.4	8.0

The simulation model reproduced the multiple social phenomena (the observed patterns in the real-world, such as growth process of a low-density suburb, expansion of urban areas, and switch from public transportation use to private automobile use) which were not directly incorporated into the model. Therefore, it was demonstrated that the simulation model can explain the real society to a certain level, and the experimental results of this research are valid.

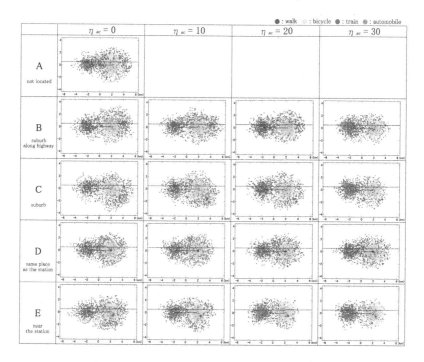

Fig. 2. Residences' final distribution of experiment 1

5   Experiment 2 - Policy to Promote Bicycle Use

This section verifies the change of the urban structure, based on the combination of the implementation of the policy to promote bicycle use with the policies mentioned in the previous section.

Table 2 and Fig. 3 show the results in this section.

By combining implementing the policy to promote bicycle use with introducing PFS and implementing a policy to promote activeness around it, the percentage of private automobile users decreased in any cases, when compared with the cases when not combing the policy. And the percentage of bicycle users and train and bicycle in combination users increased accordingly. Along with this, the total CO_2 emission reduced, and the sprawl was improved. These suggest that the synergistic effects of the policy to promote bicycle use, the proper location of the public facility for urban residents, and the policy to promote activeness around it, could impact positively on an urban environment.

Table 2. Result of experiment 2

Scenario	Percentage of representative travel modes				CO$_2$ emission	Travel time	Standard deviation	
	Walk	Bicycle	Train	Automobile			x-cor	y-cor
Ab	1.3%	4.7%	22.6%	71.5%	85.3%	8.1 min	21.5	9.1
Cb0	1.3%	3.9%	35.7%	59.2%	104.1%	30.3 min	22.8	11.3
Cb10	1.0%	3.9%	43.8%	51.3%	93.4%	29.7 min	21.4	10.8
Cb20	1.4%	4.6%	49.9%	44.1%	82.0%	29.7 min	20.3	10.5
Cb30	1.3%	5.7%	56.5%	36.5%	73.5%	29.9 min	17.3	9.9
Db0	1.1%	3.1%	40.7%	55.1%	80.3%	15.0 min	18.3	9.2
Db10	1.2%	2.9%	39.7%	56.3%	80.5%	14.9 min	18.6	9.2
Db20	1.3%	3.2%	40.8%	54.7%	79.5%	15.2 min	18.4	9.0
Db30	1.3%	3.0%	41.0%	54.6%	78.8%	15.3 min	18.5	9.0
Eb0	1.2%	3.2%	42.9%	52.8%	79.1%	18.2 min	19.7	9.6
Eb10	1.1%	3.0%	48.3%	47.5%	73.7%	17.8 min	18.6	9.1
Eb20	1.5%	3.1%	55.8%	39.6%	65.8%	18.0 min	16.4	8.5
Eb30	1.4%	3.2%	65.6%	29.8%	54.5%	22.8 min	13.9	8.2

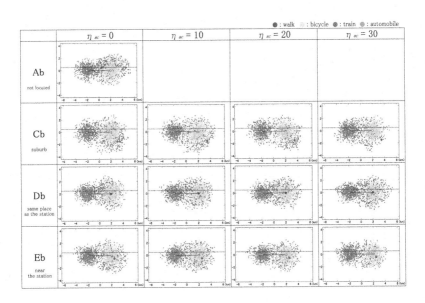

Fig. 3. Residences' final distribution of experiment 2

6   Experiment 3 - Policy to Control Private Automobile Use

This section verifies the change of the urban structure, based on the combination of the implementation of the policy to control private automobile use in an urban central area with the policies mentioned before the previous section.

Table 3 and Fig. 4 show the results in this section.

Table 3. Result of experiment 3

Scenario	Percentage of representative travel modes				CO$_2$ emission	Travel time	Standard deviation	
	Walk	Bicycle	Train	Automobile			x-cor	y-cor
Ap	1.9%	10.8%	37.5%	49.8%	72.9%	26.3 min	16.0	10.3
Cp0	1.1%	8.5%	10.8%	79.5%	151.2%	63.3 min	23.5	14.3
Cp10	1.5%	4.2%	33.1%	61.2%	127.1%	66.9 min	18.8	12.0
Cp20	2.7%	2.3%	58.1%	36.9%	86.7%	73.5 min	13.6	9.6
Cp30	3.3%	1.8%	70.1%	24.7%	64.7%	79.0 min	12.1	8.7
Dp0	1.5%	12.3%	64.9%	21.3%	42.7%	36.6 min	12.9	8.0
Dp10	1.6%	9.5%	60.0%	28.9%	52.5%	37.9 min	12.9	8.3
Dp20	2.0%	6.2%	56.4%	35.5%	61.6%	39.9 min	12.4	8.4
Dp30	3.3%	4.3%	48.4%	44.1%	74.0%	43.2 min	12.5	8.8
Ep0	1.4%	14.7%	53.8%	30.2%	55.0%	45.3 min	15.3	9.3
Ep10	2.1%	5.7%	71.9%	20.3%	42.6%	48.2 min	10.7	7.4
Ep20	2.3%	4.2%	79.5%	14.0%	34.7%	50.4 min	10.0	7.2
Ep30	2.7%	2.9%	82.4%	12.0%	31.9%	52.8 min	9.8	7.3

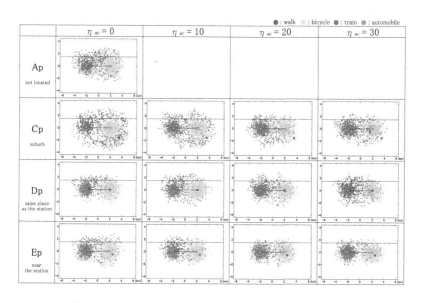

Fig. 4. Residences' final distribution of experiment 3

By combining implementing the policy to control private automobile use in an urban central area with introducing PFS and implementing the policy to promote activeness, the percentage of private automobile users decreased, the total CO$_2$ emission reduced, and the sprawl was improved remarkably in any cases, when compared with the cases when not combing the policy. Particularly, in the cases when introducing PFS in the urban central area, within the range eliminating private automobile traffic, this tendency was remarkable.

There is a slight difference whether the location of PFS is at the same place as the central station or near the station, however, as advancing the policy to promote activeness, the urban environment got worsened gradually in the former, while got improved gradually in the latter. These suggest the possibility that the synergistic effects of the policy to control private automobile use, the proper location of the public facility for urban residents, and the policy to promote activeness around it, could impact rather negatively than positively on the urban environment.

7   Conclusion

All findings described above suggest the followings. First, when a public facility for urban residents is introduced to improve an urban environment, it is necessary to pay close attention to its location and promoting activeness around it. Second, there are not only the positive but also the negative synergistic effects of transport policies implemented in combination.

References

1. White paper on land, infrastructure and transport in 2016 - the ministry of land, infrastructure and transport. http://www.mlit.go.jp/hakusyo/mlit/h28/index.html
2. Acheampong, R.A., Silva, E.: Land use-transport interaction modeling: a review of the literature and future research directions. J. Transp. Land Use **8**(3), 11–38 (2015)
3. Anderson, W.P., Kanaroglou, P.S., Miller, E.J.: Urban form, energy and the environment: a review of issues, evidence and policy. Urban Stud. **33**(1), 7–35 (1996)
4. Batty, M.: Cities and Complexity: Understanding Cities with Cellular Automata, Agent-Based Models, and Fractals. The MIT press, Cambridge (2007)
5. Behan, K., Maoh, H., Kanaroglou, P.: Smart growth strategies, transportation and urban sprawl: simulated futures for Hamilton, Ontario. Can. Geogr./Le Géographe canadien **52**(3), 291–308 (2008)
6. Brueckner, J.K., Mills, E., Kremer, M.: Urban sprawl: lessons from urban economics. In: Brookings-Wharton Papers on Urban Affairs, pp. 65–97 (2001)
7. Deal, B., Schunk, D.: Spatial dynamic modeling and urban land use transformation: a simulation approach to assessing the costs of urban sprawl. Ecol. Econ. **51**(1), 79–95 (2004)
8. Ewing, R.: Is Los Angeles-style sprawl desirable? J. Am. Plann. Assoc. **63**(1), 107–126 (1997)
9. Gilbert, N.: Agent-Based Models, vol. 153. Sage, London (2008)
10. Gimblett, R., Daniel, T., Cherry, S., Meitner, M.J.: The simulation and visualization of complex human-environment interactions. Landscape Urban Plann. **54**(1), 63–79 (2001)
11. Johnson, M.P.: Environmental impacts of urban sprawl: a survey of the literature and proposed research agenda. Environ. Plann. A **33**(4), 717–735 (2001)
12. Kaneda, T.: Modeling visitors' shopping-around behaviors in shopping district. J. Jpn. Soc. Artif. Intell. **30**(4), 423–428 (2015)

13. Lagarias, A.: Urban sprawl simulation linking macro-scale processes to micro-dynamics through cellular automata, an application in Thessaloniki, Greece. Appl. Geogr. **34**, 146–160 (2012)
14. Ligtenberg, A., Bregt, A.K., Van Lammeren, R.: Multi-actor-based land use modelling: spatial planning using agents. Landscape Urban Plann. **56**(1), 21–33 (2001)
15. Railsback, S.F., Grimm, V.: Agent-Based and Individual-Based Modeling: A Practical Introduction. Princeton University Press, Princeton (2011)
16. Schneider, A., Woodcock, C.E.: Compact, dispersed, fragmented, extensive? A comparison of urban growth in twenty-five global cities using remotely sensed data, pattern metrics and census information. Urban Stud. **45**(3), 659–692 (2008)
17. Scott, D.M., Kanaroglou, P.S., Anderson, W.P.: Impacts of commuting efficiency on congestion and emissions: case of the Hamilton CMA, Canada. Transp. Res. Part D Transp. Environ. **2**(4), 245–257 (1997)
18. Tsai, Y.H.: Quantifying urban form: compactness versus 'sprawl'. Urban Stud. **42**(1), 141–161 (2005)

Designing Healthcare Systems
with an Emphasis on Relational Quality
and Peace of Mind

Leysan Nurgalieva[1](✉)(iD), Marcos Baez[1,2](iD), Francesca Fiore[1](iD),
Fabio Casati[1,2](iD), and Maurizio Marchese[1](iD)

[1] University of Trento, Trento, Italy
{leysan.nurgalieva,marcos.baez,francesca.fiore,fabio.casati,
maurizio.marchese}@unitn.it
[2] Tomsk Polytechnic University, Tomsk, Russia

Abstract. In this paper we explore the challenges and opportunities of
designing information systems in healthcare with an emphasis on informational needs of family caregivers and work practices of professionals.
We focus particularly on the context of Nursing Homes (NH), where
family members and care professionals are often faced with challenging
situations that can affect their ability to communicate and collaborate
effectively, and thus, leading to the episodes of conflicts or mismatch
of expectations. We report on two sets of user studies with staff and
residents' family members in four nursing homes, studying current information practices, factors that influence them, and explore design alternatives that could target identified issues.

Keywords: Information sharing · Health and wellbeing
Information architecture · Nursing homes

1 Introduction

Shifting from *in-home* to *nursing home (NH)* care is a stressful transition for
both older adults and their family members (FMs), with challenges ranging from
the adaptation to a new environment to feelings of guilt and mistrust towards
the NH staff [1,8,9]. In such situations, the NH staff plays not only the role of
caregiver for the new resident, but has to carefully manage the interaction with
the FMs as well and to some extent even coordinate care, as FMs often act as
informal caregivers [2,11].

Several studies [7,10] investigated the communication between professional
and family caregivers showing that *families need more information* and a greater
involvement into the care process [3,12]. Thus, the staff-family interaction and
the kind of exchanged (or not) information is important for the wellbeing of the
FMs. The way professionals communicate residents' health related information to
their family may also significantly affect the work routine of the staff, increasing
or reducing their (often very high) workload [15].

© Springer Nature Switzerland AG 2018
S. Staab et al. (Eds.): SocInfo 2018, LNCS 11186, pp. 234–242, 2018.
https://doi.org/10.1007/978-3-030-01159-8_22

In this paper we study if and how technology can facilitate the staff-family interaction and information exchange, and which are the opportunities, critical aspects, and design considerations for doing so. Mediating and semi-automating the staff-family interaction via technology has a lot of potential in improving the information exchange, increasing its transparency, and, therefore, providing increased sense of trust and control and reducing the care related workload of the staff. On the other hand, the personal interaction is often essential, and technology may worsen it, for example, by generating unnecessary worry and doubts in FMs when information is given without the proper context or explanation for the specific recipient.

Not surprisingly, discovering the most effective ways of mediating such relations and communications using ICT is recognized as a prominent research direction [6]. However, only few studies have explored how technology can support family caregivers and staff-family interactions [4,13], so there is a little knowledge on the actual *design* of technologically mediated communication [5,14].

In the following we investigate the information seeking behavior, information expectations of FMs, and factors that define them. We also explore professional communication practices and the rationale behind them to identify if and how technology can provide a contribution. An area of specific interest, as pointed to us by NH management, was the opportunity to selectively communicate information taken from the NH information system to the FMs, possibly endowed with explanations to make information easy to understand by non professional. Specifically, we aimed at answering the following research questions:

- RQ1: What are the communication practices, perceived satisfaction and mutual attitudes regarding information sharing in NHs?
- RQ2: What are the main design considerations in technology-supported information sharing between NH staff and FMs?

We proceed by designing a set of studies, first to understand the space of problem and opportunities and then to focus on specific cases and designs. We run the studies in several NHs throughout Italy, to also capture the different NH policies and attitudes related to staff-family interactions. As we will see, the results show us that there is a space for the introduction of technology but it is rather narrow: most of the initial beliefs, not only by non-professional like us but by NH management as well and even by family members, turned out to be wrong, although there are specific situations where technology can help.

2 Methods

After the preliminary phase of informal exploratory visits in 12 Italian nursing homes (NHs), two sets of user studies were conducted in four of them, which were approved by the University of Trento Committee on Research Involving Human Beings (Application N. 2017-003). All of the NHs use the information system that stores various health and wellbeing (HWB) information updated daily for each resident. Each staff member has a defined role and information access according to it within the system and in terms of interaction with relatives but only specific personnel is allowed to report on medical information to family members.

2.1 Study 1. Communication Practices and Relational Attitudes

Focusing on emerging NH communication practices from the perspectives of the staff and family members, with this study we investigated information sharing and seeking strategies, how staff and family members deal with potentially sensitive information, and the role of technology in shaping interactions between them. Participants were recruited through the NH contacts, as to get a representative sample of family caregivers and NH staff. We conducted a total of 26 semi-structured interviews with relatives (17, 65.5 mean age and 59% of females) and professionals (9, 48.9 mean age and 55.6% of females) who volunteered to participate. Prior to the start of each interview, participants were briefed on the objective of the study and signed an informed consent.

The interviews with family caregivers focused on (i) information seeking strategies, and (ii) expectations and attitudes towards sharing of information by the NH staff. The interviews with the NH staff followed similar themes, with an emphasis on information communication practices and factors that shape them. Each interview lasted from 20 to 30 min and was carried out in full anonymity without the involvement of third parties.

2.2 Study 2. Design Considerations for HWB Information Sharing

Building on the findings from the previous interviews, we explore the specific dimensions of information exchange by navigating NH staff through low-fidelity prototypes. Overall, 9 semi-structured anonymous interviews that lasted from 20 to 40 min were conducted with NH staff members (50.6 mean age and 66.7% of females). They were asked about relevance, importance, and views on preferred ways of communicating examples of NH routine events to the FMs using ICT tools. Events included medical (sodium and glucose levels and blood pressure), daily routine events (meals, sleep, and social events), and change of therapy. Questions and surveys were specifically focused around the implications of different *design alternatives* of medical and non medical events, granularity (single events and trends) and presentation (raw events, and enriched). Regarding each screen, staff members were asked to express their informed opinion on expected reactions of the FMs upon receiving information in a given way, as well as the readiness of staff to share using given design alternative.

3 Results

3.1 Study 1. Communication Practices and Relational Attitudes

The qualitative analysis revealed specific communication practices and attitudes depending, primarily, on the type of HWB information, the role of the NH staff member, and the characteristics of the family member involved.

Communication Practices of NH Staff. Critical events are communicated proactively by the NH, for instance, a fall is always communicated *immediately* by phone but not alarms for specific health parameters like high blood pressure. Instead, upon necessary therapy changes doctor reaches family members if approval is necessary. Information is usually provided by doctors face-to-face via fixed appointment and NH staff members calling based on their competence area, and test results and daily events are communicated mostly during the visits and by request based on the resident's condition. Overall, staff communicates "trends" but not specific events, e.g., not if a person did not sleep last night but if he or she skipped several nights in a row, which is first medically evaluated. In general, for non-critical events professional judgment plays the key role in deciding what information to share.

Information Seeking by Family Caregivers. We observed three distinct types of family caregivers based on their organisation and involvement: individuals (5), care teams (6), and proxies (2). *Individuals* are family members playing the role of primary contact with little to no involvement from other relatives. *Care teams* are groups of FMs sharing care responsibility and involvement. *Proxies* are persons hired by the family to visit the resident on their behalf and deliver them HWB information.

All participants reported interactions during NH visits as a primary mode of information exchange and phone calls as another common channel, which aligns with the communication practices reported by the NH staff. However, these communications were mostly initiated by NH staff, and in two cases daily visiting participants reported not even having that. No other modes of information exchange with the NH were reported. The importance of human contact was explicitly raised by three participants from the relational perspective, while those with the loved one in a critical condition stressed the importance of the appointments with the doctor.

Phone calls were reported as the dominating mode of information exchange and coordination among family caregivers, while individual carers reported little communication with the relatives who are not involved. Proxies mentioned updating family members via phone and email. All participants reported interacting with doctors and the responsible nurses for information exchange and, interestingly, four participants also indicated the resident as their main source of information. Family information needs were determined by the resident's health condition and the level of trust on the NH. Family caregivers of residents in a non-critical condition showed either a more passive approach to information exchange, expecting the NH staff to inform them of relevant updates (e.g., *"I do not ask but if there is something [wrong], I guess they will tell me"*, F11, daughter) or contacting them when they observe an issue. Two participants with relatives in a more critical conditions preferred having access to all available information, but also reported negative past experiences with the NH staff.

General updates about the resident's situation was the dominant theme in FMs information requests (*"What is good, what is bad. Information about the day*", F10, son), while two participants (F5, proxy; F11, daughter) explicitly mention social and relational information as the most important one. Some participants were interested in general medical information relying on what the NH could communicate and deemed relevant. This aligns with the NH staff interviews, where they reported that family members rarely asked or did not even know about specific medical tests.

Mutual Views in Relation to Information Exchange. Most family caregivers were satisfied with the NH communication, especially in case of stable or non-critical condition of the resident (*"My mother takes just one medicine, there is nothing much to discuss"*, F11). In two particular cases however, participants expressed dissatisfaction, which raised a series of communication exchange problems. One family caregiver from a care team highlighted episodes of confrontation where they considered the NH did not take the appropriate actions in a case of emergency. This participant indicated that they would like to see all the test results with the exact numbers: *"I would like to see the exact numbers. Because now, for example, my mother has diabetes. [Early this year] we had a meeting with a diabetologist in [a nearby city] to see the state of the diabetes. Back then, she was under control... And now, [NH staff] controls [the progress of diabetes] just once a day. It's not enough. We asked the coordinator, how [my mother] is doing, and [the coordinator] told fine. What does it mean 'fine'? At home we measured 3 times a day and now here nothing."* The quote encapsulates several themes: the feeling that family was taking a better care of the resident at home; an apparent lack of trust in the NH practices shaped by the participant previous experiences; the involvement of third parties (experts) to verify the care practices; and issues related to expectations and understanding of the information provided by the NH staff.

Another participant expressed dissatisfaction with the doctor in particular, but for different reasons: *"He doesn't update me [on my mother health condition] if I don't ask, even if there are things to be communicated."* This participant showed different expectations on the way information should be communicated by the NH staff, more proactively. As a way to manage the situation and uncertainty, the participant wish was to be informed if only things were fine (*"If they'd [keep me informed], it's always good. It's also good to know that everything is going well"*). On that last point, all participants were aware that calls from the NH have a sort of negative connotation as the "bearer of bad news".

The **interviews with the NH staff** gave a us rich perspective into different dimensions they use to categorise and describe family members or "personas":

- Reactions to updates based on level of worry, anxiety, and irrational requests;
- Care involvement or time spent with a relative at the NH;
- Views on the NH as a facility and services it has to provide;
- Care related knowledge and experience;
- Trust on practices adopted by the NH professionals;
- Feeling of guilt towards moving their relative to the NH influenced by cultural context and society stigma;

– Expectations towards amount and quality of work from the staff members;
– Amount of questions family members ask the staff;
– Health condition of the resident.

Personal relations are very important, how comfortable staff feels to communicate certain events directly or in a less detailed fashion. However, the knowledge of the "personas" is implicit and different communication strategies scattered through the NH staff.

3.2   Study 2. Design Considerations for HWB Information Sharing

While participants agreed that introducing the technology-mediated information exchange with FMs could improve the communication, most of them were concerned of workload increase if information would have to be logged manually: *"Well, it could be nice and probably reassuring for the family members. I am asking you if a nurse who takes care of 102 residents during the night also has time to do this. I have doubts"* (P1, doctor).

Presentation of HWB Information. Discussing *raw* singular events, NH staff emphasized the importance of reference values or explanations, since family members may not know how to interpret them. However, they also noted that each case is unique and it is difficult to provide a generic explanation of the values: they depend on the specific health situation.

When shown the concept of event enrichment and explanation, which included smileys as a way to facilitate the interpretation of the event (negative, neutral, or positive), most of the professionals approved such summaries: *"If the program will let me [add]... also just a smiley, sad or red, green, anyway these are the signals that make relatives understand that there is more explanation, that it says that everything is going well"* (P4, nurse coordinator). However, one participant assumed that a smiley can also miscommunicate information: *"The family members know the resident, they can see things we do not see, if they see the red smiley and instead they know that it is not critical... [may be stressful]"* (P6, nurse coordinator).

Events communicated directly without translation by the professionals and presented only graphically could be perceived as "cold and distant": *"This one [raw event without translation] is more technical, colder, more detached. Instead this one [raw event with translation], even more visually, it makes you immediately understand the situation"* (P8, social worker).

Reports over a period of time (trends) were seen as helpful both for family and staff members, for example, to detect deviations or verify past activities and monitor overall wellbeing or therapy. *"[On the trend of having meals] I think that a graph like this would nice to have for us too. To understand better"* (P6, nurse coordinator). Regarding the time periods for such reports, most of the staff members (5 out of 9) expressed the preference towards the weekly reports.

NH staff believe that retrospective information is less stressful for family members. However, in cases when family members were not informed about some negative events or certain dynamics in their loved one's health, discovering it later in trends may raise additional questions. *"They would also ask [the NH] if they were not informed in advance. In the sense that, if things are not going well and they did not know, seeing the trend like this, they would ask "How come?". They would call immediately if they were not informed"* (P6, nurse coordinator).

Staff members were concerned that unlike trends, sending singular events would overload family members with excessive information: *"Rather than bombarding a [family member] with SMS everyday to say "today he went to the bathroom, today she walked, today he ate a beef steak"... [trend] is less invasive"* (P7, physiotherapist).

Expected Preference and Reactions. Beside the qualitative evaluation of the design alternatives, participants were asked to assess each of the randomly selected screens in relation to two main factors: preference based on efficiency and simplification of communicating events, and expected reactions and stress level of FMs upon receiving information in a given way.

Efficiency. While talking to the staff members about their views that sending *translated events* to family members could make the communication more efficient, in 75% of responses participants agreed or strongly agreed that it could, while only 12.5% did not. As for direct communication of not translated events, 58.4% of responses were positive about increasing the efficiency of such communication and 37.5% were negative.

Simplicity. For the simplicity of communication with family members, 66.7% of all comments on the design alternatives were positive that translated events could indeed simplify information the interaction. Just 8.4% disagreed. As for the design alternatives of not translated events, in more than half of their responses, staff members stated that they would share the events in this way to simplify the communication, while in 37.5% of comments they did not think so.

Anticipated Reactions by Family Members. As the response to receiving medical events, staff members would expect relatives to call the nursing home for the clarifications (occurred in 44% of responses), while the most expected reaction on daily routine updates would be asking during the visit, which was mentioned in the 38.5% of the responses.

Medical events were seen as more stressful for the FMs than daily events. In 29.2% of responses, staff would expect extreme stress in family members after receiving medical updates, while for the daily information it is just 4.2% and the most common – no stress at all (45.9%). Translation of events was considered as less stressful comparing to the direct communication. Expectations of light stress or no stress at all occurred in 79.2% of comments on translated events, while for the alternative it was 45.9%.

4   Discussion and Limitations

The results can be translated into design considerations to be taken into account when designing technology-mediated HWB information:

- **Tailor information sharing** to the "hidden" needs of the family members. Personalisation is known to increase user satisfaction but these needs are not always evident to the FMs, which can be tackled by the NH staff by mapping the relative classification (from a communication perspective) into the technology to allow for this personalization.
- **Allow for family to staff communication**, to let staff know the care preferences and habits of the resident that the family member wants to be respected if possible.
- **Consider the modalities of information sharing**, in terms of proper granularity, contextual information, and explanations. Information on trends is considered useful by both staff and family as it avoids information overload. Contextual information such as condition of the resident and historical data can help understand the data, while explanations or "translation" provide useful narrative to properly interpret information, and give an additional human touch.
- **Provide scaffolded and contextual information presentation**, from summaries from the resident's general condition to specific health parameters, giving family members the possibility to understand the situation at a glance and navigate it at their desired level of detail. Provide relevant information to the time and context, which implies thinking in terms of what information can be delivered through synchronous and asynchronous channels.
- **Provide tools to allow for coordination and information exchange** in family care teams, as well as tools to update the larger family within the limits of GDPR and related regulations.
- **Provide wellbeing and relational information:** while the interest in medical information varied, for basic questions it was overwhelming, such as how the resident slept or ate. Family members want to have the same information collected only partially by the NH today, and technology can help us gather it semi-automatically.

Overall, this work strengthens the idea that it is critical to consider both preferences of family caregivers and work practices of the NH staff in designing information services such as e-health systems. The studies have also reshaped the initial belief in communication of medical information from staff to family to the focus on (i) bidirectional interaction, (ii) social and wellbeing events, and (iii) attention to personas and personalized explanations and contextualizations.

The study has several limitations and the most frustrating one was the difficulty in approaching FMs who visit rarely due to a variety of factors including the recruitment through NH contacts. However, this means that the results are only applicable to "frequent visitors".

Acknowledgements. This project has received funding from the EU Horizon 2020 research and innovation programme under the Marie Skłodowska-Curie grant agreement No. 690962. This work was also supported by the "Collegamenti" project funded by the Province of Trento (l.p. n.6-December 13rd 1999).

References

1. Almberg, B., Grafström, M., Krichbaum, K., Winblad, B.: The interplay of institution and family caregiving: Relations between patient hassles, nursing home hassles and caregivers' burnout. Int. J. Geriatr. Psychiatry **15**(10), 931–939 (2000)

2. Blusi, M., Asplund, K., Jong, M.: Older family carers in rural areas: experiences from using caregiver support services based on information and communication technology (ICT). Eur. J. Ageing **10**(3), 191–199 (2013)

3. Carman, K.L., et al.: Patient and family engagement: a framework for understanding the elements and developing interventions and policies. Health Aff. **32**(2), 223–231 (2013)

4. Chi, N.C., Demiris, G.: A systematic review of telehealth tools and interventions to support family caregivers. J. Telemed. Telecare **21**(1), 37–44 (2015)

5. Chiu, T.M., Eysenbach, G.: Theorizing the health service usage behavior of family caregivers: a qualitative study of an internet-based intervention. Int. J. Med. Inform. **80**(11), 754–764 (2011)

6. Desai, P.M., Levine, M.E., Albers, D.J., Mamykina, L.: Pictures worth a thousand words: reflections on visualizing personal blood glucose forecasts for individuals with type 2 diabetes. In: Proceedings of the 2018 CHI Conference on Human Factors in Computing Systems, p. 538. ACM (2018)

7. Duncan, M.T., Morgan, D.L.: Sharing the caring: family caregivers' views of their relationships with nursing home staff. Gerontologist **34**(2), 235–244 (1994)

8. Eika, M., Espnes, G.A., Söderhamn, O., Hvalvik, S.: Experiences faced by next of kin during their older family members' transition into long-term care in a Norwegian nursing home. J. Clin. Nurs. **23**(15–16), 2186–2195 (2014)

9. Hertzberg, A., Ekman, S.L.: "we, not them and us?" Views on the relationships and interactions between staff and relatives of older people permanently living in nursing homes. J. Adv. Nurs. **31**(3), 614–622 (2000)

10. Maas, M.L., et al.: Outcomes of family involvement in care intervention for caregivers of individuals with dementia. Nurs. Res. **53**(2), 76–86 (2004)

11. McFall, S., Miller, B.H.: Caregiver burden and nursing home admission of frail elderly persons. J. Gerontol. **47**(2), S73–S79 (1992)

12. Stajduhar, K.I., Funk, L., Outcalt, L.: Family caregiver learning - how family caregivers learn to provide care at the end of life: a qualitative secondary analysis of four datasets. Palliat. Med. **27**(7), 657–664 (2013)

13. Thomsen, J.R., Krogh, P.G., Schnedler, J.A., Linnet, H.: Interactive interior and proxemics thresholds: empowering participants in sensitive conversations. In: Proceedings of the 2018 CHI Conference on Human Factors in Computing Systems, p. 68. ACM (2018)

14. Washington, K.T., Meadows, S.E., Elliott, S.G., Koopman, R.J.: Information needs of informal caregivers of older adults with chronic health conditions. Patient Educ. Couns. **83**(1), 37–44 (2011)

15. Zwarenstein, M., Goldman, J., Reeves, S.: Interprofessional collaboration: effects of practice-based interventions on professional practice and healthcare outcomes. The Cochrane Library (2009)

Success Factors of Electronic Petitions at Russian Public Initiative Project: The Role of Informativeness, Topic and Lexical Information

Alexander Porshnev[(✉)]

National Research University Higher School of Economics, Moscow, Russia
aporshnev@hse.ru

Abstract. Online petitions are usually regarded as one of the most popular channels to involve citizens in the political process. In our paper we have analyzed texts and voting data (pro and against) from 9705 e-petitions submitted from 2013 until 2017 at Russian Public Initiative project. Analysis of dynamics showed stabilization of interest to this resource (emergence of a new authors, growth of "strong" petitions etc.). Studying success factors of electronic petitions at the Russian public initiative project we found out that the topic and lexical information are significant factors, as well as the level of petitions.

Keywords: Text analysis · Informativeness · Topic modeling
Voting dynamics · Citizens' interest · Electronic petitions
E-petitions · Russian public initiative project

1 Introduction

The e-petitions initiatives are common nowadays and could be regarded as a natural laboratory for analysis of subjects of interest and factors (semantic and lexical) that influence voting activity. Many voting resources are available in Russia: some are international (e.g. change.org), some are local (e.g. "Наше мнение") and they demonstrate different levels of efficiency [1]. The 'Russian Public Initiative' (RPI) is one of the government-led systems similar to Petitions (https://petition.parliament.uk) or We the People (https://petitions.whitehouse.gov). At RPI the critical number of signees supporting the e-petition is 100,000 (for the federal level): after reaching it the initiative is to be considered by authorities. There has to be a review by an expert committee and the decision making should take no more than two months. This opportunity is open to any citizen of the Russian Federation over 18 years, with access to the Internet; registered on the government services site "Gosuslugi" (https://www.gosuslugi.ru/).

During the first five years of the RPI project only 15 initiatives out of over nine thousand were successful; for nine of the approved e-petitions the positive decision was made even before the votes reached the necessary threshold. A most strange situation was observed with a e-petition which was approved with 3 votes against and 2 votes pro (for a detailed analysis see [2]).

S. Staab et al. (Eds.): SocInfo 2018, LNCS 11186, pp. 243–250, 2018.
https://doi.org/10.1007/978-3-030-01159-8_23

In our research we regard the RPI initiative as a natural laboratory for determining subjects and factors of public interest. First because the PRI initiative provides fair conditions for everyone: it is free from bots and automatic increase in the number of votes, as it requires strong identification, and free from promoting petitions that were paid for. Second, the data available on the site provides the text of the petition, the author id, and what is particularly essential - the voting results (not only pro e-petition, but also against). The possibility to vote against is not common for electronic petitions web-sites and possibly can be a indicator of the tension in society.

Our paper consists of four parts: first is a problem statement, second is an analysis of submissions and votes on the RPI project to answer the question if the RPI still draws attention of society, third we analyze the influence of informativeness, topic, and lexical words markers on success of the e-petition, and in the final section we discuss the results.

2   Problem Statement

E-petitions as one of the most popular democracy tools draw attention of researchers from many countries. Wright and Scott studied how participants perceived the 'success' of their petition [3], Margetts, Hale, Yasseri model voters' behavior and investigate the role of social information [4–7], Bochel and Bochel draw attention to risks associated with e-petitions [8]. Shulman and Morozov raise an issue of the real influence of e-petitions on politics, suggest terms "slacktivism" or "clicktivism" demonstrate limited real impact of voters. Hagen, Harrison and Dumas suggest that e-petitions site can be regarded as a natural laboratory and text features of petitions could be used to model their success [9].

Hagen et al. used the following variables to model signature counts: *informativeness*, *location*, *topics (the latent Dirichlet allocation was used)*. *Day* and *the first day signature counts* were used as control variables. The exploratory results of Hagen et al. showed that an automatic description could provide valuable information about signature counts. Of a particular interest is that the topic analysis indicates that some of the topics get more votes, and that could be a source of important information about subjects of interest present in society.

In our study, we decided to follow the idea expressed by Hagen and her colleagues and duplicated their research on a sample of RPI e-petitions [9]. In their research devoted to the analysis of publicly available White House database containing data about *all* petitions displayed on the "We the People" (WtP) they tested whether the signature counts of e-petitions can be predicted using the information produced by textual analysis tools [9]. So we tried to use compatible sample of petitions associated with the Russian governmental resource.

Before running an analysis of e-petitions we have to be sure that it draws stable interest of society in spite of the controversy to its practical outcomes. So our first research question was:

RQ1. Does the RPI project draw steady interest of public?

Then, following the research of Hagen, we suggest the second research question:

RQ2. Does the number of votes pro (a) and contra (b) depend on the topic of the petition, informativeness of the text, and presence of lexical markers.

3 The Study

3.1 Description of the Sample

Using a specially created program with Python language we downloaded the texts of all the petitions posted on the RPI website on January 26, 2018. Although the site indicates that as of January 26, 2018, 11696 petitions were registered, we found information only about 9842 petitions. 1836 e-petitions were on the ballot, 7979 petitions were in the archive (not regarded by the authorities). 27 were being considered by the authorities. We assume that 1854 petitions were not published on the site, as they did not pass moderation (perhaps they contained obscene language, were considered insulting, etc.).

The following information was downloaded for each petition: the region, the petition level (municipal, regional, federal), the e-petition ID, the deadline for the ballot, the author's ID, the number of votes "pro", the number of votes 'against', the title of the e-petition as well as the text of the e-petition itself.

The overwhelming majority of e-petitions 95.26% (9350) initiate changes at the federal level. The share of the regional e-petitions is 4.42% (434) and the municipal petitions account for 0.32% (31).

Moscow residents were the most active in submitting petitions, during the period under review they posted more than 20% of petitions (2307). The other top regions were Moscow Region (Oblast) 836 (0.08%), St. Petersburg 804 (0.08%). Sverdlovsk (391), Rostov (300), Krasnodar (241), Novosibirsk (233), Volgograd (226), Nizhny Novgorod (200) and Saratov (176). The citizens from two regions of the Russian Federation: Chechnya and Chukotka submitted no petitions.

Controversy of e-petition approval (only 9 from 15 pass the threshold) did not allow us to include the successful initiatives into analysis. We analyzed petitions that failed to reach authorities for which voting was closed by 26 January 2018 (9705).

To answer the first research question we investigate dynamics of e-petitions submissions, registration of new authors and voting activity.

E-Petition Submission

Dynamics of submission showed that the interest in the resource fell after the first year, but was up later and leveled off at 2000 petitions per year in 2015 (see Table 1).

However, after a sharp decline in activity, in 2015 there was an increase in the submission of petitions. It can be assumed that this growth could be artificial and was stimulated by petitions that did not attract citizens' attention. We call them "weak"

Table 1. Dynamics of e-petition submission at RPI project

E-petition level	2013	2014	2015	2016	2017
Municipal	6	1	9	4	11
Regional	60	57	101	96	117
Federal	2251	1249	2185	1858	1774
Total	2317	1307	2295	1958	1902

Table 2. Amount of "weak" and "strong" e-petitions by the year.

	2013	2014	2015	2016	2017
Amount of "weak" e-petitions	1948	1028	1781	1353	1228
Amount of "strong" e-petitions	369	279	514	605	674

Table 3. The amount of new authors

Year of entrance	2013	2014	2015	2016	2017
Amount of new authors	1461	720	1146	983	973

petitions. In order to test this hypothesis, the top quartile of the petitions by the number of votes "pro" was selected (the threshold was 1111 votes "pro" and the petitions which gained at least 1111 votes "pro" were called "strong"). The results of the dynamics are presented in Table 2.

The growth in the number of "strong" petitions shows that PRI project still draws public attention (see Table 3).

Citizens' Activity

Since petitions are published only after authorization of citizens, each petition has an author's code. It does not disclose the gender, full name and other personal data, however, it allows us to analyze dynamics of new authors emergence.

We could see that the number of new authors halved compared to 2013 (see Table 3), but the growth in the number of submitted petitions in 2015 was caused by the emergence of new authors, which indicates an increase in interest in the resource in 2015 and its stabilization in 2016 and 2017.

Voting Activity

The number of votes 'pro' and 'against' a petition may serve as another indicator of citizens' attention. Taking into account the number of e-petitions each year, the average number of votes per petition per year was calculated (see Table 4).

Table 4. Mean amount of votes per e-petition by year.

	2013	2014	2015	2016	2017
Mean amount of votes 'pro'	1296.66	1298.14	1119.9	1234.87	1204.98
Mean amount of votes 'against'	124.43	206.92	212.03	224.07	235.81

Table 4 shows that minor changes in the average number of votes 'pro' (approx. 1200), are accompanied by a noticeable increase in the average number of votes 'against' from 124 to 235. Despite the least number of applications submitted in 2014 growth did not stop.

An increase in the average number of votes "against" may indicate a rise in civic involvement, at least related to a negative assessment of published e-petitions or might speak of a growing mistrust of users in published e-petitions.

So, answering our first question: *Does the RPI project draw steady interest of public*, we say yes. Positive dynamics of "strong" petitions, attraction of new authors, stabilizing the average amount of votes "pro" and a slight growth in the number of votes "against" demonstrate society's interest in PRI.

Regression Analysis

We analyze linguistic (amount of words and marker words) and semantic (topic modeling and informativeness) factors that may be responsible for success of petitions.

Following Hagen and her colleagues, we used logarithm of signature counts as the measure of the petition success and the same procedures of Gibs LDA sampling for topic modeling [10]. We compared several topic distributions at TopicMiner and chose division into 20 topics, as it does not generate duplicate topics [11].

Informativeness variable was populated by a ratio of the number of lemmatized unique in each document to a total amount of words in the document (we used system library for lemmatization).

As marker words first we tested the word: "запретить" ("to ban"), as we expected this word to be a marker of tension. Besides, we added "всех" ("all"), "Россия" ("Russia") as the most frequent word from the meaningful words. We added: year, petition level, region, author as control variables.

From Table 5 we can see that models are statistically significant with a relatively low R^2 value of 0.164 ("pro") and 0.286 ("contra"). The words "запретить" ("to ban") and "всех" ("all") lead to an increase in the number of votes "pro", so do the topics *"Corruption", "Document management", "Salary" and "Responsibility"*.

Table 5. Regression models for voting activity 'pro' and 'against' (non significant variables omitted to keep parsimony)

	Ln(Pro)			Ln(Against)		
	B	CI	P	B	CI	p
(Intercept)	4.66	3.45–5.87	<.001	0.09	−1.32–1.50	.904
Informativeness	−0.11	−0.39–0.16	.424	0.39	0.08–0.71	.015
Year						
year2015	0.49	0.42–0.55	<.001	0.98	0.90–1.06	<.001
year2016	0.66	0.61–0.72	<.001	1.11	1.04–1.18	<.001
year2017	0.85	0.79–0.91	<.001	1.14	1.07–1.22	<.001
year2018	1.07	0.87–1.26	<.001	1.35	1.12–1.58	<.001

(*continued*)

Table 5. *(continued)*

	Ln(Pro)			Ln(Against)		
	B	CI	P	B	CI	p
Level						
Regional	−0.00	−0.44–0.43	.985	1.60	1.09–2.10	<.001
Federal	1.01	0.58–1.43	<.001	3.21	2.71–3.70	<.001
Topic						
Work conditions	0.06	−0.05–0.18	.290	−0.18	−0.31–−0.04	.010
Internet and Telecom services	0.22	0.11–0.34	<.001	−0.55	−0.69–−0.42	<.001
History and holidays	−0.25	−0.39–−0.10	<.001	0.52	0.35–0.68	<.001
City and citizens	0.00	−0.12–0.13	.950	−0.30	−0.45–−0.16	<.001
Responsibility	0.23	0.12–0.34	<.001	−0.42	−0.54–−0.29	<.001
Housing and utilities	0.07	−0.05–0.20	.261	−0.17	−0.31–−0.02	.028
Salary	0.21	0.11–0.32	<.001	−0.18	−0.31–−0.06	.004
Religion and culture	−0.05	−0.18–0.09	.509	0.49	0.33–0.65	<.001
Children	−0.06	−0.19–0.06	.308	0.18	0.04–0.33	.015
Document management	0.12	0.01–0.24	.038	−0.48	−0.61–−0.35	<.001
Rights of citizens	0.09	−0.03–0.20	.142	−0.26	−0.40–−0.13	<.001
Weapon	0.09	−0.04–0.22	.163	−0.14	−0.29–0.02	.079
Transport networks	−0.14	−0.27–−0.01	.032	−0.23	−0.38–−0.08	.003
Corruption	0.22	0.11–0.34	<.001	−0.63	−0.77–−0.50	<.001
Respect the animals	0.11	−0.03–0.26	.131	−0.22	−0.39–−0.05	.011
"to ban" ("запретить")	0.22	0.14–0.30	<.001	0.28	0.19–0.37	<.001
"for all" ("всех")	0.11	0.03–0.19	.010	0.02	−0.08–0.11	.747
"Russia" ("Россия")	0.06	−0.00–0.12	.065	0.18	0.11–0.26	<.001
Observations	7905			7905		
R^2/adj. R^2	.164/.152			.286/.275		

In model of votes "against" a positive role is played by: informativeness, the words "запретить" ("to ban") and "Россия" ("Russia") and the topics *"Children", "Religion and culture", "History and holidays"*.

4   Discussion

We received a bigger adjusted R^2 value compared to the results provided by Hagen and el. Considering that information extracted from e-petition texts can only explain limited portion of e-petition mobilization activities at best, we view the resulted adjusted R^2 value as quite promising.

Although we expected that some topics would highlight tension in society positively influencing both on the number of votes "pro" and "contra", we do not observe such a situation. One of the topics - "Transport networks" - correlates negatively with the number of votes "pro" as well as "against" that could be a sign of lack of interest in this topic.

Unlike Hagen et al. research we could see that informativeness is a significant predictor only for votes "against".

It is worth mentioning that as we expected presence of the word "запретить" (to ban) causes tension as it increases the number of votes "pro" and "against" simultaneously.

5 Conclusion

The data analysis allows us to conclude that citizens show steady interest in the RPI project and it can be used as a natural laboratory to study subjects of interest present in Russian society.

Regression analysis of votes "pro" and "against" reveal that some topics draw more attention that others.

The word "запретить" (to ban) increases the number of votes "pro" and "against" simultaneously, so such petitions reveal tension and attract more public interest. As we found that some lexical markers could be predictors of voting activity "pro" and "against", that leads us to a question, which we plan to address in further research: "How can we extract non-topical specific markers that support or hinder voting activity?".

Acknowledgements. The study was carried out with the financial support of the Russian Foundation for Basic Research within the framework of the Scientific Project No. 18-011-00140-A "Electronic petition as a frame of social and political mobilization (Russian and cross-cultural perspectives)"

References

1. Бершадская (Видясова) Л.А.: Эффективность инструментов электронной демократии в России: анализ порталов электронных петиций и площадок для решения городских проблем, pp. 38–51 (2015)
2. Видясова, Л.А., Тенсина, Я.Д.: Исследование результативности работы портала « Российская общественная инициатива» . Материалы Научной Конференции Интернет И Современное Общество, pp. 56–65 (2017)
3. Wright, S.: 'Success' and online political participation: the case of Downing Street E-petitions. Inf. Commun. Soc. **19**, 843–857 (2016). https://doi.org/10.1080/1369118X.2015.1080285
4. Hale, S.A., John, P., Margetts, H., Yasseri, T.: Investigating Political Participation and Social Information Using Big Data and a Natural Experiment (2014). ArXiv:14083562 Phys
5. Hale, S.A., Margetts, H., Yasseri, T.: Petition growth and success rates on the UK No. 10 Downing Street website. In: Proceedings of the 5th Annual ACM Web Science Conference, pp. 132–138. ACM (2013)
6. Yasseri, T., Hale, S.A., Margetts, H.: Modeling the Rise in Internet-Based Petitions (2013). ArXiv Prepr ArXiv:13080239

7. Margetts, H., John, P., Escher, T., Reissfelder, S.: Social information and political participation on the internet: an experiment. Eur. Polit. Sci. Rev. **3**, 321–344 (2011)
8. Bochel, C., Bochel, H.: 'Reaching in'? The potential for e-petitions in local government in the United Kingdom. Inf. Commun. Soc. **20**, 683–699 (2017). https://doi.org/10.1080/1369118X.2016.1203455
9. Hagen, L., Harrison, T.M., Uzuner, Ö., et al.: E-petition popularity: do linguistic and semantic factors matter? Gov. Inf. Q. **33**, 783–795 (2016). https://doi.org/10.1016/j.giq.2016.07.006
10. Hagen, L., Harrison, T.M., Uzuner, Ö., et al.: Introducing textual analysis tools for policy informatics: a case study of e-petitions. In: Proceedings of the 16th Annual International Conference on Digital Government Research, pp. 10–19. ACM (2015)
11. Koltsov, S., Filippov, V.: TopicMiner. https://linis.hse.ru/soft-linis. Accessed 8 May 2018

With or Without Super Platforms? Analyzing Online Publishers' Strategies in the Game of Traffic

Joni Salminen[1,2]([⊠]), Dmitry Maslennikov[3], Bernard J. Jansen[1], and Rami Olkkonen[2]

[1] Qatar Computing Research Institute,
Hamad Bin Khalifa University, Doha, Qatar
{jsalminen,bjansen}@hbku.edu.qa
[2] Turku School of Economics, Turku, Finland
rami.olkkonen@utu.fi
[3] Nizhny Novgorod Technical State University, Novgorod, Russia
dmitrymaslennikov@rambler.ru

Abstract. Given the dominance of online platforms in attracting consumers and advertisers, online publishers are squeezed between declining traffic and advertising revenues from their website content. In turn, super platforms, the dominant content dissemination platforms, such as Google and Facebook, are monetizing online content at the expense of publishers by selling ad impressions in advertising auctions. In this work, we analyze publishers' possibilities of forming a coalition and show that, under a set of assumptions, the optimal strategy for publishers is cooperation against a super platform rather than posting content on the super platform. Not choosing to publish on a super platform can yield the whole coalition more traffic, enabling some individual publishers to recoup the lost traffic. We further show that if the coalition does not forbid diversification, most publishers choose both coalition and super platform.

Keywords: Media markets · Super platforms · Online content
Advertising

1 Introduction

Given the dominance of online platforms, such as Facebook and Google, for attracting consumers and advertisers, content publishers are squeezed between declining number of website visitors (later referred to as *traffic*) and shrinking advertising revenues.

The dominant platforms are relying on user- and publisher-generated content but producing no content by themselves [1]. They, in a sense, are leeching the content of others [2], typically not generating almost any content themselves [3]. By aggregating the content created by publishers and users, platforms dominate over web traffic and continuously invent ways to discourage users from leaving their ecosystem [4]. Examples of this strategic behavior include e.g. Google incorporating rich snippets in search engine results, disincentivizing users to click away from the search engine

© Springer Nature Switzerland AG 2018
S. Staab et al. (Eds.): SocInfo 2018, LNCS 11186, pp. 251–260, 2018.
https://doi.org/10.1007/978-3-030-01159-8_24

results page, and Facebook introducing instant articles. Both actions enable users to satisfy their information needs on the platforms without clicking further to publishers' websites.

With these strategies in place, the platforms have locked in users to an impressive degree. In turn, publishers that incur the cost for content creation are, in the worst case, left without the benefits when the content is monetized by the super platforms [5].

This research analyzes the 'game of traffic' between publishers and super platforms. Our purpose is to examine strategies relating to cooperation between publishers and to analyze whether a coalition is a viable option to a super platform as a source of traffic. By coalition, we refer to a cooperative organization among publishers. In practice, the coalition can be a website hosting all the content of all publishers, or can it be an ensemble of separate websites sharing content and visitors. We focus on the following questions: (1) Why and what publishers gain value from online super platforms? (2) When will publishers be better off with and without super platforms?

2   Related Literature

This research analyzes a form of self-organization that the news and content creation industry could take, namely coalition. Coalitions have been studied extensively in economics, and their primary advantages include profit maximization, increased unit outputs, and sharing risks and rewards [6–8]. In strategic management, the benefits are seen to relate to the sharing of resources and information for more effective joint value extraction [9]. In addition, coalitions can involve network effects or externalities which incentivize new members to join as the member base grows [10, 11].

In the context of the media industry, the coalition can involve externalities between content dissemination and advertising [12], by creating more feasible audiences for advertisers. The revenue from advertising can grow disproportionally with the audience growth [13]. However, not all participants necessarily yield an equal share of returns from the coalition [14]. The stability of the coalition is partly influenced by the way in which the participants extract private benefits [15]. In addition, managing a coalition can involve substantial coordination costs [16], associated with ensuring interoperability [11]. Finally, the strategies undertaken by the coalition may not always be optimal for the individual agent [17]. The combination of advantages and disadvantages, therefore, makes it meaningful to analyze coalition arrangements in greater detail.

The popularity of social media has attracted publishers to distribute their content on social media platforms [18]. Previously, the newspaper industry reacted to the threat of other media, such as television, by raising prices [19]. However, in the environment where consumers' media consumption behavior is ever more fragmented, this is no longer an option [20]. At its core, finding a functional business model refers to the ability to capture the value of online content [21]. The readers' willingness to pay has been identified as a concern in the newspaper industry [22].

In a related work, Salminen [2] analyzes the power dominance of online platforms; namely, the 'remora's curse', a condition in which startup companies can become victims of a platform's strategic decision making as they grow dependent on the incumbent platform's user base. Argentesi and Filistrucchi [12] define the newspaper industry as a two-sided market and estimate the players' market power. Despite the notable benefits of coalition arrangements, coalitions have not been widely considered by prior literature. Most points of view focus on competition between the publishers [23], instead of collaboration. Thus, we believe our analysis will be a useful addition to the body of knowledge of the strategies in the media industry.

3 Game of Monetization and Online Advertising Revenue

3.1 General Intuition

First, for dominant online content aggregators (later referred to as 'super platforms'), such as Google and Facebook, the more content created by the publishers, the better. They incur no cost for its creation and only minimal cost in retrieving it with their algorithms. Second, platforms and publishers are competing over the same total traffic, which depends on the number of consumers. This idea originates from the fact that consumers have limited time available for consumption of content that is shared among different channels [24]. Traffic is valuable because it provides revenue for publishers and super platforms that both follow the media business model, in which content is provided for free to consumers whose attention is monetized by showing advertisements. This configuration constitutes a two-sided market of advertisers and content consumers [23, 25] in which traffic is a proxy for revenue. Fourth, publishers provide traffic to super platforms and *vice versa*. The share of traffic received by each publisher may differ so that some publishers receive more traffic from a super platform than others. That is, if a publisher is publishing content on a super platform, it will get traffic from its participation, and that traffic is shown advertisements. This is referred to as 'monetization', or the media business model [26].

3.2 Assumptions and Parameters of the Model

First, there are media publishers with some content classified under some topics (e.g., news, sports, entertainment). Second, there are N channels where publishers can post their content. Every channel is characterized by consumer's efficiency in finding content there and efficiency of finding similar content in that channel. When there is much content on the channel, the increased efficiency of finding similar content helps to attract more consumers. These parameters depend on how the channel is designed. Consumers are more attracted to content published on an effective channel (with higher TT_i). Publishers are interested in sharing content to channels where their content gets more attention and their traffic share is higher. The traffic share depends on the type of content, so some content attracts higher traffic shares from social media.

Table 1 shows the parameters used for model development. Traffic share varies by channel choice and publisher. Some channel choices are more generous than others. Moreover, we assume that publishers with the best values of traffic share (TS) participate in the coalition. Another assumption is that every platform attracts attention independently without distraction effects, so the frequency of times content is seen or the order of exposure. Our analysis is based on assumption that ith channel is chosen by C_i share of publishers and then analyzing when it can be beneficial for them to switch strategy. We assume that the actions of the publisher are fully determined by their benefits of changing strategy, after which C_i shares changes.

Moreover, we assume that traffic share that a new publisher achieves in a channel choice is a linear function of C_i which is defined uniquely by $TS_{min,i}$ and $TS_{max,i}$. If the channel choice is super platform, this platform takes some of the traffic for themselves. If the channel choice is a coalition, then the share of traffic is equivalent to the coalition operating cost. In practice, the operating cost consists of development and maintenance of online traffic sharing systems. These efforts are required to ensure common traits of platform design, including compatibility, interconnection and interoperability, and coordination of technical standards [11]. Finally, in our model, the super platform moves first and then the publishers respond.

Table 1. Parameter definitions.

Parameter	Definition
$E_{c,i}$	Consumers' efficiency of finding content in a channel choice (i.e., choose super platform, coalition, or both)
$E_{s,i}$	Consumers' efficiency of finding similar content (i.e., how likely a consumer will look for similar content in this channel choice)
C_i	Number of content is published on this channel choice
$TS_{min,i}$	Minimum traffic share this channel choice gives to publishers
$TS_{max,i}$	Maximum traffic share this channel choice gives to publishers
T_i	Share of traffic to content published in this channel choice. All traffic can be distributed along channels (super platform and coalition)
$TSC_{min,i}$	Minimum traffic share for the channel. It is different from TS, because TSC is calculated for publishers taking part in this channel
$TSC_{max,i}$	Maximum traffic share for channel choice
$TSC_{av,i}$	Average traffic share for channel choice
TSC_i	Traffic share for channel that has no heterogeneity among publishers
TC_i	Total traffic attracted by content published in this channel
$P_{i,min}$	The amount of traffic a publisher gets from one unit of content in this channel, including min, max and average values for heterogeneity
P_{max}	Maximum traffic for publisher
P_{av}	Average traffic for publisher
TT_i	Traffic per content on the ith channel

3.3   Strategies for Publishers

We consider three strategies: (1) *Publish on super platform only*, (2) *Publish on coalition only*, and (3) *Publish on both super platform and coalition*. If a publisher chooses super platform, it gets more views per content unit because the platform is a popular and comfortable platform for information, but the platform takes a part of the traffic. If a publisher chooses coalition, it gets all traffic from the content unit, but many publishers should participate in the coalition to get more views using cross-references. Moreover, the coalition cannot use as much development as the super platform can, therefore, it is less efficient in attracting traffic. If a publisher puts content both on the super platform and coalition, it can take some additional expenses to conduct multiple posts, however, it can be easy if all information is just reposted to different platforms. If the publisher is not very small, such expenses are negligible. If neither channel choice imposes penalties for posting content to other platforms, then the total number of views attracted by this content will only increase. Since the coalition gives 100% of traffic and the super platform always gives less, then the average share of traffic per publisher will increase, too. Therefore, going to the coalition will always produce a higher volume of traffic than the traffic from the super platform. Then, there are only two strategies: (1) *Publish on both super platform and coalition*, and (2) *Publish on coalition only*. If the coalition forbids publishing content on Facebook, then there are two strategies: (1) *Publish on Facebook only*, (2) *Publish on coalition only*.

We assume that every unit of content posted in channel i will have 'share per content' attraction that depends on how much content on this topic is posted in the channel and how well the platform is designed for such content, as expressed in Eq. 1.

$$SPC_i = E_{c,i} + C_i E_{s,i} \qquad (1)$$

Every channel gets traffic proportional to attention attracted to all content posted on it. Since the total traffic obtained by all channels is constant, then traffic obtained by every platform can be written as Eq. 2.

$$T_i = \frac{C_i \cdot SPC_i}{\sum_{i=1...n} C_i \cdot SPC_i} \qquad (2)$$

We assume that publishers who are getting more traffic share from the super platform will go to this channel early. Then, the minimum traffic share for super platform publishers can be obtained according to Eq. 3.

$$TSC_{\min,1} = TS_{\max,1} - \left(TS_{\max,1} - TS_{\min,1}\right) C_1 \qquad (3)$$

The maximum share of traffic along publishers always equals to the potential maximum expressed in Eq. 4.

$$TSC_{\max,1} = TS_{\max,1} \qquad (4)$$

Coalition mechanics are different. First, publishers get a minimum share of traffic. Then, as the number of publishers in coalition grows, the traffic share of all publishers grows accordingly, as shown in Eqs. 5 and 6.

$$TSC_2 = TS_{\min,2} + \left(TS_{\max,2} - TS_{\min,2}\right) C_2 \qquad (5)$$

$$TSC_2 = TSC_{\max,2} = TSC_{\min,2} = TSC_{av,2} \qquad (6)$$

This is compatible with the concept of network effects, so that the more publishers there are, the more it makes sense for new publishers to join. The traffic obtained by every unit of content on ith platform can be calculated as per Eq. 7.

$$TT_i = \frac{T_i}{C_i} \tag{7}$$

The maximum and minimum traffic obtained by publishers per content consumers is denoted in Eqs. 8 and 9.

$$TC_{\max,i} = TSC_{\max,i} \cdot TT_i \tag{8}$$

$$TC_{\min,i} = TSC_{\min,i} \cdot TT_i \tag{9}$$

After a simple algebraic transformation, we obtain Eqs. 10 and 11.

$$TC_{\max,1} = TSC_{\max,1} \cdot TT_1 = TS_{\max,1} \cdot \frac{T_i}{C_i} = TS_{\max,1} \cdot \frac{E_{c,1} + C_1 E_{s,1}}{\sum_{i=1...n} C_i \cdot \left(E_{c,i} + C_i E_{s,i}\right)} \tag{10}$$

$$TC_{\min,1} = TSC_{\min,1} \cdot TT_1$$
$$= \left[TS_{\max,1} - \left(TS_{\max,1} - TS_{\min,1}\right)C_1\right] \cdot \frac{E_{c,1} + C_1 E_{s,1}}{\sum_{i=1...n} C_i \cdot \left(E_{c,i} + C_i E_{s,i}\right)} \tag{11}$$

From which we get Eqs. 12 and 13.

$$TC_{\max,1} = TS_{\max,1} \cdot \frac{E_{c,1} + C_1 E_{s,1}}{C_1 \cdot \left(E_{c,1} + C_1 E_{s,1}\right) + C_2 \cdot \left(E_{c,2} + C_2 E_{s,2}\right)} \tag{12}$$

$$TC_{\min,1} = \left[TS_{\max,1} - \left(TS_{\max,1} - TS_{\min,1}\right)C_1\right]$$
$$\cdot \frac{E_{c,1} + C_1 E_{s,1}}{C_1 \cdot \left(E_{c,1} + C_1 E_{s,1}\right) + C_2 \cdot \left(E_{c,2} + C_2 E_{s,2}\right)} \tag{13}$$

The traffic obtained by coalition users per content unit is calculated in Eq. 14.

$$TC_2 = \left[TS_{\min,2} + \left(TS_{\max,2} - TS_{\min,2}\right)C_2\right] \cdot \frac{E_{c,2} + C_2 E_{s,2}}{C_1 \cdot \left(E_{c,1} + C_1 E_{s,1}\right) + C_2 \cdot \left(E_{c,2} + C_2 E_{s,2}\right)} \tag{14}$$

For this case, we assume that every piece of content can be posted on the super platform or on coalition but not on both channels at the same time, as per Eq. 15.

$$C_2 = 1 - C_1 \tag{15}$$

We assume $E_{c,2} = 1$ because the efficiency of the coalition is a norming value.

We assume that if a publisher changes strategy, then it will be one of following two cases: (1) publishers who get the least benefit from the super platform switching to the coalition; or (2) publishers who could get the most benefit from the super platform switches to it from the coalition. Then, we compare traffic per content obtained by publisher in short term, which they can get by (1) choosing the super platform and (2) choosing the coalition. This situation is analyzed in Eqs. 16 and 17.

$$TC_{\min,1} = \frac{\left[TS_{\max,1} - \left(TS_{\max,1} - TS_{\min,1}\right)C_1\right]\left(E_{c,1} + C_1 E_{s,1}\right)}{C_1 \cdot \left(E_{c,1} + C_1 E_{s,1}\right) + (1 - C_1) \cdot \left(1 + C_2 E_{s,2}\right)} \tag{16}$$

$$TC_2 = \frac{\left[TS_{\min,2} + \left(TS_{\max,2} - TS_{\min,2}\right)(1 - C_1)\right]\left(1 + (1 - C_1)E_{s,2}\right)}{C_1 \cdot \left(E_{c,1} + C_1 E_{s,1}\right) + C_2 \cdot \left(E_{c,2} + C_2 E_{s,2}\right)} \tag{17}$$

3.4 Scenarios When Content Can Be Posted to More Than One Channel

Assume that posting content to both channels causes a negligible distraction factor, so that share per content attraction on every channel does not depend on content posting on other channels. For such scenarios, all publishers are in coalition $C_2 = 1$, and some can choose the super platform. We express this through Eqs. 18–20.

$$TC_{\min,1} = \left[TS_{\max,1} - \left(TS_{\max,1} - TS_{\min,1}\right)C_1\right] \cdot \frac{E_{c,1} + C_1 E_{s,1}}{C_1 \cdot \left(E_{c,1} + C_1 E_{s,1}\right) + \left(E_{c,2} + E_{s,2}\right)} \tag{18}$$

$$TC_{\max,1} = TS_{\max,1} \cdot \frac{E_{c,1} + C_1 E_{s,1}}{C_1 \cdot \left(E_{c,1} + C_1 E_{s,1}\right) + \left(E_{c,2} + E_{s,2}\right)} \tag{19}$$

$$TC_2 = \left[TS_{\min,2} + \left(TS_{\max,2} - TS_{\min,2}\right)\right] \cdot \frac{E_{c,2} + E_{s,2}}{C_1 \cdot \left(E_{c,1} + C_1 E_{s,1}\right) + \left(E_{c,2} + C_2 E_{s,2}\right)} \tag{20}$$

A publisher who does not post on the super platform gets TC_2. Publishers who post on both platforms get not less than $TC_2 + TC_{\min,1}$ but not more than $TC_2 + TC_{\max,1}$. If the publisher is small, it will not be able to change the situation. Then, excluding the super platform will not be a beneficial move. However, if a group of publishers who can act together decide not to engage on the super platform, they can increase value TC_2 so that it will exceed losing of TC_1. This will change the situation for other publishers, too, and can cause a chain reaction of exiting the super platform.

3.5 Scenarios When Content Can Be Posted to Only One Channel

We consider two scenarios and five sub-cases, where the amount of coalition traffic differs.

Scenario 1. If the traffic difference meets Eq. 21,

$$TC_2 - TC_{\min,1} > 0, \tag{21}$$

then publishers would choose coalition rather than publish on the super platform.

Scenario 2. If the traffic difference meets Eq. 22,

$$TC_2 - TC_{\min,1} < 0, \tag{22}$$

then publishers would more likely choose the super platform than the coalition. To further analyze, we introduce function in Eq. 23.

$$PS(C_1) = \left[TS_{\min,2} + \left(TS_{\max,2} - TS_{\min,2} \right)(1 - C_1) \right]\left(1 + (1 - C_1)E_{s,2} \right) \\ - \left[TS_{\max,1} - \left(TS_{\max,1} - TS_{\min,1} \right)C_1 \right]\left(E_{c,1} + C_1 E_{s,1} \right) \tag{23}$$

After collecting coefficients by the degree of C_1, we get the Eq. 24.

$$PS(C_1) = -E_{c,1}TS_{\max,1} + TS_{\max,2}(1 + E_{s2}) \\ + C_1\left(E_{c,1}\left(TS_{\max,1} - TS_{\min,1} \right) - E_{s,1}TS_{\max,1} - E_{s,2}\left(2 \cdot TS_{\max,2} - TS_{\min,2} \right) - \left(TS_{\max,2} - TS_{\min,2} \right) \right) \\ + C_1^2\left(E_{s,1}\left(TS_{\max,1} - TS_{\min,1} \right) + E_{s,2}\left(TS_{\max,2} - TS_{\min,2} \right) \right) \tag{24}$$

Scenario 2a. There is no heterogeneity and there is a flat coalition operating cost factor, resulting in Eqs. 25 and 26:

$$E_{s,1}\left(TS_{\max,1} - TS_{\min,1} \right) + E_{s,2}\left(TS_{\max,2} - TS_{\min,2} \right) = 0 \tag{25}$$

$$TS_{\max,1} - TS_{\min,1} = 0, \quad TS_{\max,2} = TS_{\min,2} = 1 \tag{26}$$

Thus, the function $PS(C_1)$ is linear, and the critical value of a publisher's share is:

$$C_1 = \frac{\left(TS_2\left(1 + E_{s,2} \right) - E_{c,1}TS_{\max,1} \right)}{\left(E_{s,2}TS_{\max,2} + E_{s,1}TS_{\max,1} \right)} \tag{27}$$

If there are more publishers in the coalition, others choose the coalition; otherwise, publishers exit the coalition.

Scenario 2d. As shown above, if $TS_{\max,1} - TS_{\min,1} > 0$, inequality $PS(C_1) > 0$ can either have a solution containing a single point, segment, or none. Assume solution of $PS(C_1) > 0$ is segment $[s_1, s_2]$. Then, we have the following situations.

Case 4.1. If $C_1 \in [s_1, s_2]$, then the publisher will to go to the coalition and C_1 will reduce to $\max(s_1, 0)$. If $s_1 > 0$, there are some publishers who would get much from the super platform and they are not going to the coalition.

Case 4.2. If $C_1 < s_1$, then publishers will go out of coalition until $C_1 = \min(s_1, 1)$.

Case 4.3. If $C_1 > s_2$, then publishers will go out of coalition until $C_1 = 1$.

Case 5. It is also possible to have coordinated actions of publishers. In the above cases, we showed how publishers act without coordination. However, there can be some share of publishers who can agree and go to coalition together, despite it not being beneficial in the short term. The main incentive for doing so is to create favorable conditions for other publishers to join the coalition in the future.

4 Discussion

Our analysis shows that all publishers would be better off without the super platform, since the total traffic could be shared among publishers. We also show that if the coalition does not forbid publishers to post content, all publishers choose both the super platform and coalition, except the large publishers who would lose too much traffic. The more publishers there are that only choose coalition, the more traffic the coalition can generate to recoup losses from not participating in the super platform. In this case, the total traffic for the publishers is higher than when they would cooperate with the super platform because the excess traffic can be shared.

Theoretically, an interesting notion is the relationship between content and traffic, namely, content as an antecedent to having users in the first place. If the content aggregator platform indeed depends on user-generated content, then the creators of the content yield the ultimate power, as opposed to the platforms. While publishers cannot own super platforms, they could own the coalition. This means traffic resulting from the content creation could stay among the publishers, at least to a greater degree, and not be snatched away by the content aggregators. Content could be distributed by a jointly developed system from some automatic feed. It could also be placed behind a paywall, in which case full articles are not indexable by super platforms, and the users could be encouraged to share the content within the coalition. Given that super platforms tend to cater for all content, focusing and dominating on specific topics could enable publisher coalitions to build loyal follower bases that choose to spend their online time on high-quality coalition websites rather than on mixed-content super platforms.

References

1. Goh, K.-Y., Heng, C.-S., Lin, Z.: Social media brand community and consumer behavior: quantifying the relative impact of user- and marketer-generated content. Inf. Syst. Res. **24**, 88–107 (2013)
2. Salminen, J.: Startup Dilemmas—Strategic Problems of Early-Stage Platforms on the Internet (2014). http://www.doria.fi/handle/10024/99349
3. Albuquerque, P., Pavlidis, P., Chatow, U., Chen, K.-Y., Jamal, Z.: Evaluating promotional activities in an online two-sided market of user-generated content. Market. Sci. **31**, 406–432 (2012)
4. Boudreau, K.: Open platform strategies and innovation: granting access vs. devolving control. Manag. Sci. **56**, 1849–1872 (2010)
5. Jansen, B.J., Schuster, S.: Bidding on the buying funnel for sponsored search and keyword advertising. J. Electron. Commer. Res. **12**, 1–18 (2011)
6. Arrow, K.J.: The organization of economic activity: issues pertinent to the choice of market versus nonmarket allocation. Anal Eval Public Expend. **1**, 59–73 (1969)
7. Mayes, B.T., Allen, R.W.: Toward a definition of organizational politics. Acad. Manag. Rev. **2**, 672–678 (1977)

8. Stevenson, W.B., Pearce, J.L., Porter, L.W.: The concept of "coalition" in organization theory and research. Acad. Manag. Rev. **10**, 256–268 (1985)

9. Grant, R.M., Baden-Fuller, C.: A knowledge accessing theory of strategic alliances. J. Manag. Stud. **41**, 61–84 (2004)

10. Katz, M.L., Shapiro, C.: Network externalities, competition, and compatibility. Am. Econ. Rev. **75**, 424–440 (1985)

11. Economides, N.: The economics of networks. Int. J. Ind. Organ. **14**, 673–699 (1996)

12. Argentesi, E., Filistrucchi, L.: Estimating market power in a two-sided market: the case of newspapers. J. Appl. Econom. **22**, 1247–1266 (2007)

13. Manduchi, A., Picard, R.: Circulations, revenues, and profits in a newspaper market with fixed advertising costs. J. Media Econ. **22**, 211–238 (2009)

14. Deneckere, R., Davidson, C.: Incentives to form coalitions with Bertrand competition. RAND J. Econ. 473–486 (1985)

15. Arslan, B.: The interplay of competitive and cooperative behavior and differential benefits in alliances. Strateg. Manag. J. (2017)

16. Bakos, J.Y., Brynjolfsson, E.: From vendors to partners: information technology and incomplete contracts in buyer–supplier relationships. J. Organ. Comput. Electron. Commer. **3**, 301–328 (1993)

17. Coleman, J.S.: The benefits of coalition. Public Choice **8**, 45–61 (1970)

18. Ju, A., Jeong, S.H., Chyi, H.I.: Will social media save newspapers? J. Pract. **8**, 1–17 (2014)

19. Abbring, J.H., Ours, J.C.V.: Selling news and advertising space: the economics of Dutch newspapers. De Economist **142**, 151–170 (1994)

20. Couldry, N.: Does 'the media' have a future? Eur. J. Commun. **24**, 437–449 (2009)

21. Teece, D.J.: Business models, business strategy and innovation. Long Range Plan. **43**, 172–194 (2010)

22. Umanets, E.: Effects of Obtained Benefits on Willingness to Pay and Word-of-Mouth Behavior in Newspaper Industry (2014)

23. Gabszewicz, J.J., Laussel, D., Sonnac, N.: Attitudes toward advertising and price competition in the press industry. In: Economics of Art and Culture Invited Papers at the 12th International Conference of the Association of Cultural Economics International, pp. 61–74. Emerald Group Publishing Limited (2003)

24. Voorveld, H.A.: Media multitasking and the effectiveness of combining online and radio advertising. Comput. Hum. Behav. **27**, 2200–2206 (2011)

25. Kaiser, U., Wright, J.: Price structure in two-sided markets: evidence from the magazine industry. Int. J. Ind. Organ. **24**, 1–28 (2006)

26. McPhillips, S., Merlo, O.: Media convergence and the evolving media business model: an overview and strategic opportunities. Market. Rev. **8**, 237–253 (2008)

Location2Vec: Generating Distributed Representation of Location by Using Geo-tagged Microblog Posts

Yoshiyuki Shoji[1](✉)[iD], Katsurou Takahashi[2][iD], Martin J. Dürst[1][iD],
Yusuke Yamamoto[3][iD], and Hiroaki Ohshima[2][iD]

[1] Aoyama Gakuin University, 5-10-1 Fuchinobe, Chuo-ku,
Sagamihara-shi, Kanagawa 252-5258, Japan
{shoji,duerst}@it.aoyama.ac.jp
[2] University of Hyogo, 7-1-28 Minatojima-minamimachi, Chuo-ku,
Kobe-shi, Hyogo 650-0047, Japan
{ab18y501,ohshima}@ai.u-hyogo.ac.jp
[3] Shizuoka University, 3-5-1 Johoku, Naka-ku,
Hamamatsu-shi, Shizuoka 432-8011, Japan
yamamoto@inf.shizuoka.ac.jp

Abstract. This paper proposes a method to represent the characteristics of a place (*i.e.,* use of the venue, atmosphere of the area) by using geo-tagged microblog posts around the place. It enables a vector representation of a location similar to the distributed representation of a term in Word2Vec. Our method uses a simple neural network that is trained through the task of estimating the terms that appear in tweets posted from the area. The effectiveness of our method is illustrated through an experiment of a comparison of similar locations in Tokyo and Kyoto.

Keywords: Geo-tag · Social sensing · Word2Vec
Social media analysis

1 Introduction

When we are visiting a certain location, we are concerned about its atmosphere. It is difficult to guess how the atmosphere of a location will be, and it is more difficult to search for locations with an atmosphere similar to that of a well-known location. One reason of this difficulty is lack of data; how visitors felt there or what visitors did in that place does not appear in official information or traditional Web sites. Also, we often face the situation that we need to find a location based on its usage or its atmosphere in daily life. For instance, when you move to a new city, you may look for a coffee shop that has an atmosphere similar to a familiar coffee shop in your previous home town. In such a situation, there is no point in searching for a shop with a similar name, or to search for a shop with a menu similar to the one at your familiar shop. It is more important to

© Springer Nature Switzerland AG 2018
S. Staab et al. (Eds.): SocInfo 2018, LNCS 11186, pp. 261–270, 2018.
https://doi.org/10.1007/978-3-030-01159-8_25

focus on the environment around the shop, and how other customers are feeling at the shop. There are also marketing needs; if you are the owner of a thriving shop, you want to look for a place that has similar atmosphere to your current shop's location in order to open a second shop. What kind of shops will become more popular in the area depends on the atmosphere or usage of the area.

Posts in social media are one of the most useful information sources to know the atmosphere of a location. For instance, the contents of tweets in downtown areas and residential areas are quite different. By analyzing them, we can find the difference of atmosphere between those areas.

We propose a method of generating arbitrary dimensional feature vectors of locations by using geo-tagged microblog posts. Every vector contains human information such as how people feel about the location and what people did there because it is generated from common daily social media posts. By using such feature vectors as input to machine learning methods, or for direct vector operations (e.g., similarity calculation, addition and subtraction), we can compare, analyze, or search for locations by atmosphere. For instance, similarity of vectors is likely to be a good clue for information retrieval tasks that search for a location with a similar atmosphere to a given location. It is also usable for clustering areas by their atmosphere, or for area visualization. As an application, the vector is suitable to be used as input of machine learning methods, similar to embedding of terms. It will enable a more advanced social analysis of locations by using modern machine learning techniques.

Our method uses a simple neural network to create a feature vector for an object. This approach follows the basic idea of Word2Vec [15]. Word2Vec and its derivative methods train their networks to estimate linguistic contexts of terms with those surrounding terms. Finally they use the weight of the hidden layer as the feature vector of the term. The vector is called "distributed representation" of the term, and it represents the meaning of the term. This approach is based on the hypothesis "the meaning of a term is defined by the terms around it". We formulated a similar hypothesis: "the meaning of a certain location is defined by the terms appearing around it". Here, "terms appearing around it" is related to physical distance. It means terms included in geo-tagged tweets posted close to the location. Figure 1 shows an outline of the neural network that our method uses. The weight of the edges from a dimension that represent a certain place to the middle layer can be used as a feature vector of the place, in analogy with Word2Vec.

The rest of this paper is organized as follows. Section 2 describes related work. Section 3 explains our method named "Location2Vec". Section 4 describes our experiment and its results. In Sect. 5, we examine the experimental result. We conclude with a summary of the key points in Sect. 6.

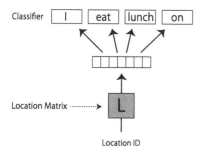

Fig. 1. Simple neural network estimating terms appearing around a given location.

Table 1. Locations in Tokyo and Kyoto sampled for the experiment.

	Statistics
Size of the area	$7,854\,\mathrm{m}^2$
# data in full dataset	256,289
# data sampled	35,211
Sampling rate	14%
Average # tweets	33.09
Median # tweets	11
Mode # tweets	0
Max # tweets	1995

2 Related Work

The purpose of our method is sensing the use or atmosphere of a location from social media posts by using a shallow neural network model. We discuss existing prior research related to our method from two view points; Social Sensing and Word2Vec-like Methods.

There is a lot of previous research in the field of Social Sensing. Social media posts are used to detect real place information or events [1,7,9,12,13,21]. Geo-tagged social media posts are good resources for subjective or empirical information. Some of research uses geo-tagged posts to find physical phenomena related to the location, such as earthquakes [19], weather events [6], intention of moving [23], and so on. Our work is also an instance of a Social Sensing approach. Our method incorporates both term features and coordinates of tweets into its algorithm.

There also exist some papers which expand topic modeling methods with location-based features. These methods use the physical distance as the relationship between terms or topics. Canh et al. [4] proposed an extended model of LDA (Latent Dirichlet Allocation) named "Spatial LDA" to find regional communities. Kurashima et al. [11] proposed the "Geo Topic Model", which is a new topic model that uses information about users and locations to estimate topics. Ahmed et al. [2] proposed a hierarchical geographical modeling method of combining location and text content in social networking services. Yin et al. [26] proposes LGTA (Latent Geographical Topic Analysis), which combines both location-driven methods and text-driven methods to detect topics appearing in geo-tagged social media posts. The method that we propose also calculates the feature vector of a place. Our vectors will have properties similar to vectors made by these topic modeling methods; containing subjective information of the place such as usage, opinion or atmosphere. The main difference is that we chose a Word2Vec-based neural network method to make a vector. Our method can accept various improvements of Word2Vec applications.

Word2Vec is a family of methods to generate distributed representations of words, proposed by Tomas Mikolov in 2013 [15]. Word2Vec has many derivative methods and applications. All of them have in common that they use a shallow neural network model. The most famous derivatives are Doc2Vec and Para-graph2Vec proposed by Mikolov himself [16]. These methods are frequently used for vectorization of words or documents. There exist many methods combining Word2Vec with other natural language processing methods in order to improve performance and create additional applications (*e.g.*, LDA2Vec [17]).

Nowadays, the Word2Vec-based approach is a popular embedding method for deep learning. There are many derivative methods which accept other kinds of data; not only terms or documents, but also graphs, multimedia data, and so on. RDF2Vec [18] creates distributed representations of graph entities. It converts sub-graphs into sequential tokens. Node2Vec [8] is another Word2Vec-based graph vectorization method. A characteristic of this method is how to sample a node's neighborhood feature; it uses random walk as a negative sampling method. As an application for multimedia data, Madjiheurem *et al.* [14] proposed Chord2Vec, which converts musical chords to a feature vector. Alcorn [3] proposed a method named "(batter—pitcher)2Vec", a unique derivative method of Word2Vec, which vectorizes major league baseball players. Place2Vec [25] is also a model which is very similar to our method. It estimates a location by its surrounding locations. The main difference is that we use physical distance instead of conceptual distance such as co-occurrence of terms or hop count in a graph.

There are some methods applying Word2Vec to social media posts. Dhingra *et al.* [5] proposes "Tweet2Vec", an approach for vectorizing non-geo-tagged tweets. It uses hash tags in Twitter as an objective of the estimation. There is another algorithm called "Tweet2Vec" [22] that does not use hash tags, but adopts a method similar to LSTM (Long short-term memory) and its auto encoder. Word2Vec is typically used to summarize sentiments and opinions from social media posts. One of the most common usages of Word2Vec in social media analysis is vectorization of the posts in the same way as other topic modeling methods or dimensionality reduction methods. Wang *et al.* uses Word2Vec to estimate the usage of the area from geo-tagged posts from Sina Weibo [24]. Seki *et al.* [20] also uses Word2Vec to estimate the sentiment of the area by analyzing Twitter posts which are posted by users who live in the area. These methods use standard Word2Vec to vectorize social media posts by using co-occurrence of terms. Our method incorporates geographical factors into the calculation itself.

3   Location2Vec Algorithm

In this section, we describe the details of our method named "Location2Vec". The novelty of our method is the data used in the estimation. Word2Vec uses surrounding terms and a central term as input and output of their estimation. Our method uses the location instead of a central term, and uses the terms appearing in the tweets posted in the area around that location instead of surrounding terms.

3.1   Training Data Creation

Our method generates a feature vector of a location from geo-tagged tweets around the location. This idea can be considered as an analogy of the concept of "context window" in Word2Vec. That is, it uses "terms that appeared in a geo-tagged tweet that was posted within 10 m from the location" instead of "terms that appeared within 10 words around a term".

A specific location, such as a shop, an institution or a restaurant has coordinates represented as longitude and latitude. The most primitive method is to use tweets posted at a location within a radius of n meters from the target venue. We calculated the distance between the venue and the location of a tweet by the Hubeny formula. Although it is a reasonable method for representing a place by using the tweets around it, there is a problem in the training of the network. Sometimes several venues are located at the same coordinate when they are in a multistory building or in a commercial complex. In addition, in dense areas, different kinds of venues will share their surrounding tweets. The training of the neural network often fails under these circumstances. For instance, it happens that the classifier has to estimate different outputs from the same input. A reasonable way to eliminate the duplication of tweets is isolating areas uniformly by a grid. In this case, instead of a certain venue, the area is expressed using the tweets included in the grid. The size of the grid will have the same effect as the window width of Word2Vec. A fixed size grid will work well if the density of tweets in the dataset is homogeneous. Yet, it should be considered how to divide the map. For example, by changing the cell size according to the density of tweets, or using area division methods such as a Voronoi diagram. There is a possibility of improving the accuracy of estimation.

3.2   Calculation

Our method follows the skip-gram model of Word2Vec. When a document ID is given, the method estimates the list of words included in the given document. Our algorithm uses physical areas on the earth, separated by certain conditions, in the same way the original algorithm uses documents. It uses words included in tweets actually tweeted within a certain area instead of words in a certain document.

The model is shown in Fig. 1. The input is a square matrix consisting of one-hot vectors. Dimensions of each vector and the number of vectors are similar to the number of locations in the dataset. The output is a set of vectors that represents which terms were used in each location. The dimension of each vector is similar to the number of terms used in the dataset, and the number of the vectors is similar to the number of locations. Thus the m-th dimension of the n-th vector is 1 if the m-th term appeared in posts around the n-th location.

4   Experiments

We evaluated our method with an application similar to analogy-based information retrieval. The aim of this experiment is to verify the usefulness of our method for an actual location search system.

We performed an evaluation task that analyzes the similarity between locations in two different cities. This task is related to analogy-based search. Analogy-based search [10] is an Information Retrieval model which accepts an example in a known domain as a query, and returns similar entities in an unknown domain. For instance, if a user wants to know "The location in Singapore that is similar to the Statue of Liberty in New York", then system should return "Merlion". This kind of search model is reasonable for search tasks with ambiguous information needs, such as the atmosphere of a place.

We conducted a experimental task that discovers pairs of areas with similar atmosphere in Tokyo and Kyoto in Japan. The reason why we choose Tokyo and Kyoto is because both are large cities in Japan (first and fourth). Therefore, it is easier to collect a large number of geo-tagged tweets, sufficient to train a neural network-based machine learning method. In addition, it is easy to find evaluators for the experiment who know both Tokyo and Kyoto.

4.1   Dataset

To compare the two areas, we collected tweets posted in the two cities, and extracted some of them. Tweets were collected from April 2016 to March 2017 from the Twitter Streaming API. Table 1 shows the statistics of the dataset. This dataset contains sampled foursquare venues located in Tokyo or Kyoto. First, we extracted venues in the rectangles of Tokyo area and Kyoto area. As both Tokyo and Kyoto are big cities, 31% (256,289/826,266) of the venues in Japan were included in the dataset. To reduce calculation cost, we randomly sampled 14% of the venues from the whole dataset. Next, we extracted tweets posted around each venue. We set a radius $r = 50$ m. Tokyo and Kyoto are high density cities. Our dataset contains many venues which share surrounding tweets with other venues. Finally, we cleansed data, as follows. Our dataset contains many useless geo-tagged posts; such as posts by bots, "Check-in" posts of geo-social networking services, and replies for friends. We removed tweets that meet any of four conditions below, and keeping 5.15% (1,165,109/22,640,460) of tweets:

- tweets that include URIs, or other users' IDs (*i.e.,* replies),
- tweets that do not contain any Japanese characters,
- tweets that contain terms characteristic for bots, and
- tweets by a user who posted more than 20 times in the same location.

4.2   Methodology

We analyzed pairs of locations in Tokyo and Kyoto. Areas have their own atmosphere, such as atmosphere of exclusive residential area, atmosphere of desolate

Table 2. Top 10 "similar" pairs in Tokyo and Kyoto. The pair in each line was estimated as places that have same atmosphere.

Place in Tokyo	Place in Kyoto
Dining district in a small station	Peaceful residential area
Dining district in high-end area	Dining district in high-end area
Commercial building in big station	Commercial building in midsize station
Dining district in a old town	Out of downtown
Road-side in commuter town	Residential area in suburb
Backstreet of shopping street	A famous temple
University	Event areas near Kyoto station
Luxury office area	Road-side in suburbs
Station in a commuter town	Interchange in suburban area
Residential area along a river	Residential area next to imperial palace

Table 3. Top 10 "dissimilar" pairs in Tokyo and Kyoto. The pair in each line was estimated as dissimilar combination.

Place in Tokyo	Place in Kyoto
Bar district	Shrine in a mountain
Shopping mall	College town
Dining area in deserted station	Famous shrine
In front of famous market	Marine museum
Subway station in residential area	Famous shrine
Suburban residential area	History museum
Anime vocational school	Marine museum
Park	Center of downtown
Station in old town	Commercial complex
Dining area in deserted station	Guest house at mountain

town and so on. First of all, we generated 200 dimensional vectors for each venue. We used "keras", the python TensorFlow library for neural network calculation. We used the default parameters of the library for estimation.

Next, we compared pairs of locations by hand. We created a ranking of pairs consisting of a location in Tokyo and a location in Kyoto by their similarity. Euclidean distance was adopted as the similarity measure in 200 dimensional vector space. Our dataset contained 31,772 venues in Tokyo, and 3,439 venues in Kyoto. We calculated the similarity of 109,263,908 pairs. Two evaluators analyzed the top 100 pairs and bottom 100 pairs one by one. They discussed locations' atmosphere, other venues around the location, usage of areas, and analyzed tweets around there.

4.3   Result

We compared pairs of two locations in Tokyo and Kyoto. The ranking of pairs is shown in Table 2. We translated the concrete location to a short description. We were able to find some pairs of dining districts at the top of the ranking. People often tweet at restaurants; they post what they ate, and the evaluation of the restaurant. In dining district, it is likely to easily find clues to calculate similarity. Our method also finds many pairs of residential areas. In these areas, we were able to find daily tweets posted by residents. Through the top part of ranking, pairs of suburban residences frequently appeared. The reason may be that they are just numerous in our dataset, and all of them are similar to each other. Conversely, Table 3 represents the ranking of the most dissimilar pairs of locations. It contains many incomprehensible combinations of locations.

5   Discussion

There is some room for improvement in the proposed method. First, a vector generated by the proposed method is affected by the amount of documents for the target place. It was assumed that tweets within a range of 50 m from the target place characterize the place itself. However, if the number of tweets is too small, we cannot calculate the characteristics of the location well. Since the appropriate distance would be different for each area, we should consider dynamic distance configuration.

The quality of the tweets is also an important factor. We deleted unnecessary tweets such as ones by bots. However, there are still many tweets that do not represent features of the target place (*e.g.,* daily reports, everyday conversations between users). A clean dataset is important for good results, even if strong data cleansing reduces the amount of available training data.

Applications using Location2Vec can also be improved. We conducted an experiment to discover similar places among different regions. We calculated the distances of vectors at two places from different regions to realize such an application. The vector of a certain place in Tokyo vaguely contains the feature of Tokyo as a whole. If we can acquire the characteristics of Tokyo as a vector, we can express the unique features of the target place in Tokyo more clearly by subtracting the vector representing the characteristics of Tokyo from the vector at the target place. One way to obtain such a vector is to acquire the average vector at every place in Tokyo in the proposed method. Alternatively, in machine learning, it is conceivable to use a neural network that takes regional hierarchy into account.

6   Conclusion

We proposed a method of generating a feature vector of a place from tweets posted around the place. Since the feature vector is made from social media data, this vector may contain subjective information such as use of the venue or atmosphere of the area. We followed the Word2Vec algorithm and its basic idea. Our method uses a simple neural network which is trained through the estimation of terms that appear in tweets posted around the place.

We conducted an experiment: a case study of analogy-based search by using geo-tagged tweets in Japan. It showed the possibility of our method for social analysis.

Acknowledgements. This work was supported by JSPS KAKENHI Grant Numbers JP18K18161, JP17K17832, JP18KT0097, JP16H02906, JP16H01756, JP17H00762, JP18H03243.

References

1. Aggarwal, C.C., Abdelzaher, T.: Social sensing. In: Aggarwal, C. (eds.) Managing and mining sensor data, pp. 237–297. Springer, Heidelberg (2013)
2. Ahmed, A., Hong, L., Smola, A.J.: Hierarchical geographical modeling of user locations from social media posts. In: Proceedings of the 22Nd International Conference on World Wide Web, pp. 25–36, WWW 2013. ACM, New York (2013). https://doi.org/10.1145/2488388.2488392
3. Alcorn, M.A.: (batter—pitcher)2vec: statistic-free talent modeling with neural player embeddings. In: MIT Sloan Sports Analytics Conference, p. 5435 (2016)
4. Canh, T.V., Gertz, M.: A spatial LDA model for discovering regional communities. In: 2013 IEEE/ACM International Conference on Advances in Social Networks Analysis and Mining (ASONAM 2013), pp. 162–168, August 2013. https://doi.org/10.1109/ASONAM.2013.6785703
5. Dhingra, B., Zhou, Z., Fitzpatrick, D., Muehl, M., Cohen, W.W.: Tweet2Vec: character-based distributed representations for social media. In: The 54th Annual Meeting of the Association for Computational Linguistics, p. 269 (2016)
6. Doran, D., Gokhale, S., Dagnino, A.: Human sensing for smart cities. In: Proceedings of the 2013 IEEE/ACM International Conference on Advances in Social Networks Analysis and Mining, pp. 1323–1330, ASONAM 2013. ACM, New York (2013). https://doi.org/10.1145/2492517.2500240
7. Giridhar, P., Wang, S., Abdelzaher, T., Al Amin, T., Kaplan, L.: Social fusion: integrating Twitter and Instagram for event monitoring. In: 2017 IEEE International Conference on Autonomic Computing (ICAC), pp. 1–10. IEEE (2017)
8. Grover, A., Leskovec, J.: node2vec: scalable feature learning for networks. In: Proceedings of the 22nd ACM SIGKDD International Conference on Knowledge Discovery and Data Mining, pp. 855–864. ACM (2016)
9. Kamath, K.Y., Caverlee, J., Lee, K., Cheng, Z.: Spatio-temporal dynamics of online memes: a study of geo-tagged tweets, pp. 667–678 (2013)
10. Kato, M.P., Ohshima, H., Oyama, S., Tanaka, K.: Query by analogical example: relational search using web search engine indices. In: Proceedings of the 18th ACM Conference on Information and Knowledge Management, pp. 27–36. ACM (2009)
11. Kurashima, T., Iwata, T., Hoshide, T., Takaya, N., Fujimura, K.: Geo topic model: joint modeling of user's activity area and interests for location recommendation. In: Proceedings of the Sixth ACM International Conference on Web Search and Data Mining, pp. 375–384. ACM (2013)

12. Lee, R., Sumiya, K.: Measuring geographical regularities of crowd behaviors for twitter-based geo-social event detection. In: Proceedings of the 2nd ACM SIGSPA-TIAL International Workshop on Location Based Social Networks, pp. 1–10. ACM (2010)
13. Liu, Y., et al.: Social sensing: a new approach to understanding our socioeconomic environments. Ann. Assoc. Am. Geogr. **105**(3), 512–530 (2015)
14. Madjiheurem, S., Qu, L., Walder, C.: Chord2Vec: learning musical chord embeddings. In: Proceedings of the Constructive Machine Learning Workshop at 30th Conference on Neural Information Processing Systems (NIPS 2016), Barcelona, Spain (2016)
15. Mikolov, T., Chen, K., Corrado, G., Dean, J.: Efficient estimation of word representations in vector space. arXiv preprint arXiv:1301.3781 (2013)
16. Mikolov, T., Sutskever, I., Chen, K., Corrado, G.S., Dean, J.: Distributed representations of words and phrases and their compositionality. In: Advances in Neural Information Processing Systems, pp. 3111–3119 (2013)
17. Moody, C.E.: Mixing Dirichlet topic models and word embeddings to make lda2vec. CoRR abs/1605.02019 (2016). http://arxiv.org/abs/1605.02019
18. Ristoski, P., Paulheim, H.: RDF2Vec: RDF graph embeddings for data mining. In: Groth, P., et al. (eds.) ISWC 2016. LNCS, vol. 9981, pp. 498–514. Springer, Cham (2016). https://doi.org/10.1007/978-3-319-46523-4_30
19. Sakaki, T., Okazaki, M., Matsuo, Y.: Earthquake shakes Twitter users: real-time event detection by social sensors, pp. 851–860 (2010)
20. Seki, Y.: Use of Twitter for analysis of public sentiment for improvement of local government service. In: 2016 IEEE International Conference on Smart Computing (SMARTCOMP), pp. 1–3, May 2016. https://doi.org/10.1109/SMARTCOMP.2016.7501726
21. Sheng, X., Tang, J., Xiao, X., Xue, G.: Sensing as a service: challenges, solutions and future directions. IEEE Sens. J. **13**(10), 3733–3741 (2013)
22. Vosoughi, S., Vijayaraghavan, P., Roy, D.: Tweet2Vec: learning tweet embeddings using character-level CNN-LSTM encoder-decoder. In: Proceedings of the 39th International ACM SIGIR conference on Research and Development in Information Retrieval, pp. 1041–1044. ACM (2016)
23. Wakamiya, S., Jatowt, A., Kawai, Y., Akiyama, T.: Analyzing global and pairwise collective spatial attention for geo-social event detection in microblogs. In: Proceedings of the 25th International Conference Companion on World Wide Web, pp. 263–266, WWW 2016 Companion, International World Wide Web Conferences Steering Committee, Republic and Canton of Geneva, Switzerland (2016). https://doi.org/10.1145/2872518.2890551
24. Wang, Y., Wang, T., Tsou, M.H., Li, H., Jiang, W., Guo, F.: Mapping dynamic urban land use patterns with crowdsourced geo-tagged social media (Sina-Weibo) and commercial points of interest collections in Beijing, China. Sustainability **8**(11), 1202 (2016)
25. Yan, B., Janowicz, K., Mai, G., Gao, S.: From ITDL to Place2Vec: reasoning about place type similarity and relatedness by learning embeddings from augmented spatial contexts. In: Proceedings of the 25th ACM SIGSPATIAL International Conference on Advances in Geographic Information Systems, pp. 35:1–35:10, SIGSPATIAL 2017. ACM, New York (2017). https://doi.org/10.1145/3139958.3140054
26. Yin, Z., Cao, L., Han, J., Zhai, C., Huang, T.: Geographical topic discovery and comparison. In: Proceedings of the 20th International Conference on World Wide Web, pp. 247–256. ACM (2011)

Graph-Based Clustering Approach for Economic and Financial Event Detection Using News Analytics Data

Sergei P. Sidorov[✉], Alexey R. Faizliev, Michael Levshunov,
Alfia Chekmareva, Alexander Gudkov, and Eugene Korobov

Saratov State University, Saratov, Russian Federation
sidorovsp@info.sgu.ru

Abstract. In recent years, one of the most extensive research topics in social media analysis has been event detection. Most of the approaches use fixed temporal and spatial resolutions to detect events. In this paper, we employ a procedure for the detection of economic and financial events using news analytics data. We use an algorithm to compute a data similarity graph at chosen scales and detect economic and financial events simultaneously by a single graph-based clustering process. Experimental results on real world data collected from news analytics providers demonstrate the effectiveness of the event detection procedure based on real-time news analytics data.

Keywords: Event detection · Spatiotemporal analysis
News analytics · Clustering

1 Introduction

News agencies, organizations, social networks, enterprises, etc. generate a huge amount of information and news in real time. The study of the characteristics and features of the news flow has become one of the recent topics in social informatics. The news stream is publicly available and reflects processes which are going on in the world. Therefore, the examination of structural properties of the news flow and the development of the methods and algorithms for processing such data are of great interest.

In this paper we restrict our analysis to the study of economic and financial news. News analytics providers (such as Media Sentiment, Thompson Reuters and Raven Pack) collect, aggregate and pre-process news from different sources including news agencies and social media (blogs, social networks, etc.). They also use so-called pre-news, i.e. SEC reports, court documents, reports of various government agencies, business resources, company reports, announcements,

The work was supported by RFBR (grant 18-37-00060).

S. Staab et al. (Eds.): SocInfo 2018, LNCS 11186, pp. 271–280, 2018.
https://doi.org/10.1007/978-3-030-01159-8_26

industrial and macroeconomic statistics. The survey of applications for news analytics tools can be found in books [14,15]. In recent years news analytics tools have been developed and used in social network analysis [4,9,12,18].

Thus, the huge amount of news analytics data enables the study of some research problems. One of such problem is the analysis of company co-mention network which has been addressed in [20,23]. This paper concerns with another such problem which is event detection. Note that news analytic data raise advantages for event detection. Using the real-time nature of news analytic services, both traders and governments may boost their awareness of real world events much quicker than with offline analysis based on traditional media sources.

Our research interest is close to the problem of event detection in Twitter. It should be noted that event detection in Twitter has long been a research topic [24] and the main problem has been detecting those events that Twitter users are discussing most. Most of the researches supposed that an increase in the usage of some related words would show when an event is happening. An event is therefore commonly characterized by a number of keywords displaying sharp burst in appearance count [10,24]. Since then the problem of event detection in Twitter has drawn a serious amount of enthusiasm from the data mining researchers [1,2,5,6,17]. The common understanding is that events in social media platforms can be loosely defined as real world happenings that occur within similar time periods and geographical locations, and that have been mentioned by the online users. Recent works include [3,7,8,11,16], among many others.

In this paper, we use an approach based on the ideas of the paper [24]. We use news analytics data for detecting events that are of similar scales and localized in time and referred to a particular company. Thus, we employ the characteristic of news items which are reflect localization in time and the similarity of their attributes.

2   Events

In this paper we define events as real world happenings that are reflected by news items that are concentrated in time and connected with a particular company or a group of companies, or an economic sector. We suppose that an important offline event attracts interest of news and information agencies as well as other news providers and news exchange participants. The more important the event, the more intense will be the corresponding news flow. We assume that an important event should cause a cascade of news. We define a cascade of news as the sequence of news items published by various news providers, which are published in the same time frame and related to one company and have one topic. As a rule, such a cascade has an initial news message (trigger), which triggers this cascade. If some news turned out to be important, other news providers and news agencies reprint this news close to the original form. In addition, they can publish news items related to the development of events caused by this news. If a published news item seems to be not important, it may be reprinted by a very few news providers, or it may not be reprinted at all. The news that did not provoke interest and did not lead to a cascade of news, in our opinion, is hardly connected with an important event. Therefore, the detection of such cascades in the flow of news items allows us to detect events in one way or another. Each such cascade is a component of connectivity in the graph of news reports. Thus, the identification of cascades and their corresponding events is reduced to the task of finding the related subgraphs (clusters) of the news graph. It can be assumed that the more news are in the cascade, the more significant the corresponding event is.

Of course, different events can exhibit different temporal scales, i.e. they can span different intervals in time.

In this paper we consider a news analytics data stream with temporal and text information. The goal of this paper is to employ an approach to identify events using the stream data of news analytics providers. We treat event detection as a graph-based clustering problem, where the vertices of the graph represent the news, and the edges reflect their similarities.

3   Event Detection via Temporal and Attributive Constraints

Economic and financial events presented in news flow may have different localization behavior in time and can have different attribution to a particular company (group of companies, sector, country). When the events are localized in the two dimensions (temporal and attributive), event detection can be adequately implemented by imposing temporal and attributive constraints on the data. In this section, we detail an approach for detecting economic and financial events that are localized both in time and attribution. It can be reduced to a clustering problem, where we assemble together the news items that describe the same real world event. We define the similarity measure between different news items n_i and n_j as follows:

$$S(n_i, n_j) = \begin{cases} 1, & \text{if } t(n_i, n_j) \leq T_t \text{ and } A(n_i) = A(n_j), \\ 0, & \text{otherwise.} \end{cases} \tag{1}$$

where $t(n_i, n_j)$ is the temporal difference in minutes between n_i and n_j and $A(n)$ is the value of attribute A (company name and news topic) for news item n.

The threshold T_t enforces strict temporal constraints of the events and A implements the shared attributes. Under such constraints, two news items n_i and n_j seem to refer to the same economical and financial event.

The graph connectivity components are found by means of the depth search approach. The main drawback of this clustering algorithm on big graphs is the high demand on the amount of RAM. However, the problem is hugely reduced due to an eminent sparsity of our graph.

Different approaches to find similarity measure for twits have been used in papers [6, 13].

Let $S(n_i, n_j)$ be the pairwise similarity between news items defined in (1). Let us define matrix W as follows:

$$W(n_i, n_j) = \begin{cases} S(n_i, n_j), & \text{if } i \neq j, \\ 0, & \text{if } i = j. \end{cases} \tag{2}$$

Matrix W is a symmetric sparse matrix. We can construct an sparse undirected $G = (V, E, W)$ for which W is the adjacency matrix. The vertices V of the graph will represent news items, $E = V \times V$ is the edge set. An edge connects two news if they are about the same company and have the same topic. If $W(n_i, n_j) \neq 0$ then there is an edge between two vertices v_i and v_j and the weight $w_{ij} = 1$.

With such a graph representation of W, event detection can then be reduced to a graph partitioning task, i.e. to divide the graph G into subgraphs. Our goal is to subdivide the vertices of the graph into disjoint clusters in such a way that each cluster would contain news items that probably correspond to the same economical or finance event. The constraints in (1) imply that the events should be localized in time and be attributed to the same company (or group of companies, or to the same economical sector, country).

Algorithm 1. Event Detection via Local and Attributive Constraints

Input: N: a set of news item with temporal, attributive, and text information; T: temporal threshold; A: attributive information

begin

> · Compute the pairwise similarities $S(n_i, n_j)$ between all news items in N using (1);
> · Compute the adjacency matrix W using (2);
> · Apply the graph partitioning algorithm to W, and retain the meaningful clusters $\{c_i\}_{i=1}^m$ after postprocessing steps;

end

Output : $\{c_i\}_{i=1}^m$: clusters that correspond to events that are localized in time and share the same attribute

---

4   Empirical Result

We now test the performance of Algorithm 1 for real world event detection problems. We first describe the data and some implementation details, and then present the event detection results.

4.1   Data Description

Providers of news analytics obtain and aggregate data from different sources (including news agencies and business reports) and social media. Our data cover the period from January 1, 2015 to January 31, 2015 (i.e. 22 trading days). We consider all the news released during this period. Initially we performed data selection and cleaning process.

Descriptive statistics of news flow can be found in Table 1. The total amount of news items issued in January was 134199. Table 1 shows that the average amount of news published per day was 4329. There were days with the very low intensity of news flow (e.g. only 30 economic and financial news items were published on January, 1 of 2015), while some days exhibit a much higher amount of published news items (e.g. 10238 news items were issued on January, 29 of 2015).

Table 1. Descriptive statistics of news flow in January, 2015

Days	31
Total amount of news items	134199
Mean per day	4329
Minimum	30
Maximum	10238
St. deviation	3122.8
Median	5360

Figure 1 shows that the average amount of holiday news items is much less than that of holidays. Therefore, we eliminate all holiday news from the study. The news flow is highly noisy and time series of news flow data exhibit self-similarity and fractality [19, 21, 22]. Examining the problem of handling the noisy information in the Twitter data, the paper [6] uses a homogeneous Poisson process as a statistical model.

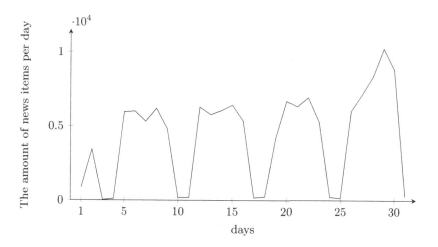

Fig. 1. Daily dynamics of the news flow in January, 2015

4.2   Event Detection Results

We would like to group similar news items into the same cluster in such a way that they could correspond to a real world event. We implement the event detection algorithm and obtain empirical results for different values of temporal threshold $\theta = 0.5, 1, 3, 6, 12\,h$ for the detection of event clusters. The results are presented in Tables 2 and 3. Table 2 exhibits the distribution of amount of cascades with dependence to the size of the cascade for different values of θ. Table 3 presents the sizes of connectivity components and temporal durations of corresponding news cascades for different values of θ.

As can be seen from Table 2, the distribution of the sizes of connectivity components is fairly stable regardless of the parameter θ. At the same time, Table 3 shows that most of the connectivity components correspond to small-sized cascades (ranging from 2 to 10 news). This small-sized cascades can not reflect an event. It is obvious that an increase of the parameter θ must lead to the appearance of larger-sized connectivity components, and corresponding cascades may last the entire period under consideration. In our opinion, taking the value of θ more than 12 h could lead to the unification of the whole news flow for a quite large company in one cascade. In our opinion, if an event occurred, then the discussion of it in the news flow will occur quite intensively. At the same time, the continuity of the working day of the world financial market will not allow to forget the event, and news will be published in Asian, European and American financial markets, and so on. Therefore, in our opinion, in order to detect events it is quite enough to take θ in the interval from 3 to 6 h.

Table 2. The amount of cascades N and the average duration of cascades T with a given size (the amount of news items in cascade), for different values of θ

Cascade sizes	$\theta = 0.5$		$\theta = 1$		$\theta = 3$		$\theta = 6$		$\theta = 12$	
	N	T	N	T	N	T	N	T	N	T
11–20	770	26 m	847	49 m	985	2 h 13 m	1071	3 h 59 m	1132	7 h 50 m
21–30	84	36 m	107	1 h 24 m	151	3 h 53 m	159	7 h 6 m	209	17 h 1 m
31–40	29	1 h 0 m	33	1 h 28 m	41	4 h 12 m	49	9 h 13 m	62	17 h 53 m
41–50	9	1 h 2 m	14	2 h 15 m	18	6 h 25 m	23	12 h 1 m	24	1d 3 h 23 m
51–60	8	1 h 1 m	10	1 h 56 m	13	5 h 15 m	16	11 h 31 m	24	21 h 6 m
61–70	1	2 h 43 m	1	2 h 43 m	6	11 h 40 m	7	22 h 28 m	7	1d 16 h 59 m
71–80	2	58 m	2	58 m	2	58 m	9	15 h 1 m	10	1d 6 h 56 m
81–90	0	-	0	-	0	-	0	-	1	2d 20 h 45 m
91–100	0	-	0	-	0	-	0	-	1	4d 6 h 51 m
101–110	0	-	0	-	0	-	0	-	1	1d 8 h 32 m

The analysis of the clustering results for Algorithm 1 show that the clusters detected by the algorithm correspond to meaningful economic and financial real world events of interest.

Below we describe a few cases of news cascades found by Algorithm 1.

Table 3. Characteristics of connectivity components' sizes and temporal durations of corresponding news cascades for different values of θ

	Temporal threshold θ				
	0.5 h	1 h	3 h	6 h	12 h
Total amount of connectivity components (with 2 and more items)	21038	21276	21382	21610	21657
Mean duration of connectivity components (with 2 and more items)	8 m	15 m	39 m	1 h 19 m	2 h 36 m
Mean size of connectivity components (with 2 and more items)	3.98	4.10	4.31	4.43	4.57
Median of connectivity components (with 2 and more items)	3	3	3	3	3
Total amount of cascades (with 11 and more items)	903	1014	1216	1334	1471
Mean duration of cascades (with 11 and more items)	29 m	56 m	2 h 37 m	4 h 57 m	10 h 32 m
Mean size of cascades (with 11 and more items)	16.16	16.49	17.05	17.54	18.29
Median of cascades (with 11 and more items)	13	14	14	14	15
Max cascade	74	74	74	76	101
Max duration	3 h 18 m	7 h 52 m	21 h 31 m	1d 16 h 59 m	4d 10 h 40 m

(1) Yahoo Inc. decided to transfer its 15% of the Chinese Alibaba Group shares to a separate company. At the closure of trading on January 26th the shares' value was estimated at $40 billion, as follows from a message on the company's website. The cascade began at 28.01.2015 02:36:07 and lasted till 28.01.2015 18:04:04. Duration 15 h 27 min 57 s. The number of news in the cascade is 22. The first news was printed by Forbes.

(2) Facebook reports fourth quarter and full year 2014 results. Its users' community was continuously growing. Revenue for the fourth quarter of 2014 totaled $3.85 billion, an increase of 49%, compared with $2.59 billion in the fourth quarter of 2013. The cascade began at 21.01.2015 21:01:12 and lasted till 22.01.2015 15:17:24. Duration 18 h 16 min 12 s. The number of news in the cascade is 48. The news was printed by Facebook.

(3) Netflix ended 2014 with 57.4 million subscribers worldwide topping expectations for overseas growth. The No. 1 subscription video-on-demand provider reported quarterly revenue of $1.48 billion, up 26% year over year. Netflix shares were up more than 13% in after-hours trading, to $395.15 per share, on the results. The cascade began at 20.01.2015 21:01:11 and lasted till 21.01.2015 15:21:30. Duration 18 h 20 min 29 s. The number of news in the cascade is 52. The first news was printed by Variety.

(4) On the morning of January 28, 2015 at 05:19:31 the BBC news service informed about record Apple's income. Apple reported about its quarterly profit of 18 billion dollars. It is a historical record for a public company. After that, the price of Apple shares increased by 5%. This statement aroused a news cascade with duration of 12 h 14 min 38 s. The cascade contained 25 news items.

(5) Tesco PLC is a British company and one of the oldest transnational trade networks. Tesco PLC owns a large trade network in British. This company controls about 30% retail of foodstuffs. On the morning of January 8, 2015 at 7:00:28 one of the largest American publications The Wall Street Journal the news was published about lower prices and closing unprofitable stores. Tesco PLC planned to close about 43 unprofitable stores and to sell a range of assets. After that, Tesco's shares increased at once by 14,97% and have reached 2.09 pounds. This information aroused a news cascade with duration of 21 h 31 min. The cascade contained 66 news items (Fig. 2).

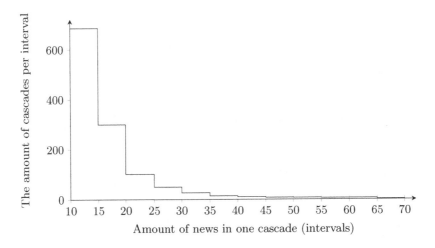

Fig. 2. The histogram for the amount of connectivity components (with 11 and more items), threshold $\theta = 3$ h

5   Conclusion

In this paper we suppose that an important economic and financial event should lead to a cascade of news. By this reason, the mining of such cascades in the news flow may be exploited to detect events. Each such cascade forms a cluster in the graph of news reports. Therefore, the mining of cascades (and associated events) can be reduced to the problem of finding the corresponding clusters in the graph. The clustering algorithm employs a similarity measure between news items that uses both the temporal and textual features of a news item. It is supposed that two news items that are generated by news agencies that describe the same event should be closely connected with a particular company, or a group of companies, or economic sector, or country. In this paper, to measure the similarity between news we use approach based on temporal and affiliation constraints. Empirical results on real world data collected from news analytics providers exhibit the capability and the efficiency of the event detection approach.

References

1. Aggarwal, C.C.: Mining text and social streams: a review. SIGKDD Explor. Newsl. **15**(2), 9–19 (2014)
2. Aggarwal, C.C., Subbian, K.: Event detection in social streams. In: Proceedings of the 2012 SIAM International Conference on Data Mining, pp. 624–635 (2012). https://epubs.siam.org/doi/abs/10.1137/1.9781611972825.54
3. Atefeh, F., Khreich, W.: A survey of techniques for event detection in twitter. Comput. Intell. **31**(1), 132–164 (2015)
4. Batrinca, B., Treleaven, P.C.: Social media analytics: a survey of techniques, tools and platforms. AI Soc. **30**(1), 89–116 (2015)
5. Becker, H., Naaman, M., Gravano, L.: Learning similarity metrics for event identification in social media. In: Proceedings of the Third ACM International Conference on Web Search and Data Mining, WSDM 2010, pp. 291–300. ACM, New York (2010)
6. Dong, X., Mavroeidis, D., Calabrese, F., Frossard, P.: Multiscale event detection in social media. Data Min. Knowl. Discov. **29**(5), 1374–1405 (2015)
7. Hasan, M., Orgun, M.A., Schwitter, R.: Real-time event detection from the twitter data stream using the TwitterNews+ framework. Information Processing & Management (2018, in press)
8. Huang, Y., Li, Y., Shan, J.: Spatial-temporal event detection from geo-tagged tweets. ISPRS Int. J. Geo-Inf. **7**(4), 150 (2018)
9. Khan, W., Daud, A., Nasir, J.A., Amjad, T.: A survey on the state-of-the-art machine learning models in the context of NLP. Kuwait J. Sci. **43**(4), 95–113 (2016)
10. Kleinberg, J.: Bursty and hierarchical structure in streams. In: Proceedings of the Eighth ACM SIGKDD International Conference on Knowledge Discovery and Data Mining, KDD 2002, pp. 91–101. ACM, New York (2002)
11. Kolchyna, O., Souza, T.T.P., Treleaven, P.C., Aste, T.: A framework for twitter events detection, differentiation and its application for retail brands. In: 2016 Future Technologies Conference (FTC), pp. 323–331, December 2016
12. Manaman, H.S., Jamali, S., AleAhmad, A.: Online reputation measurement of companies based on user-generated content in online social networks. Comput. Hum. Behav. **54**(Suppl C), 94–100 (2016)
13. Manning, C.D., Raghavan, P., Schütze, H.: Introduction to Information Retrieval. Cambridge University Press, New York (2008)
14. Mitra, G., Mitra, L. (eds.): The Handbook of News Analytics in Finance. Wiley, Chichester (2011)
15. Mitra, G., Xiang, Y. (eds.): The Handbook of Sentiment Analysis in Finance. Albury Books (2016)
16. Sakaki, T., Okazaki, M., Matsuo, Y.: Tweet analysis for real-time event detection and earthquake reporting system development. IEEE Trans. Knowl. Data Eng. **25**(4), 919–931 (2013)

17. Sayyadi, H., Hurst, M., Maykov, A.: Event detection and tracking in social streams. In: Proceedings of the International Conference on Weblogs and Social Media (ICWSM 2009). AAAI (2009)

18. Schuller, B., Mousa, A.E., Vryniotis, V.: Sentiment analysis and opinion mining: on optimal parameters and performances. Wiley Interdiscip. Rev. Data Min. Knowl. Discov. **5**(5), 255–263 (2015)

19. Sidorov, S.P., Faizliev, A.R., Balash, V.A.: Fractality and multifractality analysis of news sentiments time series. IAENG Int. J. Appl. Math. **48**(1), 90–97 (2018)

20. Sidorov, S.P.: QAP analysis of company co-mention network. In: Bonato, A., Prałat, P., Raigorodskii, A. (eds.) WAW 2018. LNCS, vol. 10836, pp. 83–98. Springer, Cham (2018). https://doi.org/10.1007/978-3-319-92871-5_7

21. Sidorov, S.P., Faizliev, A.R., Balash, V.A., Korobov, E.A.: Long-range correlation analysis of economic news flow intensity. Phys. A: Stat. Mech. Appl. **444**, 205–212 (2016)

22. Sidorov, S., Faizliev, A., Balash, V.: Scale invariance of news flow intensity time series. Nonlinear Phenom. Complex Syst. **19**(4), 368–377 (2016)

23. Sidorov, S., Faizliev, A., Balash, V., Gudkov, A.A., Chekmareva, A.Z., Anikin, P.K.: Company co-mention network analysis. In: Kalyagin, V., Pardalos, P., Prokopyev, O., Utkina, I. (eds.) Computational Aspects and Applications in Large Scale Networks, vol. 247, pp. 83–98. Springer, Cham (2018). https://doi.org/10.1007/978-3-319-96247-4_26

24. Yang, Y., Pierce, T., Carbonell, J.: A study of retrospective and on-line event detection. In: Proceedings of the 21st Annual International ACM SIGIR Conference on Research and Development in Information Retrieval, SIGIR 1998, pp. 28–36. ACM, New York (1998)

The Effect of Service Cost, Quality, and Location on the Length of Online Reviews

Antonio D. Sirianni$^{(\boxtimes)}$ (iD)

Cornell University, Ithaca, NY 14853, USA
ads334@cornell.edu

Abstract. The use of costly sanctioning by individuals has been found to enhance cooperation and pro-social behavior, especially when a centralized system of authority is either non-existent or unable to sanction anti-social behavior. Online review systems have offered a centralized location for decentralized social control: individuals who are unhappy with a service provided can offer negative feedback, harming the reputation of the service provider. The cost of services provided and the quality of service received may determine the level of motivation individuals have to compose a detailed online review. Furthermore, differences between markets and cultural norms regarding sanctioning behavior may also affect how much effort individuals will spend on online sanctioning. These relationships are tested using a corpus of reviews pulled from an online review system for various home, auto, and medical services.

Keywords: Online reviews · E-commerce · Social control

1 Introduction

What motivates individuals to contribute to a public good and not simply free ride on others' efforts? Social scientists interested in problems of cooperation and social control have noted how individuals engage in costly sanctioning, which collectively improves outcomes for the group in the long run by deterring antisocial behavior in others. Collective action problems occur when a group is better off if everyone behaves cooperatively, but individuals are better off if they behave selfishly, the classic examples being the Prisoners Dilemma in the 2-person case [1], and The Tragedy of the Commons in the n-person case [2]. Repeated interaction offers one potential solution: mimicking the pro-social or anti-social behavior of others in future interactions (tit-for-tat) can be effective in generating cooperative behavior [3]. In one shot situations, however, tit-for-tat is not available and social sanctioning may be the only option. When individuals can sanction others who have behaved selfishly, they do so at a cost to themselves. This creates a second-order free rider problem where individuals face a new dilemma: whether to punish selfish individuals at a cost to themselves [4].

In the absence of a direct reward or punishment to individuals who fail to post a review, after a transaction occurs, it is not rational for an individual to spend the time and effort necessary to compose a lengthy piece detailing the performance of their service provider. Yet it most certainly happens. By looking at the amount of energy put

© Springer Nature Switzerland AG 2018
S. Staab et al. (Eds.): SocInfo 2018, LNCS 11186, pp. 281–290, 2018.
https://doi.org/10.1007/978-3-030-01159-8_27

into reviews, mainly by measuring the overall length of reviews, we can obtain a better understanding of what motivates contributions to online review systems (and pro-social punishment more generally).

2 Prior Work

Other studies of online review systems have focused on the quality of the review system itself, including the usefulness of systems in predicting product quality [5] and the identification and removal of spam and fake reviews [6–8]. Other work has focused on what speciific components of online reviews customers find most useful for making valuations and purchasing [9, 10].

This article is interested more in the motives than the benefits of the participant. Previous literature has identified four motivating mechanisms: (1) a desire for social interaction, (2) a desire for economic incentives, (3) their concern for other customers, and (4) the potential to enhance their own self-worth [11]. The influence of mood and cost on the use of an online review system has also been shown [12].

The mechanism this article considers most directly is an intrinsic motive to retaliate at a cost to oneself when a trusted individual violates said trust. Online review sites provide an opportunity for costly sanctioning when tit-for-tat is not an option. Specifically, the cost of a service, which is partially a proxy for how often a purchase might be repeated, is included as a predictor. The quality of service as defined by the rating given by the customer, a proxy for whether service providers are shirking, is also included as a predictor of review length.

Furthermore, it has been shown experimentally that individuals from different cultures may be prone to different levels of pro-social behavior and punishment [13, 14]. For example, much work has been demonstrated the existence of a 'Culture of Honor' in portions of the Southern and Western United States, where individuals are more likely to respond to perceived threats and insults [15]. Accordingly, factor variables will be included for cities to include any baseline difference in not only the online presence of service economies, but also regional cultures. Interaction terms will be included between city variables and cost and quality variables to measure how cost and quality may differ as motivators between cities.

3 Data

Data was extracted from a popular online review site, www.angieslist.com, to measure the relationships between service cost, service quality, and online social sanctioning. This data was obtained from the website from January 18th–January 24th, 2018 - the reviews themselves were posted from 2001–2018. Reviews on providers of 26 different services were taken from four American metropolitan areas: Atlanta, Boston, Houston, and Seattle. The final data set contained information from 153,433 different customer-provider interactions, featuring 110,391 distinct customers and 14,647 distinct service providers. After filtering out reviews where there was no cost of service provided, or the cost of service was listed as less than $1(USD), 101,492 distinct reviews, 80,279 distinct customers, and 11,862 distinct service providers remained. Some reviews are indexed in multiple categories: they are assigned to each category and inversely weighted in the models estimated later in the article. Both service costs and review lengths are log-transformed to normalize their distributions; this is a necessary step for the regression framework that is employed in the paper.

Each review contains information on the reported cost of the service provided, the 'grade' given from the customer to the service provider (A–F), if the customer would hire the service provider again (a binary variable), and the total number of characters written about the service provider. Figure 1 shows the distribution of the log-transformed service cost and written review length for each category. The figures indicate that there is far more variation in terms of service cost by category, as opposed to review length. A more detailed table summarizing each category is included as an Appendix (Table 2).

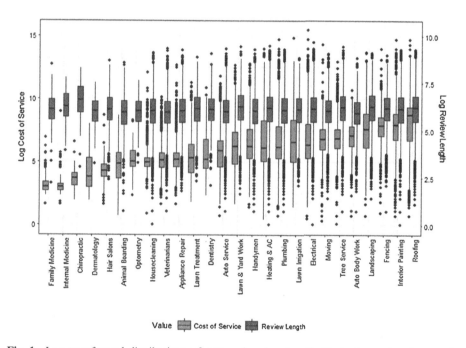

Fig. 1. Log transformed distributions of cost and review length. Each observation has equal weight in this figure.

Figure 2 shows how the relationship between the cost of service and review length vary by service quality (an A-F letter grade) and city. While Fig. 1 suggests that there is not a relationship between service cost and review length at the categorical level, Fig. 2 suggests that there is a slight but consistent relationship between the two variables in each of the 20 (5 * 4) contexts shown. Furthermore, inspection of this figure indicates that lower grades are associated with not wanting to re-hire a service provider, and also that more negative reviews tend to be longer.

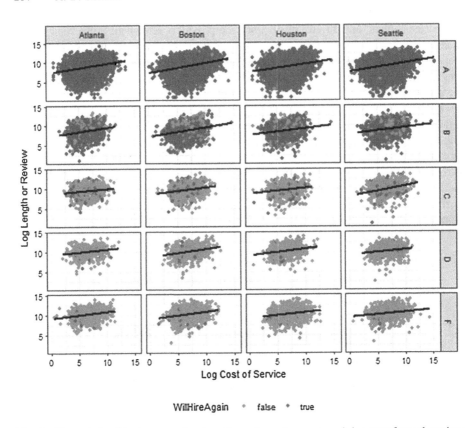

Fig. 2. The relationship between log-transformed service cost and log-transformed review length by geographic context and overall grade of review. Black lines indicate lines of best fit, blue dots correspond to cases where the reviewer indicates they would hypothetically re-hire the provider, red dots correspond to cases where they indicate they would not.

4   Models and Results

This paper is focused on what predicts different levels of effort invested in online reviews. The operationalization of effort is rather straight-forward: it is simply the (log-transformed) number of characters that an individual includes in their online review. There are three main independent variables of interest. The first and perhaps most important is cost. Cost is operationalized in a two-dimensional space - both the average cost of the service product category is considered, as well as the Z-Score of an individual service within the product category to which it belongs. For example: if a review of a plumbing service is being considered, both the average cost of a plumbing service, and the cost of that specific plumbing service relative to the average cost are included - as well as second order terms and the interaction of these two cost variables.

Quality of service is the second major dependent variable. This variable is operationalized simply with the 'overall' service grade given by the customer, which is an A, B, C, D or F. This variable is treated as a series of factor variables, as the distance between any pair of letters may not be equal (the difference between an A and a B is unlikely the same as the difference between a B and C). Furthermore, it is possible that the relationship between quality and review length is not ordinal - middling grades may in fact have the lowest or highest review lengths.

Finally, factor variables for each city are also included. This should capture any natural variation in the way that online review systems are used in each city, or alternatively compensate for average differences in product cost between cities. Interaction terms are also included between cities and quality and cost variables - as different parts of the country may be more or less sensitive and willing to respond to exceptionally good or bad (or expensive or cheap) services. This is partially predicted by the aforementioned 'Culture of Honor' hypothesis, and accordingly two of the cities selected are in the Southern United States (Atlanta and Houston).

Each of these three sets of effects are first modeled separately, and then a series of ANOVA tests are used to determine if each additional set of variables adds additional information to the model. The bulk of the explanatory power seems to come from the two cost terms (as well as their squared terms and interactions), and the overall grade given to the service by the customer. However, the addition of the city factor variable, as well as its interactions with the cost and quality variables, each make statistically significant additions to the model, as shown in Table 1.

Table 1. Explanatory power and significance of each model. Models 4–8 have F-ratios and p-values that correspond to an ANOVA test conducted between the model indicated in the 'Ref' (reference model) column.

	Cost	Quality	City	City * cost	City * quality	k	F	r^2	p-value	Ref.
1	Yes					5	1431	.0614	≈ 0	–
2		Yes				4	1121	.0394	≈ 0	–
3			Yes			3	71.36	.0020	≈ 0	–
4	Yes	Yes	Yes			9	1142	.0991	≈ 0	1
5	Yes	Yes	Yes			12	43.88	.1002	≈ 0	4
6	Yes	Yes	Yes	Yes		27	4.085	.1007	≈ 0	5
7	Yes	Yes	Yes		Yes	24	4.334	.1006	≈ 0	5
8	Yes	Yes	Yes	Yes	Yes	39	4.174	.1011	≈ 0	6

The full models are included separately for each city in Table 3 in the Appendix. (While the predicted results are the same for each observation, splitting the dataset up by city and fitting a model for each results in different overall r^2 values from Table 1). The influence of each of the sets of variables included on the overall predicted length is visualized in Fig. 3. Predictions are shown for four large service categories in all four of the cities selected.

A large contributing factor to the length of the review, somewhat surprisingly, is the cost of the product relative to the category. Perhaps less surprisingly, the customer's overall quality assessment of services received also has a large effect on the amount of effort a customer puts into writing a review. Lower grades (C's, D's, and F's) tend to be associated with longer reviews. In each of the four markets, however, A's tend to merit

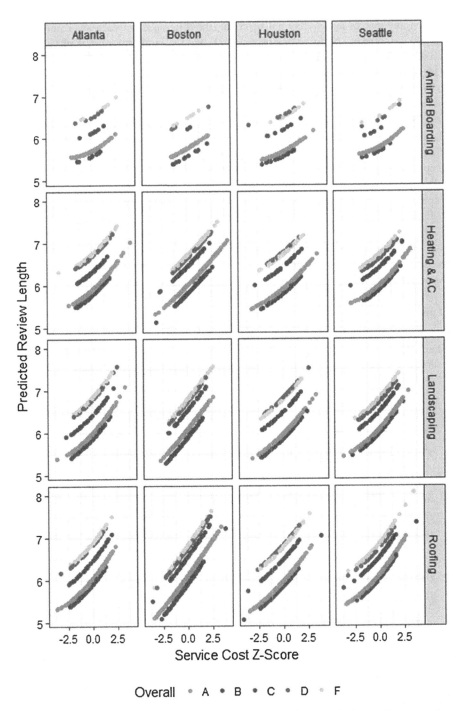

Fig. 3. Predicted review lengths by grade and relative service cost in four cities across four different service categories.

slightly longer reviews than B's (this effect is statistically significant in each city, which can be seen in Table 3 in the Appendix). This suggests that while customers may be motivated to reciprocate poor service by taking the time to write a long review, they may also be motivated to reciprocate exceptionally good service by taking the time to write extensive praise for their service provider.

5 Conclusion

Understanding what motivates contributions to online review sites is an important topic at the intersection of e-commerce and social science. It is individually irrational for individuals to contribute to online review systems, yet the existence of these systems is dependent on these contributions. The cost and quality of service may amplify an individual's willingness to contribute to these systems. An innate psychological desire to reciprocate negative service with a social sanction, or reward exceptionally good service with a social reward, may underlie what keeps these review systems intact and active.

While the overall models presented can only explain 10% of the variance seen in review length, the dataset still provides further insight into what motivates people to engage in the costly punishing or rewarding of others. Furthermore, we would expect a large part of the variance to be explained by individual characteristics of the reviewers themselves (ex: some people may be more eager and willing to share their experiences at length with others regardless of their experience, others may tend to be more succinct). This places an unknown upper-bound on the r^2 levels that could be found within the regression framework.

Both the level of customer investment and their perceived quality of service received have a large influence on the amount of time and energy they invest in online reviews. The potential curvilinear effect of service quality on review length would benefit from more research on other online platforms. Furthermore, data from a more geographically diverse data set is needed to determine how pro-social sanctioning may vary by regional culture. Just as individuals have been found to play classic game-theoretic dilemmas differently across cultures experimentally, a particularly sensitive analysis of online review data across with attention to location could sketch a map of sanctioning tendencies or even identify cultural 'fault-lines'.

The dependent variable presented here, the total character length of the customer review, is in a way derived from the most basic of all natural language processing techniques - counting letters. Further work could be supplemented through the use of sentiment-analysis or other more sophisticated NLP-techniques. Additionally, a reasonable portion of reviews contain responses from service providers, providing an opportunity to study semi-isolated interactions between individuals.

The main shortcoming of this dataset is that information is unavailable on those individuals who use service providers on the site, but do not post on the site. However, large amounts of imperfect empirical data can still be very useful. Social scientists can now use massive sets of behavioral data to build on their understanding of social control and peer punishment, instead of staying confined to the artificial environment of the lab or the hypothetical environment of computer simulation. Similarly, those who study or build online review systems can gain a better understanding of what motivates users by testing for the presence of social mechanisms that are known to motivate acts of peer-punishment or reciprocal altruism.

Appendix

See Tables 2 and 3.

Table 2. Descriptive information by service category

Category	Observations	Weighted observations	GPA	Re-hire proportion
Animal Boarding	1122	1022.3	3.67	.90
Appliance Repair	3556	3223.6	3.54	.87
Auto Body Work	1608	1507.0	3.77	.93
Auto Service	10333	9794.5	3.65	.91
Chiropractic	43	43.0	3.84	.95
Dentistry	369	369.0	3.72	.91
Dermatology	63	62.3	3.39	.79
Electrical	8968	7936.1	3.73	.91
Family Medicine	141	140.0	3.78	.96
Fencing	2707	2439.3	3.61	.89
Hair Salons	1029	1029.0	3.72	.92
Handymen	4969	4276.6	3.67	.90
Heating & AC	10063	9527.0	3.64	.90
Housecleaning	4808	4750.1	3.62	.87
Interior Painting	8714	7831.2	3.80	.93
Internal Medicine	80	79.0	3.68	.94
Landscaping	5562	4545.1	3.64	.89
Lawn & Yard Work	4348	3347.6	3.62	.88
Lawn Treatment	1340	1063.5	3.44	.84
Lawn Irrigation	2015	1689.6	3.68	.90
Moving	6495	5410.8	3.60	.88
Optometry	82	67.0	3.60	.93
Plumbing	13112	11790.2	3.65	.89
Roofing	10305	9942.9	3.67	.90
Tree Service	5615	5158.8	3.74	.93
Veterinarians	5126	4446.3	3.73	.93

The 'GPA' is the weighted average of all grades ('A' = 4, 'B' = 3, etc.)

Table 3. Regression models predicting the log of service review length in the cities of Atlanta, Boston, Houston, and Seattle.

	Atlanta	Boston	Houston	Seattle
Category average log service cost	0.124 (0.080)	0.294*** (0.058)	0.433*** (0.068)	0.187*** (0.066)
Category Z-score	−0.134*** (0.049)	−0.136*** (0.038)	−0.094** (0.045)	−0.117*** (0.042)
Category Z-score* category average	0.052*** (0.007)	0.056*** (0.006)	0.044*** (0.007)	0.049*** (0.006)
Category Average^2	−0.001 (0.006)	−0.014*** (0.004)	−0.026*** (0.005)	−0.006 (0.005)
Category Z-score^2	0.023*** (0.004)	0.007** (0.003)	0.015*** (0.004)	0.021*** (0.004)
Grade = B	−0.129*** (0.026)	−0.192*** (0.021)	−0.110*** (0.025)	−0.094*** (0.022)
Grade = C	0.425 (0.038)	0.451*** (0.032)	0.520*** (0.036)	0.421*** (0.034)
Grade = D	0.789*** (0.042)	0.650*** (0.034)	0.861*** (0.040)	0.638*** (0.038)
Grade = F	0.852*** (0.033)	0.719*** (0.029)	0.816*** (0.030)	0.740*** (0.033)
Constant	5.138*** (0.261)	4.669*** (0.187)	4.196*** (0.218)	5.000*** (0.212)
Observations	22,827	34,323	25,395	26,756
r^2	0.097	0.109	0.096	0.093
Adjusted r^2	0.097	0.109	0.096	0.092
Residual standard error	0.918 ($df = 22187$)	0.886 ($df = 34313$)	0.922 ($df = 25385$)	0.896 ($df = 26746$)
F statistic	272.502*** ($df = 9; 22817$)	465.174*** ($df = 9; 34313$)	303.202*** ($df = 9; 25385$)	303.202*** ($df = 9; 26746$)

Note: *$p < 0.01$; **$p < 0.05$; ***$p < 0.01$

References

1. Rapoport, A., Chammah, A.: Prisoner's Dilemma: A Study in Conflict and Cooperation, vol. 165. University of Michigan Press, Ann Arbor (1965)
2. Hardin, G.: The tragedy of the commons. Science **211**, 1390–1396 (1968)
3. Axelrod, R., Hamilton, W.: The evolution of cooperation. Science **162**, 1243–1248 (1981)
4. Heckathorn, D.: Collective action and the second-order free-rider problem. Ration. Soc. **1**, 78–100 (1989)
5. McGlohon, M., Glance, N., Reiter, Z.: Star quality: aggregating review to rank products and merchants. In: ICWSM, pp. 114–121 (2010)
6. Fei, G., Mukherjee, A., Liu, B., Hsu, M., Castellanos, M., Ghosh, R.: Exploiting burstiness in review for review spammer detection. In: ICWSM, pp. 175–184 (2013)
7. Mukherjee, A., Venkataraman, V., Liu, B., Glance, N.: What yelp fake review filter might be doing? In: ICWSM, pp. 409–418 (2013)

8. Akoglu, L., Chandy, R., Faloutsos, C.: Opinion fraud detection in online review by network effects. In: ICWSM, pp. 2–11 (2013)
9. Pavlou, P., Dimoka, A.: The nature and role of feedback text comments in online marketplaces: implications for trust building, price premiums, and seller differentiation. Inf. Syst. Res. **17**, 392–414 (2006)
10. Archak, N., Ghose A., Ipeirotis, G.: Show me the money! Deriving the pricing power of product features by mining customer reviews. In: SIGKDD, pp. 56–65 (2007)
11. Hennig-Thurau, T., Gwinner, K.P., Walsh, G., Gremler, D.D.: Electronic word-of-mouth via consumer-opinion platforms: what motivates consumers to articulate themselves on the Internet. J. Interact. Market. **18**, 38–52 (2004)
12. Bakashi, S, Kanuparthy, P., Gilbert, E.: Demographics, weather and online review: a study of restaurant recommendations. In: WWW, pp. 443–454 (2014)
13. Oosterbeek, H., Sloof, R., Van De Kuilen, G.: Cultural differences in ultimatum game experiments: evidence from a meta-analysis. Exp. Econ. **7**, 171–188 (2004)
14. Henrich, J., et al.: Costly punishment in human societies. Science **312**, 1767–1770 (2006)
15. Cohen, D., Nisbett, R.E.: Pers. Soc. Psychol. **20**, 551–567 (1994)

Where Is the Memorable Travel Destinations?

Miho Toyoshima[1]([✉])(iD), Masaharu Hirota[2](iD), Daiju Kato[3], Tetsuya Araki[1](iD),
and Hiroshi Ishikawa[1](iD)

[1] Graduate School of Systems Design, Tokyo Metropolitan University, Tokyo, Japan
toyoshima-miho@ed.tmu.ac.jp, {araki,ishikawa-hiroshi}@tmu.ac.jp
[2] Department of Information Science, Okayama University of Science,
Okayama, Japan
hirota@mis.ous.ac.jp
[3] Wingarc1st Inc., Tokyo, Japan
kato.d@wingarc.com

Abstract. In this paper, we propose a method to discover "memorable" travel destinations. Our hypothesis is that differences in the numbers of photographs posted to blogs for users indicate how memorable the travel destination remained to the user. We specifically examined the number of photographs posted to blogs for each user and each area. Our proposed method does not specifically examine the number of photographs simply for each place, but it examines user characteristics. We conducted experiments to demonstrate the ranking travel destinations in Japan and throughout the world using our proposed method. Results show that our method ranked not only the famous travel destinations highly but also unpopular travel destinations in terms of being memorable.

Keywords: Blog mining · Discovering travel area · Tourism

1 Introduction

Recently, the number of international tourists has increased[1]. Given these circumstances, "overtourism" has become an important problem. The cause of overtourism is that people visit areas beyond the capacity of such tourist spots to accommodate them. Inducing tourists to other areas is a useful approach to solving this problem such as the recommendation of another worthwhile tourism area. Nevertheless, it is not easy for tourists to find worthwhile sightseeing spots, irrespective of their popularity.

Our final goal is to discover and recommend "memorable" sightseeing areas, irrespective of their popularity, to people planning to take a trip. As described herein, we propose a new method to rank sightseeing areas quantitatively. Visits to "memorable" sites might enrich travel and increase the value of travel. Sightseeing areas described herein do not represent sightseeing spots or landmarks

---

[1] https://www.e-unwto.org/doi/pdf/10.18111/9789284419029.

such as the Eiffel Tower, but cities such as Paris, because over tourism have been usually not a single site problem, but a regional problem. Therefore, this research evaluates sightseeing areas. In addition, no report describes a study that includes the quantitative evaluation of travel destinations in terms of them being "memorable". Ranking based on evaluating sightseeing areas as "memorable" might be unique and novel, unlike those produced by media[2] or research institutions[3].

This study specifically examines blogs with multiple photographs to discover high-value travel destinations. This reason is that photographs represent highlights of travel (e.g., a tourist found worthwhile or unique things at a travel destination). Additionally, the frequency of posting photographs to a blog and the numbers of photographs differ among users. In this study, we quantify the worth of travel destinations to visitors. We count the photographs included in travel blogs for each area considering the user characteristics. A characteristic of a user described in this paper is "How many photographs does a blogger typically post to a single blog?" Even if the number of photographs is the same in two blogs, the importance suggested by the relative size of the average blog might be different. We also think that, given longer travel days, more photographs would be posted on the blog. This preliminary experiment uses no relation between the number of photographs in blogs and the number of days spent in a place.

Several studies discover and recommend point of interest (POI) using a blog or a social networking service (SNS) [2,6,7]. The big difference from our study is the goal. These researchers recommend travel destination or travel area, but our research focuses on the discovering worthwhile area. We can provide information to choose a travel destination by quantitative evaluation of a sightseeing area that includes sightseeing spots.

2   Related Work

Some studies discover and recommend sightseeing information using geotagged photographs. Okuyama et al. described a system for travel planning and travel path from geotagged photographs [5]. Cao et al. report a method to recommend travel information by geotagged photographs from Flickr [1]. Yuan et al. propose a system for the recommendation of a POI [7]. Ye et al. explore the influence of a user's preference, social influence, and geographic influence to provide a POI recommendation system for location-based social networks (LBSNs) [6]. In addition, Zhang et al. present a recommendation system for unknown POI [8]. The system uses a correlation between a personal check-in date, a user's social friend's check-in date, and the category of a user classified by a visited POI.

As described herein, we propose a method to discover "memorable" travel destinations. GPS exposes the information "I have been to this place". For discovering memorable travel destinations, it is necessary to use data for photographs associated with a spot. The number of photographs in a travel blog

---

[2] https://www.tripadvisor.com/TravelersChoice-Destinations.

[3] http://mkt.unwto.org/en/barometer.

might present some impression about the travel destination. In the study, we try to discover memorable travel destinations using blogs.

The blog data are beneficial information related to tourism because the text of the blog might include details related to the behavior and impressions gained during travel. Guo et al. propose a method to discover what a user enjoys about a popular spot from travel blogs [3]. Ji et al. discover landmarks in a famous tourist city from blogs to provide a personalized tourist proposal, considering the correlation between the visited place and photographs [4].

Those studies use text and some metadata in blogs. In this paper, we propose a new feature obtained from the blogs. Our method for the discovery of "memorable" travel destinations uses the number of photographs posted to blogs.

3   Preliminary Experiment

In this section, we verify the influence of the number of travel days on the number of blog photographs. It is possible that the longer the travel period for one blog, the greater the number of photographs that can be posted. Therefore, we assess our hypothesis by investigating the influence of the number of travel days on the number of photographs in blogs. We assess the following null hypothesis.

Null hypothesis *Correlation exists between the number of photographs posted on a blog and the number of travel days.*

Here, we describe the procedure to verify the null hypothesis. First, we calculate the number of travel days in each blog. We get the record of travel and define the start date of the travel as T_s and the end date as T_e. We obtain blog B_i with travel date d_i included between T_s and T_e. When i is arranged in descending order, the number of travel days D_i of the corresponding blog B_i are expressed as shown below:

$$D_i = \begin{cases} d_i - T_s & (i = 1) \\ d_i - d_{i-1} & (i > 1) \end{cases} \tag{1}$$

Next, we calculate the correlation coefficient r between the number of travel days D_i and the number of photographs P_i posted to the blog B_i. We decide whether to reject the null hypothesis according to the value of r.

We present verification results of a preliminary experiment. We obtained blogs from Travel Blog[4]. The Travel Blog has Trips which record the travel period. The number of users in Trips is 5,147. The number of Trips is 11,232. We calculate the travel period for each blog by Eq. 1. Additionally, we exclude blogs with more than 500 photographs and 500 days, which accounted for fewer than 0.1%. The correlation coefficient between the photographs and travel period is 0.083. This result shows that they do not correlate. Additionally, we calculate the correlation coefficient between photographs and the travel period for each user. As the result, 8.5% of users show correlation. The number of users who correlate is sufficiently small. Therefore, the null hypothesis is rejected.

---

[4] https://www.travelblog.org/.

4   Main Experiment

4.1   Proposed Method

In this section, we describe two scoring methods for scoring travel destinations based on the number of photographs in a blog. We assess a hypothesis that we use to discover a memorable travel destination.

Hypothesis *Difference in the numbers of photographs posted to blogs for respective users indicates how memorable the travel destinations were to users.*

The first method is scoring the travel destinations based on a standardized number of photographs posted to blogs by each user (Method 1). Here, the method of converting the features is standardized to 0 mean and 1 variance. The characteristics of this scoring method are the point that the score can be a positive or negative number. In addition, a place having large variance cannot reach a higher rank in this ranking. In this ranking, a place that many people feel memorable can be a high rank. Few people extremely feel that place unremarkable.

We describe the procedure of Method 1 to rank travel destinations based on the standardized number of photographs. First, We create the score sets Z_u for each user u and the set is composed by the standardized number of photographs. Therefore, if a user makes several blog posts about one travel destination, we add the average of the standardized number about the same travel destination to the set Z_u. At this time, we define the elements of the set Z_u as z_u.

Next, we calculate the score for each travel destination. We create the travel destination set X and define the elements of the set X as x. Also, we create the score set for each travel destination x as shown in Eq. 2.

$$Z_x = \{z_u \mid destination(z_u) = x\} \tag{2}$$

Finally, we calculate the overall score S_x for the destination x. We define the average of Z_x as S_x and rank the travel destinations based on S_x in descending order.

Secondly, the other method ranks the travel destination by the number of top $q\%$ blogs in descending order of the number of photographs in a user (Method 2). As with Method 1, Method 2 highly evaluates a travel destination that many people feel is memorable. Unlike Method 1, if some people feel that the travel destination is memorable, even if other people feel that it is extremely unremarkable, then it is evaluated highly. This is true because Method 2 does not consider a negative score.

We describe the procedure for ranking travel destinations in Method 2. Here, we create the set B_u, which is composed of blogs posted by user u and the number of photographs, as shown in Eq. 3. We define the blog posted by user u as $b_{i,u}$ and the number of photographs posted in $b_{i,u}$ as $p_{i,u}$. Also, we create the set HX_u as shown in Eq. 4.

$$B_u = \{(b_{1,u}, p_{1,u}), (b_{2,u}, p_{2,u}), ..., (b_{n,u}, p_{n,u}) \mid p_{i-1,u} \leq p_{i,u}\} \tag{3}$$

$$HX_u = \{destination(b_{i,u}) \mid |B_u| \times \frac{(100 - q)}{100} < i\} \tag{4}$$

Next, we evaluate each travel area. First, we calculate the number of users who highly valued the travel destination x. Users who assigned high scores to a travel destination x are defined as HU_x and are shown in Eq. 5.

$$HU_x = \{u \mid x \in HX_u\} \tag{5}$$

Also, we create the set U_x. The set U_x is composed of user u who post the blogs about the travel destination x. We define the score R_x as shown Eq. 6. We generate the ranking in descending order of R_x, which we calculate using the following equation:

$$R_x = \frac{|HU_x|}{|U_x|} \tag{6}$$

4.2   Experiment Dataset

This section describes a dataset in the experiment for discovering the memorable travel destination. We use the same dataset as that described in Sect. 3. It is not necessary to estimate the travel destination from the blog contents because blogs in Travel Blog are classified into a region. Users who wrote blogs only about a specific area are excluded because they might be noise. The number of users examined in the experiment was 10,166. The number of blogs was 504,233. In addition, the granularity of the travel destination is one step below the country in Travel Blog. We use the number of users that have posted about that travel destination as the BaseLine. We create ranking in descending order of scores for Method 1, Method 2, and the BaseLine.

4.3   Experiment Results

In this section, we present experimentally obtained results of ranking "memorable" travel destinations using our proposed method. In this paper, we set q to 30 in Method 2. First, we show the ranking travel destinations in Japan. In Travel Blog, the areas of Japan to be annotated to blogs are 47 prefectures and two popular areas: Nikko and Mt. Fuji. We show the top and the bottom seven areas as evaluated using Method 1, Method 2 and BaseLine in Table 1. Additionally, we show conventional ranking by a survey taken of visitors to Japan who visited the country for sightseeing[5].

In Table 1, the ranking of BaseLine is similar to the conventional ranking because the top 7 prefectures in BaseLine ranking are popular, such as Tokyo, Osaka, and Kyoto. Method 1 ranked Tottori and Tokushima as high Popular sightseeing areas such as Hokkaido and Kyoto have been ranked high also. Method 1 can at least produce a ranking that reflects popularity. In addition, Tottori is ranked seventh in the Method 2 ranking. Results show that our

---

[5] https://statistics.jnto.go.jp/graph/#graph-inbound-prefecture-ranking.

Table 1. Japan ranking

	Method 1			Method 2			BaseLine		Conventional
Rank	Area x	S_x	Users	Area x	R_x	Users	Area x	Users	Area x
1	Tottori	0.61	5	Miyagi	0.8	15	Tokyo	504	Osaka
2	Tokushima	0.60	7	Kochi	0.67	9	Kyoto	248	Tokyo
3	Hokkaido	0.51	53	Shiga	0.67	3	Hiroshima	147	Chiba
4	Kyoto	0.49	248	Okinawa	0.63	30	Osaka	139	Kyoto
5	Okinawa	0.46	30	Hokkaido	0.62	53	Kanazawa	68	Fukuoka
6	Yamanashi	0.46	9	Wakayama	0.6	20	Shizuoka	63	Aichi
7	Gunma	0.46	6	Tottori	0.6	5	Nara	61	Hokkaido
43	Yamaguchi	−0.20	14	Oita	0.27	15	Yamagata	5	Shimane
44	Niigata	−0.22	9	Akita	0.25	8	Tottori	5	Fukushima
45	Iwate	−0.32	10	Nikko	0.25	4	Nikko	4	Kochi
46	Chiba	−0.40	42	Mie	0.25	8	Shiga	3	Fukui
47	Miyazaki	−0.68	1	Hyogo	0.22	49	Fukui	3	Tokushima
48	Fukui	−0.74	3	Yamaguchi	0.21	14	Saga	1	None
49	Yamagata	−0.76	5	Yamagata	0.2	5	Miyazaki	1	None

two methods evaluate Tottori as "memorable" destination. However, Tottori is ranked 44th in the BaseLine ranking. Therefore, Tottori has not been evaluated as a popular travel destination. In addition, Yamagata and Fukui which are similar to Tottori in the BaseLine ranking, are ranked low in the Method 1 ranking. However, only Tottori moves up in the Method 1 ranking. As a result, Tottori is evaluated as a "memorable" destination using our proposed method. Tottori might be a popular travel destination. In addition, the result shows that the evaluation of users to a sightseeing area differs, even if a sightseeing area is popular. Therefore, our proposed method can extract and rank memorable travel destinations.

Method 2 and BaseLine ranked Hokkaido highly, as shown in Table 1. BaseLine ranked Kyoto as high, but Method 2 did not. In addition, Method 2 ranked Miyagi to Top in Table 1; Method 1 ranked to 16th. Therefore, the ranks of Miyagi show big differences when obtained using Method 1 and Method 2. The difference in results shows the difference between those approaches. In those rankings, a travel destination liked by many people is ranked highly.

By the characteristics of Method 1 and Method 2, everyone might feel the travel destinations such as Miyagi memorable. Those evaluations might vary among users. Posted blogs about Miyagi include the traditional Japanese festivals and views of rural areas. In addition, others post photographs about the Great East Japan Earthquake. Some areas of Miyagi were damaged by that earthquake. We guess the users felt it was memorable.

Next, we apply our proposed method to the entire world. We present the top seven areas evaluated respectively by Method 1 and Method 2 in Table 2.

Additionally, we present the ranking Best destination 2018[6] by Trip Advisor as the conventional ranking.

Table 2. World Ranking (users > 3)

	Method 1				Method 2				Trip Advisor ranking	
Rank	Country	Area	S_x	Users	Country	Area	R_x	Users	Country	Area
1	Greenland	East Greenland	3.03	4	Svalbard	Spitsbergen	1	7	France	Paris
2	Nepal	Langtang	1.77	4	Ireland	County Offaly	1	4	United Kingdom	London
3	Finland	Aland Islands	1.66	4	Greenland	East Greenland	1	4	Italy	Rome
4	Philippines	Batanes	1.57	6	Finland	Aland Islands	1	4	Indonesia	Bali
5	Svalbard	Spitsbergen	1.50	7	Bahamas	North Eleuthera	1	4	Greece	Crete
6	Isle of Man	Peel	1.49	4	Madagascar	Nosy Be	1	5	Spain	Barcelona
7	Palau	Koror	1.37	6	India	Arunachal Pradesh	1	6	Czech Republic	Prague

In Table 2, the Method 1 and Method 2 rankings differ from Best destination 2018 ranking. We can make a unique ranking using our methods. East Greenland in Greenland, Aland Islands in Finland, and Spitsbergen in Svalbard are ranked highly in Method 1 and Method 2. These areas are in northern Europe. They are not ranked highly in the conventional ranking. Using our methods, we might discover memorable travel destinations irrespective of their current popularity. The results demonstrate the novelty of our proposed methods. Areas which are ranked highly by Method 1 and Method 2 are small cities. East Greenland and Spitsbergen are polar bear habitats with rich nature. In addition, Langtang in Nepal is famous as an extremely beautiful valley. Therefore, memorable travel destinations not only have famous architecture or a large metropolis: rich natural places are memorable.

5   Discussion

We estimate that fewer visitors going to a travel destination strongly affects the evaluation of the place in individual scoring. Therefore, we think that our proposed method ranks famous sightseeing areas (i.e., the possibility of sightseeing spots that many users visit) too low. In Method 1 and Method 2, we calculate the correlation coefficient between the ranking of travel destinations and the number of users. The coefficient between the number of users and ranking in Method 1 is -0.02; that of Method 2 is 0.02. The results show no correlation among those factors. Therefore, the number of users does not affect our scoring method. In addition, the rank might be higher by some factors, but we cannot prove that the areas are the memorable travel destination. However, our proposed method can produce rankings irrespective of popularity. This paper is limited to an explanation of the first step in discovering memorable travel destinations.

---

[6] https://www.tripadvisor.com/TravelersChoice-Destinations.

6   Conclusion

As described herein, we propose a method to discover "memorable" travel destinations irrespective of their current popularity. Our hypothesis is that differences in the number of photographs posted to blogs about travel destinations by respective users affect how memorable the travel destination is. We ranked the travel destinations in Japan and all over the world using our proposed methods. Results show that our two proposed methods can rank travel destinations uniquely and show that those rankings differ from conventional one.

Future work is evaluating ranked travel destinations quantitatively and to avoid dependence on popularity. In this study, our proposed method extracts the memorable travel destinations but does not consider what destinations are memorable. Therefore, our future work shall analyze blog contents.

References

1. Cao, L., Luo, J., Gallagher, A., Jin, X., Han, J., Huang, T.S.: A worldwide tourism recommendation system based on geotaggedweb photos. In: 2010 IEEE International Conference on Acoustics Speech and Signal Processing (ICASSP), pp. 2274–2277. IEEE (2010)
2. Debnath, M., Tripathi, P.K., Elmasri, R.: Preference-aware successive POI recommendation with spatial and temporal influence. In: Spiro, E., Ahn, Y.-Y. (eds.) SocInfo 2016. LNCS, vol. 10046, pp. 347–360. Springer, Cham (2016). https://doi.org/10.1007/978-3-319-47880-7_21
3. Guo, L., Li, Z., Sun, W.: Understanding travel destinations from structured tourism blogs. In: Proceedings of 2015 Wuhan International Conference on e-Business, pp. 144–151 (2015)
4. Ji, R., Xie, X., Yao, H., Ma, W.Y.: Mining city landmarks from blogs by graph modeling. In: Proceedings of the 17th ACM international conference on Multimedia, pp. 105–114. ACM (2009)
5. Okuyama, K., Yanai, K.: A travel planning system based on travel trajectories extracted from a large number of geotagged photos on the web. In: Jin, J.S., Xu, C., Xu, M. (eds.) The Era of Interactive Media, pp. 657–670. Springer, New York (2013). https://doi.org/10.1007/978-1-4614-3501-3_54
6. Ye, M., Yin, P., Lee, W.C., Lee, D.L.: Exploiting geographical influence for collaborative point-of-interest recommendation. In: Proceedings of the 34th International ACM SIGIR Conference on Research and Development in Information Retrieval, pp. 325–334. ACM (2011)
7. Yuan, Q., Cong, G., Ma, Z., Sun, A., Thalmann, N.M.: Time-aware point-of-interest recommendation. In: Proceedings of the 36th International ACM SIGIR Conference on Research and Development in Information Retrieval, pp. 363–372. ACM (2013)
8. Zhang, J.D., Chow, C.Y.: GeoSoCa: exploiting geographical, social and categorical correlations for point-of-interest recommendations. In: Proceedings of the 38th International ACM SIGIR Conference on Research and Development in Information Retrieval, pp. 443–452. ACM (2015)

How Can We Utilize Self-service Technology Better?

Keiichi Ueda[✉][iD] and Setsuya Kurahashi

University of Tsukuba, 3-9-21, Otsuka, Bunkyo, Tokyo, Japan
s1645001@u.tsukuba.ac.jp
http://www.gsbs.tsukuba.ac.jp/en/

Abstract. Self-service technology (SST) has been broadly recognized as a promising cost-saving alternative to a workforce. Interest in SST has been increasing owing to the imminent shortage of workforce in developed countries. In such a context, the successful implementation of SST is regarded more seriously. This study focuses on a self-service kiosk at an airport to discuss how the gaming framework contributes to exploring the successful implementation of SSTs in actual service operation. We review and discuss the results of the cooperative game that equips the autonomously behaving passengers as in the real world. Through gaming, players discuss how the new technology needs to reflect old operational practices, how people embrace and adapt to SST, and how effectively the multiple players can cooperate and coordinate to minimize the waiting time of the multiple departure lobbies as a whole. Players need to manage their staff to operate an interpersonal check-in service and to guide and support passengers using technology-based self-service equipment. They communicate with each other to secure the level of service in the ambivalent ongoing conditions. Using computer simulations, we show that the extracted ideas of queue management effectively function to accomplish tolerable waiting time by utilizing the given productive resources.

Keywords: Self-service technology · Agent-based modeling · Airport Game · Simulation · Service

1 Introduction

1.1 Background

The continuous growth of the service economy and an aging society with fewer births bring a progressive and imminent issue: how to secure the services workforce. In such a context, self-service technology (SST) is a promising alternative for fulfilling future customer service requirements. However, unless SST is recognized and accepted by customers, the implementation of SST is unlikely to be successful, and as a result neither customers nor firms will enjoy the benefits of service investment.

S. Staab et al. (Eds.): SocInfo 2018, LNCS 11186, pp. 299–312, 2018.
https://doi.org/10.1007/978-3-030-01159-8_29

This study focuses on a self-service kiosk at an airport and discusses how the service provider can utilize service resources including SST. The core product of the airline is service, which has the characteristics of simultaneity and inseparability. Service staff and passengers need to work together to achieve a common goal in each process that forms the air travel experience. In particular, the check-in process is a critical starting point of the travel experience.

It is essential for both airlines and passengers to reduce the amount of waiting time. However, this is not easy in a large airport because several areas need to be covered, passengers have different characteristics and different travel conditions, and airlines cannot control which door the passenger will use to enter into the departure lobby. This esoteric issue derives from the consequence that an airline has no control over from what floor the passengers arrive into the check-in area or their choice of check-in option. Local managers need help to explore better service operations and evaluate them quantitatively and qualitatively. However, they do not currently have an examining methodology of the best practice with less operational risk.

1.2   Objective of This Study

In general, it is difficult for a computer simulation to represent an event in which human decision-making is deeply involved. In this research, we attempt to obtain suggestions of the handling strategy by using a framework of gaming that allows the player to judge how to handle variables that are difficult to formulate for the ever-changing situation. This study investigates the way to build up the handling strategy in which coordination and cooperation take place in an airport departure lobby. The gaming framework is examined to find a way to optimize the current resources of an airline. We discuss the method to extract key ideas that effectively control the service level through the cooperative game.

The objective of this research is to obtain some implications about how to deal with the complicated ever-changing situation. To achieve this, two steps are taken to uncover the fundamentals of a smoother passenger handling operation: constructing the gaming framework and conducting computer simulation under several scenarios.

2   Related Work

SST is described as technological interfaces that enable customers to produce a service without a service employee's involvement [14]. The use of SSTs can increase productivity and efficiency, while at the same time contributing to reducing labor costs [8,12,13]. First, an overview of the field of innovation diffusion and services marketing is given to provide the necessary background against which to understand the development of SST studies. Then we review an agent-based SST adoption model, as a tool to elucidate the dynamics of the phenomenon of service choosing. We also briefly review the gaming literature, which describes how to deal with complicated decision-making and how it should be designed.

2.1   Innovation and SST Studies in Service Marketing

We review studies pertaining to the adoption and diffusion of innovation, because embracing SST is an individual decision to adopt a new approach. It is well known that Rogers defined innovation as the introduction of something new: a new idea, method, or device [16]. This is accomplished by using more effective products, processes, services, technologies, or business models that are readily available in markets, governments, and society. Greater relative advantage and the effort of change agent are known to accelerate the diffusion of innovation [16].

The study of SST can be traced back to the study of convenience. Berry et al. examined and discussed convenience from two main perspectives: wait time and its management, and what consumers find convenient [1]. Davis developed a "technology acceptance model" (TAM), which is specifically meant to explain computer usage behavior [5]. The author concluded that perceived usefulness and ease of use create favorable attitudes toward SST. He also empirically examined the ability of TAM to predict and explain user acceptance and rejection of computer-based technology [6]. Bitner et al. focused on the benefits of thoughtfully managed and effectively implemented technology applications. They emphasized ways in which service encounters can be improved through the effective use of technology [2]. Meuter et al. claimed that when SST is better than the alternatives and they appreciated time saving the most, service convenience through SST resulted in consumer satisfaction [14]. SST usage depends on customer readiness for SST [3,12], however, Meuter et al. claimed that their findings show technology anxiety is a superior, more consistent predictor of SST usage than demographic variables [13]. Dabholkar and Bagozzi extended the attitudinal model of technology-based self-service and proposed that the moderating variables such as consumer traits and situational factors affect the attitude toward SST and intention to use SST [4]. Gelderman et al. claimed that technology readiness has no impact on customer decision-making, and specified that perceived crowdedness has a strong and significant impact on customers' decision to use SSTs [8].

2.2   Agent-Based Modeling: SST Adoption Model

Agent-based models (ABMs), also known as social multi-agent systems, represent the phenomena of complex social systems [11]. They enable each heterogeneous agent to behave autonomously and allow interactions to emerge in the experimental space, which is approximated to the real world. Watts and Gilbert introduced an ABM where the simulation results are evaluated by mentioning stylized facts. They are empirical regularities in the search for theoretical, causal explanations, such as statistical features [22].

Ueda and Kurahashi emulated an existing airport departure lobby (Fig. 2). They proposed the decision-making mechanism of SST use [19] into the ABM and expand it by incorporating individual traits [20]. The experiment supports the representation of the actual results in several different conditions. They also tried to uncover the cooperation between passenger and the service provider and the coordination among different service options in the process of service operation. The model is validated at different hierarchical levels (Table 3) [20, 21].

2.3 Gaming and Simulation

Representing the complicated phenomena deeply involved in people's decisions is difficult in computer simulation. Gaming is one of the ways to handle situations that change continuously, leaving judgment to participate for players to cover complicated events [18]. In addition, role-playing games are an appropriate mode of communication to convey the complexity as it allows multiple stakeholders to examine the complex systems in which they are involved [7].

Reiber introduced that the use of games and simulations is often embraced in educational settings, such as corporate and military training environments [15] because the gaming is regarded as a useful tool to learn how to deal with complicated real-world issues. All games have a core mechanic: an action or set of actions that players will repeat over and over as they move through the designed system of the game. In other words, the core mechanic is designing the expected player's experience in gaming [17]. Gaming provides opportunities to learn about responses in the real world. Greenblat proposed the design process of a game that is similar to how to construct an ABM [9].

3 Constructing the "Departure Lobby Management Game"

3.1 The Core Mechanic of the Game

We expand the agent-based SST adoption model into the business game and explain how it is employed in gaming. This game has an ambivalent structure so that an increase in the waiting time of one area leads to deterioration of the service level of the other area. We expect the game participants to learn following two things (Fig. 4): the structure of the game to find key points to make maximum use of service resources; and how to deal with real responses and endings that you see in the workplace through subjective experience and how to deal with it.

3.2 Game Settings

Game Players and Variables. The game takes place in an airport, which has two separately managed departure lobbies (Fig. 1). Each lobby has same the facilities and equipment and a responsible manager. The manager of lobby-A has nine staff the manager of lobby-B has six staff to operate service facilities. They locate their staff at check-in positions (CC), baggage dropping position (BD), and also in the lobby (CSR) to guide and advise passengers to use a self-service kiosk. Staff who are not located on the departure floor can be utilized by either manager. However, the manager of lobby-A can retrieve their staff to activate the service facility of lobby-A at any time. The arriving passenger volume and timing is different in each lobby. The ratio of passengers with checked baggage is defined differently without letting players know: lobby-A 30% and lobby-B 70%.

Passenger Behavior Rule. An arriving passenger who has heterogeneous state toward SST autonomously chooses the service option by perceiving the surrounding situation. If CSR decrease passenger's hesitation status, the passenger may head for the SST. Each passenger starts counting waiting time as soon as they join the line in front of the service facility. When the waiting time exceeds a certain threshold, the passenger's internal state changes to "angry" and the color of the passenger becomes red. After queuing for check-in, red passengers are redirected to the other lobby. This is replicating the situation where passengers in a long queue will miss the flight and need re-booking. Consequently, "angry" passengers who revisit the departure lobby from the other area take more time to process re-booking and check-in, and this causes the waiting time to increase for other passengers.

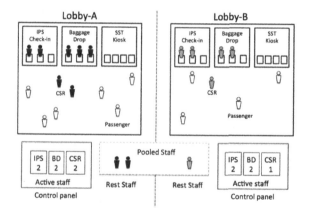

Fig. 1. "Departure lobby management game" display and control panel

4 The Result of Experiments

4.1 Gaming Results

The cooperative gaming experiment was conducted after the participants were familiarized with controlling the parameters and the gaming concept. The actual different passenger arrival times are applied in each departure lobby. Each lobby has a totally different situation. Therefore, players have to watch and predict passenger arrival carefully and then decide their action. The games were conducted three times to see how they develop their strategy and teamwork (Table 1). In Fig. 5, the horizontal axis shows time (in ticks) and the vertical axis shows

Table 1. Gaming experiment: the number of "angry" passengers

Experiment	"Angry"	BDb = 2 duration (ticks)	"Angry" span (ticks)
game-1	25	210	1463
game-2	10	40	962
game-3	20	170	1427

passenger attendance data in each lobby and the total number of "angry" passengers in both departure lobbies.

We can observe that the timing of the appearance of "angry" passengers and quantity varies. Figure 5(a) shows that the number of "angry" passengers increases at 1396 (ticks) and Fig. 7(a) indicates that Baggage Drop of lobby-B (BDb) decreases from 3 to 2 at 1174 (ticks) to 1383 (ticks) in game-1. Likewise, Fig. 5(c) shows that the number of "angry" passenger starts increasing at 1381 and Fig. 7(c) indicates that BDb decreases to 2 at 1139 to 1308 in game-3. However, in game-2, Fig. 5(b) shows that the number of "angry" passenger increases to 1465 then quickly stops increasing. This is most likely because BDb is quickly turned 3 (at 1250) after BDb decreases to 2 positions at 1211 as indicated in Fig. 7(b).

Likewise in game-2 and game-3, Fig. 7(b) and (c) describe that before the first "angry" passenger appears at the timing of 1126 (ticks) and 682 (ticks), three lobby service agents were located in lobby-B (CSRb) at 1083 (ticks) and 642 (ticks). As the role of CSR is to guide passengers to the SST, more passengers were encouraged to use SST in lobby-B and it consequently increased passengers queueing at BD because 70% of passenger held baggage after operating SST.

Findings of the Gaming Experiment. By reviewing the facts, there are two findings. Players could have achieved a better result by paying more attention to the quantity of BD. If we can predict increasing passenger queues, we should carefully examine opening the third BD. This gaming result also implicates that CSR plays an important role as a change agent. We have to note that SST users with baggage have to wait longer in total before leaving the departure lobby because they need to join the queue at BD after visiting SST. As passengers in lobby-B have a higher baggage holding rate, more SST users with baggage cause an increase in waiting time, which leads to more "angry" passengers in total. Therefore, fewer CSRs in lobby-B contributes to reducing the number of "angry" passengers.

4.2 Computer Simulation Results

The computer simulations were conducted by using the same platform as the gaming. We prepared 15 scenarios to clarify whether the findings of gaming experiments are valid (Figs. 8 and 9). The result demonstrates that the third BD works effectively to reduce the number of "angry" passengers. In addition, it displayed that more CSRs and the number of "angry" passenger has a positive correlation under 3 CCs and they have a nonlinear relationship under 2 CCs (Table 2).

Table 2. The number of "angry" passengers

Experiment	"Angry" passengers	Experiment	"Angry" passengers
CC22BD22CSR00	46.3	CC22BD33CSR00	12.1
CC22BD22CSR11	43.5	CC22BD33CSR11	9.6

These results support what players learned through gaming experiments instead of scenarios analysis by computer simulation. Thus, gaming can productively provide clues about dealing with complicated context such as responding to a situational change as time passes.

4.3 Discussion and Summary of Gaming

The Operational Strategy. The demonstrated facts through the gaming experiments and computer simulations lead us to the following conclusion. It is critical to observe arriving passengers to predict the amount of waiting time, so that players can determine whether to open the third BD. This gaming result also implies that CSR plays an important role for in queue management. Thus, local managers need to carefully watch the arrival situation of the passengers so as not to miss the timing of activating service resources according to the degree of congestion. More importantly, local managers should know the system and how they can reduce the waiting time of passengers. In that way, the players can communicate so that CSR can be arranged when needed, according to the degree of congestion. As the service resource is limited, cooperating and coordinating among stakeholders is the key to success.

In addition, the total waiting time of each passenger and waiting time as a whole could have been reduced dramatically if CSRs could intentionally invite only non-baggage passengers to use SST.

Importance of Communication. The previously mentioned findings are the outcome of communication during the gaming operation and the discussion in the debriefing of the game. The interactive questions and answers among the participants speed up the process of understanding the system structure and interactions. The discussion also unveils the background of the decision-making process of participants. These opportunities contribute to learning the "subjective experience" of other stakeholders.

5 Conclusion

Through this research, we have examined how to deal with an imminent issue, the shortage of services workforce, and how to utilize SST not only from the consumer's point of view but also from the service provider's point of view.

5.1 Summary of This Work

Owing to the nature of the service, it is essential to discuss and verify the service quality level by co-working with the service recipient. In reality, it is difficult to quantify the service quality and the opportunity to learn about this issue through actual operations is practically limited. This difficulty derives from the fact that this issue needs to deal with an ever-changing situation.

We reviewed the related interdisciplinary work about SST studies, which verify the concept model with a statistical method using quantitative data and visualized facts. Based on the agent-based SST adoption model, which reproduces the real-world context, we developed the gaming framework to discuss key factors to improve service by utilizing service resources including SST. Through practicing the gaming, players explore and exploit different strategies and gain an in-depth understanding about what to do through participating in discussions.

There are three findings from the gaming that utilizes the ABM platform. First, it is possible to deal with complicated issues related to human decision-making by gaming without exploring the enormous amount of data. The gaming participants can develop strategy. We can verify whether the strategy is effective through computer simulations using the same platform. Second, a strategy can be formulated that contributes to improving services without trying innumerable combinations according to time series or various situations. Finally, there also are findings from the communication through gaming experiments. The participants obtain a deeper understanding of practical issues and how to deal with them through discussions. The debriefing is useful and effective for formulating future strategies to enhance services. It helps players uncover the system structure and interaction with the game. It promotes mutual understanding and allows a consensus to be formed regarding a new handling policy.

5.2 For Future Study

Limitation. In this study, we dealt with the issues in the way of "Time and Space Specified" [10]. The satisfaction level of the service recipient, which is the ultimate and essential objective of the quality of service provision, is not covered by this research. The parameter values of the platform model used in this experiment are exaggerated rather than mapping the real world to emphasize the core mechanic of the game. There is much room to improve the current platform.

For Future Study. To provide more realistic learning opportunities, we would need further progress to incorporate factors and scales that explain the status of customer satisfaction better. It would be better to modify the model in terms of the timing of passenger agents getting "angry" and adding alternative CSR guiding policies. For the next step, we expect to accumulate more quantitative and qualitative data. The analytical framework can be developed by incorporating subjective experience and obtaining data through more gaming experiments.

This may be used to demonstrate the analytical development life cycle (Fig. 10) to explore the empirical solution in a complex world.

A   Airport Departure Lobby

The departure lobby has three check-in options: interpersonal check-in service (CC), baggage drop (BD), and self-service kiosk (SST). The default check-in option is the CC. Passengers who use the SST can check in their baggage at the BD. Passengers queuing in front of CC can also approach BD when there is no one waiting in front of them.

Fig. 2. Experimental space of the airport departure lobby

B   Decision Mechanism of SST Adoption

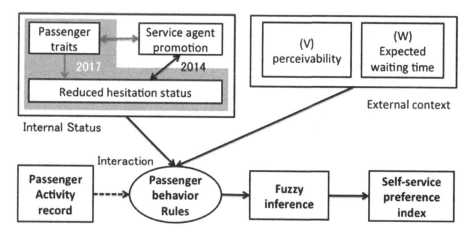

Fig. 3. Decision-making mechanism of SST adoption (Ueda et al. 2014, 2017)

C   Validation Results of the Agent-Based SST Adoption Model

Table 3. Validation results of the agent-based SST adoption model

Hierarchical level	Root Mean Square Error (actual vs simulation)
Group behavior: SST usage rate	0.039
Individual decision: prediction accuracy	0.012

D   The Core Mechanic of the "Departure Lobby Management Game"

The manager of lobby-A (player 1) has nine staff and the manager of lobby-B (player 2) has six staff to operate service facilities. The mandatory operating conditions (minimum number of operations) and maximum operating number of each service resource are set in advance in the game. Two CCs must be open, and the third position may be in operation if needed. Likewise, two BDs must always be active and the third position is optional. Resting staff are shared between the two players. Staff who are not located in the departure floor can be utilized by either manager.

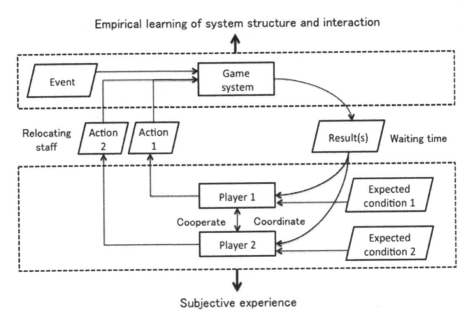

Fig. 4. The core mechanic of the "departure lobby management game"

E Gaming Experiment Results

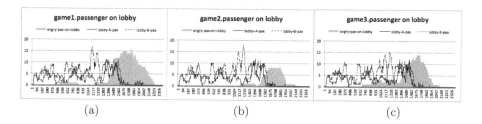

Fig. 5. Passenger appearance

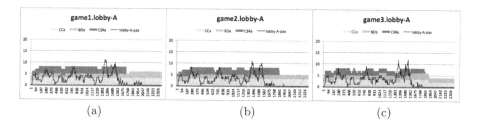

Fig. 6. Lobby-A operation process

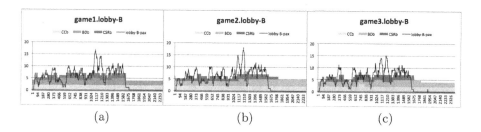

Fig. 7. Lobby-B operation process

F Computer Simulation Results

CC22BD33CSR21 denotes 2 CCs and 3 BDs are active in both lobby-A and lobby-B and there are 2 CSRs in lobby-A and 1 CSR in lobby-B.

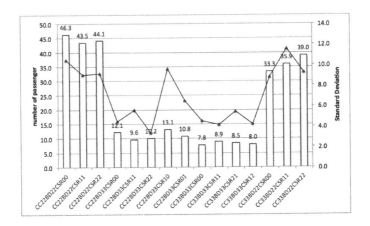

Fig. 8. Computer simulation results

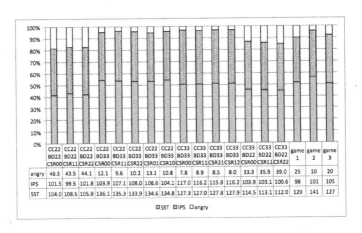

Fig. 9. Comparison of computer simulation and gaming results

G   The Analytical Development Life Cycle

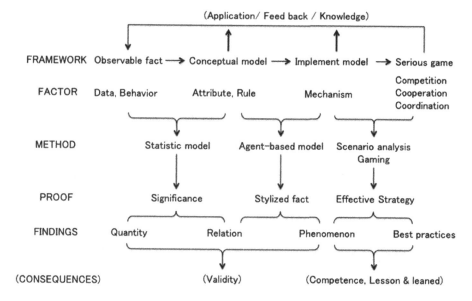

Fig. 10. The analytical development life cycle

References

1. Berry, L.L., Seiders, K., Grewal, D.: Understanding service convenience. J. Mark. **66**(3), 1–17 (2002). https://doi.org/10.1509/jmkg.66.3.1.18505
2. Bitner, M.J., Brown, S.W., Meuter, M.L.: Technology infusion in service encounters. J. Acad. Mark. Sci. **28**(1), 138–149 (2000). https://doi.org/10.1177/0092070300281013
3. Bitner, M.J., Ostrom, A.L., Meuter, M.L.: Implementing successful self-service technologies. Acad. Manag. Executive **16**(4), 96–108 (2002)
4. Dabholkar, P.A., Bagozzi, R.P.: An attitudinal model of technology-based self-service: moderating effects of consumer traits and situational factors. J. Acad. Mark. Sci. **30**(3), 184–201 (2002)
5. Davis, F.D.: A technology acceptance model for empirically testing new end-user information systems: theory and results. Ph.D. thesis, Massachusetts Institute of Technology (1986)
6. Davis, F.D.: Perceived usefulness, perceived ease of use, and user acceptance of information technology. MIS Q., 319–340 (1989). https://doi.org/10.2307/249008
7. Duke, R.D.: Gaming: The Future's Language. Wiley, Boston (1974)
8. Gelderman, C.J., Paul, W.T., Van Diemen, R.: Choosing self-service technologies or interpersonal services? The impact of situational factors and technology-related attitudes. J. Retail. Consum. Serv. **18**(5), 414–421 (2011)
9. Greenblat, C.S.: Designing Games and Simulations: An Illustrated Handbook. Sage Publications, Inc., Newbury Park (1988)

10. Ito, G., Yamakage, S.: From KISS to TASS modeling: a preliminary analysis of the segregation model incorporated with spatial data on Chicago. Jpn. J. Polit. Sci. **16**(4), 553–573 (2015)
11. Kurahashi, S.: State-of-the-art of social system research 4 model estimation and inverse simulation. J. Soc. Instrum. Control Eng. **52**(7), 588–594 (2013). (in Japanese)
12. Liljander, V., Gillberg, F., Gummerus, J., Van Riel, A.: Technology readiness and the evaluation and adoption of self-service technologies. J. Retail. Consum. Serv. **13**(3), 177–191 (2006). https://doi.org/10.1016/j.jretconser.2005.08.004
13. Meuter, M.L., Ostrom, A.L., Bitner, M.J., Roundtree, R.: The influence of technology anxiety on consumer use and experiences with self-service technologies. J. Bus. Res. **56**(11), 899–906 (2003). https://doi.org/10.1016/S0148-2963(01)00276-4
14. Meuter, M.L., Ostrom, A.L., Roundtree, R.I., Bitner, M.J.: Self-service technologies: understanding customer satisfaction with technology-based service encounters. J. Mark. **64**(3), 50–64 (2000). https://doi.org/10.1509/jmkg.64.3.50.18024
15. Rieber, L.P.: Seriously considering play: designing interactive learning environments based on the blending of microworlds, simulations, and games. Educ. Technol. Res. Dev. **44**(2), 43–58 (1996)
16. Rogers, E.M.: Diffusion of Innovations. Free Press, New York (1983)
17. Salen, K., Zimmerman, E.: Rules of Play: Game Design Fundamentals. MIT Press, Cambridge (2004)
18. Sunaguchi, H., Shirai, H., Sato, R.: Evaluation of the business strategy design method using a combination of gaming and computer simulation. Stud. Simul. Gaming **26**(1), 1–8 (2016). (in Japanese)
19. Ueda, K., Kurahashi, S.: How passenger decides a check-in option in an airport. In: Social Simulation Conference (2014)
20. Ueda, K., Kurahashi, S.: The passenger decision making mechanism of self-service kiosk at the airport. In: Kurahashi, S., Ohta, Y., Arai, S., Satoh, K., Bekki, D. (eds.) JSAI-isAI 2016. LNCS (LNAI), vol. 10247, pp. 159–175. Springer, Cham (2017). https://doi.org/10.1007/978-3-319-61572-1_11
21. Ueda, K., Kurahashi, S.: Agent-based self-service technology adoption model for air-travelers: exploring best operational practices. Front. Phys. **6**, 5 (2018)
22. Watts, C., Gilbert, N.: Simulating Innovation: Computer-Based Tools for Rethinking Innovation. Edward Elgar Publishing, Cheltenham (2014)

New/s/leak 2.0 – Multilingual Information Extraction and Visualization for Investigative Journalism

Gregor Wiedemann, Seid Muhie Yimam[(⊠)], and Chris Biemann

Language Technology Group, Department of Informatics,
MIN Faculty, Universität Hamburg, Hamburg, Germany
{gwiedemann,yimam,biemann}@informatik.uni-hamburg.de

Abstract. Investigative journalism in recent years is confronted with two major challenges: (1) vast amounts of unstructured data originating from large text collections such as leaks or answers to Freedom of Information requests, and (2) multi-lingual data due to intensified global cooperation and communication in politics, business and civil society. Faced with these challenges, journalists are increasingly cooperating in international networks. To support such collaborations, we present the new version of *new/s/leak* 2.0, our open-source software for content-based searching of leaks. It includes three novel main features: (1) automatic language detection and language-dependent information extraction for 40 languages, (2) entity and keyword visualization for efficient exploration, and (3) decentral deployment for analysis of confidential data from various formats. We illustrate the new analysis capabilities with an exemplary case study.

Keywords: Information extraction · Investigative journalism
Data journalism · Named entity recognition · Keyterm extraction

1 Investigative Journalism in the Digital Age

In the era of digitization, journalists are confronted with major changes drastically challenging the ways how news are produced for a mass audience. Not only that digital publishing and direct audience feedback through online media influences what is reported on, how and by whom. But also digital data itself becomes a source and subject of newsworthy stories – a development described by the term "data journalism". According to [12], 51% of all news organizations in 2017 already employed dedicated data journalists and most of them reported a growing demand. The systematic analysis of digital social trace data blurs the line between journalism and (computational) social science. However, social scientists and journalists differ distinctively in their goals. Confronted with a huge haystack of digital data related to some social or political phenomenon, social scientists usually are interested in quantitatively or qualitatively characterizing

S. Staab et al. (Eds.): SocInfo 2018, LNCS 11186, pp. 313–322, 2018.
https://doi.org/10.1007/978-3-030-01159-8_30

this haystack while journalists actually look for the needle in it to tell a newsworthy story. This 'needle in the haystack' problem becomes especially vital for investigative stories confronted with large and heterogeneous datasets.

Most of the information in such datasets is contained in written unstructured text form, for instance in scanned documents, letter correspondences, emails or protocols. Sources of such datasets typically range from (1) official disclosures of administrative and business documents, (2) court-ordered revelation of internal communication, (3) answers to requests based on Freedom of Information (FoI) acts, and (4) unofficial leaks of confidential information. In many cases, a public revelation of such confidential information benefits a democratic society since it contributes to reveal corruption and abuse of power, thus strengthening transparency of decisions in politics and the economy.

To support this role of investigative journalism, we introduce the second, substantially re-engineered and improved version of our software tool *new/s/leak* ("network of searchable leaks") [16]. It is developed by experts from natural language processing and visualization in computer science in cooperation with journalists from "Der Spiegel", a large German news organization.[1] *New/s/leak* 2.0 serves three central requirements that have not been addressed sufficiently by previously existing solutions for investigative and forensic text analysis:

1. Since journalists are primarily interested in stories around persons, organizations and locations, we adopt a visual exploration approach centered around named entities and keywords.
2. Many tools only work for English documents or a small number of other 'big languages'. To foster international collaboration, our tool allows for simultaneous analysis of documents from a set of currently 40 languages.
3. The work with confidential data such as from unofficial leaks requires a decentralized analysis environment, which can be used potentially disconnected from the internet. We distribute *new/s/leak* as a free, open-source server infrastructure via Docker containers, which can be easily deployed by both news organizations and single journalists.

In the following sections, we introduce related work and discuss technical aspects of *new/s/leak*. We also illustrate its analysis capabilities in a brief case study.

2   Related Work

A number of commercial and open-source software products have been developed to support data journalists in their work with large datasets. Many tools such as OpenRefine, Datawrapper, or Tabula concentrate on structured data only. For unstructured text data, there are only few options. Since licenses for commercial tools often are prohibitively expensive especially for smaller news agencies or individuals, we focus on open-source products in the following comparison.

---

[1] https://www.spiegel.de.

The most reputated application is *DocumentCloud*[2], an open platform designed for journalists to annotate and search in (scanned) text documents. It is supported by popular media partners such as the New York Times, and PBS. Besides fulltext search it provides automatic named entity recognition (NER) based on OpenCalais [15] in English, Spanish and German.

Overview [3] is a more advanced open-source application developed by computer scientists in collaboration with journalists to support investigative journalism. The application supports import of PDF, MS Office and HTML documents, document clustering based on topic similarity, a simplistic location entity detection, full-text search, and document tagging. Since this tool is already mature and has successfully been used in a number of published news stories, we adapted some of its most useful features such as document tagging and a keyword-in-context (KWIC) view for search hits. Furthermore, in *new/s/leak* we concentrate on intuitive and visually pleasing approaches to display extracted contents for a fast exploration of collections.

The *Jigsaw visual analytics* [6,7,13] system is a third tool that supports investigative analysis of textual documents. Jigsaw focuses on the extraction of entities (using multiple NER tools for English) and their correlation with metadata. It provides visualization of entities as lists and document contents as a (tree-structured) word graph. *New/s/leak* instead visualizes coherence of such information as network graphs.

Recent investigations on leaked data from off-shore money laundering companies, usually referred to as "Panama Papers" [10] and "Paradise Papers" [9] lead to the development of two software packages, which was driven by exactly those uses cases: *Aleph*[3] and *DataShare*[4]. Both packages are designed to support typical 'follow-the-money' investigations to reveal corruption. Hence, they put emphasis on integrating information extraction from text such as named entities with structured databases containing additional information about entities.

New/s/leak differs from the aforementioned software products mainly with respect to its focus on visual exploration of unknown and unstructured datasets. The idea of visualizing entity networks to explore large text collections for investigative journalism was already realized in the first version of our tool [16]. But, the software had several limitations such as (1) it only allowed processing of monolingual datasets in either English or German, (2) it only supported a predefined number of entity and meta-data types, and (3) it did not support entity extraction with user-defined dictionaries and rule patterns. Moreover, it lacked a user-friendly data import process leaving the burden of data wrangling of heterogeneous document collections to the journalist.

---

[2] https://www.documentcloud.org.
[3] https://github.com/alephdata/aleph.
[4] https://github.com/ICIJ/datashare.

3   Architecture

Figure 1 shows the architecture of *new/s/leak*. In order to allow users to analyze a wide range of document types, our system includes a document processing component, which extracts text and metadata from a variety of document types into a unified index representation.

On the extracted texts, a number of NLP processing tasks are performed in a UIMA pipeline [4]: automatic identification of the document language, segmentation of documents into appropriate paragraph, sentence and token units, and extraction of named entities, keywords and metadata. Fulltexts and extracted data are stored in an ElasticSearch index[5]. Access and real-time analysis of the data is provided by RESTful web services based on the Scala Play framework. We offer interactive information visualization technologies based on the D3 visualization library [2] composed into an AngularJS browser application.

In order to enable a seamless deployment of the tool for journalists with limited technical knowledge, we integrated all of the required components of the architecture into a Docker[6] setup. Via "docker-compose", a software to orchestrate Docker containers for complex architectures, end-users can download and run locally a preconfigured version of *new/s/leak* with only a few commands. Relying on Docker also ensures, that it runs on any Docker-compatible operating system including Linux, macOS, and Windows. Being able to process data locally and even without any internet connection is a vital prerequisite for journalists, especially if they work with sensitive leaks or FoI data. All necessary source code and installation instructions can be found on our Github page.[7]

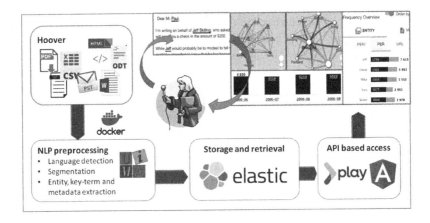

Fig. 1. "Dockerized" architecture of *new/s/leak* 2.0

---

[5]   https://www.elastic.co.

[6]   https://www.docker.com.

[7]   https://uhh-lt.github.io/newsleak.

4   Data Wrangling

Extracting text and metadata from various formats into a format readable by a specific analysis tool can be a tedious task. In an investigative journalism scenario it can even be a deal breaker since time is an especially valuable resource and file format conversion might not be a task journalists are well trained in. To offer easy access to as many file formats as possible in *new/s/leak*, we opted for a close integration with *Hoover*,[8] a set of open-source tools for text extraction and search in large text collections. Hoover is developed by the European Investigative Collaborations (EIC) network[9] with a special focus on large data leaks and heterogeneous data sets. It can extract data from various text file formats (txt, html, docx, pdf) but also extracts from archives (zip, tar, etc.) and email inbox formats (pst, mbox, eml). The text is extracted along with metadata from files (e.g. file name, creation date, file hash) and header information (e.g. subject, sender, receiver in case of emails). Extracted data is stored in an ElasticSearch index. Then, *new/s/leak* connects directly to Hoover's index to read full texts and metadata for its own information extraction pipeline.

5   Multilingual Information Extraction

The core functionality of *new/s/leak* to support investigative journalists is the automatic extraction of various kinds of entities from text to facilitate the exploration and the sense-making process from large collections. Since a lot of steps in this process involve language dependent resources, we put emphasis on supporting as many languages as possible.

Preprocessing: Information extraction is implemented as a configurable UIMA pipeline [4]. Text documents and metadata from a Hoover collection (see Sect. 4) are read in parallelized manner and put through a chain of automatic annotators. In the final step of the chain, results from annotation processes are indexed in an ElasticSearch index for later retrieval and visualization. First, we identify the language of each document. Second, we separate sentences and tokens in each text. To guarantee compatibility with various Unicode scripts in different languages, we rely on the ICU4J library [8], which provides sentence and word boundary detection.

Dictionary and Pattern Matching: In many cases, journalists follow some hypothesis to test for their investigative work. Such a proceeding can involve looking for mentions of already known terms or specific entities in the data. This can be realized by lists of dictionaries provided to the initial information extraction process. *New/s/leak* annotates every mention of a dictionary term with its respective list type. Dictionaries can be defined in a language-specific fashion, but also applied across all languages in the corpus. Extracted dictionary entities are visualized later on along with extracted named entities. In addition

---

[8]   https://hoover.github.io.
[9]   https://eic.network.

to self-defined dictionaries, we annotate email addresses, telephone numbers, and URLs with regular expression patterns. This is useful, especially for email leaks, to reveal communication networks of persons.

Temporal Expressions: Tracking documents across time of their creation can provide valuable information during investigative research. Unfortunately, many document sets (e.g. collections of scanned pages) do not come with a specific document creation date as structured metadata. To offer a temporal selection of contents to the user, we extract mentions of temporal expressions in documents. This is done by integrating the Heideltime temporal tagger [14] in our UIMA workflow. Heideltime provides automatically learned rules for temporal tagging in more than 200 languages. Extracted timestamps can be used to select and filter documents.

Named Entity Recognition: We automatically extract person, organization and location names from all documents to allow for an entity-centric exploration of the data collection. Named entity recognition is done using the *polyglot-NER* library [1]. Polyglot-NER contains sequence classification for named entities based on weakly annotated training data automatically composed from Wikipedia[10] and Freebase[11]. Relying on the automatic composition of training data allows polyglot-NER to provide pre-trained models for 40 languages (see Appendix).

Keyterm Extraction: To further summarize document contents in addition to named entities, we automatically extract keyterms and phrases from documents. For this, we have implemented our own keyterm extraction library. The approach is based on statistical comparison of document contents with generic reference data. Reference data for each language is retrieved from the Leipzig Corpora Collection [5], which provides large representative corpora for language statistics. We included resources for the 40 languages also covered by the NER library. We employ log-likelihood significance as described in [11] to measure the overuse of terms (i.e. keyterms) in our target documents compared to the generic reference data. Ongoing sequences of keyterms in target documents are concatenated to key phrases if they occur regularly in that exact same order. Regularity is determined with the Dice statistic, which allows reliably to extract multiword units such as "stock market" or "machine learning" in the documents. Since the keyterm extraction method may also extract named entities there can be a substantial overlap between the two types. To allow for a separate display of entities and keywords in a later step, we ignore keyterms that already have been identified as named entities. The remaining top keyterms are used to provide a brief summary of each document for the user.

Entity- and Keyword-Centric Visualization and Filtering: Access to unstructured text collections via named entities and keyterms is essential for journalistic investigations. To support this, we included two types of graph visualization, as it is shown in Fig. 2. The first graph, called entity network, displays

---

[10] https://wikipedia.org.
[11] https://developers.google.com/freebase.

entities in a current document selection as nodes and their joint occurrence as edges between nodes. Different node colors represent different types such as person, organization or location names. Furthermore, mentions of entities that are annotated based on dictionary lists or annotated by a given regular expression are included in the entity network graph. The second graph, called keyword network, is build based on the set of keywords representing the current document selection.

Besides to fulltext search, visualizations are the core concept to navigate in an unknown dataset. Nodes in networks as well as entities, metadata or document date ranges displayed as frequency bar charts in the user interface (see Appendix) can be added as filter to constrain the current set of documents. By this, journalists can easily drill down into interesting aspects of the dataset or zoom out again by removing filter conditions. From current sub-selections, user can easily switch to the fulltext view of a document, which also highlights extracted entities and allows for tagging of interesting parts.

6   Exemplary Case Study: Parliamentary Investigations

In the following, we present an exemplary case studies to illustrate the analysis capabilities of our tool. The scenario is centered around the parliamentary investigations of the "Nationalsozialistischer Untergrund" (NSU) case in Germany. Between 1998 and 2011, a terror network of neo-Nazis was responsible for murders of nine migrants and one policewoman. Although many informants of the police and the domestic intelligence service (Verfassungsschutz) were part of the larger network, the authorities officially did neither take notice of the group nor the racist motives behind the murder cases. Since 2012, this failure of domestic intelligence led to a number of parliamentary investigations. We collected 7 final reports from the Bundestag and federal parliaments investigating details of the NSU case. Altogether the reports comprise roughly 12,000 pages.

In *new/s/leak*, long documents such as the reports can be split into more manageable units of certain length such as paragraphs or pages. Smaller units ensure that co-occurrence of extracted entities and keywords actually represents semantic coherence. By splitting into sections of an average page size as a minimum, we receive 12,021 analysis units. For our investigation scenario, we want to follow a certain hypothesis in the data. Since the NSU core group acted against a background of national socialist ideology, we try to answer the following question: To which extent did members of the neo-Nazi network associate themselves with protagonists of former Nazi Germany?

To answer this question, we feed a list of prominent NSDAP party members collected from Wikipedia as additional dictionary into the information extraction process. The resulting entity network reveals mentioning of 17 former Nazis in the reports with Rudolf Heß as the most frequent one. He is celebrated as a martyr in the German neo-Nazi scene. In the third position, the list reveals Adolf Höh, a much less prominent NSDAP party member. Filtering down the collection to documents containing reference to this person reveals the context of

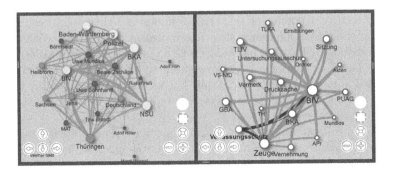

Fig. 2. The entity and keyword graphs based on the parliamentary reports (see Sect. 6). Networks are visualized interactively based on the current document selection, which can be filtered by fulltext search, entities or metadata.

the NSU murder case in Dortmund 2006. At that time an openly acting neo-Nazi group existed in Dortmund, which named itself after the former SA-member Höh who got killed by communists in 1930. The network also reveals connections to another SA-member, Walter Spangenberg, who got killed in Cologne during the 1930s as well. The fact that places of the two killings, Dortmund and Cologne, are near places of two later NSU attacks led to a specific theory about the patterns of the NSU murders in the parliamentary investigation. As the keyterm network reveals, the cases are discussed with reference to the term "Blutzeugentheorie" ('lit. trans: theory of blood witnesses') in the reports. Our combination of an external name list with the automatic extraction of location entities and keyterms quickly led us to this striking detail of the entire case.

7   Discussion

In this article, we introduced version 2.0 of *new/s/leak*, a software to support investigative journalism. It aims to support journalists throughout the entire process of analyzing large, unstructured and heterogeneous document collections: data cleaning and formatting, metadata extraction, information extraction, interactive filtering, close reading, an tagging interesting findings. We reported on technical aspects of the software based on the central idea to approach an unknown collection via extraction and display of entity and keyterm networks. As a unique feature, our tool allows a simultaneous analysis of multilingual collections for up to 40 languages. We further demonstrated in an exemplary use case that the software is able to support investigative journalists in the two major ways of proceeding research (cp. [3]): 1. exploration and story finding in an unknown collection, and 2. testing hypothesis based on previous information. Cases such as "Paradise Papers", "Dieselgate" or "Football leaks" made it especially clear that a decentralized collaboration tool for analysis across different languages is needed for effective journalistic investigation. We are convinced that our software will contribute to this goal in the work of journalists at the "Der Spiegel" news organization and, since it is released as open-source, also for other news organizations and individual journalists.

Acknowledgement. The work was funded by Volkswagen Foundation under Grant Nr. 90 847.

Appendix

New/s/leak UI Components: UI components are designed to help journalists discovering interesting stories more easily. Figure 3 presents different UI components that facilitate the close reading. The numbers in Fig. 3 mark the different types of visual components supported in our tool. (1) shows the full-text searching component, (2) presents the list of documents that are retrieved based on the current set of filters. In (3), the user can read the actual document content, but also annotate new entities ((4)), which were not detected by the NER, merging different textual references to the same entities, and remove/blacklist wrongly detected entities. The possibility to tag individual documents can be used to organize the collection with respect to any user-defined category system. (5) shows lists of keywords summarizing the document. (6), (7), and (8) displays temporal evolution, metadata and entity charts to help the reader to further filter documents. Lastly, (9) shows a history of search filters applied to the document collection so far. Not shown here: graph visualization of current document set, as depicted in Fig. 2.

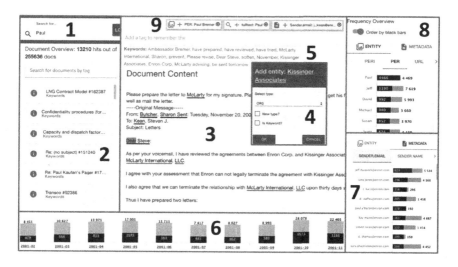

Fig. 3. Different UI components of the *new/s/leak* 2.0 system.

Supported Languages: Arabic, Bulgarian, Catalan, Chinese, Croatian, Czech, Danish, Dutch, English, Estonian, Finnish, French, German, Greek, Hebrew,

Hindi, Hungarian, Indonesian, Italian, Japanese, Korean, Latvian, Lithuanian, Malay, Norwegian, Persian, Polish, Portuguese, Romanian, Russian, Serbian, Slovak, Slovene, Spanish, Swedish, Tagalog, Thai, Turkish, Ukrainian, Vietnamese.

References

1. Al-Rfou, R., Kulkarni, V., Perozzi, B., Skiena, S.: Polyglot-NER: massive multilingual named entity recognition. In: Proceedings of the 2015 SIAM International Conference on Data Mining, Vancouver, British Columbia, Canada, 30 April – 2 May 2015 (2015)
2. Bostock, M., Ogievetsky, V., Heer, J.: D3 data-driven documents. IEEE Trans. Vis. Comput. Graph. (Proc. InfoVis) **17**(12), 2301–2309 (2011)
3. Brehmer, M., Ingram, S., Stray, J., Munzner, T.: Overview: the design, adoption, and analysis of a visual document mining tool for investigative journalists. IEEE Trans. Vis. Comput. Graph. **20**(12), 2271–2280 (2014)
4. Ferrucci, D., Lally, A.: UIMA: an architectural approach to unstructured information processing in the corporate research environment. Nat. Lang. Eng. **10**(3–4), 327–348 (2004)
5. Goldhahn, D., Eckart, T., Quasthoff, U.: Building large monolingual dictionaries at the Leipzig Corpora Collection: from 100 to 200 languages. In: Proceedings of the 8th International Conference on Language Resources and Evaluation, pp. 759–765 (2012)
6. Görg, C., Liu, Z., Kihm, J., Choo, J., Park, H., Stasko, J.: Combining computational analyses and interactive visualization for document exploration and sensemaking in jigsaw. IEEE Trans. Vis. Comput. Graph. **19**(10), 1646–1663 (2013)
7. Görg, C., Liu, Z., Stasko, J.: Reflections on the evolution of the jigsaw visual analytics system. Inf. Vis. **13**(4), 336–345 (2014)
8. ICU4J: ICU4J 61.1 API specification (2018). http://icu-project.org/apiref/icu4j
9. Obermayer, B.: Das sind die paradise papers: Ein neues Leak erschüttert Konzerne, Politiker und die Welt der Superreichen. Süddeutsche Zeitung (05112017). https://projekte.sueddeutsche.de/paradisepapers/politik/das-ist-das-leak-e229478/
10. O'Donovan, J., Wagner, H.F., Zeume, S.: The value of offshore secrets evidence from the panama papers. SSRN Electron. J. (2016). https://doi.org/10.2139/ssrn.2771095
11. Rayson, P., Berridge, D., Francis, B.: Extending the cochran rule for the comparison of word frequencies between corpora. In: Proceedings of the 7th International Conference on Statistical analysis of textual data, pp. 926–936 (2004)
12. Schwabish, S.R.J., Bowers, D.: Data Journalisim in 2017. Google News Lab (2017)
13. Stasko, J., Görg, C., Liu, Z.: Jigsaw: supporting investigative analysis through interactive visualization. Inf. Vis. **7**(2), 118–132 (2008)
14. Strötgen, J., Gertz, M.: A baseline temporal tagger for all languages. In: Proceedings of the 2015 Conference on Empirical Methods in Natural Language Processing, pp. 541–547. Lisbon, Portugal (2015)
15. Thomson Reuters: Open Calais: API user guide (2017). http://www.opencalais.com/opencalais-api
16. Yimam, S.M., et al.: new/s/leak - information extraction and visualization for investigative data journalists. In: Proceedings of ACL-2016 System Demonstrations, pp. 163–168. Berlin, Germany (2016)

False Information Detection on Social Media via a Hybrid Deep Model

Lianwei Wu⑩, Yuan Rao$^{(\boxtimes)}$, Hualei Yu, Yiming Wang,
and Ambreen Nazir

Lab of Social Intelligence and Complex Data Processing, School of Software,
Xi'an Jiaotong University, Xi'an 710049, Shaanxi, China
{stayhungry,lily_yul994,yimingwang}@stu.xjtu.edu.cn,
raoyuan@mail.xjtu.edu.cn,
Ambreen.nazir@ciitwah.edu.pk

Abstract. There is not only low-cost, easy-access, real-time and valuable information on social media, but also a large amount of false information. False information causes great harm to individuals, the society and the country. So how to detect false information? In the paper, we analyze false information further. We rationally select three information evaluation metrics to distinguish false information. We pioneer the division of information into 5 types and introduce them in detail from the definition, the focus, features, etc. Moreover, in this work, we propose a hybrid deep model to represent text semantics of information with context and capture sentiment semantics features for false information detection. Finally, we apply the model to a benchmark dataset and a Weibo dataset, which shows the model is well-performed.

Keywords: Information credibility evaluation · Rumor detection
Social media · Text classification · False information

1 Introduction

Social media based on users' generating content is represented by Facebook, Twitter, Microblog, WeChat etc., which hastens content generation, propagation and growth. Social media relies on information sharing, real time, interactivity and Diversity of content dissemination and the advantage of randomness of virtual identities, fragmented expression of sentiment, which profoundly transforms the way people access and propagate information. Nevertheless, the informational content conveyed on the social media is not always true and reliable. Recent studies of Gupta et al. [1] show that among the informative tweets, 52% of which are labeled as definitively credible, 35% of which seem credible, and 13% of which are definitively false. Besides, Lazer et al. [2] found that falsehood diffused significantly farther, faster, deeper, and broader than the truth in all categories of information. Experiment shows that the truth is about 6 times as long as falsehood to reach 1500 people. False information without identifying profoundly amplifies negative social emotions and significantly does harm to the

© Springer Nature Switzerland AG 2018
S. Staab et al. (Eds.): SocInfo 2018, LNCS 11186, pp. 323–333, 2018.
https://doi.org/10.1007/978-3-030-01159-8_31

harmony of society and country safety. For instance, Cambridge Analytica found that the events about United States presidential election were affected by fake news. Accordingly, it is one of the crucial and urgent issues that is how to classify false information quickly on social media.

To detect false information on social media, there are a series of studies aiming at detecting different types of false information. On one hand, most studies focus on a single type of false information, which main concentrates upon rumors, for example, early detection of rumors [3–5], rumor-spreading mechanism [7, 8], curbing the spread of rumors [9] et al. Some methods are interested in detecting fake news. For instance, Wang [10] releases a new, real, fake news dataset and proposes a novel model for fake news detection. Moreover, some existing algorithms inclines to detect disinformation on social media [11–13] and Bessi et al. think that disinformation is a conspiracy. Furthermore, there are many existing studies on spam detection [16–18]. On the other hand, a few researchers study several types of incredibility information, which are detecting misinformation and disinformation [20, 34], classifying fake, spam messages and legitimate messages etc. [35, 36].

Although, the existing work has made significant progress in classifying false information on social media. Unfortunately, it is obvious that the above work has several limitations. Firstly, studying on one type or several types of false information is not enough to cover all false information. Secondly, different types of false information have different characteristics. For example, rumors are controversy and unproven statements. However, fake news is unreal information. There is a lack of reasonable way to distinguish the types of false information.

To overcome the limitations mentioned, in this work, we summarize characteristics about different types of information and choose three representative dimensions of information evaluation metrics to divide the information on social media into 5 types, which are true information, rumors, biases, fake news, and spams. Next, we propose a novel hybrid deep model to classify these types of false information. In our method, we employ RCNN model to deeply capture to represent text semantics of information with context and design a model mixed with LSTM and ConvNet to learn text sentiment features. Particularly, sentiment features are the important features of classifying false information further. Lazer et al. [2] found that false rumors inspired replies expressing greater surprise, corroborating the novelty hypothesis, and greater disgust, whereas the truth inspired replies that expressed greater sadness, anticipation, joy, and trust.

Finally, the main contributions of this work are listed as follows:

- The paper firstly divides information into five types on social media, including four types of false information, and true information. We classify false information to evaluate information credibility more comprehensively.
- The paper proposes a hybrid deep model from deep semantics and sentiment features to detect false information, which significantly improves the performance of classifying false information.

2 The Types of Information

2.1 Three Information Evaluation Metrics

From a credible perspective, we can divide information into two aspects, which are true information and false information. Except this information which is confirmed authentically, scientifically, objectively and integrally. Others are false information. There are many obvious differences in false information on the social media. How to distinguish false information? Based on the issue from the three perspectives of the intention of information dissemination and the influence caused by information, the authenticity of information, we choose three representative metrics of information evaluation, which are purposiveness, harmfulness, and credibility to evaluate false information on social media.

Purposiveness is the intention, which can tell whether information dissemination has a strong orientation. We divide purposiveness of information into three types, which are purpose, purposelessness, and unclear purpose. Harmfulness refers to the negative effect of the spread of information on audience. **Harmfulness** intends to do harm to personal safety and to spawn economic loss. **Credibility** means the comprehension reflection of information receivers' subjective trust in the sources of information, objective evaluation on the quantity of information content, information disseminators' degree of trust [27]. We divide information credibility into three types, which are that information is true, information is false, and information needs to be verified.

2.2 The Types of Information

According to three information evaluation metrics and some literature [10, 12, 13, 23, 28, 29], we divide information into true information, rumors, biases, fake news and spams. The table below is a comparison of five types.

On the definition of the five types of information, true information is true, scientific, objective and complete. About the definition of the rumors, Kapferer et al. [32] reckoned that validating the trueness of the rumors needed to satisfy three factors: (1) there were reliable sources of information, (2) individuals expecting to know the truth, (3) information seeming to be true. In consequence, the paper defines that rumors are controversy and unproven statements. The definition of biases is essentially the reflection of cognition and feeling for realistic society. Biases mean exaggerating the facts, being taken out of context, and sampling bias, which affects the stance of social life and the value judgements of the public. Tandoc et al. [33] define fake news is unreal information made on purpose, which has characteristics that are fast speed of spreading, wide range of spreading and the structure of spreading that presents dispersive networks. Karlova et al. [20] also mentioned that fake news has the characteristic of deliberate deception. Spam usually includes casual and useless information, false advertisement, deceptive and trick information in the network. The existence of fake users and zombies is an important reason for spam proliferation.

Based on three information evaluation metrics, the definition of five types of information, taking into account the ease of classification of labelers, the focus of five types of information are different. Rumors focus on credibility of information that has not been confirmed. Biases tend to exaggerate of emotional language expression. Fake news focuses on the purpose of information with deliberate deception. Spam focuses on some advertising information and duplicate information. When we make sure the focus of five types of information are different, this will be five types of information that are mutually exclusive and do not overlap. Additionally, except five types of information, are there other types of information? In the recent literature, we find some researchers study misinformation. The reason why we do not classify misinformation as one type here is that the survival time of false positive information is very short. After misinformation is confirmed, it is either turned into true information, or turned into fake news.

We compare the five types of information as shown in Table 1. On purposiveness, rumors are unproven statements, which have no specific purpose. On harmfulness, different types of information credibility have difference between strong sides and weak sides. On credibility, we use true, to be confirmed, and false, levels to evaluate five types of information. In the next chapter, we will aim at classifying the five types of information.

Table 1. The comparison of the five types of information

	Characteristic	Purposiveness	Harmfulness	Credibility
True Information	True, Scientific, Objective and Complete	Yes	No	True
Rumors	Plausible, To be confirmed	Not Clear	Not too Strong	To be confirmed
Biases	Exaggerated, Fuzzy and damaging	Yes	Very strong	To be confirmed
Fake news	Deliberate deception, Misguided	Yes	Strong	False
Spams	Useless, Confused	Yes	Weak	To be confirmed

3   The Proposed Method

We have already divided information into five types in Sect. 2. In this Section, we propose a novel method to classify them on social media. The paper introduces the details of the method we proposed. Figure 1 shows the network structure of the method. We obtain semantic representation and sentiment information from social media text data. On semantic representation, we use RCNN model to obtain information with context as semantically as possible. On sentiment representation, we use ConvNet model to deeply represent sentiment features. Combined with semantic and sentiment representation, we classify the five types of information on social media. Next, the paper will show the details of the method as follows.

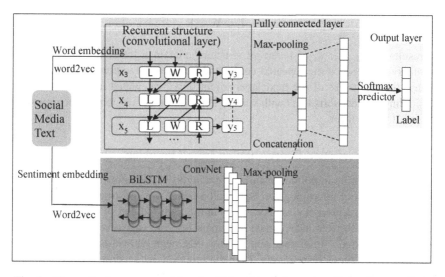

Fig. 1. The method we proposed for classifying false information (Color figure online)

3.1 Learning Text Semantic Representation from Microblog

The light blue part in Fig. 1 uses the RCNN model to describe the process of learning text semantic representation from single microblog. The RCNN model is essentially CNN model, which uses recurrent structure as the convolutional layer of CNN model. On the input of the model, we use a tool of Chinese word segmentation, which is named Jieba[1] to split text of the microblog and then remove stop words by Chinese stop words list firstly. Then we use pre-trained 50-dimensional word2vec embeddings from Chinese Wikipedia corpus. Embeddings obtained serve as the input of the RCNN model. In recurrent structure, L, R represents the semantics of all left side and right side contexts respectively, and W represents the word embedding of a specific word. The schemas of calculation of L and R are shown in Eqs. (1) and (2). We illustrate the equations with examples, we suppose that the input sentence of the recurrent structure is "Wisconsin is on pace to double the number of layoffs this year" and W_{x3}, W_{x4}, W_{x5} means "pace", "to", and "double" respectively. Then L_{x4} represents the semantics of the left side context "Wisconsin is on pace", R_{x4} represents the semantics of the right side context "double the number of layoffs this year". Next, x_4 is the concatenation of the left side context vector L_{x4}, the word embedding W_{x4} and the right side context vector R_{x4}. As shown in Eq. (3), the recurrent structure learns more semantic representation from text of microblog, compared to conventional neural network models, which only use a fixed window. We apply *tanh* activation function to x_i and send the result to the next layer y_i, which is a latent semantic vector.

$$L_{x4} = L_{x3} + W_{x5} \tag{1}$$

$$R_{x4} = R_{x5} + W_{x5} \tag{2}$$

$$x_4 = [L_{x4}; W_{x4}; R_{x4}] \qquad (3)$$

The results y_1, y_2, ..., y_n of recurrent structure contain a lot of repeated contextual information. To reduce the repeated contextual information to prevent overfitting and decrease the input size of the next layer to cut down calculated amount, we apply a max-pooling that converts texts with various lengths into a fixed-length vector and send the result to next layer.

3.2   Learning Sentiment Representation from Microblog

Sentiment features are important features to distinguish false information. To obtain the sentiment features of microblogs on Sina weibo better, we construct a ConvNet model to learn sentiment representation. As shown in the light red part of Fig. 1, on the input of sentiment model, we build Chinese sentiment lexicon[2], negative word lexicon[3] and degree adverb lexicon[4] to extract sentiment words, negative words and degree adverb words from microblogs respectively. Like the input on 3.1 section, we use pre-trained 50-dimensional word2vec embedding from Wikipedia to represent the words. We extracted and formed sentiment embedding, which is named sentiment-word2vec. Then the concatenation inputs a convNet layer to capture sentiment features better. Finally, we use max-pooling layer to extract a fix-length vector to attain more representative sentiment features from the output of the convNet layer. Additionally, the results of output is sent to next layer to wait for merging.

In conclusion, we integrate the output results of 3.1 and 3.2 section into a concatenation. Then the concatenation enters full-connected layer and subsequently passes a softmax predictor to obtain the label of different types of information mentioned in Sect. 2.2.

4   Experiments

4.1   Experimental Settings

At the beginning, on the dataset of our experiments, we split Weibo dataset we built into 70% training set and 30% testing set. Specifically, the Weibo dataset contains five types of information, 70% of which are extracted as training set in the dataset of information in every type and the remaining is testing set.

Secondly, on experimental evaluation metrics, we choose several representative evaluation metrics for our experiments, which are **accuracy**, **recall** and **F1-score**. **Accuracy** is a necessary evaluation metric for all most classification experiments. **Recall** is coverage that measures how many positive examples are divided correctly. **F1-score** is the harmonic average of accuracy and recall. Generally, for above the evaluation metrics, the larger the values of evaluation metrics are, the better the effectiveness will be.

What's more, on the hyper-parameter settings of the baseline dataset and the Weibo dataset we built. We use 50-dimensional word2vec to embedding text of microblogs as the input of the method. We set the convolution window size to be 4 and filter sizes to be 100. On the calculation of loss functions, the last layer of the network firstly processes through softmax and then uses cross-entropy to calculate loss. We set the learning rate of the optimal gradient descent to be 10^{-2} and batch size to be 50.

4.2   Data

Here, we introduce two multi-type of information datasets, which are benchmark dataset – LIAR dataset [10] and Weibo dataset we built.

LIAR Dataset: LIAR dataset is a new human-labeled benchmark dataset from POLITIFACT.COM, which includes 12,836 short statements labeled for truthfulness, subject, context/venue, speaker, state, party, and prior history. LIAR dataset contains six fine-grained labels for the truthfulness ratings: pants-fire, false, barely-true, half-true, mostly-true, and true. The distribution of labels in the LIAR dataset is relatively well-balanced: except for 1,050 pants-fire cases, the instances for all other labels range from 2,063 to 2,638. Table 2 shows some random snippets from LIAR dataset.

Table 2. The LIAR dataset statistics

Dataset statistics	Num.
Training set size	10269
Validation set size	1284
Testing set size	1283
Avg. statement length (tokens)	17.9

Weibo Dataset: Considering public multi-type information datasets lack of annotation, especially, there is a blank in Chinese information credibility field. Consequently, we construct multi-type information dataset – the Weibo dataset based on Sina weibo, one of the biggest social platforms in China.

The overall sketch of the Weibo dataset is shown in Table 3. We collect more than 40 thousand microblogs that consist of 9600 true information, 8000 rumors, 8000 biases, 8000 fake news, and 8000 spams. The average microblog length in different types of information is different. Here the average microblog length refers to the number of words of single microblog. The average length of fake news is the longest, which is 115. Oppositely, spam is the shortest, which is only 93. Based on the dataset we built, we conduct a series of experiments to verify the performance of our method.

Table 3. The overall sketch of the Weibo dataset

The types of information	True information	Rumors	Biases	Fake news	Spams
Microblogs	9600	8000	8000	8000	8000
AVG. microblog length	104	111	98	115	93
MAX forwarding volume	224.5K	213.6K	232.7K	220.1K	150.3K

4.3   Results

We compare our method with other baseline methods on classifying false information. Table 4 shows the performance of different methods, which can outperform the state-of-the-art methods. Then we analyze the experimental results based on several methods with different inputs.

Table 4. Results of comparison with different methods for different dataset

	LIAR dataset			Weibo dataset		
	Accuracy	Recall	f1-score	Accuracy	Recall	F1-score
LR + all	0.263	0.532	0.342	0.359	0.624	0.456
SVM + all	0.271	0.564	0.354	0.375	0.645	0.474
CNN + all	0.273	0.486	0.355	0.368	0.677	0.477
RCNN + text	0.304	0.557	0.391	0.402	0.701	0.511
Our method	0.337	0.597	0.431	0.433	0.749	0.549

Comparison with Methods

All means text semantic features, and sentiment features are spliced together as a concatenation.

LR + All. We use **All** features as the input of logistic regression (LR) model to classify false information. Additionally, **SVM** is Support Vector Machines. **CNN** is convolutional neural network.

RCNN + Text. We use text semantic features as the inputs of the RCNN model to classify false information. The RCNN Lai et al. [18] proposed is a text classification model, which outperforms the state-of-the-art methods, particularly on document-level datasets.

RCNN + Text + Sentiment. We use the combination of RCNN and Text, sentiment features to evaluate multiple types information.

Our Method. In our method, obtaining text semantic features with context as much as possible by RCNN model, and getting sentiment features by convNet, are integrated as a concatenation as input of our method to use CNN model to evaluate multi-type information.

Results

The experimental results are shown in Table 4.

Contrasting LR + All, SVM + All, CNN + All and our method. These methods have the same inputs, which are All. The experimental results show that our method has the better performance than other classical methods. It proves that our method uses RCNN model to capture more text semantic information with context and use convNet to extract more text sentimental features.

Contrasting RCNN + Text, RCNN + Text + Sentiment and our method. Three methods are based on CNN improved model – RCNN model. However, for different inputs, three methods show different experimental performance. The experimental results of RCNN + Text + Sentiment method are superior to RCNN + Text, which indicates that sentiment features are favorable distinguishing features for classifying false information. Meantime the performance of our method is obviously optimal in the three methods. The experiments of our method firmly confirm constructing text semantic representation and sentiment representation to classify false information is effective.

4.4 Discussion

The method proposed uses RCNN model to represent text semantic information with context as much as possible, and represent sentiment features by convNet prominently, which achieves great success on classifying false information for evaluating information credibility, even though, there still exists many issues to solve in the future. There are a couple of examples.

- On text sentiment representation of microblogs, our sentiment representation of sentiment words, negative words and degree adverb words, is slightly shallow because we have not considered the relationship of the words and their context.
- Another, there is also a problem that the volume of the Weibo dataset, including 5 types of information microblogs based on Sina weibo, is insufficient. In the future, we will continue to crawl different types of microblogs and label them to expand the Weibo dataset.

5 Conclusions

In this work, to classify false information for evaluating information credibility on social media, we propose a novel method, which captures contextual text semantic information with the recurrent structure of RCNN model, and learns sentiment representation with convNet model. On a benchmark dataset and a Weibo dataset collected from Sina weibo, the experiment demonstrates that the method we proposed outperforms the state-of-the-art methods.

References

1. Gupta, A., Kumaraguru, P., Castillo, C., Meier, P.: TweetCred: real-time credibility assessment of content on Twitter. In: Aiello, L.M., McFarland, D. (eds.) SocInfo 2014. LNCS, vol. 8851, pp. 228–243. Springer, Cham (2014). https://doi.org/10.1007/978-3-319-13734-6_16
2. Lazer, D., Baum, M., Benkler, Y., Berinsky, A.J., Greenhill, K.M.: The science of fake news. Science **359**(6380), 1094–1096 (2018)
3. Zhao, Z., Resnick, P., Mei, Q.: Enquiring minds: early detection of rumors in social media from enquiry posts. In: Proceedings of WWW, pp. 1395–1405 (2015)
4. Wu, K., Yang, S., Zhu, K.: False rumors detection on Sina Weibo by propagation structures. In: Proceedings of the 31st ICDE, pp. 651–662 (2015)
5. Ma, J., Gao, W., Wong, K.: Detect rumors in microblog posts using propagation structure via kernel learning. In: Proceedings of ACL (2017)

6. Ma, J., Gao, W., Wei, Z., Lu, Y., Wong, K.: Detect rumors using time series of social context information on microblogging websites. In: Proceedings of CIKM, pp. 1751–1754. ACM (2015)

7. Hu, Y., Pan, Q., Hou, W., He, M.: Rumor spreading model with the different attitudes towards rumors. Phys. A **502**, 331–344 (2018)

8. Wang, B., Chen, G., Fu, L.: DRIMUX: dynamic rumor influence minimization with user experience in social networks. Proc. TKDE **29**(10), 2168–2181 (2017)

9. Hamidian, S., Diab, M.: Rumor identification and belief investigation on Twitter. In: Proceedings of NAACL-HLT, pp. 3–8 (2016)

10. Wang, W.: "Liar, Liar Pants on Fire": a new benchmark dataset for fake news detection. In: Proceedings of ACL, pp. 422–426 (2017)

11. Imran, M., Castillo, C., Diaz, F., Vieweg, S.: Processing social media messages in mass emergency: survey summary. In: Proceedings of WWW, pp. 507–511 (2018)

12. Kahne, J., Bowyer, B.: Educating for democracy in a partisan age: confronting the challenges of motivated reasoning and misinformation. Am. Educ. Res. J. **54**(1), 3–34 (2017)

13. Bessi, A., Coletto, M., Davidescu, G.: Science vs. conspiracy: collective narratives in the age of misinformation. PLoS ONE **10**(2), 1–17 (2015)

14. Faris, R., Roberts, H., Etling, B., et al.: Partisanship, Propaganda, and Disinformation: Online Media and the 2016 US Presidential Election. Berkman Klein Center Research Publication (2017)

15. Marwick, A., Lewis, R.: Media Manipulation and Disinformation Online. Data & Society Research Institute, New York (2017)

16. Sedhai, S., Sun, A.: Semi-supervised spam detection in twitter stream. IEEE Trans. Comput. Soc. Syst. **5**(1), 169–175 (2018)

17. Kim, S, Chang, H., Lee, S., Yu, M., Kang, J.: Deep semantic frame-based deceptive opinion spam analysis. In: Proceedings of CIKM, pp. 1131–1140. ACM (2015)

18. Hai, Z., Zhao, P., Cheng, P., Yang, P.: Deceptive review spam detection via exploiting task relatedness and unlabeled data. In: Proceedings of EMNLP, pp. 1817–1826 (2016)

19. Chen, C., Wang, Y., Zhang, J.: Statistical features-based real-time detection of drifted Twitter spam. TIFS **12**(4), 914–925 (2017)

20. Volkova, S., Jang, J.: Misleading or falsification: inferring deceptive strategies and types in online news and social media. In: Proceedings of WWW, pp. 575–583 (2018)

21. Rajdev, M., Lee, K.: Fake and spam messages: detecting misinformation during natural disasters on social media. In: Web Intelligence and Intelligent Agent Technology, vol. 1, pp. 17–20. IEEE (2015)

22. Lai, S., Xu, L., Liu, K.: Recurrent convolutional neural networks for text classification. Proc. AAAI **333**, 2267–2273 (2015)

23. Castillo, C., Mendoza, M., Poblete, B.: Information credibility on twitter. In: Proceedings of WWW, pp. 675–684. ACM (2011)

24. Mikolov, T., Chen, K., Corrado, G.: Efficient estimation of word representations in vector space. Comput. Sci. (2013)

25. Nal, K., Grefenstette, E., Blunsom, P.: A convolutional neural network for modelling sentences. In: Proceedings of ACL, pp. 655–665 (2014)

26. Quoc, L., Mikolov, T.: Distributed representations of sentences and documents. In: Proceedings of ICML, pp. 1188–1196 (2014)

27. Tseng, S., Fogg, B.: Credibility and computing technology. Commun. ACM **42**(5), 39–44 (1999)

28. Popat, K., Mukherjee, S., Strötgen, J.: Where the truth lies: explaining the credibility of emerging claims on the web and social media. In: Proceedings of WWW, pp. 1003–1012 (2017)
29. Viviani, M., Pasi, G.: Credibility in social media: opinions, news, and health information—a survey. Wiley Interdiscip. Rev. Data Min. Knowl. Disc. **7**(5) (2017)
30. Kwon, S., Cha, S., Jung, K.: Rumor detection over varying time windows. PLoS ONE **12**(1), e0168344 (2017)
31. Choi, Y., Seo, Y., Yoon, S.: E-WOM messaging on social media: social ties, temporal distance, and message concreteness. Internet Res. **27**(3), 495–505 (2017)
32. Kapferer, J.: Rumors: Uses, Interpretation and Necessity. Routledge, London (2017)
33. Tandoc, J., Lim, Z., Ling, R.: Defining "fake news" a typology of scholarly definitions. Digit. J. **6**(2), 137–153 (2018)
34. Zhang, A., Ranganathan, A., Metz, S.: A structured response to misinformation: defining and annotating credibility indicators in news articles. In: Proceedings of WWW, pp. 603–612 (2018)
35. Ruchansky, N., Seo, S., Liu, Y.: CSI: a hybrid deep model for fake news detection. In: Proceedings of CIKM, pp. 797–806. ACM (2017)
36. Li, H., Fei, G., Wang, S.: Bimodal distribution and co-bursting in review spam detection. In: Proceedings of WWW, pp. 1063–1072 (2017)

Information Diffusion Power of Political Party Twitter Accounts During Japan's 2017 Election

Mitsuo Yoshida[1][✉][ID] and Fujio Toriumi[2][ID]

[1] Toyohashi University of Technology, Toyohashi, Aichi, Japan
yoshida@cs.tut.ac.jp
[2] The University of Tokyo, Bunkyo-ku, Tokyo, Japan
tori@sys.t.u-tokyo.ac.jp

Abstract. In modern election campaigns, political parties utilize social media to advertise their policies and candidates and to communicate to electorates. In Japan's latest general election in 2017, the 48th general election for the Lower House, social media, especially Twitter, was actively used. In this paper, we perform a detailed analysis of social graphs and users who retweeted tweets of political parties during the election. Our aim is to obtain accurate information regarding the diffusion power for each party rather than just the number of followers. The results indicate that a user following a user who follows a political party account tended to also follow the account. This means that it does not increase diversity because users who follow each other tend to share similar values. We also find that followers of a specific party frequently retweeted the tweets. However, since users following the user who follow a political party account are not diverse, political parties delivered the information only to a few political detachment users.

Keywords: Twitter · Information diffusion · Political party · Election

1 Introduction

A partial amendment of Japan's Public Officers Election Act in 2013 authorized election campaigning using the Internet. In Japan's latest general election in 2017, the 48th general election for the Lower House, social media, especially Twitter[1], was actively used. The main feature of this election is that a new party named 'The Constitutional Democratic Party of Japan' attracted many followers on social media[2]. Political parties can deliver information to their followers, but can the parties deliver to users who are not followers, political detachment users? If the followers retweet the tweets of political parties, the parties can deliver the information to political detachment users. Specifically, information diffusion

---

[1] https://twitter.com/.
[2] Bloomberg (2017): A 3-Day-Old Japanese Political Party Has Already Overtaken Abe's on Twitter.

© Springer Nature Switzerland AG 2018
S. Staab et al. (Eds.): SocInfo 2018, LNCS 11186, pp. 334–342, 2018.
https://doi.org/10.1007/978-3-030-01159-8_32

power cannot be determined by just the number of followers. We are interested in how many users have political parties' information delivered to them.

Tumasjan et al. reported that Twitter is functioning as a discussion forum for politics [13], and, there have been many studies on users' access to political information on social media. Previous studies show that users are divided regarding access to political information [1,8–10]. Such studies mainly cover political information written in the news on social media. Previous studies also show a relationship exists between the division of information and ideology [3,4,7,14]. In other words, the studies were analyzing users who tended to support specific political parties. These studies focus on users who received political information.

The number of followers is used as the attention degree of the user. The influence of the number of followers in information diffusion is not necessarily large [5], and fraudulent methods are sometimes used to gain followers [12]. Even in political communication, the hub of information cannot be determined only by the number of followers [2].

In this paper, we perform a detailed analysis of social graphs and users who retweeted tweets of political parties during the 48th general election for Japan's Lower House in 2017. Our aim is to obtain accurate information regarding the diffusion power for each party rather than just the number of followers. To this end, we address the following three research questions:

RQ1 Homogeneity of followers:
Who is following the user who is following a political party account?
RQ2 Activity level of followers:
How many tweets were retweeted by followers of a political party account?
RQ3 Information diffusion power:
How many tweets were delivered to political detachment users?

The results indicate that a user following a user who follows a political party account tended to also follow the account. This means that it does not increase diversity because users who follow each other tend to share similar values. We also find that followers of a specific party frequently retweeted the tweets. However, since users following the user who follows a political party account are not diverse, political parties delivered the information only to a few political detachment users.

2 Dataset

2.1 Development

In this study, we use Japanese retweets on Twitter collected from 28 September[3] to 23 October 2017. This period encompasses the 48th general election for the Lower House in Japan. The data were collected using the Twitter Search API[4] and consist of 42,651,648 retweets.

---

[3] The Lower House in Japan was dissolved on this day.
[4] We constantly searched by query "RT lang:ja".

Table 1. The major political parties in Japan: "The Liberal Democratic Party of Japan" and "Komeito" are the ruling party.

Party name	Screen name
The Liberal Democratic Party of Japan	@jimin_koho
The Constitutional, Democratic Party of Japan	@CDP2017
The Party of Hope	@kibounotou
Komeito	@komei_koho
The Japanese Communist Party	@jcp_cc
The Japan Innovation Party	@osaka_ishin

Table 2. The accounts of major political parties in Japan: The number of seats is the result of this election. There is no correlation between the number of seats and the number of followers.

Screen name	# of tweets	# of retweeted	# of followers	# of seats
@jimin_koho	280	110,685	134,595	284
@CDP2017	904	506,432	191,011	55
@kibounotou	410	21,559	13,529	50
@komei_koho	289	31,072	76,743	29
@jcp_cc	347	48,203	42,508	12
@osaka_ishin	281	13,163	15,999	11

To focus only on data related to politics, we targeted the official accounts of political parties and selected the accounts of the six major parties. These political parties are shown in Tables 1 and 2. In the collected retweets, we only use 732,861 retweets (84,043 users) in which the tweets of these political parties have been retweeted. Normally, tweets collected using the Twitter Streaming API and the "follow" parameter are used in this type of study. Since we started this study after the end of this election, we decided to extract necessary data from the collected retweet data.

We also used a social graph on Twitter. First, we gathered users who were following the major parties. Then, we created a set of users that combines these users and the users who have retweeted tweets of the major parties. This set includes 460,683 users. Finally, we gathered users who were following the 460,683 users on 10 November 2017 and build the social graph. As a result, the social graph consists of 16,742,073 nodes (users) and 409,741,963 edges (followee-follower paths).

2.2 Basic Statistics

Figures 1 and 2 show the number of tweets for six political parties and the number times political parties' tweets were retweeted. Under Japanese law, political

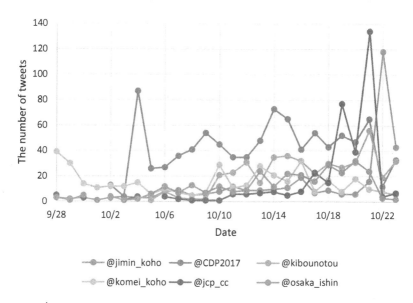

Fig. 1. The number of daily tweets: the y-axis indicates the number of tweets posted by each political party. @CDP2017 tweeted daily. The number of tweets by @jcp_cc increased on the eve of the voting day, and the number of tweets by @jimin_koho increased on the voting day.

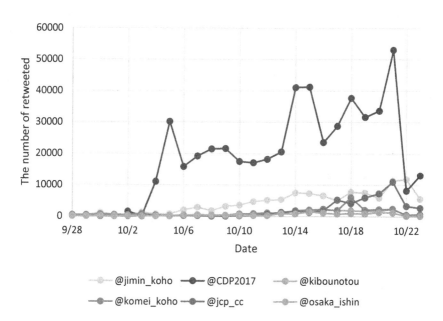

Fig. 2. The number times political parties' tweets were retweeted: the y-axis indicates the retweeting frequency. Tweets of @CDP2017 were frequently retweeted.

parties cannot call for voting during the actual voting time (7 am to 10 pm on 22 October 2017), which is why the number of tweets on the voting day was relatively low. The number of tweets by @jcp_cc increased on the eve of the voting day, and the number of tweets by @jimin_koho increased on the voting day. @jcp_cc called for voting the day before the voting day, and @jimin_koho reported each time a winner was decided. It seems that the number of times the tweets were retweeted was greatly affected by the number of followers. As shown in Table 1, the number of followers of @CDP2017 is large. As a result, the number of times tweets of @CDP2017 was retweeted increased.

Regarding information diffusion power, we focus on political detachment users. We consider "political detachment users" to be users satisfying the following criteria: they were not following any political party and did not retweet any tweets of political parties. There were 13,174,064 political detachment users, or 78.7% of the 16,742,073 users selected for this study. It is important that political parties deliver information to political detachment users because the amount of them is large.

3   Results and Discussion

3.1   RQ1: Homogeneity of Followers

Homogeneity is measured by the degree of overlap between followers of a political party and their followers. This section addresses the following research questions: who is following the user who is following a political party account? Political parties can deliver information to their followers, but cannot deliver to users who are not followers. If the followers retweet the tweets of political parties, the parties can deliver information to users other than their followers. Therefore, who the follower of a follower is will influence information diffusion power. If followers of users following a political party are composed only of followers of the political party, even if the followers retweet the tweets of the political party, the party delivers the information only to the followers.

Figure 3 shows the homogeneity of the followers of each of the political parties. Homogeneity is higher at the upper right, and homogeneity is lower at the lower left. In the followers of users following @CDP2017, 50% of the followers are users whose followers follow @CDP2017 by over 75%. If homogeneity is high, we can consider that the community of supporters (followers) was made sufficiently because the subgraph becomes dense. A new party, @CDP2017, succeeded in building a community, but the second new party @kibounotou failed.

A highly homogeneous group of followers tends to not follow other political parties. Figure 4 shows the rate of the duplicate followers for each political party. The followers of @CDP2017 typically do not follow other political parties. Such users will only receive information from a specific party. Therefore, the political parties can deliver their information to such users intensively.

3.2   RQ2: Activity Level of Followers

The activity level is mainly measured by the rate of followers who retweeted. This section addresses the following research questions: how many tweets were retweeted by followers of a political party account? For political parties to deliver information to many users, the followers need to be frequently retweeted because many users are political detachment users. If any followers of a political party did not retweet, the political party can deliver information only to the followers. Even if tweets are delivered to users by retweets, users do not necessarily see it [6,11]. In this analysis, we focus on whether political parties "can deliver" information, so we do not consider whether users actually saw the tweets.

Figure 5 shows the activity level of the followers of each of the political parties. In @CDP2017, 18% of the followers retweeted the tweets of @CDP2017. This value is higher than the values of other political parties. @CDP2017 was created on 2 October 2017, and there are no followers who have not used Twitter for a long time. Thus, if the activity level of followers was high, the followers read the tweets and may have frequently retweeted. However, the tweets of @kibounotou were retweeted by non-followers. The homogeneity of the followers of @kibouno- tou is low, and @kibounotou can deliver information to various users, and as a result, non-followers may have frequently retweeted.

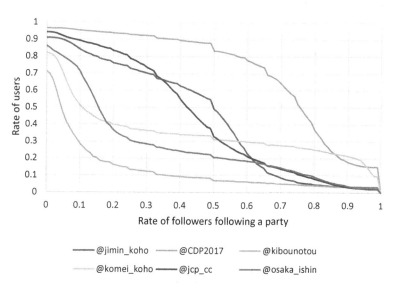

Fig. 3. Homogeneity of followers: the x-axis indicates the rate of followers following a political party. For example, if a user has ten followers, of which six followers follow a political party, then the x-axis points to 0.6. The y-axis indicates the rate of such users in the followers of a political party. Homogeneity is higher at the upper right, and homogeneity is lower at the lower left. In the followers of users following @CDP2017, 50% of the followers are users whose followers follow @CDP2017 by over 75%. In @kibounotou, 50% of the followers are users whose followers follow @kibounotou by over 4%.

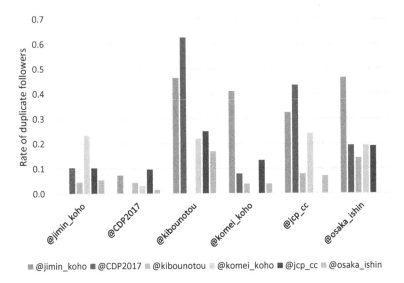

Fig. 4. Duplicate followers: the y-axis indicates the rate of followers of the x-axis following a political party. The followers of @CDP2017 typically do not follow other political parties. 63% of the followers of @kibounotou are following @CDP2017. Followers with low homogeneity tend to follow other political parties.

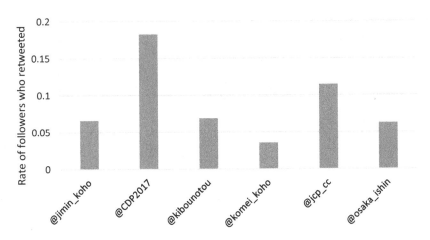

Fig. 5. Activity level of followers: how many followers retweeted. 18% of the followers of @CDP2017 retweeted the tweets of @CDP2017. The tweets of @kibounotou were retweeted by the non-followers.

3.3   RQ3: Information Diffusion Power

Information diffusion power is mainly measured by the number of users who were delivered the tweets. This section addresses the following research questions: how many tweets were delivered to political detachment users? The number of times

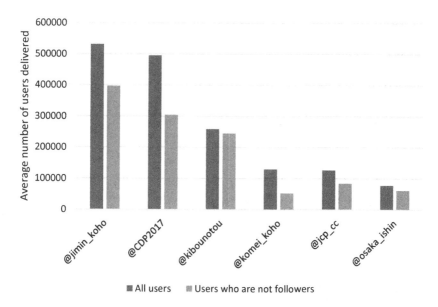

Fig. 6. Information diffusion power: the power of @jimin_koho was the strongest. @CDP2017 was the second strongest, despite having the largest number of followers. @komei_koho was weak in its power to deliver tweets to non-followers.

a user was delivered the tweets of a political party is calculated as follows: if the user is a follower of the political party, number of the tweets of political parties, else number of times that followees (followed users) of the user retweeted the tweets of the political party. We assume that a user was "delivered" the tweets of a political party because the tweet appears on the timeline of the user.

Figure 6 shows the information diffusion power of each of the political parties. The picture of the information diffusion power is the average number of users who are delivered a tweet by a political party. If the homogeneity is low and activity level is high, the information diffusion power will also be higher. The power of @CDP2017 was the second best, despite having the largest number of followers. The reason is that the homogeneity of the followers is high. Specifically, there is no diversity for followers of the followers of the political party. Clearly, the information diffusion power cannot be measured only by the number of followers. The power of @jimin_koho, which is a ruling party, is high. However, @komei_koho (Komeito) was weak in its power to deliver tweets to non-followers, despite being a ruling party.

4   Conclusion

We performed a detailed analysis of social graphs and users who retweeted tweets of political parties during the 48th general election for Japan's Lower House in 2017. Our aim is to obtain accurate information regarding the diffusion power for each party rather than just the number of followers. To this end, we addressed three research questions. The results indicate that a user following a user who follows a political party account tended to also follow the account. This means that it does not increase diversity because users who follow each other tend to share similar values. We also found that followers of a specific party frequently retweeted the tweets. However, since users following a user who follows a political party account are not diverse, political parties delivered the information only to a few political detachment users.

References

1. Adamic, L.A., Glance, N.: The political blogosphere and the 2004 U.S. election: divided they blog. In: Proceedings of the 3rd International Workshop on Link Discovery, pp. 36–43 (2005)
2. Bakshy, E., Hofman, J.M., Mason, W.A., Watts, D.J.: Everyone's an influencer: quantifying influence on Twitter. In: Proceedings of the Fourth ACM International Conference on Web Search and Data Mining, pp. 65–74 (2011)
3. Barberá, P., Jost, J.T., Nagler, J., Tucker, J.A., Bonneau, R.: Tweeting from left to right: is online political communication more than an echo chamber? Psychol. Sci. **26**(10), 1531–1542 (2015)
4. Batorski, D., Grzywińska, I.: Three dimensions of the public sphere on Facebook. Inf. Commun. Soc. **21**(3), 356–374 (2018)
5. Cha, M., Haddadi, H., Benevenuto, F., Gummadi, K.P.: Measuring user influence in Twitter: the million follower fallacy. In: Proceedings of the Fourth International AAAI Conference on Weblogs and Social Media, pp. 10–17 (2010)
6. Comarela, G., Crovella, M., Almeida, V., Benevenuto, F.: Understanding factors that affect response rates in Twitter. In: Proceedings of the 23rd ACM Conference on Hypertext and Social Media, pp. 123–132 (2012)
7. Dahlgren, P.: The internet, public spheres, and political communication: dispersion and deliberation. Polit. Commun. **22**(2), 147–162 (2005)
8. Hayat, T., Samuel-Azran, T.: "You too, Second Screeners?" Second screeners' echo chambers during the 2016 U.S. elections primaries. J. Broadcast. Electron. Media **61**(2), 291–308 (2017)
9. Hyun, K.D., Moon, S.J.: News media's role in the issue-voting process: news attention, issue proximity, and vote choice. Journalism Mass Commun. Q. **91**(4), 687–705 (2014)
10. Iyengar, S., Hahn, K.S.: Red media, blue media: evidence of ideological selectivity in media use. J. Commun. **59**(1), 19–39 (2009)
11. Rodriguez, M.G., Gummadi, K., Schoelkopf, B.: Quantifying information overload in social media and its impact on social contagions. In: Proceedings of the Eighth International AAAI Conference on Weblogs and Social Media, pp. 170–179 (2014)
12. Stringhini, G., et al.: Follow the green: growth and dynamics in Twitter follower markets. In: Proceedings of the 2013 Internet Measurement Conference, pp. 163–176 (2013)
13. Tumasjan, A., Sprenger, T., Sandner, P., Welpe, I.: Predicting elections with Twitter: what 140 characters reveal about political sentiment. In: Proceedings of the Fourth International AAAI Conference on Weblogs and Social Media, pp. 178–185 (2010)
14. Williams, H.T., McMurray, J.R., Kurz, T., Hugo Lambert, F.: Network analysis reveals open forums and echo chambers in social media discussions of climate change. Global Environ. Change **32**, 126–138 (2015)

Author Index

Abbar, Sofiane II-3
Abdulhamid, Najeeb G. I-3
Afsarmanesh Tehrani, Nazanin II-15
Ahonen, Pertti I-23
Al-Emadi, Noora II-3
Alepis, Efthimios II-148
Almeida, Virgilio I-151
Almeira, Jussara M. I-257
An, Jisun I-38
Antonie, Luiza I-242
Araki, Tetsuya II-291
Asatani, Kimitaka I-54

Baez, Marcos II-234
Bakir, Mehmet E. I-274
Balcerzak, Bartłomiej II-215
Berry, George I-67
Biemann, Chris II-313
Bochenina, Klavdiya I-439
Bontcheva, Kalina I-274
Boomgaard, Guusje I-86
Bosse, Tibor II-85, II-202
Brouwers, Thijs M. A. I-102

Caetano, Josemar I-151
Casati, Fabio II-234
Caverlee, James I-487
Cha, Meeyoung I-291
Chang, Angela II-29
Chapman, Clovis I-370
Chechulin, Andrey II-159
Chekmareva, Alfia II-271
Chen, Hao I-117
Chen, Jianqiu II-189
Chiu, Dah Ming I-471
Chung, Wen-Ting I-134
Cunha, Evandro I-151
Cutler, Andrew I-167

Dalle, Jean-Michel I-420
de Sousa Matos, Breno I-257
Delany, Sarah Jane I-117
Desnitsky, Vasily II-159

Díaz Ferreyra, Nicolás E. II-61
Dokuka, Sofia I-308
Dornostup, Olga II-40
Dubois, Antoine II-51
Dürst, Martin J. II-261

Emelyanov, Pavel II-75
Ertugrul, Ali Mert I-134

Faizliev, Alexey R. I-336, II-271
Farzan, Rosta I-196, I-348
Fatemi, Zahra I-212
Fiore, Francesca II-234
Floriana, Gargiulo I-228
Formolo, Daniel II-85
Frias-Martinez, Vanessa II-97
Funkner, Anastasia I-439

Garimella, Kiran II-51
Gatto, Laura I-242
Gomes Ferreira, Carlos Henrique I-257
Gorrell, Genevieve I-274
Grabowski, Andrzej II-118
Greenwood, Mark A. I-274
Gudkov, Alexander II-271
Guillaume, Deffuant I-228
Guleva, Valentina I-439

Hecking, Tobias II-61
Heisel, Maritta II-61
Heyko, Dar'ya I-242
High, Nathan I-67
Hirota, Masaharu II-291
Hong, Lingzi II-97

Iavarone, Benedetta I-274
Ilaria, Bertazzi I-228
Ishikawa, Hiroshi II-291

Jabeen, Fakhra II-108
Jansen, Bernard J. II-251
Jarynowski, Andrzej II-118

Kabassi, Katerina   II-148
Kalra, Gaurav   I-291
Kashefi, Armin   I-3
Kato, Daiju   II-291
Kawahata, Yasuko   I-54
Kellum, Agrippa   I-67
Kim, Daeyoung   I-291
Kocabey, Enes   II-129
Kochetkova, Nataliya   II-139
Koljonen, Juha   I-23
Koltsov, Sergei   I-308
Kontogianni, Aristea   II-148
Korobov, Eugene   II-271
Kotenko, Igor   II-159
Kovalchuk, Sergey   I-439
Kozyreva, Olga   I-322
Kulis, Brian   I-167
Kurahashi, Setsuya   II-224, II-299

Lavitt, Falko   I-86
Lee, Dongman   I-291
Lee, Hannah W.   II-168
Lee, Myeong   II-97
Levshunov, Michael   I-336, II-271
Li, Ang   I-134, I-348
Li, Yaoyiran   II-176
Liang, Qiyu   II-189
Lin, Yu-Ru   I-134
Liu, Qianqian   II-189
López, Claudia   I-196

Macy, Michael   I-67
Magnani, Matteo   I-212, II-15
Magno, Gabriel   I-151
Marchese, Maurizio   II-234
Marin, Javier   II-129
Mashhadi, Afra   I-370, II-97
Maslennikov, Dmitry   II-251
McKeever, Susan   I-117
Medeiros, Lenin   II-202
Mihalcea, Rada   I-455, II-176
Mironov, Sergei V.   I-336
Mozheikina, Liudmila   II-75

Nabożny, Aleksandra   II-215
Nagai, Hideyuki   II-224
Natali, Felicia   I-386
Nazir, Ambreen   II-323
Nurgalieva, Leysan   II-234

Ofli, Ferda   II-129
Ohshima, Hiroaki   II-261
Olkkonen, Rami   II-251
Onneweer, John P. T.   I-102

Pashakhin, Sergei   I-308
Pechina, Anna   I-322
Peng, Guoqing   II-189
Perry, Mark   I-3
Plesca, Miana   I-242
Porshnev, Alexander   II-243
Pronoza, Anton   II-159
Pronoza, Ekaterina   II-139

Rao, Yuan   II-323
Roberts, Ian   I-274

Saenko, Igor   II-159
Sakata, Ichiro   I-54
Salehi, Mostafa   I-212
Salminen, Joni   II-251
Shen, Yiting   I-455
Shoji, Yoshiyuki   II-261
Sidorov, Sergei P.   I-336, II-271
Sirianni, Antonio D.   II-281
Sirianni, Antonio   I-67
Squire, Megan   I-403
Suvorova, Alena   II-40
Sylvie, Huet   I-228

Takahashi, Katsurou   II-261
Teixeira, Douglas   I-151
Toriumi, Fujio   I-54, II-334
Torralba, Antonio   II-129
Toyoshima, Miho   II-291
Traullé, Benjamin   I-420
Treur, Jan   I-86, I-102, I-322, II-202

Ueda, Keiichi   II-299
Ulrich Hoppe, H.   II-61

Vaganov, Danila   I-439
van der Wal, Natalie   II-85
Vitkova, Lidia   II-159

Wan, Qian   II-189
Wang, Yiming   II-323
Weber, Ingmar   I-38, I-67, II-51, II-129
Wiedemann, Gregor   II-313

Wierzbicki, Adam   II-215
Wilson, Steven R.   I-455, II-176
Wu, Lianwei   II-323

Yagunova, Elena   II-139
Yamamoto, Yusuke   II-261
Yan, Muheng   I-134
Yimam, Seid Muhie   II-313
Ying, Qiu Fang   I-471
Yoshida, Mitsuo   II-334

Yu, Hualei   II-323
Yu, Minsang   I-291

Zagheni, Emilio   II-51
Zanouda, Tahar   II-3
Zegour, Rachida   II-3
Zhang, Xiaopeng   I-471
Zhao, Xing   I-487
Zhu, Feida   I-386

Printed in the United States
By Bookmasters